An Act for the Encouragement of Agriculture

(Approved February 17, 1852)

"*BE IT ENACTED by the General Assembly of the State of Indiana,...* that it shall be the duty [of the societies formed under the provisions of this act] to offer and award premiums for the improvement of soils, tillage, crops, manures, improvements, stock, articles of domestic industry, and such other articles, productions and improvements, as they may deem proper, and may perform all such acts as they may deem best calculated to promote agricultural and household manufacturing interests of the districts and of the State;

"[A]nd it shall also be their duty so to regulate the amount of premiums, and the different grades of the same, as that it shall be competent for small as well as large farmers to have an opportunity to compete therefor;

"[A]nd in making their awards, special reference shall be had to the profits which may accrue, or be likely to accrue, from the improved mode of raising the crop, or of improving the soil or stock, or of the fabrication of the articles thus offered, with the intention that the premiums shall be given for the most economical mode of improvement;

"[A]nd all persons offering to compete for premiums . . . shall be required to deliver to the awarding committee a full and correct statement of the process of such mode of tillage or production, and the expense and value of the same, with a view of showing accurately the profits derived, or attempted to be derived therefrom."

From these words sprang the great series of State Fairs which have been Indiana's heritage since the early days of the Hoosier state.

◆◆◆

> *"I know of no pursuit in which more real and important services can be rendered to any country than by improving its agriculture, its breed of useful animals, and other branches of a husbandman's cares"*
>
> – George Washington

International Standard Book Number: 0-7906-1018-3
Library of Congress Catalog Card Number: 92-60407

PROMPT™ Publications
is an imprint of
Howard W. Sams & Company
2647 Waterfront Parkway, East Drive
Indianapolis, IN 46214

Acquisition: Bruce Flanagan, Robert Hamilton

Development: Candace Drake, Wendy Ford,
Brian McCaffrey, Robert Wright, Sara Wright

Cover Design and Layout: Sara Wright

Production Coordination: Candace Drake

Printed in the United States of America

About Our Cover Girl: A comely young harvester styled after the Biblical Ruth graced the official lithographic poster for the 1886 Indiana State Fair. More Middle Eastern than Victorian-era Midwestern, her partially revealed bosom ensured readers gawked long enough to learn the Fair was September 27 to October 2. The poster created a furor, but was brought back to advertise the Fair in 1887–a bouquet of flowers modestly concealing the raven-haired Ruth's controversial anatomy.

INDIANA'S *Best!*

An Illustrated

Celebration

of the

Indiana State

Fairgrounds

1852-1992

Written by
Paul Miner

PROMPT™
PUBLICATIONS

An Imprint of
Howard W. Sams & Company
Indianapolis, Indiana

❖ Table of Contents

Thanks Go To . . .

THE MINUTES of the Indiana State Fair's earlier days; musty old files and water-ruined annual Agricultural Reports of the old Indiana State Board of Agriculture; the descendants of Jeremiah Johnson; Steve Cain of Purdue University's Agricultural Communications Service; State Statistician Ralph Gann; Marion County Central Library's reference librarians; Indiana Department of Natural Resources; Indianapolis Historic Preservation Commission; Steve Fisher of the Indiana State Data Center; *Indianapolis News; Indianapolis Star*; Maurice Williamson, retired executive secretary of Purdue Agricultural Alumni Association; Joe Collins, who answered many motor racing questions; veteran sportscaster Chuck Marlowe; the *Year Book of the State of Indiana*; Tippecanoe County Historical Association; Jefferson County Historical Society; Floyd County Historical Society; Fort Wayne Public Library; New Albany/Floyd County Library; Herb Schwomeyer, author of "Hoosier Hysteria – A History of Indiana High School Boys Basketball," who supplied all tournament statistics (and a daughter, Sandy Schwomeyer Lamb, who teaches ice skating at the Coliseum, along with another, Judy Schwomeyer Sladky, who won five U.S. Figure Skating championships); Indiana Horse Council; United States Trotting Association; Office of the Military History Project Director, Military Department of Indiana; *The Hub of the Universe*, the long-gone Board of Agriculture magazine; earlier work by former Fairgrounds staffers; the remarkable reference librarians of the Indiana State Library; "The Fox Stake," written in 1968 for the Fairgrounds by former *Indianapolis Star* sports reporter Joseph Hamelin; Ellen and her mother Margot Taylor; *Horseman & Fair World* magazine; "A Biographical Directory of the Indiana General Assembly," Volumes 1 and 2; *Lafayette Journal and Courier* farm writer Bryan Parvis; former Fairgrounds Superintendent Jess Stuckey; collector Bob Pottorff of Markleville; United States Auto Club; American Motorcyclist Association; World of Outlaws; Indiana Commission on Public Records; Indiana Historical Society; Milk Promotion Services of Indiana; *Indiana Prairie Farmer*; retired *Brownsburg Guide-Gazette* editor Bob Pearcy; J.B. Outhouse, Purdue professor emeritus and sheep extension specialist; Wm. Burford Printing Co., Indianapolis, for the use of vintage line art; Joan Champagne, my staff assistant and Fairgrounds archivist; and all the Hoosiers and happenings over the years that made it all possible.

◆◆◆

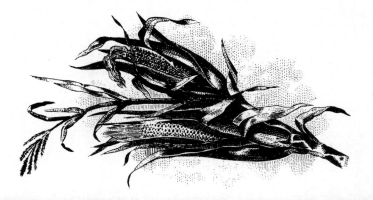

Come One, Come All!

Agrarians, agriculturists, animal husbandmen, breeders, professors, farmers, families, leaders, inventors, politicians, speakers, drummers, respected livestock judges, auctioneers, travelers, horsemen, hawkers, salesmen, exhibitors, entertainers, sideshows, musicians, and the milieu of gawkers, admirers, visitors, neighbors and competitors – all converged by horse and rail to the Hoosier capital city, Indianapolis, for the first Indiana State Fair.

It was 1852, and it was the greatest thing that ever happened to a young state only thirty-six years old.

THE REASON behind the first Fair was to share ideas, to educate, and to showcase Indiana's best. It's a reason that has remained constant ever since. It is also the reason behind this book.

This State Fairgrounds history is a history of Indiana and a tale of its people. Few aspects of Indiana life can fail to trace some involvement with the Indiana State Fairgrounds, whether during the State Fair or during one of the hundreds of events and happenings that have called the Fairgrounds home.

The Fairgrounds have always reflected the face of Indiana's people, whether in the Fair itself or in exhibits, encampments, contests, giant public shows, or championship auto races. And the strong Indiana State Board of Agriculture that founded the State Fair shaped Indiana's development, even commissioning state geological surveys and making powerful legislative overtures.

Seven different sites called the Fair theirs until, in 1892, the Indiana State Fair opened at new grounds where the Fairgrounds are today. Since then, armies of humanity have passed through the gates and turnstiles of the Great Showcase:

Presidents, foreign dignitaries, Boys' and Girls' Club graduates, blue ribbon champions, generals, the greatest horses, the greatest race drivers, the best cattle, the tallest cornstalk.

The biggest dinner gathering.

Armies in training and armies at work. World champion figure skaters. World famous entertainers.

John F. Kennedy. Franklin Delano Roosevelt in a four-door convertible. Woodrow Wilson. The Beatles.

Billy Graham, Billy Sunday, Billie Jean King. Frank Sinatra. Red Skelton. Orville Redenbacher. Astronauts. Elvis.

Dan Patch, the immortal harness horse. The boat Eisenhower almost gave to Khrushchev. Vietnamese visitors. Seventy Indianapolis Home Shows. Holiday On Ice.

Swine raised for lard, and swine raised for lean meat.

Marriage. A birth. The Coliseum explosion. Arthur Godfrey, Roy Rogers, The Beach Boys. Clarence the Cross-Eyed Lion.

◆◆◆

ALTHOUGH broad in scope, this book is by no means a complete history. It is a series of snapshots of the times and the people, as told by records and photos surviving in published documents and collections of personal mementoes. Whenever possible, actual passages and excerpts from early documents are quoted in precisely the same language and spelling originally used, preserving a historical flavor that would be otherwise lost.

During the research for this book, conflicting accounts in various "official" sources repeatedly reared their frustrating heads. There are discrepancies, for example, in the 1851-1907 Agricultural Reports, which contribute much to the story line, and we have made great efforts to check third and sometimes fourth sources for "best out of" availabilities. If the reader discerns a discrepancy yet within the text, he is invited to tell us now, inform us why he waited so long, then forever hold his peace.

◆◆◆

INDIANA'S State Fair is the sixth oldest state fair in the nation, according to records of the International Association of Fairs & Expositions (IAFE). Only New York (1841), Virginia (1846), Michigan (1849), Ohio (1850), and Wisconsin (1851) are older. The Fair has been an IAFE member since 1921, according to that association's records, or since 1885, according to the Board's 1884 Annual Report (IAFE solicited the Board's membership in late 1884). Other memberships: Indianapolis Chamber of Commerce, since October 1931; Indiana Chamber of Commerce, since the early 1920s; Indianapolis Publicity & Convention Bureau (now known as Indianapolis Convention & Visitors Association) since 1932; harness racing's Grand Circuit since 1925; and since 1939-40, the United States Trotting Association.

FORT HARRISON. IN 1812.

ROSE WELL AND BATH HOUSE.

SIR ROBERT ALEXANDER.

THE HOOSIER BY REPUTE.

STATE NORMAL SCHOOL.

STRAWBERRY HILL.

BILLY BARR.

INDIANA STATE FAIR AT TERRE HAUTE, October 1, 2, 3, 4, and 5—AMONG THE HOOSIE

❖ To Encourage the Best

REAL LIVE HOOSIERS.

SPRING HILL.

ST. AGNES HALL.

ETCHED BY J. F. GOOKING. —[SEE PAGE 698.]

Fairs didn't start in Indiana or the Americas, but a Fair is natural to an agrarian society. A great Fair is symbolic of a developing and thriving society.

A GREAT State Fair marked Indiana's turn at leadership and proud exhibition nearly fifteen decades ago.

Indiana Territory saw meetings of its trappers and early settlers. Part of a forbiddingly huge wilderness, Indiana then was navigable only by buffalo traces and its wild streams and rivers.

A fair was far from anyone's mind. Surviving was paramount. It wasn't until virgin trees were cut and burned, and until a good plow was invented, that Indiana came to realize it could become strong. This is the story of that emerging state, as reflected in its State Fair.

The First Fair

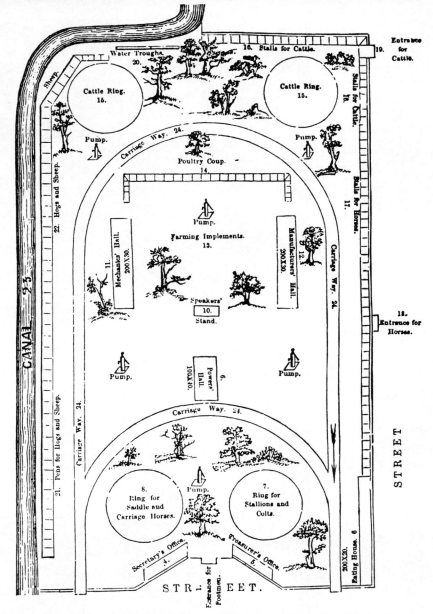

The site of the first Indiana State Fair, now known as Military Park, was at the corner of West and New York Streets in Indianapolis.

INDIANA joined the Union on December 11, 1816, but the nineteenth state was thirty-six years old before a state fair came onto the scene. The year before, sixteen men met in Indianapolis in the Hall of the House of Representatives to organize a State Board of Agriculture; the General Assembly had made provisions for it on February 14. (The Act was approved on February 17, 1852.)

It was "An Act For The Encouragement of Agriculture." Section 4 of the act gave the board true power: "The State Board . . . is hereby created a body corporate, with perpetual succession . . . under the name and style of the "Indiana State Board of Agriculture."

It was a broad definition. Their purpose was to fulfill the state's intent of allowing farmers, merchants, and manufacturers to assemble and exchange ideas to stimulate state industry. A state fair, along with many other actions, would accomplish that goal.

The first Board meeting on Tuesday, May 27, 1851, was short. State Board delegates elected Governor Joseph A. Wright president, and adjourned until the next day. According to one report, Wright, of Rockville, initially opposed the bill until backers promised to make him president.

A committee appointed to consider a "state agricultural fair in the fall of this year" recommended a day later to wait until the Fall of '52 to have the fair and then recessed until January 8.

Wright remained president four years and later went to Berlin as U.S. Minister. A state fair, he explained early in 1852, offered ". . . great advantages that result from the assembling of farmers, mechanics and manufacturers . . . in which the productions of their skill and labor are exhibited . . . [A] free interchange of views and opinions . . . stimulate industry, bring together the most distinguished mechanics of the state . . . [T]hey come together to inquire into the wants of the country, that they may return to their workshops to perfect the inventions that have been suggested by these means.

"The manufacturer exhibits the result of his inventions and labor; the farmer the mode, process and improvements of the farm; the trials, test and ex-periments . . . will create a spirit of rivalry well adapted to show the real wants of the people, and the prospects and means of supplying those wants and dependency of each; and in this laudable spirit of emulation, the country marches forward in real and substantial improvement in the true road to wealth."

Since a fair needs a fairgrounds, the Board turned to the media to spread the word: a State Fair would convene in the city which offered the most money – "take into consideration the local advantages of the different towns or cities . . . ."

The Board didn't have the money to pull off the event alone. Indianapolis made the best offer to host the inaugural affair. The Marion County Horticultural Society gave $900, so the first "Indiana Fair," spanning three days at Camp Sullivan (known today as Military Park) near downtown, opened Wednesday, October 20, each day " . . . marked by the balmy sunshine of Indian summer."

Expecting to reimburse themselves through increased shipping and passenger earnings, Lake Erie & Western Railway and Louisville, New Albany & Chicago Railway purchased the thirty-eight-acre tract and gave it to the State Board.

It was the same year the massive and ornately carved wall fixtures and matching counters found in Hook's Historic Drug Store at today's State Fairgrounds were built. Frame buildings housed the exhibits. The canal ran along one side. Livestock pens and stalls lined the perimeter. "Carriage Way" toured the grounds. Speakers' Stand, where State Board secretary John B. Dillon, a historian, gave his address, was centrally lo-

cated. Mechanics' Hall faced Manufacturers' Hall. Six pumps provided water, but the map showed no privy locations.

Shows and exhibits not allowed on the grounds set up on surrounding streets and grounds. Seventy-five years later, the *Indianapolis News'* Mabel Wheeler gleaned yellowed *Indianapolis Journal*, *Sentinel* and *Locomotive* files to learn those not allowed inside had names like the "Learned Pig," "the California Bears," "the Chinese Family," "Trained Seadogs" in "a panorama painting and the moving wax statuary." A "pyrotechnical artist" put on nightly fireworks displays west of the old State House.

A State Agricultural Ball was announced for " . . . the evening of the second day of the Fair. No pains or expenses will be spared . . . to make this one of the most brilliant and agreeable parties ever given in this State.

"One of the best Cotillion Bands in Cincinnati has been engaged and good music may be expected.

"Ticket admitting a Gentleman and two Ladies Three Dollars to be had at the Music Store of A.E. Jones; Banking House of John Woolley & Co.; and the principal Hotels. . . . Tickets should be secured at an early moment, in order that the arrangements may be more perfect to the comfort and convenience of those that attend."

All exhibitors paid $1 for State Agricultural Society (family) membership badges, which admitted the owner, his wife and all children under eighteen. Single admission tickets cost twenty cents. Complimentary tickets were sent to Indiana newspaper editors.

There were 1,365 exhibit entries. Some unknown exhibitor brought a shower bath; judges called it "ingeniously constructed and well adapted to family use."

Monroe County farmer Lewis Bollman, a county delegate (president of his county society) reporting for *Indiana Farmer*, wrote, "Listen to this medley of music, sounding out of these numerous tents on either hand, mixed with the roars of grizzly bears, and the not less unmusical voices which urge us to walk in and see the great and wonderful Giant or Giantess, or the wild mare of South America, or the Sea Dog, or something else exhibiting in the tents . . . . [provided by P.T. Barnum's "Museum and Menagerie,"

according to an August 1979 *Indiana Prairie Farmer* story.]

"What a mass of people! And what a confusion of sound! The merry laugh is almost unheard in this neighing of horses and braying of mules and lowing of cattle, and bleating of sheep and grunting of hogs."

Bollman told of "a worked cap by Miss R.T. Henderson; Ottoman covers by Mrs. W.D. Wygant; [and] fancy chair work and cushions by Mrs. J. Nicolai . . . all of Indianapolis; a 'Tidy' by D.J. Todd of Madison . . . and a lamp mat, by Miss Shafey of Putnam County. [P]aintings, in water-colors and mezzotint, by Miss Sarah Featherston of Indianapolis . . . spiral spring pad trusses, artificial legs, bandages, etc., by D.W. Daniels of Cincinnati; lasts, by Osgood of Indianapolis . . .

"These plows, made by H.S. Curtis of Albion, New York, exhibit good workmanship, but they are too unwieldy for stumps and roots of our new country . . . [T]he reapers . . . and the mowers are closely scrutinized . . . [T]hey cut fifteen acres a day, at but little more cost than one acre is now cut by the scythe.

"Over there stand various barrels of flour, which have puzzled two committees to determine the better of the best."

Indiana's State Fair was a success: " . . . It reflects honor upon all, and must make every 'Indianian' more proud of his state, for its inventive genius and skill; its persevering industry and energy.

"... No one doubts that important results will flow from this exhibition," Bollman wrote. "The spirit of progress it has infused will prompt thousands of our farmers and mechanics to strive to surpass the excellent articles here exhibited."

That year Governor Wright described to the General Assembly, "a very interesting and large exhibition of fine stock, agricultural productions, domestic manufacturers, farming implements and mechanical skill . . . ." He estimated first year's attendance at 30,000, including out-of-state tourists.

Ribbons, Gold and Silver

INDIANA State Fair blue ribbons weren't always awarded to the winner. Red once was best. Coming in second was blue. A white ribbon was complimentary notice.

Of eleven states gathered at the November 1895 State Fair Managers meeting in Chicago, only Indiana and Ohio used red for first premiums. Unheeded recommendations urged Indiana to adopt blue for first, red for second, white for "highly recommended," yellow for "commended," and royal purple for sweepstakes winners. But February 1907 rolled around before blue came first. Then second became red, third went white, fourth turned yellow, and fifth was green. The Board's diploma was "the highest commendation," awarded only as a first premium. "Its medal shall stand next in importance, and cash premium third."

Competition as early as 1856 was thrown "open to the world, except as otherwise provided herein." No premiums were allowed to anyone showing agricultural items they hadn't grown themselves.

Premium list revision was a regular order of business each year, usually during the January Board and Delegate meeting. Competition categories were regularly added or reviewed.

When premium changes were adopted in 1870, State Board men decided to "give a premium for the best boar under six months old, . . . the best sow under six months old . . . the best boar and five of his pigs under six months old; strike out five fat hogs and

A $1 Indiana State Agricultural Society member ribbon from the second Indiana State Fair, convened in 1853 in Lafayette. All exhibitors were required to join the "society" prior to entering competition.

A first-prize silver cup awarded during an early State Fair as the highest premium for "mechanical dentistry."

insert one; strike out all that relates to velocipedes."

Judges were required to "give the reasons for their decisions . . . as one great object of the Agricultural Board is to collect valuable information upon subjects connected with agriculture . . . [and] gather all the information possible from exhibitors."

Finally, "it is especially desirable that every exhibitor determine fully in what class and section he desires to compete, before making application for entries."

Enormous prizes of gold and silver were awarded, attracting competitors from far beyond state lines.

J.C. Bone of Pleasant Plains, Illinois, went home with a $50 gold medal in the 1865 cattle sweepstakes. Fifty dollars in gold certainly was welcome in the months following the war.

Fifty dollars filled the Xenia, Ohio, pockets of D. McMillan for best bull, four years old and over in the Breeding Cattle class. He took a $70 gold medal back across state lines in the Cattle Sweepstakes for "best bull, showing five best calves."

A gold medal valued at $70 rewarded breeders Jackson & Hamrick of Plainfield in the 1866 horse sweepstakes for "best stallion, of any age or class." Next year the two took the $100 gold sweepstakes medal in the same class competition.

The State Board bought hundreds of gold, silver and bronze treasures, and diplomas, and turned them over to the best in Indiana and the nation.

It was a lot of money. One gold, thirty silver and seventeen bronze medals amounted to $2,604.17 in 1871; $8,564.50 in cash was paid to exhibitors.

"Such articles as are shown by ladies" commonly won table service and cutlery. In 1857, pairs and sets of "Hunter's ebony handled" knives, forks, and butter knives were offered.

Girls under eighteen competed in a "useful and ornamental" class in 1855, vying for silver cups, tea and cream spoons, silver pencils, cash, and diplomas. Two years later, young ladies competed for butter knives, teaspoons, silver cups, gold pens, and gold dollars. Valuable cups and pitchers regularly were awarded to top exhibitors.

Early in 1856, the Board's Executive Committee gave a $30 silver pitcher and $20 silver cup to Shelby County's Nathaniel Thompson for the "best ten acres of corn grown on clay or upland soil" and "best five acres of corn grown on alluvial soil."

That year's Fair, Mrs. Powell Howland of Marion County won an engraved silver cup premium and $10 for "second best twenty pounds each, butter and cheese from one dairy."

E.J. Baldwin & Company of No. 1, Bates House, Indianapolis, provided the cup, as it had the year before.

When the State Board met during its first few Januarys, a little Winter Fair judging heightened State House excitement. More silver passed hands.

A good side of beef or twelve plucked chickens could do well in the old State House. Ten-dollar silver cups went to best-dressed pork, beef, mutton, and collections of meats at the January 1857 judging.

For the best dozen dressed fowl, J.W.L. Matlock, Hendricks County, won $6 in teaspoons. That's how Wayne County's A.H. Vestal did with the best half-dozen dressed chickens.

John Williams, Knox County, was a lucky boy in 1857: he won two copies of *Waring's Elements of Agriculture*, and two ten-dollar silver cups for the best acre of corn and acre of spring wheat.

George N. Norwood, Marion County, won all three divisions of the '57 plowing match, each awarding "Transactions" of the Board and $5. In miscellaneous judging, Marion County's Cottrell & Knight earned a diploma for their fireman's trumpet. A good one-of-a-kind was worthy of at least that.

Good coin still could be had. Young Miss R.A. Loyd of Tippecanoe County had no 1857 competitors in winning gold

This silver goblet, awarded in 1856, belonged to an ancestor of Charles Gerhing of Indianapolis. Similar goblets were awarded for the best farm implements, best butter, and champion livestock.

dollars for her geranium and phlox, and a three-dollar gold pen for her monthly rose.

By the time 1861 rolled around, "no less than fifty-four thousand dollars" in premiums had been paid in cash and silverware. All that money had the intended effect.

In the Board's opinion, to the first nine State Fairs "may be traced nine-tenths of the improvements in the way of producing large results in agriculture, stock growing, the mechanical arts and all other improvements." The Board had made the effort worth it.

Quorums were hard to come by during the Civil War summer of '62; nevertheless, enough Board members met to fix a $5,000 ceiling for cash, medals, and Board diplomas. Twenty-dollar bronze and thirty-dollar silver medals were awarded.

Hired judges were an 1862 innovation – "The exhibitors are thus kept in utter ignorance of their committee until the examinations commence," *Indiana Farmer* informed readers.

"The committee having no excuses for hurrying half thoroughly over their work, have done it here we think with much more than ordinary satisfaction to the exhibitors. The executive committee [is] ready to hear any complaints or remonstrances and have them decided on the spot."

Diplomas were awarded for nearly anything Indianians could produce, as well as to concerns outside the state. Judging considered virtually anything made, discovered, or sold in the state. Exhibits which didn't fit into any conventional category were designated "Non-Enumerated." If judged worthy, they received diplomas, and sometimes judges' "recommendations."

In 1882 "Geology, Natural History, Etc." competition, for "one of the best cases of insects (classified in orders)," W.J. Chambers of Kent in Jefferson County won the judging committee's diploma and recommendation.

Art ranked equally with science. Fort Wayne's P.S. Underhill received a Fair-time Non-enumerated List diploma in 1866 for his marble statue of a female figure.

Awards in the form of medals cost $1,540, and 188 diplomas set the 1868 Board back $1,680. Premiums, "payable in Cash, Gold and Silver Medals, and Diplomas of new and elegant design" amounting to $20,000 were offered at the 1873 Fair and Exposition. Enormous premiums, even by today's standards, were offered for the best farming implements, but only after actual tests. In 1876, nine different combined reapers and mowers "hotly contested" for the $100 "grand gold medal"

awarded to The Buckeye Senior, manufactured by Aultman & Miller of Akron, Ohio.

Eight single reapers and single mowers vied for $50 gold medals. Soon however, mechanical and machinery exhibits came just for show and sale. A good judges' inspection guaranteed mention and possibly an engraving (if provided) in the ensuing State Board Agricultural Report. That was good advertising. One mechanical exhibitor at 1865's State Fair in Fort Wayne, representing the American hay and cotton press, donated his cash premium to the "society," and instead secured a medal.

The Traveling Fairs

INDIANA agriculture was growing. Forty-five county agricultural societies had been established under the "Encouragement" act by January 1853.

Spirited competition began over which Indiana city would host the Fair. Best offers were sought. Railroad deals were cut.

Lafayette hosted the second extravaganza, on twenty acres atop what is today known as Fourth Street Hill. By then, the iron horse linked Indianapolis with the Tippecanoe County town.

A strong rivalry with "Indianapolitans" appeared in the newspaper. *Indiana Farmer* had made disparaging remarks about Lafayette.

Lafayette's *Daily Courier* barbed back at Indianapolis: "It is natural enough that where the Capitol of a State is located at a small, new place, that there an entirely different kind of population will be drawn together from that which must, necessarily, compose an important commercial town. In the one case, the main living of the people is derived from feeding, lodging, drinking, carrying the trunks, and blacking the boots of the strangers attracted by the sessions of the Legislature, Courts &c., &c."

The *Daily Courier* reported that the Tippecanoe County town put on a better Fair. Better lodging and eating was claimed.

On October 1, the paper contended, "We are satisfied Lafayette has prettier women than any other city in the State." Their daguerreotypes would be found superior, the newspaper was certain.

"Prof. Wm. Dunckelburg and Gideon Lane . . . have opened a Daguerrean room on the north-east corner of the square, and if any of our numerous *pretty* (italics in original) women wish correct likeness of themselves taken, for exhibition at the State Fair, or for home use, these gentlemen can accommodate them."

Madison hosted the third Fair, although Indianapolis, "having the greatest facilities of access" had been recommended in January if citizens offered as much "as any other place."

Although Indianapolis citizens promised their fairgrounds "would be fitted up in a style equal to, if not superior, to . . . Lafayette, . . . the great mass of our citizens would prefer that it should be held elsewhere." The main reason for this gallant deferral was "the fear . . . that it would . . . be the means of engendering a jealous strife between cities and towns which should not exist – a feeling which we have no desire to see continued."

Heavy rains made Madison a wash-out, and the next four State Fairs convened back at Military Park. Then distant New Albany was selected for 1859's Fair. New Albany's *Daily Ledger* looked forward to "an immediate week of glorious sunshine. Then may we look for a concourse almost innumerable of free white inhabitants, male and female, as they were created. Let them come and let them bring their innocent progeny with them."

When the gates opened at seven on a bright sunny morning, Fairgoers stepped onto the "magnificent acres" owned by Floyd County Agricultural and Mechanical Association to an "unparalleled and almost unapproachable spectacle. Three thousand dollars were promiscuously scattered during the past year in necessary preparation."

Carriage arrivals at the Charlestown gate espied a certain Mr. Ben Smith, a man "fully prepared to take care of horses and buggies in any number," according to a purchased commendation in the New Albany *Daily Ledger*. "Mr. Smith is entirely trustworthy . . . ." Those who came saw more than livestock and machines. "Within the enclosure" were the Fat Boy, "Snake and Alligator," the Grizzly Bear, Fat Woman, the "Kickapoo Giantess" and the "Great American sword swallower."

◆◆ **William M. French of Jeffersonville "exhibited himself" for the Secretary of State's job, the paper reported. "Mr. French entered well, with head up and tail up, prancing and snorting, and he had our abundant wishes that his head may be decorated with the red ribbon."**

"Professor" W.H. Rarey, "the celebrated horse tamer," offered to tame "WILD" and "UNGOVERNABLE" horses at no charge. "Any one can learn this art who has ordinary intelligence," the *Ledger* reported. "Most of the celebrated turfmen of England have learned this art, and given high testimony . . . all horseman and stock dealers should be in possession of the art." Three days of rain diminished seekers of the spectacle.

The newspaper remarked on the difference between the Kentuckian and the Hoosier. "You can tell incontinently a Kentucky agriculturist. His badge is gracefully fled through the ring of his watch chain, or through a button hole in his coat, and he steps about with cocked hat and an air which unmistakably indicates that he knows where he is. The Hoosier farmer . . . wears his badge spread

This 1870 Braden & Burford engraving features the Camp Morton Fairgrounds. The original engraving is on display at the Indianapolis Fairgrounds, where descendent Burford "Bo" Danner still handles the State Fair printing. Smoke pours from the power halls at the left; the Speed Ring and Amphitheater are at the rear. Livestock stalls line three sides. Because of city expansion, Indianapolis soon would envelop the grounds.

about the size of a stable door over his Mackinaw, and is diffident and doubtful until he takes the premium upon what he knows is the very best bull or ass ever exhibited. Then he breaks for home and blows."

Gypsies arrived in town with their livestock too late for judging. General Solomon Meredith arrived on time from Wayne County with three freight cars of livestock, among them an imported bull called "Crusader," and a broodmare which already had claimed premiums at three previous Fairs.

The *Ledger* heaped accolades on New Albany firemen, "first in war, first in peace, and first in the hearts of their countrywomen." Hoosier Fire Company fared best in a "throwing" contest against the Oceola Company; Hoosier's best throw, its second, shot 160 feet, seven inches through fifty feet of fire hose. The Hoosiers championed again in the hose carriage race "in true fireman style. After ringing the fire bell in the judges' stand . . . the carriages were started." Hoosier time, fifty-three seconds, was five faster than Oceola. It was perhaps the first "Gentlemen, start your engines" ever recorded in Indiana.

◆◆◆

Indianapolis' Otis Grove/Camp Morton

THE BOARD was nearly bankrupt early in 1860. Even so, an arrangement secured a new Fairgrounds in Indianapolis. The process involved a tripartite committee of three from the Board, directors of three railroads and three City Council members.

Railroad money paid for the land. The ten-year agreement guaranteed the rail lines exclusive Fair-related traffic. Reasonable rates were promised. Each year the Board would collect $2,095.50. Railroaders had the right to hold their own celebrations and "picnics," provided the Board wasn't using the grounds at the time. If for any reason a Fair were to be held somewhere else during the ensuing decade, the railroads would be released from their obligations.

The City Council held an election to discover how Indianapolis citizens regarded the proposition of a $5,000 appropriation. "The exact vote was nine and one-fourth in favor to one against." While the precise site for the Fairgrounds was being decided, the city treasurer refused to give up the money, arguing that "it was *unconstitutional* [italics in the original] to appropriate money out of the city treasury to be expended outside the corporate limits of the city." Luckily, "eager" capital city citizens held a fund-raiser and came up with the money.

After reviewing twelve tracts, the railroad and City Council committees chose Otis Grove, "a beautiful tract of ground north of the city, recently known as Camp Morton." The thirty-acre area was bounded by today's 19th Street, Talbott, 22nd Street and Central Avenue (an 1875 Indianapolis map identifies 19th as Ninth). The main entrance opened where 19th and Alabama Streets are now. It was considered far enough from the city that it wouldn't interfere with Indianapolis residents. The Board itself paid for another six acres. The entire thirty-six acres, "being the most beautiful and complete structure of the kind in the northwest," was surrounded

Union Army troops at the entrance to the infamous Camp Morton prisoner of war camp, photographed in 1864. Photograph originally owned by R.W. Lowery, Indianapolis.

with a cedar post and pine board fence, six feet and a half high.

The 1860 Fair, "as an exhibition, was a success perhaps never excelled by any former State Fair."

After the Civil War started in the spring of 1861, volunteer troops occupied the Fairgrounds. The grounds were severely damaged. Trees were peeled and killed. Blue grass sod "which spread its green mantle of rich verdure" also was despoiled.

With the war over in the spring of 1865, the Board was left to collect for war's ravages at Camp Morton. Damage was too great to convene a Fair there that year. Instead, Fort Wayne claimed the first Fair after the war. Allen County agriculturists paid expenses at the 26-1/3 acre site in an agreement where the Board made half-fare railroad arrangements. A "good time track of not less than one-half a mile in extent" mandated whether Fort Wayne was to win that year's Fair.

Much of the Fair ". . . stretched through a portion of what is now Lawton Park, in the neighborhood of the present City Power Plant. "A pontoon bridge was laid across the St. Marys River to make the grounds more accessible to the downtown area . . . The swamp area was cleared of brush and converted into an attractive lake . . . A fountain splashed across its surface, fed by pumped-in [St. Marys] waters." Governor Morton was key speaker, holding forth from the Aveline House balcony. The National Pomological Society convened during the Fair.

Piano exhibitors showed up during the Fort Wayne stop-off, unanimously asking that all pianos manufactured outside Indiana be "stricken" from premium competition. Instead, they wanted diplomas awarded for the best grand pianos, semi-grands, square pianos, uprights, church and parlor organs, and melodeons, all "made anywhere." The Board acquiesced.

The Vigo Agricultural Society grounds near Terre Haute were chosen for 1867's Indiana State Fair, held from September 30 to October 5. A special $1,000 "President's premium" was paid to the fastest trotting mare or gelding. Second took $200 and third paid $100. Reportedly, 1,552 exhibits, "a much larger number" of animals and exhibit articles than any previous State Fair, arrived for judging at Terre Haute.

Problems developed in Fine and Common Wool, and Mutton Sheep judging, as the committee charged with this task reported to President Hamrick they "proceeded to discharge that duty, under what to us, seemed to be very unfavorable circumstances. "The sheep were exhibited without the benefit of shelter, and were, consequently, by the seveer (sic) shower that preceded our examination, rendered totally unfit for exhibition."

"Upwards" of 55,000 admission tickets were sold at the best attended Fair ever, 11,000 more than any since 1860, although the Terre Haute stop-off saw receipts drop slightly to $17,148.05. Premiums, out of $7,000 offered, reached an all-time high at $6,331.

◆◆◆

The Sinker & Company Boiler Explosion

DURING the 1869 Fair, a Sinker & Company saw-mill steam boiler exploded right after its trial in "a most terrible accident" around 4 in the afternoon, Friday, October 1, "scattering death and terror in every direction" and killing nearly thirty persons, including the engineer, who died instantly.

Doctors and nurses from throughout Indianapolis, including the Indiana Surgical Institute and City Hospital, rushed in to care for the injured. Frank Johnson of Indianapolis, exhibiting light Brahma chickens, corn and wheat, went to the Fair Grounds Saturday to pick up his entries. "I went into the Agricultural building to get my corn and wheat," he recalled in 1927, "but the displays were scattered all over the ground, and there were no sacks to be found. The Agricultural building had been used as an emergency hospital and the grain had been dumped out, the sacks used for bandages."

Although the press censured Sinker & Company, their dead engineer and the Board for allowing steam-operated machinery tests, Board Secretary Fielding Beeler wrote, "this terrible catastrophe was the result of an unforeseen accident not unusual where steam is now employed."

"Every man of business . . . is continually exposed to them," Beeler wrote in that year's Agricultural Report. "He can scarcely turn, even in the heart of our crowded cities but machinery run by steam in some form is in full view. Steamboat boilers burst; steamers and other vessels burn; railroad trains collide, fall through bridges, or burn up, carrying in their trail hundreds of victims; but such accidents are so common that they are regarded without alarm . . . [H]ere is chronicled the first accident of the kind that has ever happened in the United States . . .We should rather look at these oft repeated accidents as . . . 'unforeseen' and 'unavoidable' misfortunes that we can not prevent but must endure."

If the Fairgoer was "attentive, studies the lesson day by day as opportunity presents, the old couplet, 'I never had a piece of toast/Particularly good and wide/But fell upon the sanded floor/And always on the buttered side,' /will not in any wise apply . . . ." From then on, a committee, with "at least one competent engineer" safeguarded all precautions. All who failed to adhere to these requirements were barred from the Fair.

◆◆◆

The Grand Exposition

"NOT abating in zeal for the industries which have long been its chief care," the State Board in 1872 fatefully decided "the time has arrived when a higher field of usefulness shall be initiated . . . Indiana . . . should institute a State Exposition . . . [to] more fully and satisfactorily exhibit the advances . . . in all the leading industries of our people." They planned "a more thorough and complete exhibition of the Agricultural, Mechanical, Mineral, and Productive Industries of Indiana, including those Arts of Peace, which give life and beauty to the civilization of the nineteenth century." Indianapolis citizens contributed money to fund a new $62,769.07 two-story brick "Grand Hall" (or "Exposition Building") as the 308-by-150 foot centerpiece for the new thirty-day September 10 to October 10 Indiana State Fair and Exposition.

Inside "the best lighted public building on the continent" were 10,600 feet of gas pipe, 202 reflectors, and 1,362 burners consuming 570,900 cubic feet of gas. Elevated galleries offered visitors the best view possible of "the greatest inland city on the continent." Just in front of the main entrance stood a "colossal bronze figure of Justice resting upon a large block of granite . . . ." A counterfeit grotto in the east end of Floral Hall was "at once a triumph of art and mechanical skill." One admirer couldn't restrain claiming the grotto "may be fairly said to surpass any

thing of the kind heretofore attempted, at least in the Western country . . . [O]ld citizens of Indianapolis were overheard remarking that they had lived in the city for forty years without knowing that such a place existed so near them, and wondering that it had not long since become a place of fashionable resort."

Indianapolis was indebted to the Board, according to Mayor James Mitchell, "and to those liberal gentlemen (numbering 420, according to a January 1874 report) whose guarantee . . . of one hundred thousand dollars has given to us this beautiful building . . . [W]e have one grand panorama of the productions of art, labor, taste, skill and genius."

Senator Oliver P. Morton toasted the Fair's opening: ". . . This is a step out of the old beaten path of the ordinary State Fair . . . [I]t is a school of knowledge, which there can be no higher – no better . . . [T]he money spent in an enterprise of this kind, is as much devoted to the cause of education as money spent in the support of Common Schools. The farmer . . . can learn more in three days than he can learn on his farm in twenty-five years . . . [T]he mechanic . . . comes to see what new tools have been made and what new improvements have been made in his trade; and he will carry away more new ideas with him, after a week spent here, than he would gain in his shop in twenty years." Morton told listeners, ". . . India-

napolis is to-day the largest inland city in the United States . . . [with] thirteen railroads running into the city . . . ."

Of great ironic significance at the 1873 Fair & Exposition was a diploma awarded to Isaac Lawrence of Plainville, Ohio, for "best stump puller." An *Indianapolis Star* account revealed that a factory accepted Lawrence's patented invention on sight and wanted to manufacture it on a fifty-fifty basis. Unfortunately, a disagreement on terms soured the deal. Two years later the advent of dynamite made stump pullers obsolete. The Fair before, Lawrence also took a diploma for best stump puller.

Even though the Exposition was a success, "the [national] financial panic" which struck as it opened "affected the receipts very materially." The Exposition was a great financial mistake. The Board had allowed itself to be talked into the Exposition "Chestnut," as it would later be called. From the public's point of view, the awesome opportunity to witness the spectacle and to be a part of it all was fantastic. But its financial after-effects plagued the Board for years – all the way through 1891's Fair.

◆◆◆

Worthy of Praise

ITS WORK was "almost unlimited in extent, in promoting the interests of agriculture, to show the vast resources of the State and how to best protect them," the Board declared in 1880. An important resource was its 900-volume library. Every existing state agricultural organization but one had been organized "within a period of nine years," in the Board secretary's office. The National Association of Short-horn Breeders, and Swine Breeders, were also first organized in the Board's State House rooms. The Board was first "to remove all limits of competition," and "the first of the States West, to own State Fair grounds, and with the largest and best buildings . . . and run their State Fair at half the price of admission charged by other States."

The Indiana State Fair was first to pay jurors awards for their service, and first to introduce the feature of no premiums on implements or machinery without a test, with recognition of merit by expert committees. "State Fair interests have become so closely identified with the material welfare of the city, that its people no longer regard you as strangers," Mayor Caleb S. Denny told January 1888's annual gathering. Indiana had "at last come to fully understand and adequately appreciate the importance of the agricultural interests. [M]y interest is doubled, for I know that success for your Association means improvement and success for the city, also."

Somewhere Over the Railroad

WITHIN three decades after the Indiana State Board of Agriculture settled the Fair at Camp Morton, Indianapolis had prospered, eventually enveloping the Fairgrounds. Camp Morton now was valuable urban property; driving livestock from Union train station nearly two miles through Indianapolis' finer neighborhoods wasn't the wisest move. One delegate to the Board, a long-time swine exhibitor, had grown tired of the location's inconvenience. "If I arrive in the city at 4 o'clock, it takes until midnight to reach the ground," he complained in 1887. "If we could have [the Fair Grounds] located near the Belt Road the expenses would be much less." He wasn't alone in calling for a site beyond the great Belt Railroad surrounding the capital city.

Indianapolis Mayor Denny recommended a similar move in his 1887 and 1888 Delegate Board addresses. Denny questioned the Board's "wisdom" when it purchased twenty more acres in 1887.

Early in 1891, the State Board "Committee on Sale of Fair Grounds" recommended $300,000 after early bids were opened and found to be too low. The bidding call went out again. By November 11, all bids were rejected and the Board lowered the price to $275,000. That got results. Camp Morton was sold on December 22 to Judge Elijah Bishop Martindale, Willard W. Hubbard, and Edward F. Claypool for $275,100. Jay G. Voss' Farm two miles northeast

Indiana Pioneers

MUSIC Hall filled with old settlers October 2, 1878, responding to a search for old-timers from the days "when pluck and undaunted courage were the crowning virtues." All pioneers over seventy with forty years' residence in Indiana were admitted free to the State Fair that day. Free railroad passes were arranged.

At least seven hundred Indiana pioneers showed up, and perhaps "not less than a thousand others" considered "entitled to rank as old settlers." The Pioneers drew up a constitution and

organized as the Indiana Pioneer Society that afternoon. Judge Charles H. Test of Marion County was elected Society president. Its most important article concerned "collecting, preserving and from time to time publishing biographical sketches of the early settlers . . . ."

Young James Whitcomb Riley recited "Old Settlers," a poem heard earlier at an Oaklandon "old settlers' meeting." Mrs. Sarah T. Bolton of Indianapolis recited "The Last Adventure and Death of George Pogue, The First White Settler in Marion County." It was said that Pogue built Indianapolis' first log cabin in 1822. "It was a gathering of old people as was never seen in this city before."

◆◆◆

of the old grounds on the north edge of town was selected on Christmas Eve.

Planning began for railway and street car transportation. Water pumping negotiations opened with Schofield Mill Company just past the grounds' northeast tip.

Jeremiah Johnson opened seventy-six acres on Fall Creek's west bank in 1821 and received a land grant personally signed by President James Monroe on November 13, 1822. The deal wasn't finalized until January. Board President William A. Banks told the Board and Delegate meeting January 6, ". . . [W]e are not orphans, we have a home. We have bought a farm, the trade was consummated last night, quite late."

The *Western Horseman* announced the big move five days earlier: ". . . [A]n attractive park and a first-class mile track is one of the certainties of the near future." The Board had conducted a "thorough and impartial examination" of the several sites before selecting the Voss Farm, the *Western Horseman* editorialist noted. "[I]n making this selection in opposition to the heavy special pressure . . . for other selections, the Board demonstrated its independent ability to handle the subject at hand." Voss Farm was "admirably adapted" for a fairgrounds and track "and is in easy access to the city. Indiana will not only have the greatest fair . . . but Indianapolis will become one of the greatest trotting and pacing horse centers in the country."

Board men asked Voss, seller on behalf of his sister Mrs. Theresa H. Smith, to "furnish certain guarantees from the railroads – Monon and [Lake] Erie [& Western] – and the street railway, Indianapolis gas and water companies . . . ." Voss told the *Sentinel* January 3 "guarantees would be forthcoming, notwithstanding reports to the contrary that were being circulated by parties interested in other fair sites."

Everything was ready except for street car transportation. "As to the street car difficulty, Mr. Voss states that if the Citizens' company refuses to construct an electric line to the grounds, the line will be built by other parties who are interested in real estate on the line of the proposed road, and that a number of wealthy land owners will bind themselves to have an electric line in operation by the time of the next state fair."

Indiana Farmer claimed only a mile of road was needed for Citizens' to reach the new Fairgrounds. By Fair-time, a double track electric street car line dropped visitors at the 30th Street entrance – today's 38th Street.

President Banks, from Door Village, recommended a mile race track and setting aside forty acres for an Indianapolis zoological garden. He also suggested leaving space for the state horticultural society and state florists "to cultivate and beautify." "Nature has done about all it could in making beautiful grounds," *Indiana Farmer* apprised. "On the west side is a very handsome park of natural growth of young timber, affording ample shade. This is well set in blue grass." Monon

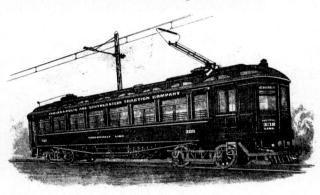

Railroad on the west and the Lake Erie & Western to the east provided "ample siding and platforms." Unloading directly onto the Fairgrounds saved exhibitors "much annoyance and expense."

Along the way, however, a smell arose. *Indianapolis Sentinel* learned "by what appeared to be good authority" that former president Robert McBride Lockhart had been offered $1,000 to vote against the Voss deal in favor of another farm. "Approached [and] questioned," Lockhart "flatly denied" the allegation. When an evening paper published the charge, Lockhart was "again sought out and found in his room at the Denison . . . again questioned . . . [He] refused flatly to deny or confirm the rumor . . . ."

According to the bribery accusation, the money was deposited in Secretary Leon Bagley's safe, but that charge also was gainsaid. *Sentinel* readers learned ". . . $1,000 had been received since the [annual] report was made out, and some of the delegates infer that this amount was necessary in order that certain subsequent events might transpire. It remains to be seen." Treasurer Sylvester Johnson reported that the money came from "the proceeds from sales of a lot at the old grounds. . . ." Tenacious, the *Sentinel* kept on the bribery trail. During a January 7 Columbia Club evening meeting hosted by attorney Albert W. Wishard, one unidentified Board member acknowledged an investigation had indeed been launched.

Board members finally concocted a somewhat unbelievable story

1892 Construction Costs for the Indiana State Fairgrounds

Building	Contract	Amount Paid
Women's Building	$ 8,600	$ 7,850
Horticultural and Floral Hall	4,2276	4,461.36
Administration Building	4,340	4,315
Dairy Building	2,088	2,232
Grandstand	21,165	19,990
Swine Barn	7,600	7,600
Sheep Building	4,500	4,475
Agricultural Hall	3,200	3,558
8 Speed Barns	10,168	10,068
10 Cattle Barns	12,750	13,670
8 Show Horse Barns	12,00	13,670
Entrances	1,050	1,050
Lavatories	1,720	1,720
Water Works	—	5,965.13
Track	—	16,843.60
Engineer's Payroll	—	1,093.77
Superintendent's Payroll	—	10,862.87
Architect	—	2,000
Miscellaneous	—	21,955.32
TOTAL	**$93,457**	**$151,725.05**

that the entire Lockhart issue was a set-up to draw out the briber. Prosecuting Attorney John W. Holtzman issued a subpoena for Lockhart, but Lockhart already had departed for his Waterloo home. Eventually, the issue died down and was forgotten.

An old horticultural building was picked up and moved north for poultry. Orders were given "to remove four of the horse barnes [sic] to the new grounds . . . [and] the north-west part of the ground was dedicated for the use of the city of Indianapolis, in the event they would elect to equip it, as a park." The new land was directly north of Frank Johnson's homestead, where he had settled in 1870. During the summer of 1892, the tremendous building project began. By fall, Johnson, great grandson of Jeremiah, had trouble concentrating on his wheat plowing directly south of the main entrance, across Maple Lane. "Thirty-eighth street then was only a private [Maple] lane, running but a short distance east of Central avenue. [Johnson] extended the road to a point near Fall creek, hauling gravel and grading the road bed . . . 80 rods, by himself," an unknown journalist wrote in 1927. Street cars not far behind cut Johnson's farm in half. Soon he sold all but four acres.

"Excessive" rains held up construction "until it began to look as if the 19th of September would find us not ready for the Fair," 1892 President John M. Boggs of Lafayette said later. Although open, the buildings weren't finished until after the Fair was over.

All told, the new Fairgrounds contained seventy-two buildings. The 440-by-57 foot grandstand, "a model of beauty and convenience," seated 6,000 people. A fifty-foot-high, 1,600-barrel capacity water tank fed nearly five miles of pipe.

Horsemen in 1892 called the regulation mile track "second to none." Completed July 19, it required 17,000 yards of soil hauled 25 miles. Within twenty-four hours, in a speed trial, Silvertail, "driven by a lady, went the fastest mile of his life – 2:07 – and would have gone at least two seconds faster but for a break." Horsemen wasted no time scheduling races.

In the May 13 *Western Horseman*, an unnamed Independence, Iowa, correspondent noted that "Indianapolis is one of the greatest railroad centers [fifteen railroads centered at Indianapolis, with connecting lines] in the United States and has to exceed 100,000 population. . . [T]he national game of base ball is well patronized in the large cities, but by a class of people now the votaries of such gambling contrivances as the pool box. . . . at the present time the English method of racing to saddle at the uncivilized gait of the runaway horse has a first mortgage upon all cities of upwards of 100,000 population . . . If . . . the Indianapolis *Sentinel* and the *Journal* could be induced to favor the turf upon which the people's race horse the sulky-carriage [performs] . . . in preference [to] the turf of the gamblers' race horse, the runner, the people

of Indianapolis may have an opportunity of witnessing as many racing contests of legitimate speed as now take place in the smaller cities."

The Board's September 16 ad in *Western Horseman* invited everyone to "The Banner Meeting at Indianapolis . . . With the Choicest Lot of Horses that ever answered the Starters' Bell in Indiana . . . see some of the Records Smashed Over the Newest and Fastest Track in the Union. Electric Cars Every Five Minutes, Steam Cars Every Seven Minutes. . . ."

Since state law forbade it from owning more than eighty acres, the Board leased an additional 134 acres from Mrs. Smith just north, then lobbied the General Assembly for buying approval. The purchase wasn't consummated until 1904.

There almost wasn't any kind of buy, and the State Board of Agriculture nearly ended. Fair cancellation rumors circulated. Acting on complaints that the Board was "self-perpetuating," the 1891 General Assembly passed a law creating a "commission for the purpose of managing the agricultural, mechanical, and stock interests of the state." The annual $10,000 appropriation, due April 1, was refused.

The old Fairgrounds sale was held up, as was the new land purchase. "Without a single dollar in the treasury," Fair planning nevertheless continued, and the Board hired an Indianapolis law firm to test the constitutionality of Senate Bill No. 61 which had passed both houses by a large majority. Several months later, the Indiana Supreme Court declared the new law unconstitutional, and the Board retained its powers. But the scare was on and the Board revised its rules. Agricultural districts were reorganized on a more nearly equal population basis.

The Fairgrounds officially opened September 19, 1892, nine months after Ellis Island. Opening day was a comfortable 67 degrees and it didn't rain. The livestock show was "large and fine, requiring [some 50] additional pens to our supposed ample accommodations in the Swine Department [1,011 hogs exhibited]," Boggs recounted. Poultry was also cramped. The new grounds hosted the state's largest-ever cattle show; of 610 entries, 337 were beef breeds. Premiums reached $19,875.50, the highest ever in the Fair's history, and the highest, ultimately, of the century.

◆◆◆

Camp Mount

AT THE outbreak of the Spanish American War in 1898 (Spain declared on April 24, the U.S. retroactively declared April 21), Camp Mount was established. Governor James A. Mount received a War Department call for troops at 6:15 the evening of April 25; Indiana National Guardsmen began arriving April 26.

As with the Civil War Army of the Republic, occupation damages were great. Troops stayed until November 1899. "[T]he grounds . . . were in deplorable condition . . . vast amount of rubbish and destruction wrought . . . ." Claims lingered through 1905. Damages totalled $9,037.50.

"So interwoven are the interests of the State Board and the Fair . . . the advancement of either marks the progress of the agricultural interests of Indiana," Board members disclosed in 1902, their fiftieth anniversary.

"Through the Fair, too, the State Board has . . . brought before the farmers the best of the herds and the flocks of Indiana and the country, and . . . the best and newest machinery that comes within the needs of the tiller of the soil."

In its half-century history, the Board had distributed half a million dollars in premiums. "I know of no association of men who do more for the city of Indianapolis than you do," Mayor John W. Holtzman told the annual Delegate Board meeting in January 1905, "and I hope that the . . . Legislators . . . will realize that you are doing as much as any body of men to build up the State as well as the capital. . . ."

Capital city growth continued and soon would envelop the Fairgrounds once again. Land surrounding the Fairgrounds was selling from $500 to $1,000 an acre, "a good deal of it having been cut up into small tracts, upon which preten-tious suburban homes have been erected."

The Fair could expand "for fifty years without outgrowing its location," outgoing president John C. Haines asserted. "The interests of the State Board of Agriculture and of the business people

◆◆ "Indiana is in the habit of setting the pace for the other states in the Union in every line of public endeavor." Gov. J.P. Goodrich, 1919

of Indianapolis are identical . . . for time to come neither should ever be a prey upon the other."

By Fair time in 1905, the Fall Creek bridge at College Avenue was expected to be completed, giving Indianapolis Traction and Terminal Company three "distinct" street railway lines to the Fair.

Haines called for legislative help to pay for the land purchase, and buildings "of brick and steel that exhibitors may have ample protection . . . [W]e need

The Fairgrounds' first Coliseum, "America's newest and largest," was dedicated in 1907. The 12,000-seat edifice, built on a "pretentious scale," was considered crucial to Indiana's continuing competitiveness in livestock exhibition.

a coliseum for our live stock shows – a building of magnitude and on pretentious scale." Loosening legislative purse strings wouldn't happen without support from the livestock breeders and the exhibitors.

Debt relief occasioned a legislative act early in 1905. The Board now was roughly $45,000 in debt; it couldn't pay for the land it had insisted on purchasing. State money helped cover new building costs.

"No more ring shows in scorching sun, or sudden rain, or stuffy tent" – America's newest and largest livestock show Pavilion, just south of "Central Avenue," west of the streetcar loop, opened in 1907 with seats for 12,000.

"You have builded well," Governor J. Frank Hanly remarked at the Coliseum dedication. "The foundation of our wealth and progress and attainment is agriculture. Upon it all depends . . . It is the root of all commerce; the basis of all industry. Its prosperity means national prosperity; its impairment, national distress.

By 1918, the Board had acquired "by its own efforts . . . practically without cost to the taxpayers . . . grounds now worth over $1,000,000," *Hub of the Universe* readers learned. (The *Hub* was an old Board magazine.) "[T]he Indiana State Fair is an institution belonging to all the people of the state, yet unlike the other state institutions it receives no help from the taxpayers except an annual [premium] appropriation of $10,000." With the exception of state money in 1907 for the Coliseum, taxpayers had contributed nothing in building the Fairgrounds.

Growth plans would "give Indianapolis a new park. . . ." When the Fair wasn't in session, the grounds would be open to the public, while not interfering with speed horse training on the mile and half-mile tracks.

The Fairgrounds were now "bordered along the south side by Maple Road, one of the broadest and best-made boulevards in the United States." Maple Road reached Fall Creek boulevard along the Fairgrounds' east side, "and this boulevard extends into the Millersville pike, a beautiful highway that reaches Fort Benjamin Harrison, some miles to the east. Maple Road runs across the north edge of Indianapolis and at its west end, about three miles from the State Fair gates, it is to be extended into a boulevard that will connect with Riverside park and boulevard, and these will give connections with the boulevard now built along the edge of White river down into the city."

From 1918 to 1920, Indiana contributed one-half million dollars for Fairgrounds building construction. The Manufacturers' and Women's Buildings had joined the Fairgrounds roster.

"More work along that line ought to be done and will be done . . . to make it the best State Fair in the United States," Governor James P. Goodrich said.

A "more imposing and more attractive and convenient" 620-stall brick, steel and frame Draft Horse Barn went up in time for the 1922 Fair on the same site as the Brick Horse Barn which fire had destroyed early in the year. Money came from the State Finance Committee.

Before the 1940s ended, a growing number of Fair-time saddle horses (and raucous drinking parties in the stalls)

were pushing draft horses out of the 400-by-194 foot building. Only four Fairs after it was built, the giant building, "believed to be fully adequate for all future needs, only house[d] about two-thirds the number entered."

The Swine Barn was built in 1923 where the old wooden swine pavilion had stood. Brick, steel, and concrete, the 308-by-340 foot open pavilion with a brick colonnade and offices at its front blended in with the other grand edifices. One large section of the old dismantled Swine Pavilion – dating to 1912 – was moved east of the Administration Building and remodeled into a modern cafeteria, or "refreshment pavilion." Soon afterward, the Indiana Farm Bureau used it as a Farmer's Building until sometime in the early 1950s.

Another section of the old swine pavilion was moved east of the Grandstand and converted into an eating pavilion. Board men called both establishments "semi-permanent"; more were planned, "that visitors . . . may be provided with meals and refreshments."

Two show arenas, a thousand cement-floored pens and an original 2,500-animal capacity made it one of the nation's "largest and best appointed." Exhibitors stayed in a southeast side basement dormitory. Expansion in 1947 increased capacity to 4,000 swine. Sixty-seven years after it was built, the Swine Barn hosted its first BMX moto cross race on a specially created 1,250-foot, hairpin-curved dirt track.

The Fairgrounds hotel, open year round, was moved to a new site just north of the east gate to make room for the Swine Barn, then it was thoroughly re-

modeled and enlarged. Of frame construction with gray stucco outer walls and red fire-resistant roof, "State Fair Inn" featured a new kitchen in its basement. On the main floor, visitors discovered the lobby and office, a main and private room; upstairs there were 20 sleeping rooms. Open to horsemen training at the track, hotel accommodations served the public as well.

Land west of Fall Creek and north of the 39th Street bridge, running north to the railroad bridge and on Noblesville Pike's east side was rented to Hawthorne Tennis Club. The agreement opened the semi-community courts not only to Hawthorne members but also to boys and girls for nominal dues. Western Lawn Tennis Association also used the grounds.

By 1925, the Fairgrounds had evolved from "a few run-down, dilapidated wooden buildings to one of the

The 1923 open pavilion Swine Barn still stands at the Fairgrounds' east side; the Board of Agriculture called it one of the nation's "largest and best appointed." Several national swine shows have convened there, as well as BMX moto cross races.

most modern and best equipped exposition grounds in America, adequate to meet the needs of Indiana's agriculture for the next fifty years." All that was needed was a new grandstand, administration and poultry buildings, and the Fairgrounds would "stand out first among exposition grounds in the United States."

Former Board president E.J. Barker of Thorntown was named

MODELED IN PURE LARD

Presidential candidates Franklin Delano Roosevelt and Wendell Willkie astride their "party animals" were modeled from pure lard at the 1940 Indiana State Fair.

secretary-treasurer in 1926. From his State House office, Barker guided the State Board and the Fair to some of its greatest triumphs. Barker stayed nine years until his January 1, 1934, no-choice resignation, blamed on "politics."

Road improvements surrounding the Fairgrounds were rapidly making it more accessible to visitors. By mid-October 1926, Fall Creek Parkway was graded and covered with crushed rock and oil, "making a good thoroughfare." Road developers then turned their attention to a thirty-foot street on the Fairgrounds' north side.

Although Governor Ed Jackson supported plans for a new grandstand and main gate, by 1928, times were growing hard. Black Tuesday, October 29, 1929, when the Stock Market crashed, was but a scant year away. "This year," Jackson noted, "we will collect from the taxpayers . . . over four million dollars less than . . . 1924 to pay operating expenses of the State government."

A surety bond covered the Board when State Savings and Trust Bank closed on April 25, 1930, with $7,695.06 of its money in a checking account. Unluckily for bookkeeper Minnie Fisher, her paycheck had been drawn on that bank. Another check was issued at Meyer-Kiser Bank, where a temporary checking account had been established, and Minnie got her pay.

By November 13, "a couple of good reliable gentlemen in the State House passed the information . . . [that] if the Board had any large amount of money in the Meyer-Kiser Bank, it had better distribute it." The Board promptly changed its account to Indiana National Bank.

Board members took a bus to Muncie on April 14, 1931, to attend the funeral of Board member W.W. Wilson. Times had grown hard. So hard that Board members' per diems were deferred at least once. So hard that a Boys' Club Camp request for 200 sheets of stationery was turned down. Grandstand planning confidently went ahead in 1931 even though the money wasn't there.

By March 3, the Board's [increased] mil tax bill became law. The next day wrecking bids were opened. Eight days later bonding bids were reviewed. A huge new grandstand, with 7,144 reserved seats and 2,272 box seats, replaced the old amphitheater.

A dismal *first* was recorded on January 3, 1934, during the annual conference and delegate meeting. "This is the first time that I recall when we have had our meeting in a hotel [the Claypool]," President Russell G. East of Shelbyville mourned. "We have always had it at the State House."

Legislation had reared its legal head with a March 9, 1933, act creating a Division of Agriculture under the Department of Commerce and Industries. Board of Agriculture members were demoted to a "non-executive board in an advisory capacity to the division of agriculture under the department of commerce and industries" with the power to convene state fairs "subject to the approval of the governor." Three days earlier, President Roosevelt had closed all the banks. And now this.

◆◆ "There is one Indiana State Fair . . . shaping the ideals of the community. [A] fair is a show place and, oftentimes . . . a post-graduate school for the breeders." Board President Guy Cantwell, 1927

Board member/State Senator John Bright Webb pointed out ten years later that legislators attempted to operate the Secretary/Fair Manager's office "by political means entirely and we saw it displayed with an overwhelming opinion that the agricultural people were against it."

It was indeed a time for change, with not much of anything to spare; there wasn't enough money to print the 1932 annual report. Instead, it was mimeographed, as were all others throughout the remainder of the decade.

Board offices were moved from the State House to the Fairgrounds Administration Building.

A 1934 view of the Federal Economic Recovery Act "Alphabet Building," located immediately west of the Administration Building. "By actual count," 116,878 visited the modernistic structure which educated the public about programs to put the nation back on its feet.

of Agriculture. No more long-winded speeches in Indianapolis hotels. Elections took place in the districts. No more meetings in the Lieutenant Governor's office at the State House.

And the Board answered to no one beyond themselves, despite the fact that a portion of Indiana property taxes went into its coffers for whatever purpose they decided was appropriate.

Individual Board member power ran deep, as Secretary-Manager Earl J. Bailey of Lowell wrote in response to fact-finding questions from the Iowa governor's office in 1962: "Each director of the Fair . . . is appointed by the president to a certain department. After general policies are established by the board, this director is in complete control of his own department and can make all decisions without the necessity of reporting to any member of the board – even the president."

The 1952 Fair took the trophy for "Finest Agricultural Fair in the Nation." ". . . [T]he board through its various members has accomplished many important projects that affect our daily lives," Centennial program readers learned. The Board took credit for better roads, "because its weight was felt in providing enabling laws. First crop and weather reports were sent by county delegates. First authentic surveys of the state's natural resources were provided by the board's geologists. Development of industry was encouraged. Establishment of a U.S. Department of Agriculture was advocated."

Board "agitation . . . resulted in the establishment of Purdue University. Breed organizations, resulting in improvement of livestock, were born under the wing of the board. Organization of the State Fish and Game Association resulted in the present Department of Conservation. Conservation practices being urged today were not new to pioneer board members and delegates.

"[A]n appraisal of its first 100 years reveals that the work of the board's members through the years has made it the most valuable department of

The Board and its committees met in many locations over the years – in Tomlinson Hall, various chambers and offices in the original and current State House, the Young Men's Reading Room, Chicago hotels, the Claypool Hotel Assembly Room, the Fairgrounds Administration Building – but the January 5, 1940, meeting in the visiting hockey team's locker room in the Coliseum reigns as oddest. Absolutely no one yelled at them to try harder.

Legislative action in 1947 set up a nineteen-member Indiana State Fair Board, of which eleven were elected from the state's eleven agricultural districts by recognized farm group delegates. The structure of the Indiana State Fair Board remained unchanged until 1989.

Five members were appointed by the governor (no more than three from one political party). The remaining members, all ex officio, were the governor, lieutenant governor and Purdue University's Agricultural Extension Service director.

Each county in an agricultural district sent one delegate or voting member to represent each agricultural interest for elections called by the Commissioner

Franklin Delano Roosevelt's Public Works Administration put men to work during the Depression. In this June 17, 1939, scene, the Coliseum ("Livestock Pavilion") is under construction, as seen from the south. The power house is in the foreground.

The Farmer's Building on the Fairgrounds' Machinery Field north side was completed in 1955, replacing the old Farm Bureau Building (a former sheep barn pressed into service around 1923) east of the Administration Building. It housed a cafeteria and kitchen, a 1,000 seat auditorium, and a display area.

AGRICULTURE & HORTICULTURE

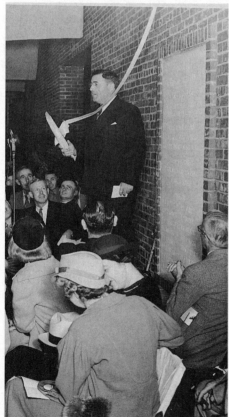

The September 5, 1937, Saddle Horse Barn formal dedication ceremony saw Governor M. Clifford Townsend christening the barn with a fourteen-inch ear of corn submitted by Hamilton County farmer N.E. Boyer. Townsend claimed that the act was more noteworthy than the christening of a battleship.

government of the state of Indiana that was ever conceived."

The Board had always been "a non-political board much to the advantage of the state, the Indiana State Fair and agriculture in general. Much credit should be given to the activity of this board during these many years for the improvement of live stock, grain and other crops in Indiana."

The Farmers' Building fulfilling the dreams of farmers and farm organizations was completed for $450,000 in 1955, featuring a 400-seat cafeteria, a kitchen, an auditorium large enough for 1,000, and a 1,900 square foot display area. Yet political dissatisfaction over Board activities was brewing. Complaints from high offices arose repeatedly, only to gasp before slipping powerlessly below the surface.

While U.S. Bankruptcy Judge Richard W. Vandiver was Governor Roger D. Branigan's press aide, he learned that the Fair Board was considered "aloof and unaccountable," according to the *Indianapolis Star* in 1989. In a memo to Branigan, Vandiver suggested selling the Fairgrounds and using the land for a parimutuel race track. Land sale proceeds would then build a new Fairgrounds west of the State Office Building. The site wasn't far from the first Fairgrounds.

Vandiver's memo "had hardly reached the governor's desk when it came

The Board of Agriculture hoped displays in the 1921 Agriculture/ Horticulture Building would "be made by county organizations until each county is represented by a pretentious showing of what it yields from the soil, the orchards and the vineyards of its farms."

flying back, with this note from Branigan: 'Vandiver, have you met the state fair board?'

"The group was so unaccountable, the governor said, that their financial records weren't even subject to audits by the State Board of Accounts. . . ."

◆◆◆

JOSEPH L. Quinn Jr. of Terre Haute, a sanitary engineer and officer of Terre Haute Gas Corporation, took over the 1970 Board presidency. Quinn's term was marked by a series of public relations setbacks.

Sometime before the 1970 Fair, *Indianapolis News'* "City Desk Memos" questioned, "Has Politics Taken Over State Fair?

"There's whispering in rural areas of the state that's the case. Joe Quinn, Jr. . . . at a Board meeting made a big pitch about Handley & Miller Inc., the advertising agency here. The Handley in the agency is former Gov. Harold Handley.

"After his pitch, Quinn said he would entertain a motion that the Fair Board hire the agency on a retainer basis for the 1970 Fair.

"His nephew, James Quinn, representing Gov. Edgar D. Whitcomb on the board, quickly responded: "'I so move.' "With little debate, the board hired the agency . . . ."

State and city officials "indicated" repairing the Fairgrounds would be "too prohibitive," *Indianapolis News'*

John Carpenter reported on July 29. An Indianapolis Department of Metropolitan Development report also was analyzing the Fairgrounds for future land use, "if it is abandoned." The report looked at sites inside and outside Marion County.

"Problems concerning the fair's future at the 38th Street location reached a climax last month when a section of the old grandstand collapsed just before the start of the Indiana Classic stock car race," Carpenter wrote.

Actually, part of the Grandstand dropped eighteen inches, according to former grounds superintendent Jesse Stuckey. "Quinn wanted me to jack it back up."

An *Indianapolis Star* report disclosed that Metropolitan Development would release a future land use report on the Fairgrounds – and possible sites for a new Fairgrounds in rural Marion County.

The day after "Indiana State Fair Expo 70," opened, radio station WFBM editorialized, "Why A New Fairgrounds?

"It's been suggested the present Fairgrounds is not large enough, not accessible enough, and too valuable for such

A 1926 Fair scene looking west. The "new" Poultry Building is still a year away, but the old one can be seen in the background, behind the Indiana Daily Student "Daily Fair Edition" newspaper headquarters.

limited use. Some have concluded rehabilitation or replacement of present buildings cannot be justified.

"[P]urchase and development of a new location would cost many millions more than could be realized from sale of the present Fairgrounds. Any large amount of construction funds the state can raise is desperately needed at our mental and correctional institutions. [A] crowded, high-speed expressway is no place for traffic jams . . . [C]rowds are the essence of fairs, anyway.

"Obviously, many Fairgrounds buildings are being maintained poorly or not at all. Some need rebuilding or replacing. But since the Fair Board reports it's barely breaking even financially, we believe a thorough study of purposes, policies and financing should be the first step."

State Representative Kenneth B. Bays of Anderson had suggested state-owned farmland near the Indiana Reformatory at Pendleton for a new fairgrounds. Doubtless, grounds help would be cheaply available.

Meanwhile, Quinn said "go first class." Quinn wanted every Fairgrounds building air conditioned. "'You can't afford to modernize the old place . . . you'd only wind up with a second-class facility,'" he told the *Indianapolis News*.

By Quinn's figuring, $12 million was needed to renovate the 38th Street Fairgrounds. He wanted a new grandstand and an updated race track "to satisfy the United States Auto Club," a new main gate, and "other improvements." Quinn also was Indianapolis Motor Speedway safety director.

He also saw to it that a scaffolding stood where the old brick tower once greeted hundreds of thousands since 1928. Forty years after it rose, the Board dynamited it.

According to Quinn, several potential new sites included one west of Plainfield on U.S. 40, a northeastern Marion County spot near 82nd Street, and north of Indianapolis off Interstate 65. Quinn told *Indianapolis News*' Frank Salzarulo that the Indianapolis Chamber of Commerce had suggested a location "beyond the I-465 loop."

◆◆◆

THE BOARD was having trouble conducting some Fair entertainment business at a professional level. Contracts for Gooding's Million Dollar Midway, Jack Kochman's Thrill Show, and the rodeo "had been declared illegal because the Fair did not advertise for bids." This was nothing unusual for the Fair Board.

"The procedure was so loose," *Star* reporter Jep Cadou wrote, "that Hal Eifort, general manager of the firm who had requested quick awarding of the contract, simply was told to draw up the new contract on the same basis as the old three-

The 1928 Main Gate brick tower was dynamited in August 1968 after a Board member convinced his fellows to destroy it. Construction scaffolding with sign barking "Rock 'n Roll Dixieland—Circus Acts and more, more, more!" replaced it in this 1970 photograph which Indianapolis News' *Frank Salzarulo captioned "Our beautiful entrance – or Quinn's Folly."*

year pact which had expired with the end of the 1970 Fair on Labor Day."

A week before Salzarulo's article, the *News'* Bob Basler talked to area residents about Fair expansion plans. None were pleased.

Already, twenty-seven out of 250 properties belonged to the Board, which had "eyes focused on owning the rest of it eventually." Some didn't want to sell. Others would, "but [would] remain bitter toward what they consider 'unfair' practices being used by the Fair Board to 'lower property values.'"

Three houses had been torn down in the past year, but additional purchases had been halted until talk about moving the Fairgrounds was resolved.

Interviews with area residents revealed that the Board had become a slum landlord, failing to repair or improve the properties. Others were afraid to improve their homes; no one knew how much longer they'd be allowed to live there.

Expansion was the practical financial move, according to Howard E. Abbott, who said the acquired lots would be used for parking.

"Another factor," he mentioned in the interview with the *News* "is this talk about a sports arena. The appropriate place for this would be on the fairgrounds, but as things stand now we couldn't accommodate all the cars." But Market Square Arena was built downtown.

◆◆◆

"WAY OF doing business" dishonor was heaped higher on the Board when the *Star* disclosed that the members had been accepting "elaborate gifts" from Gooding's Million Dollar Midway for three years.

Marion County Prosecutor Noble R. Pearcy was in the midst of making up his mind whether to call a Grand Jury investigation. He had returned from the Department of Justice in Washington September 30 after checking on Gooding's possible underworld connections.

October 1, Pearcy said he now knew Gooding's had "'absolutely no connections with the Mafia.'" An inaccurate report in the *Wall Street Journal* had linked the two. Pearcy still was on the trail of no-bid contracts, "gifts," and "other connections between the board and the firm," since the Mafia lead had grown cold.

The Board and "key staff personnel" fared well while Gooding's nudged in close. The year 1968 was good for Fair-time gifts of General Electric portable vacuum cleaners. Gooding's gave G.E. dual speaker AM-FM radios in 1969. Westinghouse bacon grills followed in 1970 only two weeks before the Board breezed through awarding Gooding's another two-year contract.

"One of the persons who received the gifts from Gooding said that they formerly were given rather openly when Fair Board members and key staff personnel visited the midway at Gooding's invitation to ride on all the rides and see all the shows – free, of course.

"But the firm 'has been operating more coyly lately,' he said. Current technique is to leave the gifts at the board members' offices while they are out." Gooding's had mastered the technique of knowing when every director was out.

Two color television sets mysteriously appeared at the Administration Building around that time. Unclaimed since the last day of the '70 Fair, the TVs were meant for "some board members," Quinn said. "We don't know who sent them here and now nobody will claim them."

Meanwhile, the *Star* learned Quinn had cancelled October's Board meeting while he toured central Africa. Governor Whitcomb was waiting for the results of an Indiana State Police and State Board of Accounts investigation into the Board and the Midway contract.

"I thought and still think that the Indiana State Fair Board is no different from any other state agency such as the Highway Commission," Quinn told Jep Cadou. "A contract involving this much money (an approximate $400,000 gross to Gooding's) should have been subject to competitive bids."

An earlier Cadou article disclosed Board member Robert M. Morse of LaPorte had purchased a 1969 Dodge for $1 from the Jack Kochman Hell Driver Show. "Morse originally paid only 2 cents state sales tax on the transaction but after an investigation by the Indiana State Revenue Department, he finally paid $24 . . . Morse said he got the 'bargain basement' price not because of any spadework he did [for] Kochman . . . which . as played the State Fair for many years."

A salesman, Morse was selling outdoor advertising at the time of his appointment by Governor Branigan, and

was secretary-manager of the LaPorte County Fair. Morse claimed the bargain price resulted from "ground work" with another thrill show which bought its cars from Kochman's Show.

He saw no conflict of interest and denied using his influence to secure Kochman's State Fair contract. *Star* investigation also discovered that Board member Oren Wright operated the Greenwood auto license branch. "Such dual job-holding is prohibited by the Indiana Constitution, according to [Attorney General Theodore] Sendak." Sendak overlooked the fact that Governor Whitcomb appointed Wright to operate the license branch, and that Whitcomb had certified Wright's board seat.

◆◆◆

A SPECIAL governor's committee recommended the Fairgrounds remain where it was on East 38th Street, according to a February 3, 1971, *Indianapolis News* story. The report called for year-round professional management at the venerable home of blue ribbons. Indiana University-Purdue University management experts, in preparing the report, reached their "stay put" conclusion because of the enormous amount of money a move would require.

The Fair was one of very few which was "self-supporting for all practical purposes," according to the *News*. By 1971, the Board received $340,000 in mil tax for building maintenance, a figure approximately 13 percent of its annual income in 1970.

But that apparently wasn't enough for improvements because the Board had been asked to remodel Exposition Hall for a black-tie dinner as part of the May 25-28 World Conference of Mayors. Costs, including installing air conditioning, had been estimated at $650,000. "The board, however, is not expected to follow through because of lack of funds."

Otis R. Bowen, M.D., of Bremen governed the state for two terms beginning in 1973. A decade after he left office, Bowen recalled the Board during his eight years in office: "During the term before me there was Board turmoil. Once that was resolved, the Board functioned better.

"[Actually,] during my term the Board functioned well," Bowen said. He recalled some of the best fairs in the coun-

try. "Although I tried hard to keep track of what was going on, I did not interfere in their decisions. I did not try to run the Board.

"The only problem apparently was apprehensiveness that the Fair was lopsided toward agriculture and too light on industry and other activities," Bowen said in May 1991. "But I didn't interfere," he said. "If it ain't broke, don't fix it."

Bowen recalled one item with a small amount of humor. "There were two different [appointed] positions in the state [which everyone clamored for]: the State Fair Board and trustees for the [state universities] boards."

Early in 1975, the Logansport Rotary Club's newsletter claimed "the structure of the body governing the State Fair is unique in the country. . . . Other state fairs are not nearly as efficiently financed. . . . The Indiana State Fair pays 78 percent of its own way. State aid for the fair comes to one [per]cent of the real estate tax, which is used for maintenance and improvement of the facilities."

A $673,000 Fairgrounds facelift greeted '75 Fair visitors. A new $98,000 38th Street main gate of three twenty-eight-foot carved Indiana limestone pylons faced on structural concrete, was set off by connecting black iron gates. Pylons honored the five areas of commerce: Agriculture, Education, Labor, Trade and Industry. Funds were provided by the General Assembly.

A 1974 steel shortage delayed opening the new $513,000 Pavilion east of the Coliseum, the last new Fairgrounds building. Legislators had appropriated $455,000 to make it happen. Constructed of brick and steel, the 78,000 square foot Pavilion replaced the fifty-three-year-old Draft Horse Barn; multi-purpose plans called for year-round use. New lighting, painting, and other work totalling $25,000 touched up the Draft Horse Barn's remaining section. The addition didn't resemble the original in the slightest.

◆◆◆

A MASTER plan introduced in November 1977 recommended "future planning for expansion should be directed toward increasing the intensity and scale of year-round activities and improving and upgrading [the] existing physical structure as well as planning for additional new facilities . . . .

"With the construction of the Market Square Arena in downtown Indianapolis, some events that made use of the Coliseum have been lost due to seating capacity, no air conditioning and quality of acoustics. Planning for improvement of some of these conditions is not being implemented . . . ." The master plan report noted that year round use of all facilities should be increased. The plan was never implemented.

On the Monday before 1984's Opening Day, Governor Robert D. Orr and Lieutenant Governor John Mutz unveiled a Fairgrounds master plan and a miniature model of the proposed new look for the grounds. The $32 million plan would carry the facility well into the 21st century – an outdoor sunken festival grounds, new carnival and Pioneer Village areas, an exhibit park, a limestone "quarry" passage, Exposition Hall expansion, a new train station, and an Agri-Center and hotel-office complex where the IUPUI 38th Street campus was located, an addition to the 4-H complex, and state office buildings. Nothing ever came of it.

◆◆◆

"THE Indiana State Fair is ready for its journey into the 21st Century," the "21 Plan" brochure proclaimed. Not yet it wasn't.

Late in 1982, the *Muncie Star*'s Bob Barnet called the plan a land grab. "Members of the state fair board who haven't been recruited into one of the new 'committees' [splintered from the original 21 Committee] are telling their constituents that they had better start talking to members of the state legislature about this Indianapolis advertising-agency-type raid on some land that belongs to all Indiana citizens."

The downtown movers and shakers likely would change the Fairgrounds "so much that its best friends never again will recognize it," Barnet argued. "There is a feeling that the present push and shove session that started in the statehouse and the downtown area could result in the Indiana State Fair Board being told, more or less politely, 'We'll let you run your state fair each year but during the rest of the time we'll make the decisions and operate the fairground.'"

In "An Open Letter" in the Winter 1984 "State Fair News," Fair Board President Bruce Walkup, from Sullivan, wrote: "Change for change's sake will not be tolerated and certain principles will not be affected by change. For example, the fair will never change its dedication to the agricultural excellence of this state. Nor will it change its search for this excellence.

"It will not change its concern for the youth of Indiana, which is expressed each year by the participation of over 40,000 young people in State Fair events, competitions, and demonstrations.

"Changes will and must take place, but only when your board feels it will serve more and serve better."

And the Board really wasn't ready yet. At the January 5, 1985, Board meeting, the Board directed the Howard Needles Tammen & Bergendoff architec-

tural firm to prepare cost estimates for the 4-H complex renovation and landscaping.

A month later, the $6 million "conceptual design" called for major 4-H dorm rehabilitation, adding four- and eight-person suites, furnishing both dorms, sitework and renovating the 4-H Exhibit Hall to make it useable year-round. Landscaping was recommended for the 38th Street/Fall Creek Gate 6 and the area by the Tee Pee restaurant.

The Board took no action on the plan. Financial problems were plaguing the Fairgrounds. Secretary Manager Sid Hutchcraft told an agricultural paper in October, "It's to the point where we absolutely have to cut expenses or generate revenue."

As of September 30, the Board's bank balance had dropped to $2,179, compared to $184,524 in 1984. Gate receipts dropped an estimated $100,000.

Most of the Fairgrounds revenue by then came directly from the annual Fair – $4.1 million in 1984. And although the mil tax brought in $1 million out of the overall $3.1 million, it wasn't enough to reverse the downward trend; higher utility costs, building repairs, and maintenance were massing faster than income.

The Coliseum, once the only major venue in town, was now rarely used during the summer months and required air conditioning if it was to compete with the newer downtown facilities. That alone would cost $1 million.

"Renovating the 4-H buildings will take priority over the Coliseum, however," farm readers learned. "[T]he Fair Board already has targeted that as the first phase in its new master plan. But that project took at least a two-year setback last spring when the General Assembly failed to grant the Board's appropriation request."

With state money years away at best, master planning would never get off the ground; by 1991, the 4-H dorms were closed for safety reasons, with unrealized hopes that they might reopen in time for the Fairgrounds centennial. The Coliseum stayed cool only when it snowed.

In the Board's June newsletter, President John Merlau of New Palestine remarked, "Unlike the majority of state fairs throughout the nation, the Indiana Board members have full management and budgetary responsibility for the departments.

"In addition, board members direct the overall policy for the year 'round use of the Fairgrounds."

The policy would be called archaic and impossible by a later and extremely short-termed secretary-manager in 1989.

"Fiscal responsibility is a major concern to the Board," Merlau wrote. "Of the Fairgrounds' $8.5 million annual operating budget, less than $1 million comes from public funds. The remainder of the Fairgrounds' operating budget is generated from the State Fair, Indy Super Pull and other Board-sponsored events."

After the Fair, former president Walkup, an appointee, said the Board should be changed, according to the *Indianapolis Star*. He suggested reducing the Board to eight appointed members, with a ninth as the secretary-manager. Walkup called the established method archaic and said that elected members often weren't chosen based on business skills.

◆◆◆

FAIRGROUNDS marketing got serious in 1988, implementing scientific surveys to determine precisely who attends the Indiana State Fair. Results revealed visitors primarily come from within a 60-70 mile radius, and less than ten percent are involved in farming. More than one-fourth are in managerial or professional positions. Fair visitors spend millions in the Indianapolis area each year.

Secretary-Manager J. Patrick Buchen resigned on February 27, 1989, after seven months on the job, "sharply criticizing fair operations and the structure of the fair's board of directors," according to *Indianapolis Star* coverage.

Buchen charged that the Board's structure "in which each director serves as both a policy-maker and department manager" was holding the Fair back. "Because of the extreme competitiveness and complexities of this business, it is equally unfair to place a director in a department where he or she may have little or no experience or expertise," Buchen said in announcing his resignation.

"The Board has to take a serious look at themselves, or the legislators will," Buchen said.

Almost immediately, Donald W. Moreau Sr. was named interim secretary-manager. Soon after, a television report inadvertently, but rather prophetically, called Moreau "Secretary-General." He would become the most powerful executive and administrative head of the Fairgrounds' modern era. Moreau rewrote the way the Fair and Fairgrounds were operated, and ran them according to his management style.

Moreau immediately identified poor conditions of Fairground buildings as a leading problem behind sinking year-round income. With renovation, he was certain the aging structures would provide far more than the estimated 20 percent contribution non-Fair related events made to the Fairgrounds' annual income.

Within hours of his appointment, Moreau estimated that $5 million

was required to repair the buildings. He later revised his estimate to $50 million. Twelve days after his appointment, Moreau brought in interested legislators for a tour of the Fairgrounds. One lawmaker was overheard remarking that the 4-H dorms, built in 1939, were in worse condition than Indiana's prisons. After the dorms were condemned in 1991, the 4-H Leadership School and other activities had to convene at the Indiana School for the Deaf, just north of the Fairgrounds' northwest side.

Three days before Moreau's appointment, an amendment to House Bill 1493 called for the establishment of the Indiana State Fair Legislative Oversight Committee. House members voted 92-8 in favor of it, indicating that the time had come for a change – major change. Fair Board president Homer McDonald later dared Oversight Committee members to

change the 1947 law governing the Fairgrounds. Neither he, nor most of the current Board directors wanted any change or would admit that problems existed at the Fairgrounds. None thought the unthinkable could occur.

Former governor Orr testified on March 28 at a Senate Agriculture and Small Business Committee that the Fairgrounds' problems were far worse than nearly everyone realized.

"There are no checks and balances," Orr told the committee. "The ones who set policy do the work." Orr wanted the legislature to restructure the Board to make it accountable to taxpayers, who, through the mil tax, had contributed millions to the Fairgrounds since the 1947 law which gave Indiana governors no authority except one vote during Board meetings.

McDonald told the committee the Fair's problems "just kinda evolved." He claimed the Orr administration had promised but not delivered financial help from the General Assembly.

◆◆◆

RESTORATION 1995, the ambitious $50 million fund-raising campaign to restore the Fairgrounds to pre-World War II's glory and to fund an endowment for programs, was supplemented by $1.14 million from the General Assembly.

The following year $1.4 million arrived from Hoosier Lottery "Build Indiana" funds.

In a March 1989 letter, McDonald wrote Governor Evan Bayh proposing a State Fair Capital Improvement Board "to monitor funds appropriated for capital improvements" at the Fairgrounds. "We regret the need to request additional assistance from you and the General Assembly, but after forty-two years of trying to maintain this large, aging facility with diminishing public resources we can no longer fulfill our statutory responsibilities without new monies to meet basic needs."

McDonald, on behalf of the Board, proposed this other board to be composed of: the Board's president, vice president, and treasurer; three governor appointees; the state budget director; the co-chairman of the House Ways and Means Committee and Senate Finance Committee as ex officio members; and a chairperson also appointed by Bayh. But House Enrolled Act 1347 took the wind out of those sails. It was too late: Bayh didn't care to give the State Fair Board a chance.

◆◆◆

"WHO or what is to blame for the mess at the Indiana State Fair?" asked an *Indianapolis Star* editorial on April 2, 1989. "Testimony before a legislative committee fingered a variety of culprits, among them uninterested state administrators, poor management, neglect of facilities and a lack of direction, expertise and long-term planning.

"[T]here is more than enough blame to go around . . .The fair is not a private venture, nor should it be treated as the exclusive province of a few special interests.

"The state provides about $1 million of the $8 million annual fair budget. The state and its taxpayers should have an accounting of how the money is spent.

"Beyond oversight, however, state administrations – current and future – should exert greater involvement in fair policy and operations. A strong state presence is needed on the board. The consequences of distance and lack of interest are all too apparent."

Time was running short for the nineteen ensconced in the paneled board room. The Indiana State Fair Advisory Commission voted December 22 to abandon the Board regime with a governor-appointed commission. The commission would run the Fairgrounds. Another governor-picked group, a "committee," would put on the Fair.

"The present State Fair Board has shown itself to be unable to run the operation as efficiently as many would like," *Indianapolis Star*'s "Behind Closed Doors" gossiper wrote. "Believe it or not, the legislature has no present control over fair board operations." It was an obscure fact most overlooked, dating to 1947.

"Many believe those directors have created fiefdoms [State Senator Louis Mahern's word] . . . and have extended their control by giving away free tickets to events at the fair to those who vote for them."

Governor Bayh's complete support of the recommendation was considered essential. He supported the change: ending an almost completely autonomous reign unchanged since 1947, the Indiana State Fair Board was abolished in 1990.

At the second regular session of the 106th General Assembly, the death knell sounded. A new law established the Indiana State Fair Commission and the Indiana State Fair Committee. The Commission, a separate corporate and politic body, consisted of five governor-appointed members, one presiding offi-cer, and the commissioner of agriculture. Commission members alone determined the Fairgrounds' course; Moreau was named executive director.

The Board lost its identity and its very name. The new State Fair Committee had seventeen members, including the governor or his designated appointee, the commissioner of agriculture, the director of Purdue University's cooperative extension service or his designee, seven governor-appointed members with agricultural backgrounds, and one member from each of the seven new agricultural districts.

Under the new law, one Fair is held annually with the emphasis on agriculture and agribusiness. That was the Committee's only job. The Commission employed Moreau as executive director and chief administrative officer. "Housekeeping" legislation the following year

♦♦ **Today, professionals operate the Fairgrounds 365 days, allowing the Board to concentrate on producing the greatest State Fair to showcase the best Indiana has to offer to its citizens, the nation, and ultimately the world.**

restored "Board" to the group's title, since "commission" and "committee" were too alike and created confusion.

The Fair Commission requested $48.8 million from the Hoosier Lottery's Build Indiana Fund to renovate the facilities over the next several years, the second-largest request in the state.

An economic impact study released following the 1991 Fair (for September 1990 to August 1991) revealed the Fairgrounds' contribution to Indianapolis:

♦ $609,418,663 in total direct and indirect sales and receipts – direct spending by Fairgrounds visitors and exhibitors amounted to almost $194 million; and more than $415 million in indirect spending;

♦ More than half the direct spending was on food and lodging – including Fair-time;

♦ $30,470,933 in earnings as a result of Fairgrounds tourism-related activities;

♦ Total attendance at Fairgrounds events in 1991 exceeded five million, including the annual State Fair. More than two million vehicles passed through Fairgrounds gates in 1991.

The Indiana State Fair Board of tomorrow, descendent of the 1851 Indiana State Board of Agriculture, again answers to the Governor, but it has little power and slighter still resemblance to the original. Streamlined, its role is purely the production and the management of the Indiana State Fair.

The first Board met in the old State House, eventually in their own Agricultural Rooms, and rarely in a body at the Fair Grounds except for special inspections, and during Fair Week. There were winter meetings where business was interspersed with important discussions and winter premium awards.

Then the Administration Building was built at the "Great Grounds" and meetings of increasingly short-sighted impact and more intense micro-management convened monthly.

The Board today no longer sets Fairgrounds policy or publishes every known agricultural, atmospheric/meteorologic, and mineral fact about Indiana.

Throughout the relocations, war cancellations, political maneuverings, attitude shifts, financial successes, and difficulties, the State Fair is still Indiana's best!

♦♦♦

❖Hurry! Hurry! Hurry!

A stolen kiss at the top of the ferris wheel. The lush dietary suicide of elephant ears, funnel cakes, and barbecued pork chops. The envious glances as you carry away the huge blue stuffed bear. . .

ALL are part of the undeniable pull of the Indiana State Fair.

The hazy swelter of Summer only serves to brighten the thrills of the Midway, and what could appeal more than a night of music under the warm open sky. The Fair has played host to many entertainers from around the globe. From John Phillip Sousa and the Beatles to the more exotic attractions of Roberta Roberts and Delores Pollard, there is something of interest for every Fair visitor.

1853 The Newhall Family singers accompanied Horace Greeley's address with "two of their choicest songs" at the second Indiana State Fair, convened in 1853 at Lafayette. Fletcher & McElrath paid $240 for the "exclusive privilege of [the] eating house at the Fair Grounds."

1859 The State Board men wanted legislators to empower agricultural societies to prohibit or remove "any temporary huckstering, gambling, or other nuisances" to a mile away from any fairgrounds. That year wasn't shaping up well for idle men of vice.

Then three days of rain bewetted fun seekers at the New Albany spectacle. Those who came were entertained by Levi J. North's Circus troupe. Sons of Malta paraded and the Silver Band performed.

1862 Despite "considerable misgivings," the State Board convened a Fair. "The troubles on the border, the large enlistments from the country, all seemed to point to a small show and attendance," according to *Prairie Farmer*, but the Otis Grove legal obligation with the railroads demanded a Fair.

"With these things in view the management took hold in earnest to make it pay, by the licensing inside of the grounds of all manner of side shows of sickening monstrocities (sic), eating saloons, patent medicine vendors, auctioneer stands, tight rope performances [a Mr. Donaldson was hired to walk the rope for $25 each of three days], etc., giving the Babel character. . . ."

The Nineteenth United States Infantry bandsmen made martial music at $25 per day on Wednesday, Thursday, and Friday in an agreement allowing only fifty dollars "should the fair prove a failure." Donaldson the rope walker received the same terms.

1863 One-hundred dollars secured Mademoiselle Carolista for four performances on the tight rope. The Indianapolis Brass Band played one day for $50.

1865 Despite purifying efforts, vice frequently found its way into the Fairgrounds. During Fort Wayne's Fair, the Board told Superintendent J. A. Grosvenor, who had arranged for the "side-shows" and "eating stalls," "to remove . . . all

A special "Sanitary Fair" exhibit of war trophies and other articles "of interest" was presented, then auctioned off, during the 1864 Fair under the auspices of the State Sanitary Commission. The auction proceeds, less Board expenses, were donated to benefit sick and wounded Union soldiers.

gambling tables, and establishments for gambling . . . .[T]hey [must] desist immediately."

1869 Fair planners recommended converting the old Dining Hall back to just that instead of its 1868 duty of exhibiting carriages and wagons. The Amphitheatre basement could serve for a Carriage and Wagon Hall, in their opinion.

Once Fair dates were set, Secretary Andrew J. Holmes telegraphed the adjoining states with the news. On the Fair's second day, Board vice president John Sutherland contracted with a Professor Wilbur to make balloon ascensions on Thursday and Friday, at $100 each performance.

Side saddles were offered to the top "Lady Equestrianism" performances.

"Much interest was manifested in this novel exhibition on Indiana fair ground." The three entrants were Mrs. Rena Brooks, Miss Kate Mayhew, both of Indianapolis, and Mrs. Lemuel Hackney of Edinburgh. Miss Mayhew was "mounted on a bad horse, and was consequently beaten." Our Mrs. Brooks won the $75 side saddle, while Mrs. Hackney settled for the $50 second-place prize.

Yet another novelty appeared: Velocipedestrianism. In the mile trial, W.V. Hoddy, Terre Haute, pedaled to a $50 first prize over eight other entrants with a time of 8:45. George Thudium of Indianapolis received a $25 second prize, with a time of 10:02. More novel still, in the "most artistic management of veloci- pedes," Willie Domm of Mt. Healthy in Hamilton County, Ohio, scored the $25 first premium. In the three-man competi- tion, Indianapolis William Hindman came in a $15 second. T.C. Redding of Indianapolis, received a $5 award for ex- hibiting his two-wheel velocipede.

1870 Superintendent John B. Sullivan was "thoroughly persuaded that . . . all side shows, auction stands, fat women, white negroes, snake shows and all classes of similar exhibitions" should be prohibited, since the Encouragement Act made no provisions for them.

"They bring in their trail the worst classes of thieves and scoundrels of low and high degree; besides, no good emanates from their exhibitions. [T]he young are especially attracted by their flaming handbills, and the sugared words of the showmen . . . for they amount to little else than an alluring bait to just that class of people who . . . visit your annual exhibitions for information touching ag- riculture or mechanical sciences, of which the State Fair is presumed to be an exposition."

Sullivan wondered whether "the young lad remember[s] more of Fine Art Hall than of the snake show? . . . Is it as important to give the rising generation instruction in the side show business as it is to teach them in stock growing and the various arts connected with farming and mechanism?" He thought all agreed that "the custom of admitting auction stands and trinket lotteries [was not] very much better." The area used by these purveyors of vice was needed for displaying reapers, plows, threshers, and other farm machinery.

The argument worked and the Board barred all side shows in 1870. The ban "partially got rid of their annoyance . . . and it may have decreased the amount of your receipts some four or five hun- dred dollars," but Board president James D. "Blue Jeans" Williams was convinced the space it gave machinery and farm implement exhibits "was of more value to the sensible portion of the community."

1871 Sideshows nearly were barred again, but after "argument and discus- sion," the Board decided to allow "the glass blowing exhibitors, steam man, and perpetual motion . . . each exhibitor pay- ing therefore the sum of one hundred and fifty dollars." That was for inside the grounds. Those outside the fence paid "reasonable" fees to the sideshow com- mittee, which decided "the propriety of permitting . . . excluded shows, to erect their canvas outside of the grounds of the Society: provided, that they are not of an immoral, or pernicious tendency . . . ."

Arriving bands discovered the Board unprepared to receive them; some had traveled far to perform. Embarrassed, the Board resolved that any still around on Thursday and Friday would find a place to perform. Those found "deserv- ing and meritorious" were given "consid- eration . . . in the shape of a silver medal."

Fort Wayne's 21-member Silver Cornet Band, under Professor Charles A. Jones' direction, won that silver medal, "with a suitable inscription, significant of their superior skill as musicians." The band also took $50 on the long trip home. With "the reputation of being one of the best . . . in the Northwest," the band per- formed throughout the next Fair. Benham Brothers awarded the band $50 for "best musical instrument band," although no others entered. After all, the band was "the best in the States, or in the West."

Benham awarded Jones himself a $60 E-flat cornet.

1872 No side shows or "exhibitions of any kind" were allowed on the grounds, although Ohio Steam Dental Company's first display of false teeth and dental in- struments was found in the Fine Art Hall. "Despite the ghastliness of this array, it is a point of great interest, because of a little machine, constantly in operation, show- ing the action of the human jaws, with false teeth inserted."

1874 Fair President John Sutherland discovered "most positive proof" that ven- dors "grossly and defiantly violated . . . the laws of the State by selling intoxicat- ing liquors" at 1873's gala.

Once again, the Board resolved "to absolutely prohibit" liquor sales dur- ing the Fair. Almost immediately, an- other member honed the ban to include all malt liquors. Superintendent Hezekiah Caldwell recommended selling popcorn, candy, cider, lemonade and cigar stands to the highest cash bidder; and barring all "small peddling institutions, patent right, medicine, lung testers, lifting ma- chines, etc."

1875 Opening exercises convened in the Music Hall, with the Anderson Cornet Band blaring. Ten musicians per- formed "first-class music" for two and one-half hours each morning, afternoon and evening for $31 each day.

Indianapolis women had free use of the Music Hall for a three-day Centen- nial tea party during the Exposition. Pro- fessor Gresh was turned down, however, when he asked to rent it "for dancing purposes." The learned Indianapolis man provided Exposition music "at thirty-three dollars per day" the next Fair, only to be struck from the program as a loss-cutting measure.

1876 Serious alcohol problems led to one of the Board's famous WHEREAS's: ". . . the trafic (sic) in ardent spirits . . . during the exhibitions . . . has given rise to the false impression, as expressed by cer- tain journals, public lecturers and advo- cates of the temperance cause, that due precautionary measures were not being used . . . to guard against the evil influences of this great source of profit to those engaged in its trafic . . . ." Stronger measures were taken to guard against spirits.

1878 No night exhibitions were secured. Daylight was needed for Maurice Thompson's archery tournament. The Crawfordsville man recommended a gold bugle horn badge for "best skill at one-hundred yards," but only a diploma for "best skill at 50 yards."

Harry Gilbert, aeronaut, was paid $450 "on account of the balloon race; provided, an ascension [was] made [October 3] at 3 o'clock, P.M." That afternoon, Mr. Stacy, Indianapolis Gas Company superintendent, obtained assurance of a $150 payment "on account of the balloon race, before he would refill the balloon for the ascension to be made tomorrow." Three months later, Boardmen rejected Gilbert's request for "an appropriation . . . on account of the injury to himself and balloon in the attempted ascension at the fairground ."

During the 1880s, Belle L. Closser performed at the Baldwin Piano display in the center of the Grand Hall's first floor on a platform about three feet high surrounded by a fence made of wooden slats and covered with a bright carpet, recalled Charlotte Cathcart in her 1965 book, *Indianapolis From Our Old Corner*. Cathcart was born in 1877. Closser played "against a background noise of lowing or protesting farm animals. It was the only music at the Fair."

1880 Octagonal lunch stands were moved and converted into sheep pens. Forty-four years later, an old sheep barn was moved to the old Fish and Game building location and equipped as a dining hall, while another was moved south of the new Sheep Barn and converted into yet another dining establishment.

1882 When Captain Richardson of Richardson Zouaves proposed to give an exhibition drill on Friday afternoon, the proposition was accepted "with thanks."

That evening, with an "objection being made to the proposed performance of a certain band of negro minstrels and a certain Italian band upon the grounds for exhibitors in the Mechanical Department,

it was moved . . . that they be allowed to perform during *good behavior* (italics added) . . . . [F]ive voted in the affirmative and five in the negative." Board president Lebbeus B. Custer then broke the tie, voting for the performers. But the Board had second thoughts. The following afternoon, "after due consideration," Custer was sent to talk to the bands' managers "and, if possible, persuade them to abandon the same."

1884 Professor S.A. King was hired to make balloon ascensions. Shows with "immoral and other objectional features" were banned. Indianapolis Light Infantry Company offered to put on a one-day exhibition drill for $150, but a counter offer paid $75 for the best drilled and uniformed company on Wednesday, October 1.

On Opening Day, Captain Richardson's Broom Brigade was admitted free in exchange for a free exhibition.

1887 Overcrowding led president W.B. Seward to recommend "a more careful distribution" of exhibitions, and "rigidly excluding side shows of every description . . . so that the fat woman and the five-legged calf will be seen there no more, forever."

Indianapolis Mayor Caleb Denny called for a night parade "including illuminations" to keep people overnight in the capital city. Seven years later, Denny still wanted the Board to devise attractions to hold visitors' attention for more than a mere day.

The *Indianapolis News* reported on some of the more disturbing attractions: a fat woman, a boa constrictor and the "Caucasian Beauty." Not so disturbing was the Women's Christian Temperance Union ice cream emporium.

1888 "The Fair," a promotional circular, touted Thursday night's fun amid a clutter of advertisers: "Evening Exhibition in the Main Hall – Music and promenade concerts from 7 to 10 p.m. Novel entertainment by Model Clothing Co."

A cyclorama, "a pictorial representation, usually of a battle or landscape, displayed on a circular wall in imitation of natural perspective, and viewed from a central point" (*Webster's*), came to the Fair this year. Spectators were invited to see the "Battle of Atlanta" on Market Street, between the State House and Circle Street. "The Most Magnificent Cyclorama in the United States – Fifty Feet High, Four Hundred Feet In Circumference. 30,000 Soldiers in Action. Larger and Finer than the Famous Gettysburg, of Chicago."

1891 The Juvenile Band provided musical entertainment at the last Camp Morton State Fair. No privileges were sold "for the sale of liquors, games of chance or immoral shows."

1892 Secretary Leon T. Bagley was quite assured that "in the matter of 'special attractions' . . . people of to-day will not come 75 to 100 miles to see a balloon go 3,000 feet in the air, or to see the noted 'Moose and Elk Attraction,' but on the other hand they will come to see some noted horse go against time, or in a matched race, or some celebrated herd of cattle, breed of horses . . . ."

1896 "Objectionable show" complaints led to eviction threats.

The Art Hall gallery offered an X-ray exhibit during the Fair, courtesy of Caldwell and Haywood.

1897 After the Fairgrounds was "thoroughly washed" of the "pollution they received by fake shows and other disreputable concerns and gambling devices," visitors were no longer "contaminated."

1898 A $3,500 bad decision was made when Pain's Fireworks Company was hired for the "Battle of Manila." The show flopped and the Board paid only $3,000 of the original price. Secretary Charles Downing claimed the Board owed

John Phillip Sousa's band, "a great drawing card," performed several State Fair concerts from 1899-1903. Sousa was the first nationally prominent musician at the Fair. Sousa and his band cost $3,500 in 1901-03. For 1903, Sousa played two afternoon concerts at the Fair and two evenings at Tomlinson Hall downtown on Market Street.

social visit with friends, and not be annoyed by seeing or hearing on or near the grounds anything that would offend refined tastes, or in any way injure or debase innocent childhood. . . . [F]airs are and should be for the best elements of society."

The Sousa Band played for $3,500. The Odd Fellows maneuver drills cost $1,000.

1902 John Phillip Sousa and his band performed Wednesday and Thursday afternoons and evenings that fiftieth Fair for $3,500. Three harness races followed. The Woman's Building hosted a 9 'til noon and a 1 to 4 o'clock concert the same days as the Sousa performances.

1903 Negotiations for the John Phillip Sousa concerts were initiated early in January. Agreed upon by March, Sousa played four concerts: Wednesday and Thursday afternoons at the Fair, and both evenings at Tomlinson Hall downtown on Market Street for $3,500.

The owner of Dan Patch, Marion Willis Savage of Minneapolis, offered the famed horse for an exhibition race.

1904 Dare Devil Tilden and E.J. McGowan's diving horses provided Fair thrills. McGowan was reimbursed for half the cost for digging a diving pit for the horses and for filling the hole with water.

1906 Cavalry and artillery drills arranged "on the spur of the moment proved so very popular" that president H.L. Nowlin wanted a bigger program in 1907. Colonel Russell B. Harrison and General Carter helped make the military show possible entirely through "good will . . . wholly to gratify the people" at no charge.

An "airship" (a dirigible) was specially featured at that Fair. Although it "seemed to give universal satisfaction, it was one of the most uncertain things on the grounds." Nowlin didn't want an airship back "until it is more certain."

patrons "an apology . . . especially those who saw it on the opening night. To say that the Board was disappointed is putting it mildly. We have information that the production was tame . . . ."

Victorian morality raged unabated as the era ended. "No question-able features of any kind or character were permitted to enter . . . at any time . . . ."

1899 John Phillip Sousa's band, "a great drawing card," performed two Fair-time concerts; music costs reached $3,259.50. A "drilling chorus" cost $105.

1901 "[T]he management sought to make this fair . . . appeal to the best element of society – a fair where the most refined and Christian lady could take her children and enjoy a day in viewing the wonderful progress displayed on every hand from factory, farm, orchard, garden and home, and at the same time have a

1907 The 1907 Fair was "Interesting in Character! Educational in Scope!" Daily amusements featured airship flights, John

C. Weber's Cincinnati band, local bands and vaudeville attractions – all free every day.

1908 One thousand dollars was appropriated for the six-horse team exhibits "such as are owned by Nelson Morris, Swift & Co., Armour & Co., and S&S of Chicago."

J.A. Craig of Greenwood proposed a Greenwood Juvenile Band concert, and a zouave drill. The Juvenile Band was approved for a one-day concert on September 8.

1909 The following is a taste of 56th Fair entertainment: the thirty-five musician Indianapolis Military Band; bands from Muncie and Plainfield; the *Indianapolis News* Newsboys Band (J.B. Vanderworker organized the 50-boy band in March, 1900; a second band had 45 boys); the Six Abdallahs acrobatic novelty act; the Four Kellys in a hazardous high wire act; and Nicholas Chefalo, who did "Looping the Death Trap," the "Loop, etc."

Also appearing were the La Tell Sisters, "The Flying Fairies," the Marco Twins – "Vaudeville's Laughing Fit," Hill and Silviany in a new and exciting bicycle act, Miss Royal and Her Horses, the Ishkawa Jap Troupe of Acrobats, and The Herbert A. Kline Shows.

Those seeking "privileges" learned "It is useless to write for privileges for gaming, questionable shows, or the sale of intoxicating liquors, including hop ale and near beer." No intoxicating liquors were allowed for gifts, either. Also

"no monstrosities or beggars [were] allowed on the grounds."

1910 Pain's Fireworks Company secured Board approval for its "The Battle in the Clouds" show. John C. Weber's Band was engaged.

1911 President Isaac Newton Brown lined up a Mr. Bumbaugh for three "aeroplane" flights priced at $250 each.

1914 The Board considered special attractions including monoplanes, air balloons, and Wright flying machines. Thompson the aviator was engaged to make flights "after the manner of Clem Peachy."

Natiello's Band of Louisville performed. Also present were Mangean Troupe vaudeville, Namba Japs, Reno & Dailey, Forbes-Cameron Troupe and Castine & Devalles. Tom W. Allen Company handled the carnival.

1915 Fortune tellers were excluded from concessions.

Miss Ruth Law, aviatrix, brought a parachute act to the Fair, with one flight and parachute jump each day, for $1,250. She threw in fancy flying at no charge.

Miss Law was the Fair's first woman flyer, recalls old-timer and retired newspaperman Richard Jackson of Greencastle. "She landed on the track and took off . . . and I was one of the scouts who kept the people in line.

J.B. Vanderworker organized the fifty-boy Indianapolis News NewsBoys Band in March 1900; a second band had forty-five younger boys. The band took first prize in the juvenile band contest at the 1904 Louisiana Purchase Exhibition World's Fair in St. Louis. "Practically all the boys attend school regularly," an old News *record reveals.*

"She was much like Amelia Earhart . . . she had a harsh face," Jackson remembers. "It looked like she had lived hard."

1916 A 2,000-foot "high speed roller coaster" was erected on the Fairgrounds that year. Schoepflin Indianapolis Coaster Company invested $10,000 in the project; Mahan-Keenan Construction of Oklahoma City built it. Old-timer Jackson remembers an amusement park in connection with the Fair. "At basketball sectional time, at noon on sunshiny days we'd climb all over that giant roller coaster – all the way to the top."

◆◆◆

AN ERA ended late in 1916 with the death of taffy-maker Caroline Jessop (March 3, 1840 – December 10, 1916). "Known to Millions," Mrs. Jessop's "Good, Clean Taffy Brought Prosperity to [a] Woman of Unusual Ability," according to May 1918's *Hub of the Universe*, which belatedly told the story of a widow of forty years and her "candymaking outfit."

"Visitors to the Indiana Fair last fall who sought their annual treat of

"Uncle Ed" Jessop (far left), an unidentified man, Orin Morgan (whom Uncle Ed raised), Grandma Caroline Jessop, and her son Joseph await customers at the "Mrs. Jessop, The Lady Confectioner" stand sometime before 1917. Today, the fifth generation family business still sells taffy at the Fair.

chewing candy, found the candy as usual in Mrs. Caroline Jessop's pavilion on the north side of the Fine Arts building, but . . . she died . . . and her death marked the passing of one of the Hoosier exposition's oldest concessionaires."

According to the *Hub*, "in the beginning she carried her candy-making outfit from one fair to another in a trunk, but in her later years the business had grown to an extent where two large motor trucks and two touring cars were used to transport the crew of workers and outfit from one fair to another."

For years she did all the work of her "traveling candy factory . . . her candy was always known for its purity, her tent for its cleanliness, and she was an insistent follower of all public health rules. The candy was made from a recipe of her own and she also originated the flavoring."

She left her business to her son Charles, from Connersville. His son Daniel Jessop and his wife Mary carried on the tradition.

"They used to make long strips of taffy here," Mary recalled in 1991. "Charles would pull it with a hook." During World War II, with widespread rationing, the Jessops were the only concessions with candy at the Fairgrounds, she said. "Sometimes we'd use malt syrup."

Mary's daughter Jan Jessop Burton took over after her retirement, and Jan's children still work at the Fair. Today, Jessop Taffy is sold at five state fairs and many county fairs, but 'way back then, when their banner read "Mrs. C. Jessop, The Lady Confectioner," the Jessop name was familiar all over the country.

◆◆◆

1918 Auto polo, with stripped-down Ford Model Ts sporting roll bars as big as wagon wheels, was booked to perform. A framework over the radiator allowed the cars to bump a six-foot ball around the race track.

1921 In its first Fair appearance, the eighty-man Purdue University Military Band agreed to perform a week of music.

1925 In April, a Mr. Baumbaugh proposed to build the largest balloon in the world, "200 feet high, 17-1/2 tons lifting capacity." The Board offered ground space for the project.

The 240-singer Indianapolis Oratorio Society performed throughout Fair week.

The Riding Lloyds and Ed Holder's Ebenezer were secured to perform, along with Barry Circus, Robison's Elephants, the Sinclair Highlanders and the Fighting Fords. Harry M. Snodgrass, "King of the Ivories," was there. "Egypt," a Gordon Fireworks show, was at the Grandstand.

A massive auto exhibit and a display about Los Angeles County, California, could be found in the Manufacturer's Building.

The Greater Sheesley Shows, "the largest carnival company in the country," arrived at the Midway in forty rail cars.

The Belgian Draft Horse Association put on a Horse Pulling contest. Pulls soon became a standard bill of "Fair."

"Cleopatra," a tremendous five-hundred-foot-long spectacle and fireworks show starred sixteen ballet and thirty-two other dancers. "Colored" auto races and a "colored revue" included fireworks.

1926 Orpheum and Keith lined up the Frank J. Sidney #1 bicycle act, the Australian Whip Crackers, the Kasewell Sisters Aerialists, the Flying Melzers, and Reine & Caruse, who played basketball and polo on bicycles. Also included in the contract were the Daro-pole act, Nochols-Chefalo looping death trap, and the "Cotton Pickers" and Scotch Lassies bands. A ninety-minute fireworks show featured the "Hawaiian Volcano" spectacle.

Greater Sheesley Shows brought in the 1926 carnival, with twenty shows and "twelve high class riding devices." The "Hayday," a new ride, took the place of the scenic railway. No fortune tellers were promised. The carnival employed four hundred workers and forty rail cars brought it to town.

Eastern's Educated Horse was paid $400 to show. A rodeo cost half that amount. The U.S. Navy received free recruiting space. Indianapolis Military Band and the 54-boy Franklin Masonic Band made Fair music.

1927 Mr. Baumbaugh returned in July with a plan for the world's largest balloon: one and one-half million cubic feet, or five times larger than anything ever built, capable of carrying newspapermen, radio experts, motion picture men – the first "talkie" motion picture, starring Al Jolson in "The Jazz Singer," was shown in New York City October 6 – and others. One thousand soldiers would be required to hold the balloon in place. The estimated cost of the project was $35,000-$50,000. Baumbaugh asked the Board to pick up $10,000 of the costs. They asked to see the plan in writing and never formally discussed it again.

1928 Fireworks were out and the rodeo was in: A.C. Rowland's Flying X Rodeo was a twenty-five cowboy and cowgirl group, with a ten-piece band, 150

head of wild horses "shipped direct from Montana," and fifteen Indians. The Indians raced, and there were also chariot races, Roman standing and relay races. Rowland offered to bring in a buffalo which would be ridden every day, then "on Friday have Indian hunt, kill buffalo, barbecue it and serve in sandwiches on Saturday. Will furnish Indian to cut sandwiches and the bread." (Indians made sandwiches?)

The deal almost fell through when Rowland wired that he couldn't obtain bonding. By July, "satisfactory arrangements" were made, and the Board advanced him money because he didn't have enough to pay freight and other expenses.

Lester, Bell & Griffin clown act, "Five Fearless Fliers," four elephants, six auto polo cars, and a twelve-minute tumbling act "composed of Japs" provided free entertainment.

Indiana Farm Bureau offered a new Fair feature: a contest in every county "to discover the best quartet" through eliminations, as judged by the State Federation of Music Clubs.

Military entertainment at the 1928 Fair was potentially lethal. Colonel McIlroy of Fort Harrison staged Tuesday and Friday Grandstand parades of five hundred troops, three machine gun companies, mule teams and a band.

Four sirens in cotton tights did night-time Grandstand shows sometime in the '30s.

Wabash County Farm Bureau's 1930 Whoopee Band and other amateur groups were relied upon for much State Fair entertainment.

Delaware County's Farm Bureau quartet won second prize in the 1930 Indiana State Fair annual singing contest: (l-r) Walter L. Jester, Raymond Gibson, Omer Brown, Merrill Waite.

1929 No time was wasted hiring Walter Stanton & Company's giant rooster comedy act.

After the Fair, Secretary-Treasurer E.J. Barker recommended and received full Board approval that "all eating places must keep their menus and prices posted in plain sight of the public and the following prices for certain articles are hereby established."

Cold ham sandwich	10 cents
Hamburger	10 cents
Frankfurter	10 cents
Hot pork and beef	15 cents
Fish	15 cents
Coffee	10 cents
Lemonade	10 cents
Orangeade	10 cents
Pop drinks	10 cents
Juices	10 cents
Dry beer	15 cents

The Board reserved the right to change prices "provided they notify the concessionaires."

1930 Four Fairs later, Gordon Fireworks Company each evening presented 'Hawaiian Nights" – what a spectacle! "[A] remarkable, vivid and realistic portrayal of life in the Island Home of Love

1933 The WLS Barn Dance began that year in the Coliseum. The great Chicago radio station brought its crew for a first Saturday night program from nine to midnight. WLS collected admissions up to $3,000 and turned the rest over to the Board. One stipulation was that the Fairgrounds gates were to be thrown open at 6 p.m. The deal went through, and the WLS Barn Dance became a part of Indiana State Fair history.

Hudson Fireworks Display Company brought a 292-shell "Victory of the Air" show. Hudson offered a sweet deal: "...if the board is not satisfied in any respect, they can deduct whatever they see fit from the amount due [us] without any recourse from [us]." After the Fair, nearby resident Ancil T. Brown protested the 11 p.m. nightly fireworks and cannonading, calling it "disturbing and unnecessary." Boardmen filed his letter.

D.D. Murphy Shows furnished midway fun. The shows, "rated as the best in the country, include[d] fourteen major riding devices and sixteen of the highest type shows obtainable." Murphy Shows arrived in its own train of thirty double length railroad cars, with more than 500 persons on the payroll. "Among the special features . . . 'Melody Maids,' featuring Miss Alice Melville and her Hollywood Troupe of Dancers; the 'Georgia Minstrels' a splendid company of thirty colored musicians; several large collections of real freaks and many others."

1933 Beer came to the Fairgrounds, but only after Governor Paul V. McNutt, informed in August that the Board was evenly split on the issue and wanted his tie-breaking vote, said he was for beer. Purdue Dean John Harrison Skinner voted against it.

1936 Captain F.F. Frakes' September 6 Thrill Day eclipsed nearly every other known stunt when he crashed his air-

and Romance," featuring a Mount Mauna Loa eruption, the destruction of a village, and a cast of three hundred "living actors."

1931 The Indiana National Guard's 113th Observation Squadron needed more flying time, but Great Depression gasoline was at a premium. In January, Boardmen learned that the Guard had ten "big airships" for a "grand aerial maneuver" planned for the final Saturday of the Fair.

The problem was that the Guard's fuel allotment was running on empty. Planes would fly if the Board donated either the gas or the money. The Guard "would be glad to get five-thousand (gallons), probably at ten cents." The rest of the program built around 139th Field Artillery units from Fort Harrison.

By May the deal had shaped into a $575 fuel donation, later bargained to $625, leaving $20 for a six-mule team attraction. The September 12 aviation spectacular – an auto-gyro ship, aerobatics, aerial combat, bombing and formation flying – today would have a hard time with the Federal Aviation Administration.

A Guard airplane flew over Danville September 3 and dropped handbills depicting an aerial view of the Fairgrounds. Altogether, twenty-two towns surrounding Indianapolis were barraged by 100,000 bills. Two hundred red ones were good for free admission September 12. (One red bill still exists at the Indiana State Library.)

plane into a house built in front of the Grandstand. Eleven other acts included: head-on crashes, trick and fancy motorcycle riding, "and other almost suicidal feats."

Major Al Williams brought in his Flying Circus. Luke J. Pasco had a sheep dog act, performing twice daily.

1934 Troutman's YMCA Band had one-hundred and fifty players, as did the American Legion Band. No drum corps show was booked since the Legion's convention was scheduled too close to the Fair. Other bands such as the Newsboys' Band, Lions' All State Band, and the (I.U.) Hoosier Music Festival performed.

The I.U. Band, a 156-piece "massed band" of outstanding young male musicians from each county, formed the nucleus of the Festival. The group was housed in the barracks vacated by the Indiana National Guard north of the track.

Conductor-composer Frank Simon co-directed with I.U.'s Frederick E. Green.

Every evening, Barnes-Carruthers staged an elaborate revue, stage show and water ballet, capped off with fireworks.

1938 Children under twelve were admitted free on War Veterans Day. Many ran to see Lucky Teter's Hell Drivers Sunday afternoon thrill show at the Grandstand.

Teter's premium book ad claimed Teter, "world's champion daredevil, and his internationally famous Hell Drivers will smash, crash, and race his stunt automobiles and motorcycles in rapid succession . . . Teter himself will attempt his hazardous double somersault, rolling a stock sedan over at terrific speed, sending it end-over-end and side-over-side. The brilliant stunt star will also jump a stock car over row after row of automobiles

placed in front of him and will crash another car through a flaming solid timber barrier . . . while traveling at top speed in mid-air."

The "Parade of Stars" revue featured "A Parisien Fantasy," the Cosmopolitan Mixed Octette, Alvis Lynn the Prima Donna, premier danseuse Ruth Pryor, and Carl Freed's Harmonica Lads.

Captain Frakes returned with an even more amazing aerial show, this time with two planes crashing in midair.

The WLS Prairie Farmer National Barn Dance's Saturday night program, with its entire original cast, was re-broadcast nationally "over NBC chain" from a Grandstand stage. "Due to several different times in effect on that date, the show will run continuous from 6:30 until after 11 P.M."

Daily until midnight, Johnny J. Jones' "Mighty Exposition" offered free acts and bands such as the Gay New Yorkers, International Casino, Temple des

Rhumba, Darktown Follies, Circus Side Show, Globe of Death (a motordrome with alligators, girls, and seals, although the seals weren't guaranteed), a Giant Stratoship, a $10,000 Skooter Ride, and four Ferris Wheels.

1939 The Board nixed a proposition for a three-balloon race awarding prizes for top altitude, time, and distance. Instead of the "ordinary balloon ascension of coming down in a parachute," the rejected proposal had the pilots riding them down. ◆◆◆

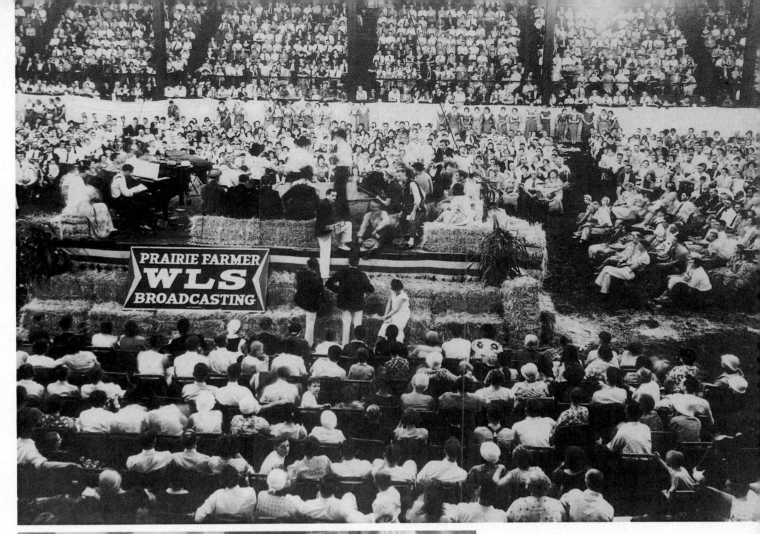

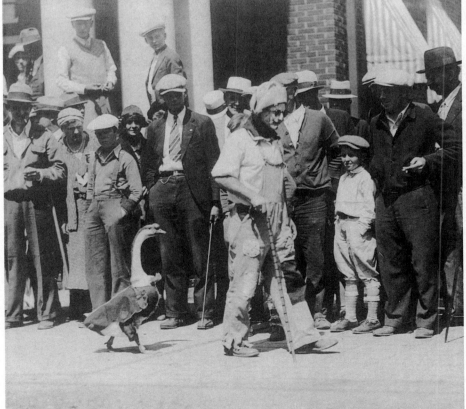

Gooding Greater Shows' barkers hound spectators into the '34 "all alive" freak tent which starred Roberta Roberts the hermaphrodite.

Madame Bedini performed with her trained white circus horses in 1932.

Scene from the first Prairie Farmer WLS Barn Dance, broadcast coast-to-coast from the Coliseum in 1933.

Clown farmer Gerald Duncan of Columbus Junction, Iowa, and his trained Brown Chinese gander "Chink" advertised the '32 Poultry Show.

Indianapolis Police Sergeant Arvil "Jigger" Hudson and vaudeville's "Shorty the Cop" in '32.

Labor Day crowds throng the Midway in '34; some paid to visit the Bug House.

Hand-car rides attracted children to South Bend-based J. C. Weer Carnival Company's 1933 Midway.

Carolyn East, granddaughter of '33 Board President Russell East of Shelbyville, prepares to try her hand at the kiddie rides.

The American Legion's 1934 Drum and Bugle Corps contest attracted 600 Legionnaires; an estimated twelve thousand watched the second annual event.

Lucky Teter's Last Leap

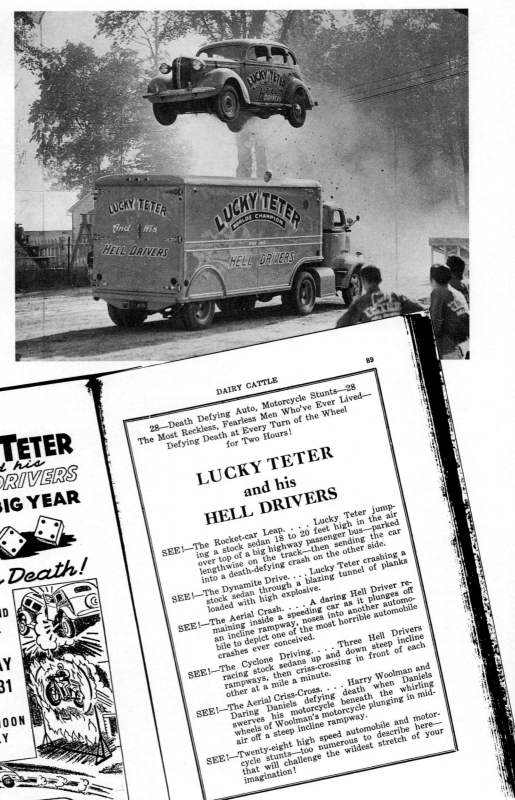

EARL "LUCKY" TETER of Noblesville, who had brought his "Hell Drivers" auto daredevils to the Fairgrounds many times, died attempting a show-climaxing stunt in front of a 12,000-person Grandstand crowd on July 5, 1942. Staged for the Army Emergency Relief Fund, the show was to be his last for the duration of World War II.

Teter began his stunt career in 1932 and was believed to be the first man ever to purposely turn over a car. For safety (and probably luck), he wore a regulation football helmet and the same pair of heavy black boots for nine years until his death at age thirty-nine.

Only Teter performed the dread "leap" – driving up a ramp at high speed,

LUCKY TETER *and his* **HELL DRIVERS** **8TH BIG YEAR**

Still Defying Death!

GRANDSTAND FEATURE

SUNDAY AUG. 31

AFTERNOON ONLY

89

DAIRY CATTLE

28—Death Defying Auto, Motorcycle Stunts—28
The Most Reckless, Fearless Men Who've Ever Lived—
Defying Death at Every Turn of the Wheel
for Two Hours!

LUCKY TETER and his HELL DRIVERS

SEE!—The Rocket-car Leap. . . . Lucky Teter jumping a stock sedan 18 to 20 feet high in the air over top of a big highway passenger bus—parked lengthwise on the track—then sending the car into a death-defying crash on the other side.

SEE!—The Dynamite Drive. . . . Lucky Teter crashing a stock sedan through a blazing tunnel of planks loaded with high explosive.

SEE!—The Aerial Crash. . . . A daring Hell Driver remaining inside a speeding car as it plunges off an incline rampway, noses into another automobile to depict one of the most horrible automobile crashes ever conceived.

SEE!—The Cyclone Driving. . . . Three Hell Drivers racing stock sedans up and down steep incline rampways, then criss-crossing in front of each other at a mile a minute.

SEE!—The Aerial Criss-Cross. . . . Harry Woolman and Daring Daniels defying death when Daniels swerves his motorcycle beneath the whirling wheels of Woolman's motorcycle plunging in mid-air off a steep incline rampway.

SEE!—Twenty-eight high speed automobile and motorcycle stunts—too numerous to describe here—that will challenge the wildest stretch of your imagination!

jumping over a truck and a clear span, and then landing on another ramp.

Before beginning his ill-fated performance, Teter, who talked of "joining up," told the crowd it probably would be his last until after the war.

Teter's last words were, "I want to thank the officers and soldiers in Indianapolis and I'm dedicating this last stunt, not only to the soldiers here, but to all the boys in Uncle Sam's armed forces throughout the world."

As Teter's car rounded the curve before starting up the ramp, it went into a slide, raising a cloud of dust. Assistants said they heard the motor miss, probably as a result of dust clogging the carburetor air intake. They believed the loss of speed then caused the accident. The car left the ramp, barely cleared the transport truck, then nosed underneath the second ramp. Supporting timbers shattered, the ramp fell on top of the car, crushing in the top and pinning Teter under the wheel, according to their report.

Earl "Lucky" Teter brought the Fair its first auto daredevil thrill show in the 1930s. Teter's show guaranteed stunts performed by the "most reckless men who've ever lived." After Teter's death in '42, Joie Chitwood took over the show.

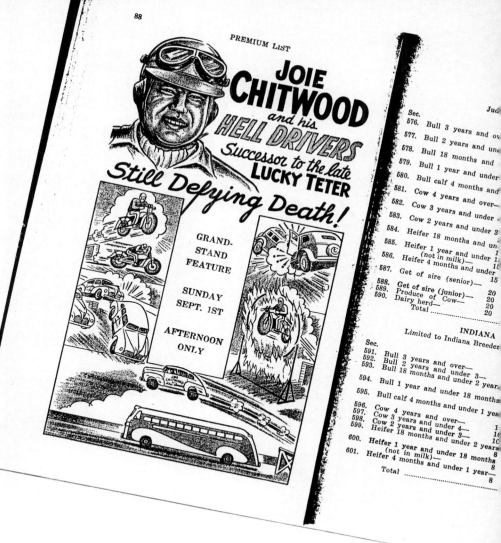

He was dead on arrival at City Hospital. (Wishard Hospital today, but City Hospital from 1862 or so to 1951, then changed in 1951 to Marion County General Hospital, and in 1975 changed to Wishard. "City" hospital is the oldest in Indiana and in the region.)

Jack Kochman then took over the show and brought it back to the fair for many years afterward, according to disputable Fairgrounds publicity records. Kochman's top thrill act was the "T-Bone" crash, once banned in New York City as too risky on public land, although the climax to his program was yet another dangerous ramp-to-ramp 70-foot "flight" of a pick-up truck.

Joie Chitwood also claimed credit for taking over the Teter operation. Following the accident, as a favor to Teter's widow, Chitwood, then an American Automobile Association race driver, originally intended to handle the sale of his late friend's equipment. When there were no takers, Chitwood borrowed $20,000, bought the show and taught himself the

stunts. Chitwood apparently not only took over the show, but used virtually the same advertisements as well.

Joie Chitwood's Original Auto Daredevils played their first show on July 4, 1943, in Williams Grove, Pennsylvania, thirteen years before Kochman showed up at the Indiana State Fair.

Early in 1946, Chitwood told the Board he had purchased Lucky Teter's equipment. Claiming to be the "number one entry" at that year's Indianapolis 500, Chitwood advised, "If I win the race, naturally it will be very valuable for the Fair." Speedway president Wilbur Shaw called Lieutenant Governor Richard T. James, offering to publicize Chitwood before the 500. That was good enough.

◆◆◆

1943 Rudy Vallee and his orchestra appeared for $100 on September 9 in a "Victory Celebration" entitled "This is the Infantry." The Board bought a

Midgets and other circus freaks were common Midway attractions. These midgets were part of the post-war Cetlin & Wilson Carnival.

Girlie shows were a regular bill of fare with Gooding's Million Dollar Midway, as this 1969 photo reveals.

$100,000 war bond; an estimated 12,000 attended.

Moving pictures were shown every night. But there also was fun to be considered – fun that poured cash back into Board coffers. Johnny J. Jones Exposition, the "Mighty Monarch of the Tented World," now on its 44th annual tour, again was tapped, this time for an abbreviated Machinery Field Midway of eight major rides, one eating tent, and two "grab joints."

The Board, however, needed certain assurances since the 4-H Club Fair was built around youth. Jones had a girl show. "It is a revue show the same as you

might see in a theatre here," Jones' representative Charles Abbott informed Boardmen. "One thing," director U.C. Brouse commented. "When no one is around they put on some strong stuff – very suggestive. They have put them on when our backs are turned. We have boys and girls that will be out there all week. The fathers and mothers will come and see that and the Farm Press will write us up."

Abbott offered the Colored Minstrel Show in place of the girl show. Now hold on a minute. "A good girl show is all right," former President Francis M. Overstreet maintained. "I don't think the last years [have seen] so much criticism." Brouse concurred, although the 1940 show had been another matter. Jones promised not to bring a "posing" girl show.

(In January 1927, outgoing Board president Roscoe Conkling "Rock" Jenkins of Orleans announced, "I am certain that our Midway is an educational institution.")

1946 On the last day of January, Secretary-Manager Orval C. Pratt reported "many demands" for one-night whiskey sales in the Manufacturers' Building as opposed to "bootlegging it in." Board consent ruled out whiskey altogether.

Boardwoman Karolyn Holloway questioned, "Aren't you going to have fewer beer permits since the law [not] to sell intoxicating beverages to minors is in effect?"

Brouse, "thinking about our coming generation," was against beer at the Fairgrounds.

The following day, Concessions and Mechanical Field Director Overstreet observed, "in the past, anyone who wanted beer paid for their space and paid their license fee and a little additional. We had twenty-seven."

"Off hand it seems like twenty would be enough," Lt. Governor James observed.

"What are we going to do about this law that prohibits minors?" Boardman Charles R. Morris asked. He suggested putting up "No Minors" signs. A firm decision, if reached, was not recorded.

There was going to be an Indiana State Victory Fair! And on Daylight Savings Time! Six nights of Interstate Fireworks Display's fireworks lit the Fair's evening sky with alternating shows at the Grandstand.

In Show One, ninety shells were fired. Scenes depicted a farmer plowing, stalks of tasseled corn, hogs eating corn, and closing with a map of Indiana and two large American flags. The second show included "bombing trees," shooting stars, "prismatic squares" of silver and gold fire with revolving wheels in the center, and a scene showing people arriving at the Fair.

1947 Fewer than twenty-five bands competed on September 3 in the first Indiana State Fair High School Marching Band Contest. Grant County's Combined Band won in Class A, Rochester won in Class B, while Class C went to Francesville.

It was the first and last time a divisional contest was held, although beginning in 1989, large and small bands were afforded the opportunity to win, with an overall champion named.

1948 Sam Levy's Barnes-Carruthers Theatrical Enterprises brought its "State Fair Revue." The show opened with "Circus Days," which Levy called a "Big Top Phantasy [sic] with thrills and gaiety." His "In the Land of Egypt" featured the music of Aida, the Girl in the Moon. Another Barnes show: "Romany Nights," depicting gypsy life, "with real gypsy wagons and music." Levy threw in "Stairitone," where girls played music by dancing up huge stair steps. Levy also threw in free acts between the harness races.

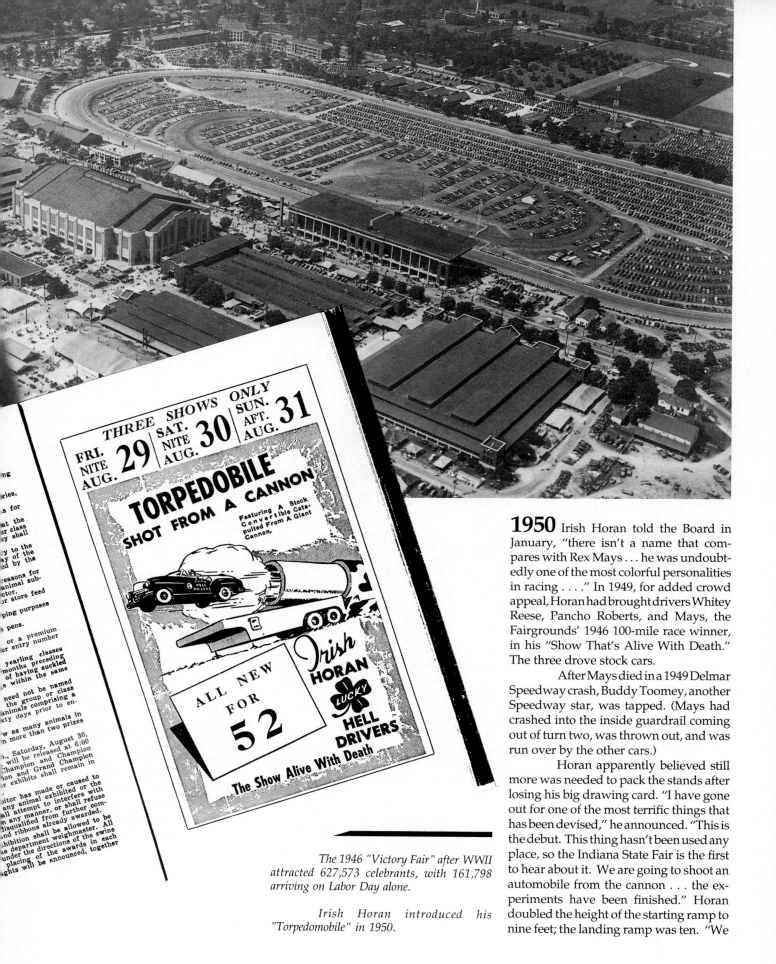

The 1946 "Victory Fair" after WWII attracted 627,573 celebrants, with 161,798 arriving on Labor Day alone.

Irish Horan introduced his "Torpedomobile" in 1950.

1950 Irish Horan told the Board in January, "there isn't a name that compares with Rex Mays . . . he was undoubtedly one of the most colorful personalities in racing . . . ." In 1949, for added crowd appeal, Horan had brought drivers Whitey Reese, Pancho Roberts, and Mays, the Fairgrounds' 1946 100-mile race winner, in his "Show That's Alive With Death." The three drove stock cars.

After Mays died in a 1949 Delmar Speedway crash, Buddy Toomey, another Speedway star, was tapped. (Mays had crashed into the inside guardrail coming out of turn two, was thrown out, and was run over by the other cars.)

Horan apparently believed still more was needed to pack the stands after losing his big drawing card. "I have gone out for one of the most terrific things that has been devised," he announced. "This is the debut. This thing hasn't been used any place, so the Indiana State Fair is the first to hear about it. We are going to shoot an automobile from the cannon . . . the experiments have been finished." Horan doubled the height of the starting ramp to nine feet; the landing ramp was ten. "We

A "colored revue" in 1948 brought in by Celtin & Wilson performed at the Fair. No burlesque girl or "donation" shows were allowed that year.

are going to go nineteen feet in the air. With a roadster."

One of Horan's autos had been an Indianapolis 500 pace car, yet another attraction. He also promised the Fair would have him exclusively in Indiana. He got the contract.

1948 Beer had been sold at the Fair since 1933, but the Board eliminated it for the 1948 Fair. Consumer interest was there, however. The United Press, in an item datelined September 8 (no year shown), reported that, "The Indianapolis Brewing Company, holder of the beer concession at the Indiana State Fair, today reported that 400 barrels of beverage were delivered on the grounds yesterday. Figuring 31 gallons to the barrel, brewery statisticians reported that the delivery amounted to 12,400 gallons, enough to serve 1.3 bottles (12 oz.) to each of the

approximately 100,000 visitors to the fair yesterday."

1951 Six nights of Jimmy Dorsey's Orchestra during the nationally prominent State Fair Horse Show featured Pat O'Connor, the Cuban Army equestrian jumping team, the Criollo horses, along with Roman riding. Less adventuresome Fairgoers competed in a crochet race in the Women's Building.

1952 Cetlin & Wilson Shows, open a day earlier than the Fair, had the Midway with "25 sensational rides, 20 big shows"; they arrived at the Fairgrounds on forty-five double-length railroad cars.

The "Hollywood on Parade" show brought in Hollywood and "South Pacific" singing star Peter Garey. Hoosier bumpkins marveled at "Siska, the girl with the green hair." Along with the "Hi Steppers of 1952" girl show and "Little Egypt," the Lion Motor Drome, a circus sideshow, fun and glass houses, the Monkey Circus, and more novelties appeared.

The State Fair Follies of 1952 were described as "a Super-Spectacular Musical Extravaganza of Colossal Proportions and Glittering Splendor" with 150 of "the World's most talented artists."

Phil Harris and his band performed in the Coliseum, while Herb Shriner's "Homespun Humor" made Fairgoers laugh. The 4-H State Dress Revue convened in the Coliseum as well.

1953 Three nights of Guy Lombardo and his Royal Canadians were found in the Coliseum as well as Patti Page the "Singing Rage," the Ink Spots, starring Bill Kenny, and TV Stars of 1953.

Texas Rangers' Rodeo and the South of the Border Show made its first Indiana appearance, starring Grand Ole Opry hillbilly artist George Morgan. A $1,000 prize was offered to any spectator who could ride "'Old Blue,' the bad Brahma bull, for 10 seconds."

1954 Barnes-Carruthers presented "the World's Finest Grandstand Show" for the State Fair Follies in 1954. Advertising hacks promised something "more elaborate and

Grandstand ushers line up for a group photo in 1951.

A big farmer welcomed a young Machinery Field visitor in 1954.

spectacular than ever before. All new, with a breath-taking array of fresh and sparkling entertainers, recruited from the top ten percent of the world's most accomplished artists." Among the acts were Adriana & Charly, a trampoline act; and Bent Blue & Yvette's unicycling and juggling act.

Also performing at the Fair were the "Cisco Kid and Pancho" Rodeo, and Irish Horan's Lucky Hell Drivers, still firing cars from giant cannons. Coliseum entertainment starred Julius LaRosa, the Mills Brothers, Eddie Fisher long before he married Elizabeth Taylor, and the Jan Garber Orchestra with the Night Horse Show.

1955 Headline entertainment for this year included Frankie "Mr. Rhythm" Lane, Nat "King" Cole, Russ Morgan's Orchestra, Irish Horan's Lucky Hell Drivers (back

again with their "H-Blast Cannon" firing a turbo jet automobile), Tennessee Ernie Ford, Ray Sullenger, Red Ingle, Bonnie Ann Shaw, and Gene Holter's Racing Ostriches and Wild Animal Show.

1957 The All Western Horse Show starred Smiley Burnette, Kenne Duncan, Leon McAuliffe, and the Rin-Tin-Tin Troupe (Rinny, Rusty, and Rip). State Fair Follies of 1957 featured The Lennon Sisters (they were made honorary 4-H Club members in a Grandstand ceremony), Nip Nelson, The Marshalls, McKay & Charles, Wazzan Troupe, The Brunos, and the twenty-four Hild Dancers. Mr. Green Jeans and Circus Boy from the Captain Kangaroo Show were there on Family Day.

1958 The $55,000 Horse Show starred Arthur Godfrey and "Goldie" his dressage-trained Palomino horse, with the Jan Garber Orchestra. An "Arthur Godfrey Room" was reserved in the Saddle Horse Barn for the great showman. Godfrey maintained a private bar in the room, according to long-time Fair employee Bob Heilwagen.

1960 Mrs. Frank Krahulik and Robert Sisson were tied at five wins each in a ten-year Spelling Bee running battle.

1961 The prestigious, colossal, and deafening Rooster Crowing Contest woke up fairgoers for the first time in 1961. The contest gained national and world recognition. Entries were "open to the world." Purdue's Roscoe Fraser of Monticello started the contest which had its roots in contests which western miners originally used for gambling in the 1800s.

    Dick Clark brought his Caravan of Stars, and the stars from the Andy Griffith Show made an appearance. Duke Ellington, Al Hirt, and George Shearing performed jazz on Friday night. Johnny Cash came with Lester Flatt, Earl Scruggs and The Foggy Mountain Boys, Rose Maddox, The Tennessee Two, and Gordon Terry.

    The *Indianapolis News'* Newsboys Band delivered two concerts nearly every day from their bandstand between the Women's Building and the Indiana Board of Health Building – the site where Better Babies once played.

    The Cisco Kid and Pancho on the Nickel Plate railroad in 1954 with Board Secretary-Manager Kenneth Blackwell.

    The Lennon Sisters, seen here in '58, visited the Fair several times; in '57, "the nation's singing sweethearts" were made honorary 4-H Club members.

    Eddie Fisher disembarks, eager for his 1954 Indiana State Fair appearance.

Yeah! Yeah! Yeah!

ON FEBRUARY 9, 1964, the "Fab Four" made their American debut on "The Ed Sullivan Show." Come Fairtime, the four mop-heads from Britain touched down in Indianapolis; destination: the Fairgrounds. People still talk about those two September 3, 1964, State Fair Concerts – they saw the Beatles.

Every seat sold out before the official State Fair program was printed. Board President William F. Johnson, Secretary-Manager Hal L. Royce, and Lieutenant Governor Richard O. Ristine ensured their names were on each $3, $4, and $5 ticket.

Coliseum and Fairgrounds officials sent back six thousand unopened pieces of mail, all pleas for tickets to the Fairtime shows. Teenagers wrote to Congressmen begging them to use their influence to procure Beatles concert tickets. "Could you use all the influence you can possibly muster?" asked one eighteen-year-old. "I'll cry a lot if you can't help me get the tickets, and you wouldn't want that now would you?" But even U.S. Congressmen couldn't get tickets.

The entire affair created embarrassing headaches for some. "Our Fair City," a column by the *Indianapolis Times* city room staff, told readers "The Beatles Have Fair Board In Jam With Teens and Press.

"The State Fair Board, which has had problems with musicians, horse show enthusiasts and a myriad of other ticklish situations in the past few years, may have topped all previous 'faux pas' with its handling of The Beatles. . . . [I]t was revealed that 1,900 of the precious tickets had been reserved for purchase by the 16 Fair Board members, plus Governor Matthew Welsh, Ristine and Earl Butz, dean of the school of agriculture at Purdue. That . . . brought hurried vows from Welsh and Ristine that they would return their 100 tickets."

Richard K. Shull's "Mailbag" fired two salvos, the first a reader's comment about the disclosure: ". . . These men (including Governor Welsh, Lieutenant Governor Ristine and whoever Earl Butz is) are entitled to tickets, but 1,900! The men who direct the fair are nothing but farmers."

"No one ever accused them of being smart," Shull responded.

Then a reader asked, "Is it still possible to get tickets to the Beatles State Fair show?"

"That would depend on whether or not you're a member of the Fair Board," Shull wrote back.

Fearing the onslaught of fans, the Fair Board met with the Indianapolis Police and Fire Departments, Marion County Sheriff's Office, Civil Defense, the Red Cross, and Indiana State Police. A disaster plan was implemented – just in case.

The Beatles' two-concert visit drew an afternoon panic of 12,513 in the Coliseum. They did it again at nine-thirty in front of almost 17,000 screaming fans in the Grandstand. Doctors and nurses constantly were running up and down the Grandstand aisles helping hysterical girls. According to one witness who got into the concert because he "knew someone," he watched two girls running from both sides of the Grandstand down to Main Street after the concert. Running, screaming, crying, they dashed in zigzags before crashing head-on into each other.

After the excitement, and after the screams subsided, Ringo couldn't sleep,

so Indiana State Trooper John Marks took him home after a quick tour of Indianapolis; his wife refused to fix the drummer breakfast.

John, Paul, George, and Ringo were tough to deal with. An August 10, 1964, letter from General Artists Corporation requested special treatment:

Paul McCartney, John Lennon, Ringo Starr, and George Harrison arrive at Weir Cook Airport.

Lennon yells and shakes his mop top during the afternoon Coliseum concert.

Janet Harding (nee Coats, second from right) and her friends needed no urging to become excited about their idols' visit.

Indiana State Police troopers escort the Fab Four to their concert. Jane O'Neill, Holly Hill, Connie Miller, Arlene King, Bonnie Ernst, Betsey Williams, and Jean Dieslser came from Harrisburg, Pennsylvania, with their special B-E-A-T-L-E-S welcome.

"With reference to the engagement of THE BEATLES, we would appreciate very much if you would have in their dressing rooms, prior to their arrival, a supply of clean towels, chairs, a case of cold Coca Cola, and if at all possible, a portable TV set. Also, please make sure the dressing rooms and lavatory are clean."

◆◆◆

1967 Grand Ole Opry stars headlined a Country & Western Spectacular: Minnie Pearl, Porter Wagoner and the Wagon Masters, Roy "Wabash Cannonball" Acuff and his Smoky Mountain Boys, and Don Gibson, Norma Jean, Bobbi Staff, and Bobby Bare.

A second day of country and western stars were there for the State Fair Jubilee – Sonny James and the Southern Gentlemen, Ernest Tubb and the Texas Troubadours, Dottie West and The Heartaches, and guest host Rusty Draper, star of NBC's daytime color series "Swingin' Country." Backing them up were Little Jimmy Dickens and The Country Boys, Charlie Walker, Red Sovine, Merle Travis, and the Duke of Paducah.

EXPO 1967 ATTRACTION

LIVE Delores Pollard The AMAZON GIRL

Rowan & Martin brought their big "Laugh In," Ed Ames sang, and Andy Williams and Henry Mancini charmed the crowds.

Lawrence Welk and his Champagne Music Makers were there for some of the bubbly. Eddy Arnold, "the Frank Sinatra of pop country music," was packaged with the cigar-smoking Baja Marimba Band. Herb Alpert and the Tijuana Brass headlined, with Don Rice.

1969 Two hundred truckloads of Gooding's Million Dollar Midways, billed as the world's largest traveling amusement and tented theater extravaganza, arrived with a chorus line of pretty New York show girls in "Star and Garter" and "Gay New Orleans," an all-star black musical. For the rube, Gooding offered a torture show, giants, a teenage fat show, a chamber of horrors, a circus sideshow, snakes, and a wax museum.

A big entertainment package included two Bob Hope shows (with The

Golddiggers, Diane Shelton, Mary Lou Collins and orchestra leader Richard Hayman), The King Family, The Association and The Ventures, six performances of the Glen Campbell Show, Jack

♦♦♦
Believe It Or Not Time:
Herman's Hermits headlined an act opened by the Blues Magoos (America's first psychedelic rock band) and the Who, "a British group like the Hermits" who "helped start the mod trend in London."
♦♦♦

Kochman's Hell Drivers, and the six-performance English Horse Show starring Anita Bryant.

Teens went to the "Nitty Gritty" show in a special pavilion tent between

One visitor can't get a close enough look at Amazon Girl Delores Pollard in 1969.

Hook's Historic Drugs and the International Building. The 1969 version was not "a warmed-over" version of the Young America Fair, which was discontinued after the 1968 Fair. This one featured "Battle of the Bands," a Youth for Christ musical.

Dairy goat milking contestants met in the Sheep Barn basement.

The Indiana Chicken Barbecue Cook-Out Contest smoked in the secretary-manager's front yard. The Farmers' Building hosted the "Fair Goer's Song Fest," and a "Sing Out Dearborn (Ind.) 'Up With People'" presentation.

A high school choral group contest first appeared following unanimous Board approval; Coca Cola and others sponsored the event. Incoming Board President Joseph L. Quinn, Jr. had personally called the choral directors. Skitch

Henderson directed the five finalists during Century pre-race activities.

1970 A demolition derby crashed onto the mile track in a new Joe Quinn Grandstand program. Participants requested their entry forms directly from him.

The Indiana State Fair Organ Contest August 31 in University Building East attracted sixty-five contestants. George Smith, 1969's winner, performed during the Quarter Horse races, the Auctioneer's and Fiddlers Contests, and Quinn's Demolition Derby. Smith also won the 1970 Organ Contest.

Shriners paraded on "All American Day."

Art Linkletter's show – on "Art Linkletter Day" – featured Paul Revere & The Raiders. Buck Owens was packaged with the stars of "Hee Haw." Bob Hope – on "Bob Hope Day" – did a free Grandstand show with trampoline artist Dick Albers and the Three Degrees. Ray Coniff and Johnny Cash also performed. The Blackwood Brothers Quartet, the Statesmen, and J.D. Sumner and the Stamps Quartet sang gospel, and the Kochman Hell Drivers returned.

1973 Opening day, the Schlitz forty-horse hitch, driven by one man, welcomed Fairgoers. Later, driver and noted Belgian breeder Dick Sparrow drove his huge

Hog caller Harvey O. Harris of Whitestown hollered but failed to win in 1970.

Amy Robinson of Indianapolis took a senior division third place in the 1988 chicken barbecue contest.

The Schlitz forty-horse hitch had plenty of room for riders in 1973, including first-term Governor Otis Bowen. The hitch stretched more than half a city block.

team in the Farmers' Day Parade. Each horse weighed a ton.

Sparrow's seven-ton bandwagon was the first big, circus-style parade wagon brought to the Fair in more than fifty

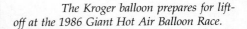

Giant Balloon Race. Publicity touted it as the first major contest since the 1910 National Balloon Races in Indianapolis. Conducted as a "hare and hound" contest, the race attracted world-class aerostatic aviators, but something went wrong – the weather. Originally scheduled for August 14, the race was delayed twice before the August 16 maiden lift-off. Five of the original seventeen entries lifted off.

And the winner? The Sprite balloon, piloted by seventeen-year-old Denise Weiderkehr of St. Paul, Minnesota. She dropped a bag of Indiana corn within 146 feet of the State Fair "hare" balloon after traveling 15.5 miles to just west of Cumberland. Meanwhile, the Lark balloon landed on I-465's Emerson Street bridge.

1976 Entertainment during the country's bicentennial Fair included Neil Sedaka (who presented the Archway Home Style Cookie Award to Mrs. Richard [Jamie] Clayton of Greenfield), Mac Davis, Johnny Cash and June Carter Cash, Bobby Vinton, Chicago, Heart, and Bachman Turner Overdrive. Kochman's Hell Drivers made another exciting appearance.

1977 Husband-calling champion Linda Johnson of Fountaintown received telephone calls from as far away as Texas and Oregon requesting recordings of her award-winning husband summons.

Marilyn McCoo & Billy Davis, John Davidson (replacing Tony Orlando & Dawn – Orlando had announced he was retiring from the stage), The Keane Brothers, Dolly Parton hosting the Steiner Championship Rodeo, The Captain & Tennille, The Beach Boys (who played to an estimated crowd of 20,000), Linda Ronstadt, The Bay City Rollers, Kansas, The Outlaws, and Jack Kochman's Hell Drivers provided entertainment.

Jambalaya was served from a three-hundred and fifty-gallon iron pot, which was cast in 1849; the ton of "whompin up" Creole food was enough to feed 3,000 at a time. If that was too hot, there was plenty of cool, nutritious milk from the Dairy Bar to soften the burn. A

years. It had not been publicly displayed since the Barnum and Bailey Circus Parade of 1904. [Another appearance did occur, however, on July 4 the year before at the Schlitz Circus Parade in Milwaukee.] The horses pulled it four abreast in four teams; the hitch stretched more than half a city block.

The Horseshoe Pitching Contest was the biggest in its history: 250 entered in all divisions, including thirty-five women and seventy-five men in the father and son tourney.

Concerts for the Fair included The Jackson Five from Gary, Ind.; Jim Nabors with The Hagers; The Osmond Brothers; Tanya Tucker; Tom T. Hall; Don Gibson; Tommy Cash; Jackson Browne; Sonny & Cher; Donna Fargo, headlining the Championship Rodeo; America; and gospel music from the Singing Hemphills, the Sego Brothers, and Naomi. Gooding's Million Dollar Midway featured its 1973 edition of "the Gay New Orleans Revue with a comely Creole chorus and the Casino Royale Show featuring a bevy of beauties direct from leading night clubs in Las Vegas."

1975 First-day visitors had expected a great State Fair greeting from something truly large – the first annual State Fair

post-Fair report showed 30,000 grilled cheese sandwiches and 64,000 milk shakes were sold in what was certainly one of the most nutritionally rewarding promotions at the Fair.

1978 This year's entertainment included the Tex Beneke Orchestra with Helen O'Connell and Bob Eberly; Roy Clark; Indiana's own Crystal Gayle; Mel Tillis; and the Oak Ridge Boys with Barnes Rodeo. Styx set a Grandstand general admission record of 18,001 which wasn't broken until New Kids on the Block's 18,509 mark in 1989. Bob Welch, Heart, Mac Davis, and The Osmonds with Donnie and Marie also performed.

1978 Jack Kochman's Hell Drivers, the Four Wheel Drive Pick-Up Truck Pull, and the NPTA-sanctioned Tractor Pull provided powerful and dangerous fun.

On the night of August 16, a clutch blew out of a puller competitor's tractor, injuring twelve spectators, two of them seriously enough that they spent time in the hospital. The NTPA sanctioned event in front of a 12,000-fan crowd had met all safety requirements.

The following day, Fair officials called a press conference. The offending tractor was displayed on a trailer with a hand-painted sign warning against touching the evidence.

"Pictures of the exploding tractor taken by an off-duty photographer (Eric Gruelich) who was being paid by fair officials to take publicity photos were released to the media Friday," the *Indianapolis Star* reported August 18.

Gruelich had offered the photos Thursday night, "but fair officials withheld them until Friday because of 'insurance problems.'" President R.J. "Steve" Panke, Zionsville, defended the decision. "'I think he owes his first loyalty to us.'"

1978 Sixteen crossbred pigs claimed the distinction of racing in the first annual Pig Races. Supplied by Producers Marketing Association, the pigs' training relied upon conditioned response. Named after prominent Hoosiers, the line-up included Otis and Borr, vying for a whopping purse of Indiana-grown apples. The Coliseum clean-up crew swept up an estimated half million soft drink cups.

Girls with the Kokomo High School Band cavort for the camera during 1986 Band Day activities.

1979 A Frisbee Contest debuted this year, with classes for distance, accuracy, team freestyle, and K-9.

The new Indiana State Fair Balloon, a Cameron O-65 manufactured in England, premiered in 1979. When inflated, it held 65,000 cubic feet of air, and was seventy-eight feet high and fifty feet in diameter. The maiden voyage was on May 17, with approximately sixty appearances scheduled for the summer.

1982 A "Clog-Off" competition was offered for the first time, sponsored by the Indiana State Cloggers Association.

1983 Hoosiers took the train to the Fair for the first time in many years. A special ten-car FairTrain travelled the old Monon Railroad right-of-way, bringing passengers from a Carmel depot to the Fairgrounds' west gate. A restored 1930s dining car and power from an early streamlined diesel locomotive, commissioned in the 1940s, reminded Hoosiers of their rail

heritage. The Indiana Transportation Museum in Noblesville provided the train as a fund-raising project for the growing museum and for restoration of rail equipment. FairTrain appeared in 1984, 1985, and in 1990-1992.

Concert acts that year were Beach Boys (who were nearly rained out), Oak Ridge Boys, Loverboy, and the Statler Brothers. Willie Nelson, Wayne Newton, Anne Murray, Cheap Trick, Kenny Rogers and Dottie West, and the Greg Kihn Band rounded out the line-up.

1984 Concerts for the Fair included Rod Stewart (rumored to have insisted on a swimming pool and two dozen soccer balls to throw from the stage), Willie Nelson and Waylon Jennings, Jefferson Starship, The Stray Cats and Weird Al Yankovic, Alabama, Wayne Newton, Kool & The Gang with Deniece Williams, Conway Twitty and Ronnie Milsap, Merle Haggard and Tammy Wynette, the Bar Kays and Mtume, and the Bill Gaither Trio with Joyce Lighty and Mike Smith.

1985 Marvin E. Routzong of Springfield, Ohio, won the Hog Calling Contest with his rendition of "Figaro." Lee Ann Brubeck of Rockville was best husband caller. "Whitey" the rooster let loose 155 times to clinch the Rooster Crowing title for Doris Stauffer of Apple Creek, Ohio. Two sessions of the State Fair Championship Tractor and Truck Pull and a nearly mired Combine Demolition Derby – agricultural armageddon – entertained Grandstand crowds.

Big name entertainment needed feeding: Willie Nelson asked for Texas Jailhouse Chili; Tom Jones dined on beef burgundy; and the Oak Ridge Boys settled for grilled steaks. Night Ranger's contract called for pina colada chicken. Alabama ordered one-hundred-sixty country-style barbecue ribs and three dozen Tootsie Pops.

Appearing that year at the Fair: Lee Greenwood, Statler Brothers, George Strait, Exile, the Judds, Vern Gosdin, Sammy Hall, Sylvia, "the pride of Kokomo," Neil Young and the International Harvesters with David Allan Coe, and Bill Medley. The Amazing Kreskin extended his famous standing offer of $100,000 to anyone who could scientifically prove that a hypnotic trance or state exists, and the Barnes Rodeo bucked, bronc'ed, and rode in the Coliseum.

1988 Even those who couldn't come to "Bringin' Back The Glory" festivities wanted to hear about it. Unable to make it to a concert, a Lone Star State caller asked someone in the Press Room to walk to the pay phones across from the Grandstand, return and give her a number, whereupon she proposed to load up on change, call, the staffer would answer, then leave the phone off the hook so she could enjoy the show long distance. The answer? Sorry, ma'am.

A cowboy rides Geronimo the trained buffalo through a ring of fire in 1986.

Waylon Jennings and Jessi Colter visit the Midway.

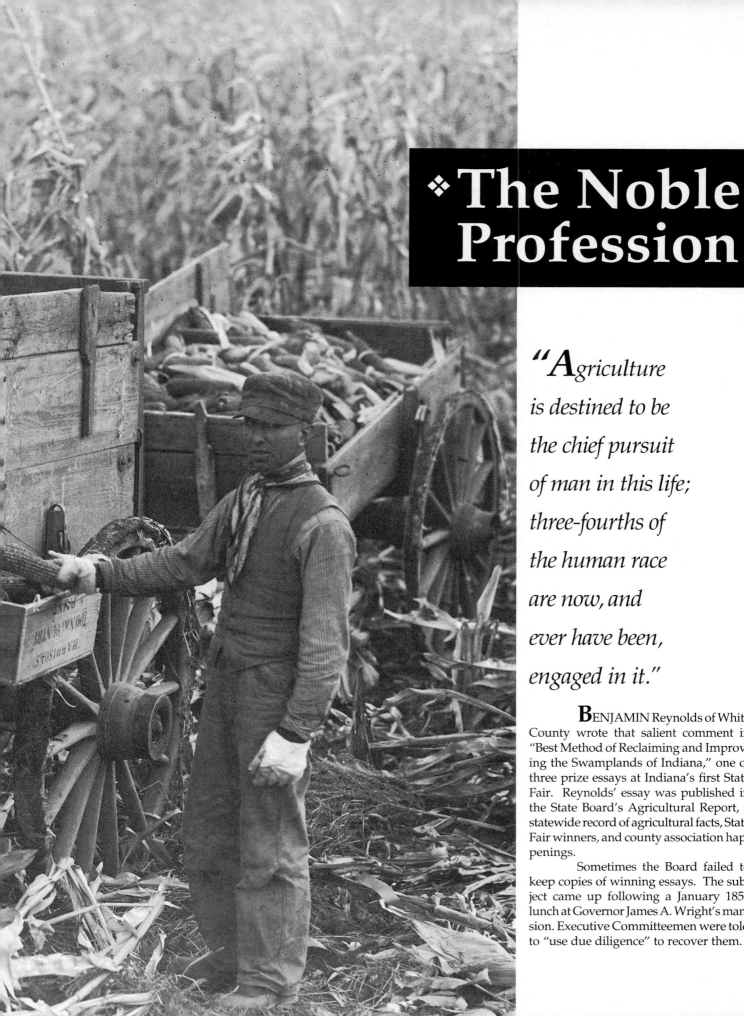

❖ The Noble Profession

*"**A**griculture is destined to be the chief pursuit of man in this life; three-fourths of the human race are now, and ever have been, engaged in it."*

BENJAMIN Reynolds of White County wrote that salient comment in "Best Method of Reclaiming and Improving the Swamplands of Indiana," one of three prize essays at Indiana's first State Fair. Reynolds' essay was published in the State Board's Agricultural Report, a statewide record of agricultural facts, State Fair winners, and county association happenings.

Sometimes the Board failed to keep copies of winning essays. The subject came up following a January 1855 lunch at Governor James A. Wright's mansion. Executive Committeemen were told to "use due diligence" to recover them.

FAR FROM scientific, the essays generally described methods a wise individual had successfully devised to overcome the harsh elements of a young, undisciplined state. Long before there was an Indiana agricultural college, decades before a Farmers' Institute, these successful "agriculturists" shared their insight with all who cared to read about it.

"To apply a specific and uniform course of treatment to every variety of soils, would be as arrant quackery as to propose to cure all the maladies of humanity by the same remedy," Ryland T. Brown, M.D., wrote in the third Board report's prize essay.

The Crawfordsville doctor had observed that the soils in his part of the Wabash Valley were either prairie, "hazle barrens," rolling sandy loam, "heavily timbered with sugar maple, walnut, pop-

lar," or "summit, clay lands, timbered with a dense growth of oak, hickory, beech, elm, &c."

Brown prescribed drainage, subsoil plowing, and the alkali from lime for prairie soil treatment. Crop rotation improved barrens. He recommended preserving alluvial "bottom" lands, giving that soil a "rest in clover" if its essential minerals were depleted. Clearing plain land alleviated excessive dampness.

Each year, the Agricultural Reports – and the State Board's Geological Survey – were sent throughout the state to county agricultural societies and public libraries; throughout the nation; and even to Europe to encourage immigration.

Oliver Albertson, Washington County, published his essays "On Manures" and "On Field Fencing and Shade

Three harvesters bring in the hay with a horse-drawn loader under a quiet afternoon sky.

Trees" in the 1855 Agricultural Report. In his essay "To Improve the Soil and the Mind," he wrote, "John Quincy Adams has said 'if there was one business, profession or calling, more independent than another, one that could be called more noble, it was Agriculture.'"

Albertson was correct. Agriculture was more than noble. As a later State Board secretary wrote, "The first garden, according to the Holy Writ, must have been planted by the hand of God, the great Agriculturist of the world."

◆◆◆

A Greater Purpose

LITTLE WAS known about Indiana in the 1850s. Its natural resources were hardly identified, and agriculture was not yet a science. The Indiana State Board of Agriculture knew something had to be done; they also knew it would be their task to lead the way.

Indiana's agricultural statistics were "so many dead letters," State Board secretary William A. Loomis wrote in 1856, "and for the credit of the great industrial interests of our State, these laws should be so amended by the next General Assembly, as to secure correct statistical tables of all our products." Progress was made despite legislative reticence.

By 1860, in the Board's opinion, "nine-tenths of the improvements in the way of producing large results in agriculture, stock growing, the mechanical arts and all other improvements . . ." could be traced to the first nine State Fairs.

Having not lost sight of its primary charge for "the encouragement of agriculture," the Board in 1864 offered premiums for the best dairy cattle, specifically Ayrshires (alternately spelled Ayershires), Aldernays, Herefords, and Keeney (alternately spelled Kerry), or Devon, "for the purpose of encouraging their introduction in Indiana."

The Board also asked agricultural society delegates to contact their Congressmen, urging appropriations for "practical experiments for making sugar economically from some of the sugar-bearing plants adapted to our climate, and for instituting investigations to find some variety of cotton better adapted to our latitude, and for experiments to cottonize the fibre of flax, and for raising the ailanthus silk worm."

"We can form no conception of the value of our annual products other than mere conjecture," Board secretary Fielding Beeler wrote in the Agricultural Report for 1869.

"Not a word is said about new and improved modes of culture, or the advantages of one system over another;

the success of new varieties of cereals, vegetables, and fruits; the best time in which to plant the crop or gather the harvest; all is blank."

The State Fair was "a rare school of general instruction to those of the many thousands interested who are present, but utterly useless to the remaining thousands who are absent."

A February 11, 1874, letter from Secretary of State W.W. Curry asked the State Board to martial all the "influence you can exert" for a state bureau of statistics.

"I need only remind you that the inductive phylosophy (sic) which deduces to principles from a collection of facts, is

THE GRAIN THRESHING FLOOR.

the only one which gives us theories of practical value . . . [Y]our society is formed for the purpose of advancing the interests of the farming community, you are expected to keep them informed of the best methods of procedure, the most profitable branches of their business, the most valuable inventions to assist their labors.

"But how can you do this without such a collection of facts as will enable you to compare and analyze, and so present results with accuracy . . . [H]ave you such tables . . . as will enable you to say with certainty whether your premium[s are] awarded from the accident of a superior soil, or the intention of

a superior cultivation.

"Year by year you award premiums for fast horses, but do your tables inform you as to the cost and value of such stock so that the ordinary farmer can tell whether it is, or is not, profitable to raise fast horses."

The Agricultural Department in the nation's distant capital was the "only reliance" for crop reports, Board Secretary Alexander Heron wrote in 1875. "This is comparatively meagre, but is gradually improving."

Indiana, for all practical purposes, simply had no method of collecting agricultural statistics, and it would remain a persistent condition for years to come. The State Auditor collected and compiled statistics provided by tax assessors, but the public waited nearly a year after harvest before learning anything. "Also, the collection of the statistics being optionary with the assessor, the returns are but partial."

At that point in Indiana's history, the national department compiled information by laughable standards: "The information is collected by a system of correspondence from a chief and three assistants in each county. The opinions of each are averaged, and the result reported accordingly. Of the ninety-two counties in this State, fifty-five are so reported and given as the average of the whole.

"As a remedy for this imperfect system (as applied to a single State), a bill was prepared and presented to the Legislature of 1873, creating a bureau of statistics."

That bill lost in a final Senate reading and was tabled again in 1875. Yet another bill proposed collecting agricultural statistics through Agricultural Department assessors, but "this also received but little encouragement," Secretary Heron wrote.

"Finally a bill was prepared providing for the collection of statistics of products of all kinds, including all raw materials, by the road supervisors in their respective districts, they to report to the County Auditors by the 15th of November, and the returns to be forwarded to the State Board of Agriculture by the 10th of December of each year, and be published within the year collected. . . .

"This bill . . . met with universal favor. It was presented to the Legislature in proper form, near the close of the last session, but met the fate of the other bill, owing to an unpleasant feeling or 'dead lock' existing between the Senate and House . . . [F]or another two years we can give only partial statements of the resources of the great State of Indiana."

Statistics were critically needed to "properly present the true state of the agricultural and other industrial interests as they deserve," secretary Heron wrote a year later. "'Statistics stand guard over the farmer's interests, foil the schemes of the speculator, and save the producer's money.'"

"Believing that current farm literature has a very important influence upon the prosperity and development of the country, we heartily congratulate the farmers of Indiana," State Board secretary Andrew J. Holmes of Rochester wrote in an 1868 endorsement of *North-Western Farmer*. That journal was "destined to prove a great blessing, not only to the State and the great north-west, but also the nation." T.A. Bland, M.D., edited the esteemed Indianapolis-based paper which premiered in 1865.

"Already," Holmes wrote, "it enjoys a circulation wider, perhaps, than any similar journal in the west, and is on a handsome paying basis, which places it beyond the reach of failure and among the permanent and reliable institutions of the country." *North-Western Farmer* was "equal to any similar publication in America, and far superior to any other farm journal in the west."

"Indiana has two hundred thousand farmers," Holmes wrote, "yet it has been said she could not sustain one agricultural paper. Let this slander be effectually silenced, by every one of them subscribing for our home paper, the *North-Western Farmer*."

In 1875, the State Board noted "an increasing interest in agricultural progress . . . [T]he march of improvement is steady . . . [In] years past the interest seemed to center on cattle; at present all live stock attract a fair share of attention. Heavy draft horses vie with roaders; Short-horns are dividing the interest with Aldernays as milking qualities are as important as beef. What is the best breed of hogs is a problem yet to be solved. The

same is true of sheep. Poultry is attracting a wonderful interest, not only in this, but in all the States."

"The farming community is receiving an impetus in the encouragement of agricultural education and intellectual development," secretary Heron wrote for 1876. "[T]he social education which has been aided and encouraged by and through the introduction of the Granges has done much to elevate farm life and cultivate a spirit of contentment and happiness."

The State Board of Agriculture took one of its most important steps in 1882 when, at President Henry C. Meredith's urging, it officially sponsored the first Farmers' Institute. The meetings, held March 8-9 in Columbus, brought in lecturers and others on an agricultural

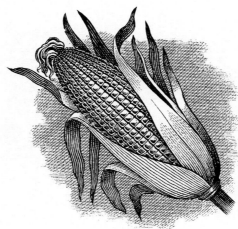

Average Yield per Acre and Average Prices of Three Crops Compared ◆ 1852 and 1991 ◆

Crop	Avg. Yield	Avg. Price
1852		
Wheat	15 bu.	$0.55-.60
Corn	30-40 bu.	.25-.30
Soybeans	N/A	
1991		
Wheat	38.7 bu.	$2.90
Corn	128 bu.	2.40
Soybeans	36 bu.	6.25

education mission. The Institutes ultimately led to the agricultural Extension Service itself.

Purdue University president E.E. White had called for farmers' institutes as a cooperative effort between Purdue and the Board as early as 1877, in a January 3 speech to the Delegate Board. Seven years later, the General Assembly passed the Farmers' Institute Act. Purdue Agriculture Professor William C. Latta was placed in charge; by 1890-91, he had organized institutes in all but two Indiana counties.

President W.B. Seward, from Bloomington, was a "humble visitor" at the first State Fair. Proud that he had missed only three Fairs, Seward, too, favored state aid in 1887, especially in light of the progress since 1852.

"I do not suppose that we will ever succeed in raising fried spring chicken . . . or produce automatons that will do all our work. Yet he would be a reckless prognosticator of future events that dared claim that improvement will in time fall far short of this." In Seward's opinion, the Board was "just entering upon our mission of usefulness."

In an 1898 Board address, Governor James A. Mount stated his concern about the continuing urban migration. "A few evenings since[,] I heard a discussion . . . [I]t was the consensus of opinion that the most discouraging outlook for agriculture was found in the fact that so many young men were leaving the farm."

Statistics and observation had led Mount to that conclusion. But why were the children leaving the farm? "Young men are full of hope, buoyant with expectations," Mount declaimed. "They desire to enter the field that offers the broadest opportunities that promises the highest success. Farmers, as a rule, are inclined to talk farming down, instead of exalting its possibilities."

One of Mount's acquaintances laid the blame on education. "'The tendency of our educational system is away from the farm. The enjoyment of the beauties of farm life, the study of nature, the possibilities of the farmer being able to utilize the forces of nature's great laboratory and make them subservient to his will, do not occur to the farmer as one of his great privileges.'"

"When the farmer realizes that the mind is the important factor leading to success, then will he cultivate his reasoning powers. Books and papers will be multiplied, modern improvements will find their way into the farm home."

With success, "the tide will then be turned from the city to the farm," Mount concluded. "The young men will see possibilities for as grand success on the farm as are offered in any of the business or professional pursuits."

Mount was on the money, as far as the Board was concerned. "A farmer is a man who lives upon his farm," commented a delegate who acknowledged Mount knew of what he spoke. "An agriculturalist is a man who owns a farm and lives in town and carries on some other business to pay the expenses of his farm."

Purdue University president E.E. White spoke at length on "The Education of the Farmer" at January 1878's annual meeting. White laid three blames to "the present disrespect for labor, and especially for what is termed service. The first of these is the influence of slavery, which once permeated the entire country with degrading views of labor. It will take a hundred years to recover from the influence of the slave code with its 'mudsill' theory of labor.

"Another cause is immigration, which has filled nearly every department of common labor with ignorant and cheap workmen, crowding out intelligence or subjecting it to unpleasant social conditions. It was once a common thing for the sons and daughters of persons in good circumstances 'to go out to service,' and they were treated as the equals socially of other young people . . . [W]hen domestic service in New England was subjected to social degradation, the American girl turned to the mills and the factories . . . [W]hen ignorant foreign labor took possession of these she turned to the store,

the telegraph office, the school-room, and other occupations demanding intelligence and granting some social recognition . . . [W]orkmen as a class, not their tools, determine the dignity of their employment.

"A third cause is the rapid development of the country . . . causing a rush . . . from the farm into the towns and cities, which have sprung up on every hand as if by magic."

A fourth cause was "the influence of our free institutions. The political and social ideas which are the common inheritance of Americans, have done much to incite the ambitious and aspiring to seek those employments which more directly lead to public life and official position."

Against the "three dogmas of aristocracy (Caste, Capital, Culture), White

submitted the propositions that "Education promotes industry and lessens idleness"; that "Education makes labor more skillful and more productive"; and that "Education improves the condition of the laborer."

With the philosophical conversation over, the Board and delegates settled into a discussion on the merits of wheat strains, bone dust fertilizer, threshing machines, and soil pulverization.

◆◆◆

OLD Dr. Ryland T. Brown of Crawfordsville recalled during the January 1878 meeting, "A long while ago I followed the plow; but the plow that I followed, you would now be ashamed of."

A prolific essayist and State Board member in 1856-57, Brown was hired in 1854 by Governor Wright to "prosecute" the state's first geological "examination." Brown, according to an 1887 Board tribute on the occasion celebrating his eighty-second year, "traversed the entire length of the State several times on foot from Lake Michigan to the Ohio River in locating the coal fields. The accuracy of his work has never been disputed."

Brown recalled times, and his studies had told him more, when few people lived in American cities. By his statistics, in 1810, one man in every twenty-five lived in cities or large towns. The urban side had grown to one-fifth by 1870. "Right there is the key to the whole trouble," Brown knew.

"As a rule . . . the men who live in the country make money, produce wealth, while the men of the cities accumulate wealth which other men have

(Two-horse Corn Plow. Exhibited by Ferrell, Ludlow & Rodgers, Springfield, Ohio.)

Number of Indiana Farms in 1870 by Acreage	
1-3 acres	1,565
3-10 acres	7,270
10-19 acres	13,506
20-49 acres	55,821
50-99 acres	52,614
100-499 acres	29,433
500-999 acres	1,004
1000 or more	76
TOTAL	161,289

made. There has been a passion all over the United States to accumulate money rather than make it. Men have deserted the fields . . . left the plow, and have gone to speculating – that is accumulating money without making it.

"The man who can make money most surely is the farmer; he knows how much his farm will produce in a year, and can therefore judge how much credit he has a right to ask for; but a prudent man will not venture much.

"No man should be so free from debt as the farmer; in this respect he should be an example to the whole country; but too often they yield to the temptation to put mortgages on their farms, and incur a heavier debt than their farms can bear."

Another speaker that day could speak with the greatest authority – John B. Dillon, first State Board secretary.

"Considerable difficulty was experienced in selecting men from different parts of the State to act upon this Board when it was just established, and a great deal of credit was due to . . . David P. Holloway . . . who was then a member of the Legislature.

"Governor Wright . . . loved to brag about anything with which he was connected . . . When he was Minister at Berlin he wrote to me to collect for him and send, for exhibition in that city, specimens of the different agricultural products of this State . . . [T]hat year was very favorable for the growth of corn, and I sent him over several remarkable ears. When the box was opened on its arrival at Berlin many prominent men were present, and some Americans. Governor Wright took up ear after ear, and viewed them with a look of dissatisfaction and disappointment, while the foreigners and Americans who were looking on viewed the specimens with astonishment, because they were the best they had ever seen. Mr. Wright . . . only remarked, in a tone of voice intended to convey great disappointment, 'I sent to Indiana for some of the largest ears of corn that could be found.'"

> ◆◆ "The farmer's son, not satisfied with his father's simple and laborious life, joins the eager chase for easily acquired wealth." – Grover Cleveland, fourth annual message to Congress, December 3, 1888

Dillon believed he'd seen better fruit exhibitions at the earliest society meetings than "those of more recent years."

He claimed that "one of the best results of the early efforts of the State Board was the establishment of the county fairs . . . [and, as well,] a boy might spend a large sum of money traveling and not acquire the practical knowledge which he can get in attending a State fair."

GOVERNOR Claude Matthews told 1894 annual meeting listeners the farmer was destined to be someone "whose quiet, earnest, intelligent thought on the farm and at the fireside shall find expression in the world through earnest, noble action. With you, gentlemen, largely rests the sacred duty to assist in finding out, or to blaze the way that leads to these higher plains."

Secretary Charles F. Kennedy, of Indianapolis, reported an apparent State Board shortcoming:

"The one thing that has impressed me most is our lack of ability to touch the masses of that class of farmers who have learned to read, and to benefit themselves by the information thus obtained, and thus grow into a more useful existence to those about them who are not disposed to avail themselves of the various sources of information."

The federal government had by now created the Bureau of Agriculture. Many states published agricultural reports, but the State Board was still without a method to gather statistics for transmittal to Indiana's Bureau of Statistics or

Principal Agricultural Products as Reported by the U. S. Department of Agriculture for 1871			
Crop	Bushels	per Bushel	per Acre
Corn	35.7	$ 0.37	$13.20
Wheat	12.0	1.26	15.12
Rye	13.9	.72	10.00
Oats	28.8	.33	9.50
Barley	24.4	.72	19.72
Buckwheat	13.5	.75	10.12
Potatoes	64.0	.82	52.48
Tobacco (Lbs.)	70.2	1.085*	59.67
Hay (Tons)	1.19	12.78†	15.20

*Price per pound.
†Price per ton.

to Professor Henry Augustus Huston, of Purdue's Experiment Station.

Kennedy offered to shoulder the responsibilities for bringing about these capabilities, "but . . . if you want the Indiana State Board of Agriculture to grow in usefulness, you must let yourselves and your neighbors become interested, and let us see if some of the great sums of money that are expended by the State every year can not be used in the interest of the farmer, the stockman, the mechanic and the artist."

"[A]griculture is a business of the first importance, requiring special skill and scientific knowledge," Governor J. Frank Hanly remarked at the September 9, 1907, Coliseum dedication.

"Industry, science and invention, supplemented by a dozen years of bountiful harvests and high prices and the prosperity resulting therefrom, have transformed and revolutionized farm life in Indiana.

"The average Hoosier farmer has bade farewell forever to the isolation of the past. Free rural mail delivery, bringing the story of the daily happenings of the world to his door; the telephone, placing him in instant communication . . . at the volition of his own will; the electric railway, bringing to his gate the means of quick, convenient, comfortable and cheap transportation to county-seat and state capital, make him and his a part of the social, business and political world to a degree undreamed of a generation ago."

Randolph Adams, a young Martinsville farmer, amassed $83 winning sixteen premiums at the 1925 Fair, in a story "Special" to the *Indianapolis News*: "The value of vocational training, coupled with a determination to

accomplish something worth while, is proved by the record of Randolph Adams. . . .

"The remarkable thing about his work as an exhibitor is the number and importance of his prizes. He won the first prize in . . . ten pecks of Irish potatoes, one peck Early Ohio potatoes, largest and best display of watermelons, largest watermelon, light green watermelons, display of alfalfa and timothy seed." Adams took four second and five third prizes. He had won numerous prizes during the past several years.

◆◆◆

A SECOND World War had done as much for agriculture as it sustained combatants. The struggle which annihilated thousands of farm youth rapidly produced technological advances to replace them.

In January 1945, Fair Board secretary Guy Cantwell wound up his remarks about the abbreviated 1944 4-H Club Fair by cautioning directors and delegates to shoulder the peacetime mission of showcasing what science had done. Farming depended upon it; there was a crop surplus, and surpluses had caught farmers unprepared in the aftermath of World War I, according to Cantwell. The State Fair offered safeguards against a repeat of what "broke the farmers' economic back seven years before the final economic crash in 1929."

"Since World War I we have found many new uses for farm crops beside that of food. We have too much food. Agricultural food production has outstripped the growth of people in numbers the world over and especially in the

Livestock Statistics as Reported for 1872

Animal	Number	Average Price
Horses	663,000	$66.78
Mules	35,300	68.66
Oxen, Cattle	785,000	22.26
Milch Cows	444,200	33.57
Sheep	1,953,000	2.54
Hogs	2,489,900	4.93

Richard Jordan of Knightstown brought a sixteen-foot, one-inch cornstalk to the Fair in 1938. It was tall enough to reach the balcony of the Administration Building.

United States. Farm Chemurgy offers large possibilities of diversion of farm food and fiber materials into plastics, building materials, industry in general, motor cars and fuels, etc. Twenty-five to thirty per cent of plastics are now derived from farm crops. Community centers of processing farm crops either as plastics, clothing, building materials, [and] fuels, may easily be established – thus decentralizing industry, reducing many costs of transportation and labor and stabilizing demand for farm crops. Think it over briefly, then do something. We should not let the calamity occur again. Were the big Fair to be given this year – a big Chemurgic exhibit in place of many crop exhibits should be on hand to let us in farm life see how chemistry and industry can combine to give Indiana basic prosperity from crop abundance with profit, friendship and good living for all. Without such an easy object lesson we must work out this problem as we investigate and educate concerning possible uses of crop abundance. The Fair should always be a show window of agriculture and industry. Its value just now would be far above normal to livestock breeders, crops men and the industrial people of Indiana." These remarks . . . from an Indiana farmer.

One hundred years of progress caused the State Fair Board in the 1952 Centennial Fair program to recall the events leading up to that point:

"In addition to sponsoring county and district agricultural and mechanical organizations throughout the state to better inform the citizens, the board through its various members has accomplished many important projects that affect our daily lives.

"Its influence is felt today in better roads, because its weight was felt in providing enabling laws. First crop and weather reports were sent by county delegates. First authentic surveys of the state's natural resources were provided by the board's geologists. Development of industry was encouraged. Establishment of a U.S. Department of Agriculture was advocated.

"Agitation for an Indiana Agricultural College resulted in the establishment of Purdue University. Breed organizations, resulting in improvement of livestock, were born under the wing of the board. Organization of the State Fish and Game Association resulted in the present Department of Conservation. Conservation practices being urged today were not new to pioneer board members and delegates.

"[I]t is safe to say that an appraisal of its first 100 years reveals that the work of the board's members through the years has made it the most valuable department of government of the state of Indiana that was ever conceived."

In 1990, Our Land Pavilion, a vision of agriculture's future, took quarters in a renovated Universities Building leading Fairgoers through a science, space, and technology showcase. Pioneer Hi-Bred International funding made building renovation possible. Through computers, satellite imaging, Purdue University, and commodity group exhibits, Our Land Pavilion carries on the Indiana State Fair's tradition of educational excellence.

Average Yield per Acre and Field Crop Prices for 1871

Crop	Bushels	Acres	Value
Indian Corn	79,205,000	2,218,627	$29,305,850
Wheat	19,190,000	1,599,166	24,179,400
Rye	423,000	30,321	304,560
Oats	11,784,000	409,166	3,888,720
Barley	352,000	12,846	253,440
Buckwheat	154,000	11,407	115,500
Potatoes	2,436,000	38,062	1,997,520
Tobacco (Lbs.)	8,316,000	11,840	706,860
Hay (Tons)	826,000	694,117	10,556,280

INDIANA AGRICULTURAL COLLEGE,
Purdue University at La Fayette.

Braden & Burford, Lith. In

A School For Agriculture

THE Indiana State Board of Agriculture's first meeting of 1852 convened on January 8 in the Hall of the House of Representatives, Hendricks County Agricultural Society delegate Enion Singer submitted a resolution: "That this Board appoint a committee to take into consideration the propriety of suggesting some feasible plan for the establishment of an agricultural school." It was tabled.

Two years later during the January 5, 1854, evening session, the Board and delegates told the Premium List committee to "inquire into the expediency of offering a premium for the best essay on the subject of establishing an Agricultural College in Indiana . . . [also] to inquire into the expediency of memorializing the Legislature on the subject of establishing an Agricultural School in connection with the University" (eventually Indiana University).

Two more years later, during the January 10-12, 1856, Winter Meeting, the Board adopted a resolution that "Agriculture is rapidly assuming its proper place, among the natural sciences, and schools of scientific and practical agricul-

ture are being opened in several of the States, and, as Indiana . . . has no school in which the sciences are taught, with special reference to their application to farming . . . a committee of three [was] appointed to inquire into the necessity and practicability of establishing a school of scientific agriculture, under the direction and control of the State Board of Agriculture."

The following day the committee reported the necessity but questioned a school's "practicality." Costs were beyond the Board's control, since a "commodious college edifice with attached work-shops, out-buildings, &c." was needed "on an eligible site." Land was needed for a model farm "of the first class," in the committee's opinion. Modern farm implements were needed, and a library, chemical laboratory, and "philosophical apparatus."

Even though that dream was beyond the State Board's ability, Dr. Ryland T. Brown, committee spokesman, wasn't for neglecting "to do what may be done.

Nature works on the principle of progressive development. She produces great results from small and seemingly improbable beginnings."

Agricultural science lectures could begin as early as the following December 1, by committee reckoning, "divided among three or more teachers, somewhat on the plan of a Medical College." A $10 "tax" per ticket or $30 per course could be charged students at first. As soon as enough money came in to pay teachers $500 each, the "residue" could be applied toward growth and improvements.

Eighteen years later, Purdue University opened its doors, but not under Board control.

◆◆◆

Fair receipts from 1857 were for the first time "large enough to defray all current expenses, and still leave a surplus . . . [S]uch a result was not generally expected by the friends of the enterprize. It was due partly to the fine weather during . . . the exhibition, and partly to the strenuous efforts for months prior to the fair to attract the attention of the people."

"Society" accounts were in good shape and "its prospects . . . brighter than at any former period . . . firmly established, and . . . [with] little to fear in the future," leading it to recommend that the General Assembly give it the power "to institute an Agricultural School, or to purchase an experimental farm. Either, or both of these agencies when combined with the annual fairs, would extend and perpetuate the influence now exerted by the Society on the agriculture of the State." A "liberal" appropriation was required before either would happen.

Board members in January 1858 urged Indiana's U.S. senators and representatives to support U.S. Senator Justin Smith Morrill of Vermont. Morrill had introduced a Congressional bill donating 6,340,000 acres of Federal land to states and territories, "20,000 acres to each Senator and Representative in Congress, and to each Territory 60,000 acres – for the purpose of endowing agricultural colleges, and other means of agricultural improvements." This bill passed in 1862 as the Morrill Act.

Dr. Brown, serving on the Board's agricultural school committee, reported that the state's associations were beginning to call for schools "on the various branches of science connected with agricultural and mechanical arts, in their practical application to the business of life." Brown's committee recommended a school "under the patronage of the Society" where the business of farming was taught "as a science and as an art."

Ohio already had two or three such schools just leaving infancy. Michigan had an endowed university "with ample grounds for the practical application of the principles taught, and for all experiments in crops, implements, modes of culture, &c."

Without courses on agricultural lecture, "[w]e are certainly falling behind the age," Brown and committee reported. But the report was as far as the Board went. A motion to send the committee back to discover a way to provide agricultural education for "the young farmers" was withdrawn.

On July 2, 1862, President Abraham Lincoln signed the Land-Grant College Act. The following January 7, a five-member State Board committee was appointed "to examine the law." A day later the committee reported the act was "feasible and should be favorably considered by the Board."

A three-member Board committee joined in January 1864 with an equally-sized State Pomological Society committee to urge Indiana's Congressmen to buy more time to allow the General Assembly to accept "the congressional agricultural college land grant." The committee was given until the next annual meeting to submit a progress report. Deadlines, however, wouldn't allow a year to go by.

The next day, a concerned joint committee dispatched an urgent request to the United States Senate and House of Representatives: ". . . Indiana has failed to take, through its legislature, the steps required by law, to secure the munificent donation offered to the State for the establishment of agricultural colleges . . . [S]aid failure has not resulted from the want of appreciation of the importance of the proffered gift, but from the facts, first, that causes already sufficiently understood by the public, prevented the legislature of our State from holding during the past year, a session in which it was possible to take such action as is required by the terms of the donation; and, secondly, that, as the legislature of Indiana meets, not annually, but biennially, it can not meet again until the time allowed by law (July 2, 1864) shall have expired."

Representing the full voice of all its associations, the Board asked for an extension until state lawmakers could "accept in due form, your very liberal donation."

Professor J.S. Campbell of Wabash University appeared before the January 1865 Board and delegate meeting – convening in the Young Men's Reading Room – and read a bill "respecting agricultural colleges" as provided under the Morrill Act.

His bill divided the fund equally between five different existing colleges, "providing for agricultural professorships in each, with a department of research at the capitol, where analysis of soils, &c., &c., should be conducted; in fact a central college, or headquarters, where all scientific researches should be made." That day Campbell and Cyrus Nutt, D.D., president of the "University at Bloomington," were made honorary Board members.

Before the meeting ended for the morning, a Board and delegate committee recommended legislative acceptance of Campbell's bill and the Morrill Act's

Purdue University's Mechanics Hall, erected in 1885.

"liberal" land donation. Board member and state geologist E.T. Cox of New Harmony in Posey County (assistant to the late state geologist David Dale Owen) disagreed and made a "speech" against the committee's report.

Discussion wasn't over yet. After lunch, detail hammering picked up again. Dr. Nutt moved to strike the committee's report "so much as relates to recommending Professor Campbell's bill," offering instead a plan "hitching" the agricultural college "to the Bloomington University." Rather than sharing with the others, Nutt argued "with much sincerity and eloquence" on behalf of his university.

After "lengthy discussion," outlines of Nutt's and Campbell's bills, along with the committee report, were recommended for Board and General Assembly consideration "in the disposition of said congressional grant."

The next January, Professor J.A. Thompson, District of Edinburgh delegate, urged taking full advantage of the Morrill Act land grant by establishing "not less than two nor more than five departments of agriculture in endowed colleges suitably located" throughout Indiana based on soil classes. All graduating classes at these competitive colleges would earn degrees from the same "board of examiners." Soil studies would involve "thorough" examinations and experiments.

Although two Board members argued against Thompson's resolution, he saw them adopted. But an agricultural college still didn't open in Indiana, and in 1869 the Board grew impatient. Board member Alexander Heron offered a promptly adopted resolution:

"The chief aim and object . . . in creating the Board of Agriculture was to guard the agricultural and industrial interests of the State; and such interest is promoted by other means than State Fairs alone;

"The National Congress has tendered a liberal assistance toward promoting agricultural education, which has so long been neglected by our State Legislature . . .

"Resolved, That a special committee . . . confer with members of the Legislature, and request them to leave the question of locating the proposed Agricultural College . . . in the hands of this Board, believing the same to be proper and appropriate."

Convening January 4, 1871, State Board men sent five members to tell General Assembly lawmakers about the "importance of having the Indiana State Agricultural Society represented in the Purdue Agricultural College . . . ."

◆◆◆

THE SCHOOL opened its doors in the Fall of 1874, so the Board must have been planning in advance.

By March, Board minutes record "the last General Assembly passed a law authorizing the State Board of Agriculture to select three of their number to act as trustees of the Purdue University." Delegate Isaac De Graff Nelson of Fort Wayne, a state representative in 1851-52 (credited as the state's first drain tile manufacturer, in 1853), was selected, along with New Harmony's delegate L.A. Burke, and Board member John Sutherland from Laporte. (Sutherland began a three-year term as Board president in 1872, serving through 1874.)

One day during the February 1873 meetings, "Mr. Purdue, of LaFayette,

Purdue students labor at the old university foundry, circa 1894.

was introduced and was requested to give his views concerning the different breeds of hogs . . . [A]lthough having had in years past much experience as a 'packer of pork' he asked to be excused from speaking upon that subject and after some general remarks . . . made some interesting statements in regard to the progress of Purdue University."

◆◆◆

IN A 1904 Delegate Board address, Purdue Professor H.E. Van Norman described the genesis of the university's name: "An old bachelor, John Purdue, who had made much money on the Wabash Canal, proposed to the Indiana Legislature that it accept this Government land grant [the Morrill Act] and establish the Indiana Agriculture College on lands in West Lafayette, which he with others would donate. This offer was accepted, and out of respect for John Purdue and his work the name was changed from Indiana Agriculture College to Purdue University."

Another version of the story appeared in a thin black volume commemorating the 50th anniversary of Indiana's Cooperative Extension Service: Purdue was a merchant and banker "who dreamed what the great possibilities" of Indiana's own Land Grant college could mean to Indiana. Purdue offered the state $150,000 and 80 acres "if they would put

the institution in Tippecanoe County, give it his name and make him a trustee for the rest of his life." The offer was immediately accepted.

◆◆◆

PRESIDENT Sutherland closed his January 5, 1875, written address calling attention to the "coming Centennial of '76, and the Purdue University at LaFayette, both of which are of vital interest to us as a State, and the last named to us as a Board, it being so closely connected with all that pertains to agriculture.

"The Agricultural College of Indiana is no longer a myth but an Institution, found[ed] on the broad basis of free education to those of our youth who feel disposed to avail themselves of its advantages . . . which necessarily secures for its students that amount of exercise so essential to a sound mind and body, and yet too often neglected in many of our colleges."

Could it be that the Indiana State Board of Agriculture was dissatisfied with the university in Bloomington? Almost as old as the state itself, apparently Indiana University wasn't teaching enough agriculture to satisfy State Board men.

◆ 71 ◆

[Indiana University was founded January 20, 1820, as the State Seminary. Later it was named "Indiana College" in 1828, before its present name was adopted in 1838.] The Board should have the interests of Purdue at heart, Sutherland adjured.

◆◆◆

WHILE THE State Board of Agriculture was one means the General Assembly had adopted "to encourage, by all suitable means, moral, intellectual, scientific and agricultural improvement," there was another "and even higher, through the State Agricultural College, unfortunately christened Purdue University.

"These institutions are not only co-laborers in reality, but are made so legally," outgoing (1880) Board president William Henry Ragan reminded fellow Board members. The Board was authorized to select two trustees to Purdue, which "yet in her infancy," already had made its "benign influence" felt throughout the state. "One of the highest duties of this Board is to guard well the trust herein conferred," Ragan avowed.

Oration occupied much of the January 1887 Board meeting. Colonel J.B. Maynard of Indianapolis held forth about "The State Board of Agriculture as an Educator," reminding the Board it met annually for "deliberation and consultation as to the wants, prospects and conditions of agricultural interests throughout the State. . . .

"The Board was not only to instruct the people, but the Legislature as well," the colonel intoned. "The results . . . [of educating] the Legislature have not been, it appears to me, specially flattering.

"If . . . education is as desirable as men would have us believe, it occurs to me that agriculturists should be the best educated men in the State, and that the State should expend more money to

advance agriculture as an occupation, an industry, a science, than for any other educational specialty."

During the past 11 years the Legislature had appropriated, for agricultural education, only $16,500 to the Board, Maynard pointed out. Purdue University had received the bulk of the money, amounting to $173,000.

"Think of it, work for it; in time it must come," adjured outgoing State Board President W.B. Seward in 1888, arguing for greater state appropriations which would allow "nominal" Fair admission, thus opening its "object lessons" to many more.

"In this connection, and in direct line with the idea just mentioned, I am glad to be able to report that the 'Hatch Bill,' appropriating fifteen thousand dollars per year to each State having an Agricultural College, for . . . an experimental farming station, has become a law, and I understand Indiana has, or soon will receive her portion of the money."

In 1919, State Board President John Isenbarger had "found after soliciting information from many other States that the Agriculture College and experiment stations in some instances, has absorbed or had thrust upon it the mission and function of an Administrative Department. I think you'll agree with me

The Purdue Building rose in 1924, west of the Administration Building. More than 7,000 people visited every hour. Exhibits inside shared modern information needed to "make agriculture the most important industry in Indiana."

that the College is to teach and the duties of the experiment station ought to be confined to just what its title suggests.

". . . Purdue University does a whole lot of police duty . . . regulates the State Chemical Department, the manufacture of stock foods control, manufacture of fertilizers, the enrollment of stallions and many other departments of state that should not belong to it. . . .

"These powers should be delegated to the State Board of Agriculture as in other States and I believe that if the present legislature is properly approached we shall be given the power that our title implies . . . ."

The 1962 Fair shared in the centennial celebration of the Morrill Act which created the nation's sixty-eight land grant colleges. It also was the one hundredth year of the United States Department of Agriculture.

The Board letterhead sported Purdue University Land Grant and State of Indiana seals, and the slogan "Agriculture, Science, Technology."

A FAIR wouldn't be a fair without contests. From the first plowing match to today's horse pulls, the spirit of competition has never flagged in Indiana. Hard-fought victories and clear-cut wins are chronicled, along with protests and bitter rivalries.

1852 The plowing match, set for "9 o'clock A.M." on Thursday of the Fair, actually began "at a late hour." Contestants plowed an average of twenty-three minutes at Calvin Fletcher's farm. Benoni Newby took the $5 premium and a diploma for best specimen of "not less than six inches deep" plowing. Judges reported twelve entries in this class, "and with one exception, the plowing was of very high character."

Each plowman was required to "mark out" his site, "and finish it up." Competitors "managed" two or three horses or one or two pairs of oxen. There were three entries in ten-inch deep plowing, "and the committee decide that no ties of kin or letters or figures, are more closely connected than the samples of

Struggling to tow the load, this world champion team took second place in the 1940 heavyweight pulling competition. The team was owned by C.B. Kiehl of Bradford, Ohio.

plowmanship in this class. They, therefore, award to Benoni Newby and his two sons William and Daniel, the diploma and two premiums of $5 and $3."

1857 A $50 silver pitcher was awarded to Wayne County's Horton Ferguson for the best over-two-year-old boar in 1857 competition. In the twenty-four-entry sweepstakes, his boar "Warren" made him a second pitcher richer.

1859 Judging some premium contests lasted days; decisions took weeks. Consider the 1859 class for 145-acre farms. Decisions on this arduous judging task weren't completed and reported until the following January. The fates of David G. Rabb, of Ohio County, and Valentine Linginfelter, who hailed from Hendricks County, were decided based on the rules "adopted for . . . correct conclusions 'in reference to the cultivation of the soil, the net profits per acre, the completeness of out buildings, fences, orchards,' &c., by a personal visit to the farms owned by . . . exhibitors, and by receiving from them a very satisfactory account of the number of bushels of farm products, tuns [sic] of hay, &c., raised by each . . . ."

Although Linginfelter was, in the Awarding Committee's opinion, "Lord

Hotly Contested

of the Manor," he kept no record of expenditures and profits which would have enabled "proper comparisons."

Rabb had kept a three-year record of proceeds and net profits during thirteen years farming "on the banks of the Ohio river, near the village of Rising Sun," and judges awarded him the $50 prize. His property was valued at $14,550. His expenses for 1859 totalled $2,850.64. He grew wheat, barley, corn, hay, and Irish and sweet potatoes. Rabb also kept apple and peach orchards and a vegetable garden. Coincidentally, he was also a member of the State Board.

1867 Mechanical exhibitor complaints over unfair competition at the '66 Fair led the State Board in January 1867 to resolve: "That in the trial of drag saws they shall be tested by requiring each exhibitor to saw on the same log, and that the said log shall not be less than from thirty to forty inches in diameter." A.B.J. Flowers of Indianapolis had protested that trial, and had written; and, "on account of the disrespectful language and temper of the communication," the Board spurned his dissent.

day of the Fair, A. Wallace of Indianapolis filed a protest against Moses Crawford of Clayton, who had won the $15 premium for "best 25 varieties of apples." Wallace complained "for the following reasons:

1st. We are informed he has no orchard.

2nd. That he borrowed apples of William Reagan [Ragan] to make his collection.

3rd. Dr. [Allen] Furnace [Furnas] put up the apples, and marked them.

4th. Dr. Furnace [Furnas] was Chairman of the Committee."

The protest was never picked up.

1871 Things to feed a growing Indiana attracted gifted competitors. Sally A. Hartsock of Lawrence took the $10 best "five pounds of butter made in June" premium offered October 3 at the 1871 Fair.

What was her secret? "The butter was made from the milk of six cows. The milk, after being strained into stone crocks, was left to stand until the cream became thick. It was then skimmed off and put into a jar, left twenty-four hours and then churned in an adjustable churn. Took out the butter, salted it and worked slightly, and then left for twenty-four hours, and then worked thoroughly, and then packed it in a stone jar – covering it with brine, in which condition it has been since kept. The jar has been kept standing in cool spring water."

Precise rules governed the Plowing Match. Plows were tested "by an actual trial with a dynamometer," the Board finding ground in which to make the trial, under the following rules: "The plows to be held by the competitors, or persons appointed by them; Each plow shall open and plow four rounds, back furrowing; the last furrow to be not less than seven inches deep and thirteen wide; In testing the draft the same plowman shall hold the plow who did the trial plowing; the third and fourth rounds to be the test, which shall be of the size above indicated. Not more than two plows for the same purpose shall be used in the trial."

Committeemen charged with determining plow merits accessed the gross draught; the weight of the plows; the loss of power in overcoming friction; the net power required to cut and turn a furrow slice; the width of a furrow slice; the depth of a furrow slice; the comparative draught; and the simplicity of structure, the materials, the workmanship, the durability, and the price.

Protests sometimes called attention to the patently obvious. On the final

On a hot summer day in rural Indiana, four men work hard grinding limestone into lime. A steam engine powers the grinder with the belt seen in the foreground.

Horse-drawn cream deliveries by the high-water buggy were a common sight on Indiana's country roads.

1937 On Wednesday of the Fair, International Harvester was begrudgingly allowed ten minutes to present its National 4-H Club prize for farm accounting to young Ward Love of Lapel. It was the first time an Indiana youth had won the national honor. WLS carried the Grandstand ceremony during the National Farm Hour.

1953 The '53 State 4-H Tractor Operator Contest at the Grandstand selected junior and senior champions. Each received a seventeen-jewel Elgin wristwatch from Standard Oil Company and a Sterling silver trophy from Indiana Implement Dealers Association.

Holding five of 1940's first prize 4-H Club pullets: (l-r) Marion County's Billey Maines, Bruce McNeal, Charles Jack, and Marion Burden.

Harry Templeton, State Fair Manager, and the 1937 tomato queen prepare to slice into a gigantic tomato at the Purdue tomato exhibit.

At the poultry Building, a "Chicken of Tomorrow" contest, specially authorized by Indiana Junior Chicken-of-Tomorrow, was open to any ten- to twenty-one-year-old boy or girl. Exhibitors competed for $450 in cash prizes. Birds were displayed in the cooler at the building's east side.

A $185 Governor's Tomato Trophy (rotating) and the year-long "State Tomato King" title was offered to the farmer who grew and displayed the State Fair Sweepstakes hamper of canning tomatoes.

1960 The National Junior Sheep Shearing Contest convened for the first time at the 1960 Fair. Adults already had their contest in place. Sunbeam Corporation offered winning youth four cash college scholarships. Both contests taught the proper use of shearing equipment and the value of correct shearing methods.

Animals, Animals

INFORMING livestock breeders about better breeds was a Fair goal from the start. The Earl of Seaham, a roan Shorthorn bull, was one of the first animals imported directly from England for stock improvement. Arriving in New York in August 1850, his reputation was so great by the time he reached Indiana that he was withheld from first Fair competition.

1855 State Board of Agriculture reporter/farmer Lewis Bollman, on assignment to cover the 1855 State Fair, purchased two Poland pig pairs at the Fair; "their ears very broad and hanging down nearly to the point of their short nose; but more industrious, active, feed-hunting pigs I have never had." While common stock tore up rain-softened pasture with their long snouts, "the Polands graze more sensibly, letting the roots remain for future yield." Not only that, but Polands "do not put up their bristles and dash off with a booh! booh! when the owner comes near, but run to meet him as gentle as pet sheep."

Shoveling corn for the hogs consumed farmers' time; a flexible feeding base, the wagon could be moved once the surrounding ground was too trodden for a feeding floor.

When the Poland China swine breed was introduced into the United States, the pigs were considered to be "as gentle as sheep." June, a junior yearling Spotted Poland China sow, took first prize for Ralph E. Ponsler, Greensburg, in 1946.

Junior Hobson, Monrovia, and his Berkshire Grand Champion barrow in 1937.

A champion Hampshire sow and her fourteen-pig litter, shown in 1954 by the Walker family of Greenfield.

Horses were classed into farm, draft, carriage, and riding, but Bollman was unable to trace their stock line, "for nearly every horse had a stock after his own name, indicating a mixture of breeds not calculated to perfect the horse ≈ an error that has been avoided in the breeding of nearly all other stock except the common stock of our country."

Farm horses had shown "too much coarseness and awkwardness . . . the progeny of these coarse brutes fill our State; and at every cross roads one of these two dollar and fifty cent animals may be found. It is hoped that they will be discarded from our fairs."

1872 A.C. and Gus. Shropshire of Paris, Kentucky, entered "Fanny Forester," a 1,782-pound red short-horn Durham heifer valued "at the enormous sum of twelve thousand dollars," in 1872 competition. Fanny, " the renowned cow of the world, no animal of a like character approaching her perfection . . . walked away with another red [first-place] ribbon . . . fairly outdistancing all its competitors in the three-year-old show. The animal is a truly wonderful creature."

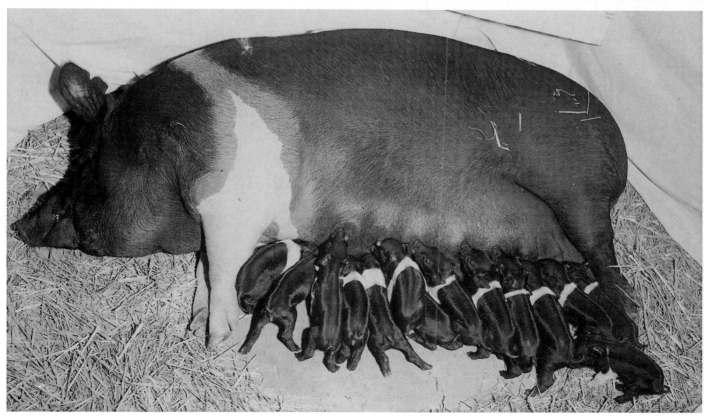

1876 Indiana Wool Growers Association organized October 21, in Franklin; there were then two million, four hundred thousand sheep on Indiana's farms. The group is now Indiana's oldest livestock organization in continuous existence.

In support of all sheep growers, in January 1876, the State Board adopted a resolution after considerable discussion: "Whereas, Dogs are a nuisance . . . his canine majesty is a great hindrance to the successful raising of improved sheep, therefore be it Resolved, That this Board recommend our coming Legislature to pass a stringent law, making it a penal offense to keep or harbor dogs."

By 1887, "sheep killed by dogs, etc." reached 31,800. In 1888, 28,850 perished by the fang. By 1889, the statistic dropped to 25,248.

Mildred Harper, Ligonier, with one of her prize-winning Shropshire lambs at the 1937 Shropshire 4-H Club Show.
A champion draft horse at the 1954 Fair at the old Draft Horse Barn.

1877 Indiana swine breeders met January 3, 1877, in the State House Agricultural Room and organized the state's first Indiana Swine Breeders' Association.

Section 2 of Article I stated, "Its object shall be to encourage the interest and promote improvement in the breeding and management of the various breeds of swine; first, by the dissemination of reliable and practical information . . . second, by co-operating with the officers of the State Board of Agriculture in making large and attractive exhibitions of hogs at the annual Indiana State Fair." W.A. Macy of Lewisville was elected first president.

1893 Unfavorable scheduling the same time as the Chicago "Columbian Exposition" World's Fair resulted in a dismal showing at the 1893 Indiana State Fair. Sheep, however, exceeded any previous State Fair – 478 head. Interestingly, musicians performed "some three or four pieces" during sheep judging, "and you have no idea how inspiring that was." Sheep Superintendent Stephen W. Dungan of Franklin called it a "love feast."

Nerva, the 1940 Grand Champion Percheron mare owned by Fairhome Farm, Lewisville, with Mary Jane Hale, daughter of farm manager Elmer Hale.

A packed Coliseum crowd watches judges reviewing Belgian mares during the 1941 State Fair, the last Fair before World War II.

Dungan, an Indiana Wool Growers Association organizer, and others had learned "that sheep could appreciate fine music as well as other domestic animals, especially horses. You know it has been the custom at our fairs that our bands play altogether for the horse shows and for the races . . . but we were fortunate in getting the boys to come down and play for the sheep."

1928 J.E. Morrison of the Indiana Pigeon Club pledged two hundred birds and eighty-six coops if the Board would create a pigeon fanciers class in 1928, which they did. A goat class request was refused.

1948 Dairy goats finally got into the Fair. "Our modern dairy goat . . . is one of the finest and oldest and highest bred animal there is," Indiana Milk Goat Association President Edgar W. Johnson successfully argued. He estimated nearly 2,000 registered goats could be found in Indiana, divided into four breeds.

Definitely distinctive, this sheep, one of several breeds captured in stone on the sides of the Sheep Barn, sports dread locks and an attitude.

Four gentlemen displaying H. H. Cherry's champion Oxford flock at the 1915 Indiana State Fair.

Pig Love at the Fairgrounds! Barrows snuggle in the Swine Barn in 1986.

Sporting a more than quizzical expression, a farrier prepares a horse for the show ring by trimming its hooves.

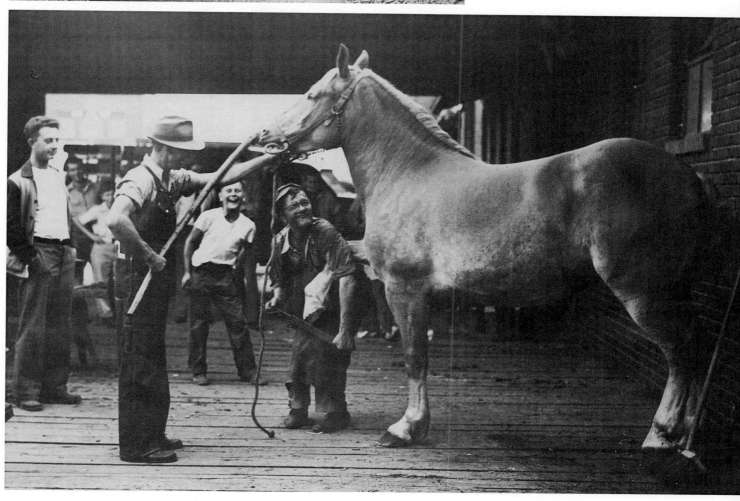

Board discussion after the 1948 Fair disclosed that no one was willing to build a show horse barn "when we have cattle out in the weather." Big as the Cattle Barn was, roughly seven hundred head of cattle still were kept under tents.

But when January rolled around, Charles O. House of Arcadia, Indiana, Draft Horse & Mule Breeder Association president, complained draft horses were losing space to saddle horsemen. "We feel that we got rather 'a slap in the face' last year," House said. More than half of the Draft Horse Barn had been turned over to saddle horse exhibitors.

1976 Wotan the boar and Erikka the sow visited the 1976 Fair. Both European wild hogs, also known as Russian boars (*Sus scrofa scrofa*), the pair were ancestral types of modern-day domestic farm animals. Rare mule-footed hogs were also on display.

A country girl and her steer at the Union Stock Yards office at the 1923 Indiana State Fair.

Ray Bottema of rural Indianapolis, "a consistent winner," with his Holstein cow which won the 1940 championship of breeds in the 4-H Club Show.

A young man leads his cattle down Main Street at the Fairgrounds in 1954.

Boys in club beanies show off their winning Angus steers in the 1923 4-H Club show.

Anna Demberger, daughter of Louis J. Demberger, Stewartsville, with her Japanese Silky chicken—a chicken with no feathers—at the 1940 State Fair.

Stephanie Dunlap displaying her Fair winnings as the Rabbit Queen.

An unidentified girl and her Polled Shorthorn steer.

William Burford "Bo" Danner (in short pants and saddle shoes) hands the winner's ribbon to Saddlebred horseman Max Bonham in this September 1948 Coliseum scene, while father Henry Burford Danner (left) watches. The Danner Family printed numerous Fair materials as early as the 1870s when the Fairgrounds were located at Camp Morton.

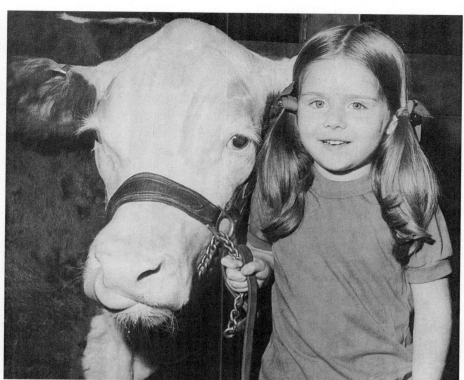

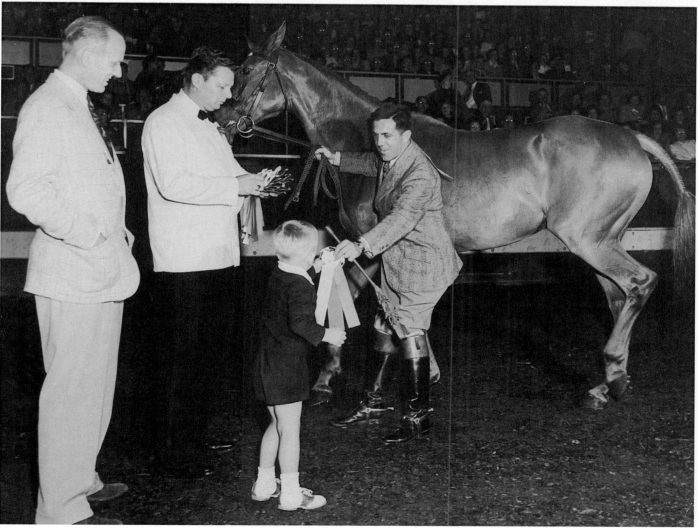

Newfangled Contraptions

ANOTHER popular part of the Fair has been the display and competition in new technology fields.

1856 Beard & Sinex, Wayne County, showed the best plows for clay, light sandy, and alluvial or muck soil, and the best subsoil and general use plows in a forty-plow show.

S.F. Jones, Decatur County, showed the best – and sole – hurdle fence.

A.M. Collins & Company, Philadelphia, had best apple parer. John M. Hutchings, Floyd County, had the best "scientific climax" churn.

The Geizer patent thresher and separator took first premium. Powered by circling horses, the machine was manufactured by Hasselman & Vinton, Washington Foundry, Indianapolis.

1872 Most of the March 21 morning session centered on buggy plow discussion. Edinburgh's Jacob Mutz, general superintendent beginning in 1871, opposed giving premiums for riding plows.

"He looked upon it as a new-fangled invention of no practical value, and was of the opinion that the inventor should pay for exhibiting it instead of having the State Board advertise it.

"Messrs. [W.B.] Seward and [A.B.] Claypool took the opposite ground, on the principle that the State Board was organized for the encouragement of every labor saving machine.

"Mr. [Secretary Joseph] Poole seconded them on the ground of gallantry and humanity. He had seen ladies drive a reaping machine by the day. If a practicable or convenient riding plow could be invented another wide field would be opened for the [other] sex. There was also a large class of infirm or crippled men who could use the riding plow to advantage."

Ed "Papaw" Eller, grandfather of Lee Eller of Arcadia, astride a horse-drawn mower many seasons before powerful tractors replaced every farmer's beasts of burden.

1876 The State Fair report described Sinker & Davis' "new fangled" internal combustion engine "of one horsepower, made at their shops, and operated by successive explosions of gas.

"A heavy piston is raised in a vertical cylinder by the explosion of a mixture of common illuminating gas and atmospheric air, which, descending by the force of gravity and the vacuum in the cylinder, communicates motion to a heavy fly wheel which, by its momentum, renders the motion uniform though the power is applied by successive impulses. A machine of one horse power consumes 100 cubic feet of gas, worth twenty-five cents in five hours. It requires no fireman nor engineer to run it."

A field trial of agricultural machinery and farm implements at Purdue University's farm near Lafayette convened June 27-29 under Board direction earlier that year. Three thousand copies of trial rules were printed and distributed to manufacturers and farm machinery dealers "throughout the country." Executive Committeemen took "general control" of the trial; General Superintendent John L. Hanna ensured it was "conducted in all respects as prescribed by the rules and regulations."

The site was "peculiarly appropriate" because of the different types of soils found there for plow tests, corn varieties for the cultivators, and grains and grasses – all "secured within a radius of three-fourths of a mile, on each side of a main road."

Twenty-six reapers and mowers, thirty-five breaking-plows (including general purpose, sod, gang and sulky-plows), twelve two-horse corn cultivators (including riding and walking plows with and without tongues), "several" one-horse plows and cultivators, one- and two-horse corn drills, check-row markers, harrows, and rollers, "each of which received its share of attention." In fact, "each machine has its admirers and was shown to the best advantage, while the best of good feeling prevailed among the exhibitors." Premiums were awarded at the end of the State Fair.

"Eastern manufacturers and others who have attended such trials in years past, stated that the late trial was the most thorough test of reapers and mowers, and plows that had ever taken place in the United States."

Despite "unpropitious" weather which rendered judging nearly impossible, attendance at one point was estimated at "near two thousand." In their report, judges insisted that "the importance of the field trial . . . can only be appreciated by those familiar with the wonderful improvements in agricultural implements of all kinds, and the astonishing number of devices to the different machines, each claiming superiority.

"Not only to the farmer, who wishes to see the operations of the different implements and select for himself, did this trial afford a rare opportunity, but to the inventor and manufacturer it was an occasion by which they could profit in several ways, see the working of the latest improvements, and by an interchange of ideas, produce results which could be developed hereafter."

1877 In Miscellaneous Articles, T.R. Cook of Mooresville showed "an apparatus for equalizing the draft where three horses are worked abreast. It is an ingenious device and is especially adapted to breaking colts or balky horses."

S. J. Hains, Prairie City, Iowa, showed a hog trap. "It often becomes necessary," the Special Committee on the Merits of Exhibits / Miscellaneous wrote, "to catch pigs on a farm . . . Hain's trap does away with all this trouble."

1895 Two hundred fifty-four exhibitors drummed up business at the Mechanical Department, seventy-one more than the year before. Moline Plow Company; Rude Brothers Manufacturing Company of Liberty; and Clay Whiteley & Company, Indianapolis, all erected new buildings. Altogether, 800 "traveling men" worked the

A young farmer behind an Oliver horse-drawn walking plow turns a winter furrow early in November 1919.

Fairgoers of 1912 found the Dawn of Plenty exhibit at the International Harvester tent. Exhibitors' plowing took place on the Fairgrounds' northeast side. The steering wheel is on the right hand side in the auto in the foreground.

John Deere Plow Company offered its steel-wheeled tractors after the company bought out the Waterloo Boy line of tractors. This scene takes place in the old Mechanical Field south of the Fairgrounds Sheep Barn, with the old Coliseum looming in the background.

Salesmen at 1923's Mechanical Field sold the crank-start, tiller-steered, steel-wheeled General Ordinance 'GO' tractor – lubricated with Gulf Tractor Oil – which cost $515, F.O.B. Indianapolis. Fordson Tractors were displayed as well.

Mechanical exhibit. By 1896, one-hundred ninety-six "Machinery" exhibitors were on hand. Advanced though the implements might be, all remained horse-drawn or steam-powered. A few more furrows were still to plow.

1917 Tractors were essential "to the man who is looking for something to take the place of the boy . . . 'over there,'" Board President Leonard B. Clore remarked, referring to WWI.

1918 "The growing interest in farm tractors . . . will make the show at the Indiana Fair one of the most important features," a state board *Hub of the Universe* news magazine told readers. "As in the display of passenger cars, the show of tractors will include all of the important makes."

The Lyons Atlas tractor, "An All Year Tractor – A One Man Tractor – Made In Indianapolis," was shown at the Fair.

Former Boy Scout and retired newspaperman Richard Jackson of Greencastle recalled a family friend who was the Indiana distributor for Moline plows and tractors sometime around the late 'teens.

"Tractors were just coming in," he said in May 1991. "He would set one of his tractors going in a circle. And it would just go all the time, all day long. People would come and look at it, and watch. And no one in the seat."

1938 John Deere had a "mammoth" display at Machinery Field, then located south of the Sheep Barn. WFBM's daily broadcast, sponsored in the International Harvester Tent, presented "Blue Ribbon Melodies" by the McCormick-Deering Haymakers and Dorothy Robards, the International Sweetheart.

1950 A 10,000-square-foot Atomic Energy Exhibit in the Education Building attracted thousands. The State Fair Board actually built an atomic pile replica according to instructions provided by the American Museum of Atomic Energy, operated for the U.S. Atomic Energy Commission by Oak Ridge Institute of Nuclear Studies. Wisconsin leased the replica for its next State Fair.

1951 Atomic energy returned this year, with exhibits few Hoosiers had ever seen: "Dagwood Splits the Atom," a Van de Graaff generator, a Wilson cloud chamber, Dunning's "Splitting the Atom," a bomb sight, and "Fission – Servant or Master."

◆◆◆

Mud surrounds the Holland Creamery Company in Holland, Indiana. Planks are placed across the street for easier crossing.

An International Harvester Farmall Super H tractor, made in 1953-54, pulls a corn wagon in from a nearly harvested corn field.

Hereford Calf Club entries in the 1928 4-H Show in the old Coliseum.

Although the first State Fair was confined to adults, concern over properly prepared youth led the Board of Agriculture to open competition to boys by 1855's Fair. The sheep pen was moved, and a tent was erected for "young men's work." A special $1,000 State appropriation fixed premiums in 1856 "for young ladies and young gentlemen" from Indiana. A Young Men's Department hall "after the manner and style of the other halls" was built for that Fair.

1871 A boy under 16 could win $20 if his acre of corn was judged best. Judging, naturally, was done in the field. Alfred Welton Jr. of Vincennes was awarded the prize during the January 1872 annual delegate meeting. Young Welton's yield: 128 bushels, 48 pounds, sworn before notary public Gerard Reiter Jr., September 23, 1871, and recorded in the 13th Annual Report.

1904 John F. Haines, Hamilton County superintendent of schools, planned the first "junior club." After two instructional meetings on growing corn, Haines' club exhibited in the fall. That "junior club" became 4-H.

1909 The State Fair Judging Contest for Boys under twenty offered $500 in scholarships – $150, $125, $100, $75 and $50 – to the Purdue School of Agriculture.

Professor G.I. Christie of Lafayette was in charge; the Coliseum contest covered horse, cattle, sheep, swine, and corn classes. The top three winners applied prizes toward regular courses, while the $75 and $50 awards were established for regular course work or a Winter Course in agriculture. Scholarship money was paid out in $20 per month increments; boys were required to enroll in the School of Agriculture no later than one year after winning. A fifty-cent entry fee gave a boy the chance to change his future.

Each was required to judge one ring each of draft horses, beef cattle, mut-ton sheep, and lard hogs, "and not less than two varieties of corn (white and yellow)." Contestants were allowed twenty-five minutes to amass up to seven hundred possible points; written reasons for their judging decision were mandatory.

1912 This year was the first for 4-H Club work in Indiana; Zora Mayo Smith was appointed State 4-H Club leader September 1.

1915 The first 4-H class, market hogs, was offered at the State Fair. The Board set aside $250 for the 1915 Boys' Corn Contest. A class competition was instituted that year for Spotted Poland China hogs.

1921 Girls had a Canning Club, inaugurated this year. Other 4-H clubs: Beef Calf (beginning in 1921), Dairy Calf, Jersey Calf, Holstein Calf, Ayrshire Calf, Boys' and Girls' Lamb, Spotted Poland China Pig, Duroc-Jersey Pig, Yorkshire Pig, Boys' and Girls' Poultry – and more.

The 4-H Club vegetable exhibit filled most of the Agricultural and Horticultural Building at the 1949 Fair.

Boys in 4-H Club beanies, judges, and officials ring prize Shorthorn in the old Coliseum.

The 1953 4-H Parade of Champions filled a packed Coliseum with floats and equine color guards as 4-H Club members paraded in by county.

Loral W. Sears, Lapel, took the 1933 4-H Club first prize with his Chester White gilt.

1922 By this time, five 4-H classes were established.

1923 A Corn Club Class was added; the Board was "especially active," and many more "educational enterprises" were developed.

    The Boys' Judging Contest, one of the modern Fair's older educational features, drew 160 boys from forty-two counties. "It is a kind of practical schooling, too," taught by the State Board, "which not only helps oncoming generations to a higher plane of living and to greater prosperity, but will add to the rating of Indiana as an agricultural and livestock state."

1924 A Potato Club Class including Early Ohio and Irish Cobbler was added. By this year, there were seven pig club classes.

◆◆◆

Tastefully symmetrical, long-gone Crop Arts exhibits filled the Agricultural and Horticultural Building with harvest colors in this 1928 display.

David Williams proudly displays his prize-winning dressed chickens at the 1954 Fair.

Boys of the State Fair Club Camp gathered for a group shot sometime in the late 1930s outside a reconditioned Sheep Barn where the 4-H Buildings now stand. A train on the old Monon Line can be seen in the background. The Camp opened in 1924; thousands of boys had attended by the time the nation was drawn into World War II.

Boys Club campers drink tomato juice during a 1938 meal.

SOME TIME before the 1924 Fair, three sheep barns, two for bunks, one for a mess hall, were moved to the Fairgrounds' northwest side near the Monon line, secluded in the north grove. They opened as the first eight-day Indiana State Fair Boys' Agricultural Club Camp, to 150 youths fourteen to nineteen years old, for $1 and a $5 deposit.

Instructional and recreational, the camp followed a strict regimen. A 5:30 a.m. bugle awakening was followed twenty-five minutes later with flag raising. Bunks were inspected at 7:45 a.m. Every boy brought khaki trousers and shirts, the regulation camp uniform, from home; and two blankets, a comforter and pillow. Tin plates, knives, forks, spoons, and tin cups were sold at camp. Livestock were fed three times daily, and so were the boys. M.L. Hall of Lafayette was the first superintendent.

Two class periods were devoted to health, nature study, and agriculture (corn, livestock, and crops judging and selection; horticulture; poultry; and soils.) State YMCA, State Board of Health, and others provided cooperative instruction. Taps played at 9:30 every evening.

The *Indianapolis Star* offered three $100 Purdue scholarships to Camp Club members, for the four-year Agriculture course, or the eight-week short course. Winners were selected on the basis of accumulated points.

1927 Around 2,200 entries were produced by 4-H members during this Fair, up from 1,400 the previous year.

1928 More than 20,000 boys and girls were involved in 4-H club work by 1928. Indiana's youth now came to "the place where the future leaders of the State are gathered, rub shoulders with them and get acquainted with them." Those future leaders were forming associations invaluable not only to them in later years, but to the agricultural state as well.

Indiana Future Farmers of America secured the nineteenth state charter on September 6. Twelve chapters received their charters during an October 18-19 convention: Battleground, Kempton, Pierceton, Martinsville, Middleburg, Madison Township of St. Joseph County, Nappanee, Columbia City, Monrovia, Paragon, Seymour, and Wea Township of Tippecanoe County. Later the vocational agriculture education group shortened its name to merely "FFA."

1935 Loral Sears of West Lafayette won a Boys' State Fair Club Camp scholarship at the '35 Fair; he wrote his appreciation the following May:

"[T]he only way I can see to improve . . . is to give more of them. A scholarship means every thing to a farm boy who must work his way through school. I am endeavoring to make the best possible use of my chance to attend college and hope that more farm boys will have the opportunity in the future."

Sears was one of 239 boys and 12 leaders educated at the twelfth annual camp, 106 more than the Fair before.

1936 Eighty-five counties dispatched 3,277 4-H Club exhibits in 1936; planning had begun for something more than three old sheep barns and crowded space in the Women's Building, Fair program readers learned.

"The fact that about 1,500 exhibitors of club products and members of livestock judging teams can stay on the ground during fair week, will be an asset to the fair that will be greatly enhanced with the completion of the new building by 1939."

Boys' Camp and 4-H Clubs still met in the grove of trees at the Fairgrounds' northwest corner. That year,

A very proud young man with his prize watermelon at the 1952 Centennial Fair.

Prize barrows fail to intimidate this young farmer who is more concerned with herding them to the show ring during a recent State Fair.

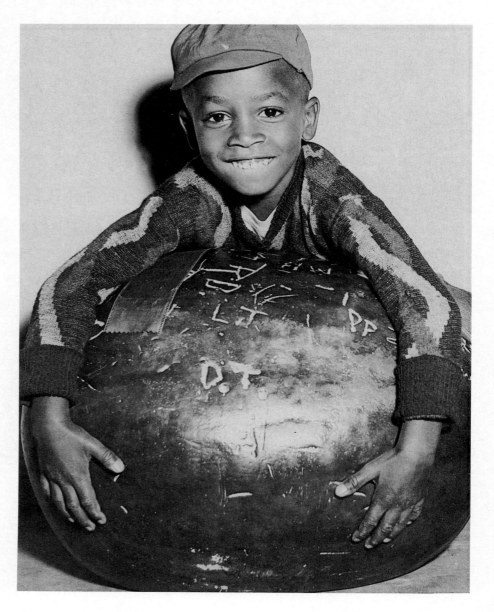

250 boys and leaders attended; for the second year, a tent went up to shelter the overflow.

1941 In its fifth year at the Fairgrounds, Boys State quartered in the Youth Buildings. Howard Myers, directing the eight-year-old program, told Executive Committeemen there were "no limitations as to race or creed. They are all treated alike . . . they have yet to have the first objection from any of the boys. They never have more than four or five col-ored boys and they are the cream of the crop."

1949 In the spring, Kiwanis International convened their first 4-H Junior Leaders Training Conference since 1941 in the 4-H buildings. Fair Board President Homer E. Schuman of Columbia City, who had dropped in, was impressed and wanted them back.

"I think possibly the State Fair Board should lean a little backwards to get organizations such as these to hold their meetings on the grounds and not to charge them any more than actual expenses. "They are the cream of the crop in the State of Indiana and we can create more goodwill in the State by doing this."

1963 Indiana Future Farmers of America initiated its first Young McDonald's Farm at the 1963 Fair in a forty-by-sixty foot tent at the west end of the Track of Champions. Visitors saw and petted small farm animals.

1974 FFA moved to a permanent location just east of the Natural Resources Building, with a wood building, a greenhouse, a twenty-seven-by-one hundred foot tent, another forty-by-one hundred foot tent, and outdoor exhibit space for large wood and metal products.

1975 Seventeen-year-old Todd Cunningham of Kempton became the second 4-H'er to ever succeed himself as owner of the Grand Champion 4-H Steer. Todd also was 1975 FFA State Hoosier Farmer.

John F. McKee of Lafayette claimed the first distinction; records show he won in 1928, then again in 1929.

1986 Two records were set in 4-H livestock exhibitions: 1,094 barrows and 1,016 sheep. Steers' biggest year went all the way back to 1977, when 712 paraded for judges' inspections.

1989 The Lindley scholarship was established when Chad Lindley of Tipton County exhibited both the Grand Champion 4-H Barrow and Grand Champion 4-H Wether. According to guidelines of the Spotlite Sale, a 4-H member can receive proceeds from only one Spotlite Sale animal. As a result, Lindley donated the $10,000 his Grand Champion wether brought to the Indiana 4-H Foundation to establish the scholarship.

1990 Amber Hoffman of Princeton in Gibson County won the Fair's first annual Lindley 4-H Sheep Scholarship in 1990. The $1,000 annual scholarship is awarded to an Indiana 4-H sheep exhibitor who has shown one or more 4-H wethers for at least seven out of the last 10 years. Recipients must be in their last year of 4-H.

1991 More than 1,800 FFA exhibits greeted Fair visitors – small farm animals, agribusiness, agricultural production, natural resources, sales and services, various products, horticulture, aquaculture, hydroponics, mechanics, and chapter activities.

Louise Newton, fifteen-year-old 4-H Club girl from Washington, Indiana, with her 1940 breed champion Jersey cow.

Jesse Gant of near Greencastle won a polled Shorthorn heifer during the 1970 State Fair from Mr. and Mrs. Jim Humphrey of Wolcott. Indiana Beef Queen Mary Beth Dysert looked on. Gant was the first winner in a promotional effort to get youth interested in raising cattle, particularly Shorthorns. Humprey's brother John recalled, "I think Jesse went on to become a veterinarian." Gant, who lived with his grandfather, showed up one day of the Fair and asked if he could help, according to then breed manager Barry Jordan of Rensselaer.

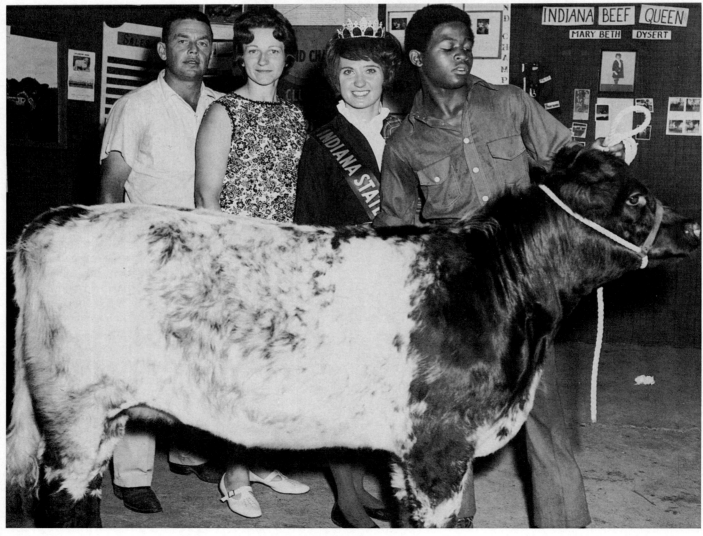

Boys sheep judging at the 1915 State Fair. An electric street car can be seen in the left background.

Amy Maddox, nineteen, of Carmel, sold her 4-H champion Hereford steer for $5,300 during 1991's 21st Annual Spotlite Sale of 4-H Champions. With Amy are (l-r) her brother Clay and two of the buyers, George Faerber and Doug Smith of Faerber Bee Windows.

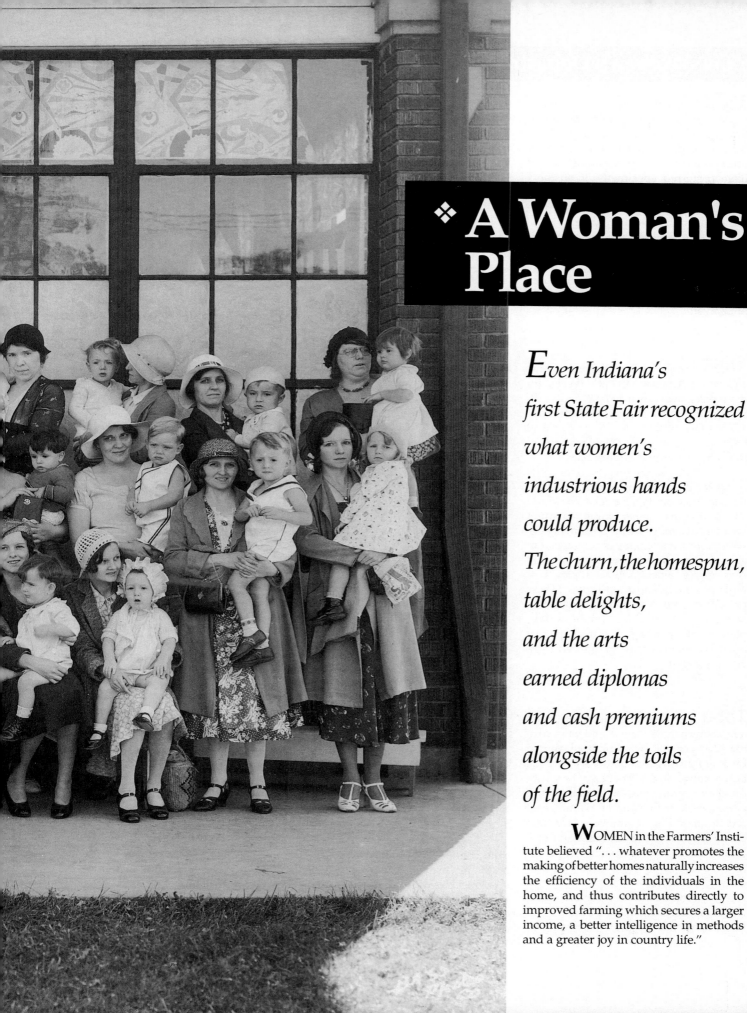

❖ A Woman's Place

*Even Indiana's
first State Fair recognized
what women's
industrious hands
could produce.
The churn, the homespun,
table delights,
and the arts
earned diplomas
and cash premiums
alongside the toils
of the field.*

WOMEN in the Farmers' Institute believed ". . . whatever promotes the making of better homes naturally increases the efficiency of the individuals in the home, and thus contributes directly to improved farming which secures a larger income, a better intelligence in methods and a greater joy in country life."

The Women's Department

1853 One of the popular competitions in the miscellaneous section was handwriting. All eleven penmanship entries were "ornamental, and many of them very fine specimens, but the committee would have preferred specimens of business hand writing." W.W. Wilson of New Albany and N. Loring of Chicago, nevertheless each won $2 and a diploma.

Judges also gave awards to Daguerreotypes and an Ornamental Hair Wreath, "wrought of the hair of sixty [deceased] persons, all members of one family," exhibited by Mrs. S.M. Miskelly of Lafayette.

1855 In the General Division of Miscellaneous Articles, Mrs. J.G. Weeks, Indianapolis, was awarded $3 and a diploma for her bride's head dresses. "These beautiful articles were gazed at with longing eyes by 'Maidens fair, of dimpled cheeks and auburn hair.'"

"May she be preserved forever!" remarked the awarding committee in giving Marion County's Pamelia Wood $10 and a diploma for her preserved water melon rinds, musk melon, citron, raisins, wine grapes, winter grapes, tomatoes, English ground cherry, green apples, wild crab apples, Siberian Crab apples, currants, pears, figs, and dried apples. "These preserves were in an excellent condition of preservation, and the committee take pleasure of awarding . . . in the hope that other housewives may be induced to go and preserve likewise."

1856 The Board decided that "Hunter's ebony handled knives and forks, costing $2.75 per sett, [would] be substituted for $3 gold pens, and that ivory handled butter knives, at $1.50 per pair, be substituted for $2 gold pens, and twenty setts of ivory handled knives and forks, at $6 per sett, be offered as premiums . . . ." Hunter charged $42 to fill seven knife and fork orders for the January exhibition premiums, and $312 for eighty-five Fair-time cutlery premiums.

Worsted work by twelve-year-old Catharine E. Michael of Indianapolis was "very neat for a girl so young. It

deserve[d] a small premium." A wax candlestick shown by Mrs. M.M. Griffith of Bartholomew County was "a new article." She also showed four-year-old pickles which "seem[ed] to be perfect," and cotton and wool Kersey blankets. Wool dog stockings were "more singular than serviceable." No record exists for who exhibited them.

1857 Mrs. Powell Howland of Marion County had the best ten pounds of butter made in June and shown at the Fair, the second best year-old twenty-five pound cheese (which won an award of knives and forks), the best twenty pounds each of butter and cheese from a single dairy, and

thirds in fruit butter collections and "jellies, preserves, pickles, and canned fruit, by one exhibitor."

1872 Mrs. James Thornburg of Wabash won $5 for showing the best under garments in "Embroidery, Braiding, etc." in the Domestic Arts. Amelia Gilmore, Bloomington, showed the best worsted braiding.

Thirteen-year-old Alice Lockridge, Terre Haute, received Miscellaneous honorable mention for her penmanship specimen. So did Indianapolis' Mrs. E. Hartwell for her knit corset, and Covington's Susan H. Sharon for her knit drawers.

1875 Mrs. M. Leibhard of Knightstown won $2 for her "best embroidered infants' sack." Virginia C. Meredith, Cambridge City, wife of Henry Clay Meredith, 1882's tragic president, won $8 for "best gown, chemise and drawers."

Captain (and 1881 Republican state representative from Wayne County) Henry Clay Meredith of near Cambridge City was 1882 Board president from January until his death at home July 5, twelve days short of his thirty-ninth birthday. Meredith suffered twelve days following a trip to Chicago; he "took cold, probably from over-exertion, and was taken down with strong symptoms of pneumonia." Three respected physicians could not save him, "despite their utmost professional skill. This sad death seems even more sad . . . [because] with his death his line became extinct, he being the last male member of a family known and honored throughout the State, and, indeed, the whole country."

Meredith widowed the former Virginia Claypool, who would go on to become "Indiana's most widely known woman farmer who bred and managed a notable Shorthorn family for many years, [and] was the first woman speaker to appear on the [Farmers'] Institute program in Indiana," according to *A History of Fifty Years of Cooperative Extension Service in Indiana*.

1876 Brownsburg's Mrs. Laura Smith won $2 for best crocheted opera hood. Miss Elizabeth Howland, Indianapolis, embroidered the best gored yoke and sleeves, winning $3. Miss Melinda Hill, Greensburg, took $8 for her hand-sewn gown, chemise, and drawers. A toilet cushion was worthy of $2; congratulations, Mrs. James Deathe of Knightstown!

1877 A map of the United States worked "in worsted, with brilliant colors" by Indianapolis' J.W. Nicholson was "quite accurate, and shows no common degree of skill and patience."

An Excelsior quilter exhibited by Zionsville's Mrs. Augusta Hoover was described as a "frame for quilting by a sewing machine. The frame travels on a slightly inclined railroad, on which the feed of the machine moves it readily." Committeemen acknowledged "it is a first class labor-saving machine, but will not be popular with young folks, as it abolishes quiltings."

1878 Femininity's role was officially recognized three weeks before the Fair when the Board of Agriculture authorized a Women's Department. Mrs. Mary E. Haggart was named the president of the group; Miss Mary D. Naylor, the corresponding secretary; Mrs. Joseph E. Cobb, the recording secretary; and Mrs. Ruth Wales, treasurer. Each woman was from Indianapolis. Along with the executive committee, a committee of "lady journalists" was appointed.

The Equal Suffrage Society of Indianapolis was organized that year. May Wright Thompson, a widow, was the society's secretary; she later remarried and became May Wright Sewall. In an address delivered ten years later to the Delegate Board of Agriculture, Sewall reminded listeners, "In antiquity, women were suffered to live that they might bear children for a state in whose defence or for whose aggrandizement the male children . . . would, as men, almost certainly be called to die . . . .The progress of civilization . . . has transformed the relations between home and state – almost reversed them. If formerly the home existed to maintain the state, now it is equally true that the state exists to protect the home and to serve its widening interests." Sewall later became president of the International and National Council of Women.

In the Textile Fabrics competition, miscellaneous awards were given to: Miss Alice Darby, Avon, for sixteen pencil drawings – "excellent taste and skill displayed"; Mrs. J.M. Elliott, Indianapolis, for a "meritorious" sampler made in 1820 and a "very fine" infant cap made in 1828; Sisters of St. Francis, Oldenburg, for a specimen of crochet work and embroidery and two pairs of shoes; and the Sisters of the Good Shepherd, Indianapolis, for a "beautiful" fancy quilt and a "very good" embroidered infant robe.

1879 The "Domestic and Miscellaneous" Department was created in 1879. The following January, President W.B. Seward, after "considering the short time in which they had to work it up," believed the Ladies' Department "was simply wonderful, and was one of the most interesting features of our fair . . . I hope to see [it] grow . . . ."

1880 The Woman's Board of Industry took over the textile and domestic departments in 1880, and women gained complete control over the Woman's Department.

1884 Woman's State Fair Association President Mrs. A.M. Noe claimed the women's petition, "'It will mark a new era in woman's industrial relations . . . it will be as bread cast upon the waters, to return, not after many days, but at once . . . and continue returning, increased a thousand fold' has more than been fulfilled."

1885 "To-day, Indiana's State Board of Agriculture stands before the world as the only one showing this confidence in women," Mrs. Noe informed the Board in

Board President Frank J. Claypool of Muncie and his sister Mrs. Virginia C. Meredith of West Lafayette at the 1934 Fair. Mrs. Meredith was the first woman speaker on the Farmers' Institute program.

January. "[I]t has given them the opportunity to prove their ability to carry on such an enterprise, and to bring before the public the labor of their hands and brains on an equal footing with that of men. The efficacy of the organization has been demonstrated in the display made in the Woman's Department of the World's Industrial Exposition at New Orleans . . . a creditable exhibit . . . in position before any other State in the department allotted to such displays."

A family outfits scene from the 1923 L.S. Ayres & Company Style Show in the Women's Building.

Two participants in the 1935 Style Show wear old-fashioned dresses.

Models on the L.S. Ayres runway at the 1961 Fair.

Lucile Morris of Marion County took the 1934 championship in the 4-H Club Dress Revue.

1900 "Table Luxuries" embraced everything from homemade cheese, maple syrup, wheat bread, rusk (a twice-baked sweet bread), fruit cake, cheese straws, Saratoga chips, spiced pears and peaches, catsup, gelatine dessert, and fruit butters.

Mrs. Madge Waggaman of Kokomo was awarded $1.50 in the Art Department for knitting the best infant's shirt. Mrs. L.A. Moore of Terre Haute won the same amount of money for her Battenburg lace specimen and an embroidered picture frame.

Absolutely the highest "Art" premium, $3, went to Mrs. D.P. Stagg of Greensburg for showing her ladies' underwear.

1919 Art Hall was long past its prime, the Board remarked in its *State Year Book* report. "Neglected until it [was] no longer fit for the use of the women of Indiana," the ancient frame was replaced with the imposing concrete and brick "Woman's Building," which housed "the things most important to women: fine art, domestic art, applied art, and culinary and Girls' Club work."

1922 A Women's Advisory Committee composed of representatives of "various State organizations . . . active in the promotion of the well being of women in Indiana" was set up early in 1922. Members included: Mrs. Charles Lindley of Salem in Washington County, Mrs. Charles W. Sewell (Indiana Farmers' Federation) of Otterbein, Purdue's Miss Lella R. Gaddis of Lafayette, Mrs. Lawrence G. Vannice of Amo, and Mrs. W.J. Torrance of Evansville (Indiana Federation of Women's Clubs). Former president John Isenbarger directed the department. Ironically, a man remained in charge of the Women's Department until 1945.

L.S. Ayres inaugurated its style show, climaxing with a wedding gown showing. The Ayres tradition lasted through 1967. "Home Economics Day"

Floriculture judges at the 1937 gladiolus competition; J.L. Coomler of Fairland, the Indianapolis Gladioli Society secretary, and division head C.R. Green of Indianapolis.

The Soldiers and Sailors Monument took third prize in the 1954 Floriculture competition.

Dresses and other 4-H sewing projects displayed in the 4-H Exhibit Hall.

Mrs. Hubert Sayler, Crawfordsville, won the Women's Building Sweepstakes Award for her angel food cake.

sought the state's fastest crocheter; State Fair employees were not eligible to compete.

Premiums were offered for first through fourth-best one-hundred-year-old coverlids and shawls. Century-old antiques were sought in premium competition – coffee mills, fans, music and snuff boxes, pictures made of hair, tin-type photographs, and State Fair souvenirs. The Women's Building Cafeteria offered the finest of foods prepared by hotel chefs.

1953 The Grand Champion Pie was worth a $25 premium. Contestants squared off in fine, domestic and applied arts contests, culinary skills judging, the Crochet Contest, and the Spelling Bee. Fashion plans were made with the L.S. Ayres' Style Show. Pie Day was September 8.

"Buy All Your Farm and Household Supplies in Cotton Bags and Save Money" – women and girls were invited to enter the new statewide "Save With Cotton Bags" Contest. A "lovely" Model 130 Pfaff Zig-Zag sewing machine and cash awards awaited the creator of the most skillful and ingenious clothing and

pounds, also took first in the watermelon display. A winter squash with a seven-foot circumference, and weighing one-hundred and seventy-three pounds, broke all state fair records, much to the pleasure of Max Zaring of Fillmore.

Sandy Newhard of Markleville scared better than thirty others in the "Halloween in August" jack-o-lantern contest. Nearby, the Home & Family Arts Building, with a "Fashions Alive in '75" theme, hosted belly dancing demonstrations, courtesy of "Roxanne."

1976 Military Miniatures at the Home & Family Arts Building featured authentic, tiny lead soldiers varying in height from twenty-two to eighty millimeters; they were painted and equipped by using tweezers and a magnifying glass.

1977 Mrs. Richard (Jamie) Clayton of Greenfield, the 1976 Indiana State Fair Archway Home Style Cookie Contest winner, was judged best in the nation with her "Glazed Apple Cookies" recipe. Nancy Schuman of Wabash, now three-time victor in Archway's contest, received her award from Dolly Parton.

Needle Arts competition added machine embroidery and machine knitting, while Craft Potpourri added string art, sand art, and quilting. The Cake Department displayed cakes depicting past and present Indiana life in the Hoosier Heritage Cake Decoration Contest.

1978 The Home & Family Arts Department celebrated its 100th anniversary. First known in 1878 as the Women's Department, men had invaded woman's sole domain many years earlier.

1967 Barbara J. Stillwell, Frankfort, joined the State Fair Board in 1967, replacing Ida Wright. She resigned just before the 1969 Fair. Hortense Kaufman of Shelbyville replaced Stillwell, followed by Lola Yoder of Goshen who was appointed September 6, 1973, when Kaufman died.

1973 Because of a scheduled "First Family" member's visit, the Secret Service emptied the Home & Family Arts Building on the evening of August 20. Possibly exploding preserves were defused. Julie Nixon Eisenhower spoke the next day; the topic of her talk? A woman's choice.

1975 A "Roadside Market" at the Agriculture-Horticulture Building was guaranteed to delight vegetarians, while an all-day Rose Show invited sweet-smellers inside. Cheryl Stuckwish of Vallonia took first place in the "largest single watermelon" contest with her ninety-three and one-half pound entry. Her fifty-five watermelons, averaging eighty-eight

1983 Catherine C. Conner of Remington, then of Indianapolis, was appointed to the State Fair Board , the seventh woman to claim the distinction. Conner served through the 1986 Fair.

Computers in the kitchen made their first Home & Family Arts Building appearance with "Housewives' Computers for Home and Farm." Housewives watched domestic applications of the personal computer.

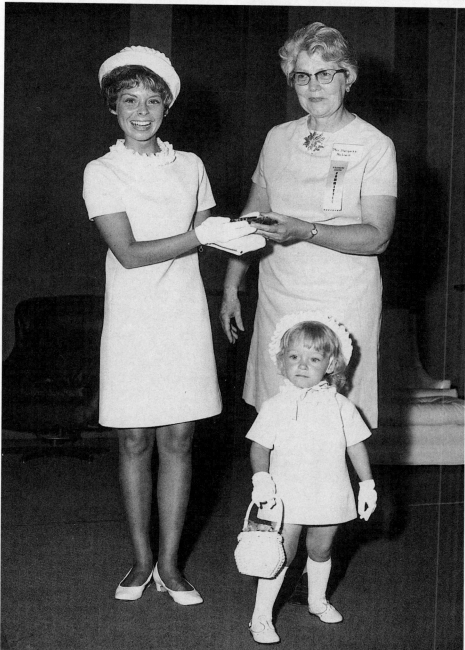

Josinah Allen, Wayne County (left), was named 1936 Dress Revue champion, and Mary Stoner, Clark County, was reserve champion.

A 1923 display exhibiting the proof that the advice of the 1855 award committee has been heeded – the women of Indiana have "go[ne] and preserve[d] likewise."

Judi K. Merkel and her daughter Angie took reserve honors in the 1970 Family Outfits Professional Division; show committee member Mrs. Margaret McClain presented the award. Merkel, from tiny Berne, was appointed to the Fair Board for '87, then rose to Board presidency in 1991. Although other women joined the Board beginning in 1977, only eight have headed the Women's/Home &Family Arts Department as full directors. Before then, men commanded the department charged with "the things most important to women."

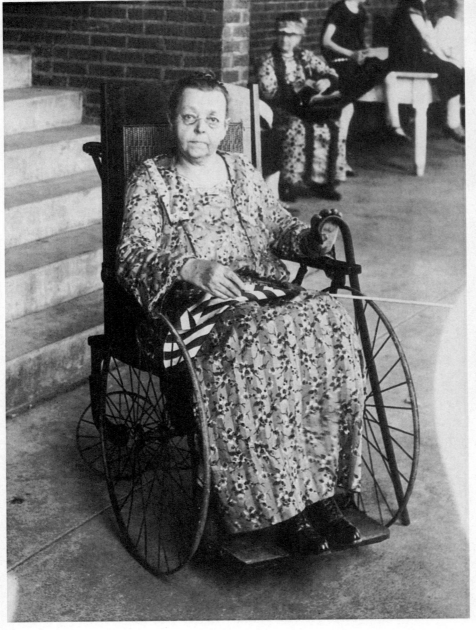

Mrs. Julia Goff of Russellville won first prize for her display of canned products during the 1940 Fair.

A patriotic woman in a wheelchair outside the Women's Building during the 1927 Golden Jubilee Fair.

Mrs. George Jones of Rockport and her 1940 first-prize devil's food cake. Mrs. Jones was one of the oldest exhibitors in the Women's Department Culinary Division.

Jean Sheets of Frankfort took a Culinary Arts first and second with her entry.

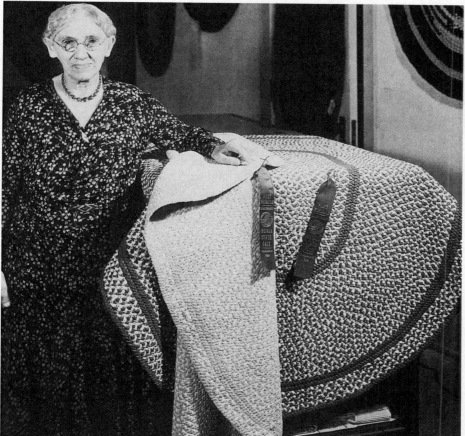

Winners in the 1936 Women's Department cake exhibit competition.

Mrs. Louise Christie of Indianapolis and her 1934 first-prize winning braided cotton rug.

Mrs. Mabel E. Thompson of Indianapolis with her 1940 first-prize birthday cake.

Mrs. George Boyd of Montezuma displays her Grand Sweepstakes winning cake in 1940.

Mrs. M.E. Rynerson of Clayton holds the pie and cake with which she won the Grand Sweepstakes of 1937.

Cooking group of Indiana State Fair School making peach rolls.

The Home Economics School for Girls

*"W*OMEN'S year at the Indiana State Fair!" *The Hub of the Universe* trumpeted in June 1919. The new Women's Building was joining the ranks of modern structures at the Fairgrounds.

"The second floor is to be given over largely to a new school of domestic science and home economics . . . for girls from the ninety-two counties . . . ."

A Home Economics School for Girls ages sixteen to thirty, "as now in vogue at Illinois State Fair," was approved early in 1919; it was inaugurated as soon as the new Women's Building contract was assigned in May. Mrs. Charles Lindley of Salem in Washington County, referred to only as "Mrs. Charles" whenever mentioned, was selected to serve as the chairperson of the first Home Economics School Board of Lady Managers.

Years earlier, a group of Board members traveled to the Illinois State Fair "and one of the things which particularly impressed them was the School of Home Economics held during the week of the Exposition," according to *The Hub*. Illinois had operated its own version for more than two decades.

Good Lady Lindley is credited with the idea for such a school in Indiana. Husband Charles Lindley had directed the 1917 Woman's Department. In 1919 he was merely the Board president.

Mrs. Charles W. Sewell of Otterbein, the director of foods, and dormitory director Mrs. Lewis Taylor of Newburg formed the Board of Managers with Mrs. Lindley. Mrs. Nellie K. Jones and Mrs. Edna H. Edmondson were instructor/chaperones.

The school, a product of the Board's vision, was "a new movement . . . in the expansion of the policy it has followed since 1852 – to help in all practical ways to spread enlightenment among the people of the state that the farming resources of Indiana may be increased."

Teachers, lecturers, and assistants welcomed girls to "a well organized and equipped school for the work which instructs the girl in home experience not provided nor found in any other school. This the board points to as a great stride in the support of better homes and a wider knowledge of all and every part of home life," the 1919 *State Year Book* recorded.

The fifty-two girls – each "from the best of families throughout the state of Indiana" –attending the first ten-day Home Economics School were allowed to see Woodrow Wilson, their nation's president, and enjoyed entertainment at the Claypool Hotel and the Hippodrome. President Wilson visited Indianapolis on September 4, then appeared in the Coliseum that evening, offering his argument for the League of Nations. By noon forty thousand persons had crowded onto the Fairgrounds, according to the *Indianapolis News*, "with ten thousand arriving each hour." Twenty acres were covered with closely packed automobiles.

Although the "Women's Art Building" second floor wasn't completed in time for the Fair, and the school didn't fully open until Thursday of the Fair, the girls "thoroughly enjoyed" their training. They stayed in a downtown hotel while their rooms were finished, according to *The Hub*. They visited the theatre, took a sight-seeing trip of greater Indianapolis on a specially provided Indianapolis Street Railway car, visited the State House, and shopped the city's large stores.

Each girl paid $10 tuition and brought her own bedding. Transportation was covered by sponsoring

organizations, among them county women's committees.

As planned, the building's entire second floor had enough dormitory space for 120 girls, including class, study, and lecture rooms plus a library. An auditorium seated six hundred. A sewing room and "cooking laboratory" were in the basement.

There also was a "model home" inside the "largest and most complete building used for showing the arts and crafts on an American fair ground." The home where School girls acquired "practical instruction in all phases of homemaking," consisted of dining, living, bed and bath rooms, with a kitchen and pantry.

"A new day had come to the Indiana farm girl," Mrs. Sewell wrote in *The Hub*. "Not many years ago she with her parents and brothers were caricatured and ridiculed. But today, with the teaching of domestic science in the centralized rural high school, and girls' club and the home demonstration agent, things have changed. The country girl who capably helps her mother serve real cream with

the family's breakfast cereal or coffee, instead of condensed milk . . . who eats an egg she knows is yester-laid . . . is the subject of a new feeling—and that is envy."

The first graduates of the school and their counties were: Esta Fleming, Adams; Louise Brockman, Bartholomew; scholarship alternate winner Bernice Lewis, Benton; Lula Hites, Blackford; Emmalyne Miash, Boone; Arthusia Phillips, Cass; Ina Northway, Clay; Gladys Hamilton, Delaware; Roberta Wilson, Dubois; Fern Cotterill, Elkhart; Eva Beason and Gertrude Gettinger, Fayette; Marie Gast and Mary Hire, Fulton; Ruth Flora, Grant; Pearl Simpson, Green; Margaret Follett, Ruth Barker, Virginia White, and Juanita Rush, Hamilton; Martha Shepherd, Henry; Irene Poer, Hancock; Fern Grable, Harrison; Ethel Kenney, Hendricks; Blanche Smith, Howard; Leah Barber, Jefferson; Harriet Benjamin, Lake; Mildred Eaton, Lagrange; Fern VanSickle and Marcia Orme, Marion; Lulu Leitzman and Marie Brown, Morgan; Melva Hendricks, Montgomery; Elizabeth Voris, Noble; Gladys Stockton and Addie Murphy, Newton; Dora Blime,

Girls of the 1923 School of Home Economics make peach rolls in the Women's Building basement.

A basket-weaving class during an early 1920s School of Home Economics.

Pulaski; Mrs. Guy Collings, Parke; Elizabeth Brown, Posey; Opal Schockney, Randolph; Faye Baughman, Sullivan; Velma Everett and Mable Hester, Scott; Velma Smith, Steuben; Mable Bouse, Tipton; Purdue scholarship winner Grace McCutcheon, Vanderburgh; Doris Bryan, Wabash; Irene Newton and Margaret Stecker, Washington; Edith Beeler and Beth Garrett, Wells; Mida Abbott, Whitley.

The "womanhood of Indiana" could take pride in the Women's Art Building, President Lindley remarked during his final address in January 1920. The first floor, planned for exhibition, "was the mecca for the ladies who were interested in fine art, domestic art or culinary products." Gas and water lines served the build-

Dinner time during the 1923 School of Home Economics.

The sole man in the photo is director and 1918 Board president John Isenbarger of North Manchester. Girls of the 1935 State Fair School of Home Economics. Ida Ray, one of that year's Honor Girls, is in the front row, third from the right.

Cooking class at the Fair.

A 1934 meat cooking demonstration by Miss Mildred Batz of the National Meat Board. With her are: (l-r) Kathryn Kidwell, Hancock County; Dixin Wilson, Warren County; Marjory Pierce, Henry County; School director Mrs. Calvin Perdue; Purdue's Miss Lela Gaddis; Mary Passwater, Hancock County; and Maudellen Chappell, Hancock County.

ing, which wouldn't sport the gold lettering identifying it as the Women's Building for another nine years.

The School of Home Economics, designed to provide home economic training and demonstration work to "a girl from each county" was "completely equipped with modern conveniences" donated by Indianapolis merchants.

The following July, Mrs. Lindley wrote about an important aspect of School education: "Some few girls who came to the school with what seems to be the 'stylish languorous swing of the fashionable lady' straightened up into the dignified, straight-ahead walk of the wide-awake, healthy American girl. All of the girls soon grasped the idea that a sound, healthy, well-cared for body is a girl's greatest asset."

In its first full term of September 1 to 11, a longer engagement than the Fair itself, the 1920 State Fair School of Home Economics remained under Board of Lady Managers direction, "a team of workers who work with both hands and brains."

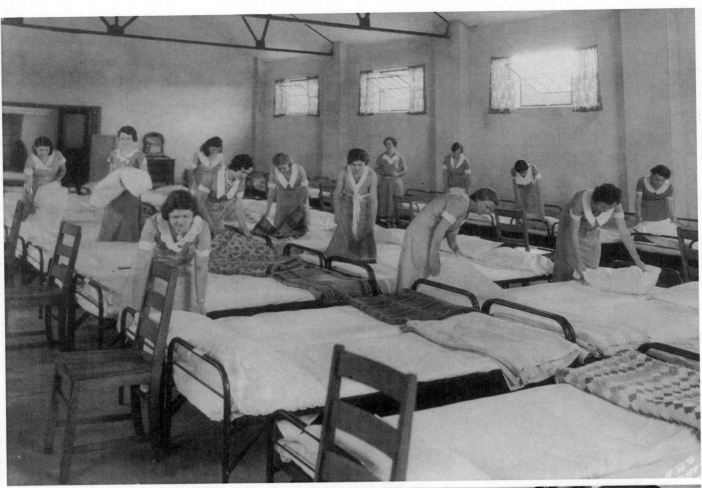

Bed-making class at the 1922 School of Home Economics.

Girls' School members of 1934 studied washing machine use and the best laundry methods.

Marion County's (l-r) Alice Springer, Mary Mowry, and Lillie Stine helped serve the food during the 1940 Boys Club Camp.

Instructors were selected on the basis of their "broad sympathy" for farm and small town girls. They knew and understood "a girl's ambitions and why a girl on the farm can be lured away to city life." They taught the rural girl "how to get the last degree of comfort and contentment out of a home."

The sole mission of the school was "to train young women in better and scientific methods of housekeeping; and . . . associating with a splendid group of teachers and pupils, to inspire them to love the profession of homemaking.

"[M]uch was accomplished. The school is intensely practical. Each girl must do her bit. She put into practice daily the lessons given on foods, table service, dormitory work and health. The real knowledge acquired through practice will give her greater efficiency in her own home; [and] give each girl something worth while to carry to the Domestic Science Clubs and Farmers' Institutes back home. The inspiration she received in living for ten days with this group of live Hoosier girls and in performing with them the useful tasks of homemaking and enjoying to-

gether the pleasures planned for them will go far toward giving these girls wholesome ideas."

Now open to "any girl, wife or mother of Indiana between the ages of sixteen to twenty-five years," the School was designed "along the same lines that any well-regulated home should be planned . . . sitting room, dormitory, bath room, clothes room, hospital, lecture rooms and large corridor upstairs [and] . . . in the basement . . . [a] large school kitchen, dining room and demonstration corridor."

Seventy-one girls from sixty-two counties (that year all were single, sixteen were in grammar school, twenty-three were high schoolers, six attended college, nine were teachers, seventeen already were housekeepers) divided into work groups for meal preparation, baking, serving, dish drying, and dormitory. Group captains ensured that everyone did their work; each group performed a different task daily.

Girls were sponsored by their schools' home economics classes, county farm bureaus, county fair associations,

Directors and Instructors at the 1940 State Fair School of Home Economics: (l-r) Mrs. L. Stewart, Indianapolis; Mrs. Morris Hansen, Fremont; Miss Jeanette Reffett, Covington; Mrs. Elmer Walters, Lafayette; Mrs. Wilbur Elshoff, Huntingburg; School Director Della Hemmer, Greencastle; Miss Jean Hollis, Princeton; Mrs. Howard Taylor, Indianapolis; and Mrs. Dan Hey, Shelbyville.

"or any organization recognized by the Indiana State Board of Agriculture." A $15 fee covered food costs. The sponsors paid all other costs. That year, however, five paid their own way.

Each instructor and supervisor was admirably suited for her role. Purdue's Miss Florence Boston was a lecturer and food demonstrator. Her "charming personality" complemented her reputation as "the best food expert in the State." Mrs. Guy Collings, Parke County's club supervisor, was Miss Boston's assistant. Collings, a graduate of the first school whose "splendid personality did much toward establishing a high standard" in 1919, had helped with "many perplexing problems." She started the Honor Girl tradition lasting well into the 1960s. Each year's Honor Girl was selected on the basis of top performance; directors chose the girls to return to help manage the following year's School as assistant directors. Assistant directors supervised one of the groups at the school. Honor girls, all of whom demonstrated leadership quali-

ties and high scores, were selected by girls attending the school, school supervisors, and instructors.

Dr. Ada Schweitzer, from the Indiana State Board of Health, taught health lessons. She impressed students with "the truth and the beauty of the things she advocated." While in her classes, girls received practical instructions on baby care and feeding.

Mrs. B.M. (alternately W.B.) Stoddard was the art supervisor from Washington Township Schools of Marion County. One skill Stoddard taught was pine needle basket weaving. Most of the girls finished their baskets by school's end.

Miss Eleanor Throckmorton, a Purdue Graduate in charge of Lafayette High School's cafeteria, supervised meal preperation, but her main lesson to the girls was efficiency.

Miss Blanche Zaring, from the Salem High School Domestic Science Department, taught baking skills. Zaring's "quiet ladylike manner and carefulness in doing things just right" proved invaluable.

Miss Laura Moore, a domestic science teacher, instructed the girls in dining room skills. "Quiet and unassuming," Moore taught attention to detail.

Mrs. Ida Piatt of Evansville was in charge of lessons in the girls' dormitory. With "many years in the interest of domestic science club work," Piatt gave bed-making lessons. "She maintained always a system of perfect order and [the dorm's] eighty-five beds, and the bath room, and clothes room were at all times open for inspection."

The house nurse, Miss Bertha Lips of the Red Cross in Washington County, taught bandaging and home care. Nurse Lips "proved invaluable. One case of infectious sore throat was cared for promptly and skillfully. None other appeared among the girls. Miss Lips endeared herself to all by her readiness to entertain the girls with her overseas experiences; to chaperone and to work in any capacity for the success of the school."

The school was universally accepted and embraced, *State Year Book* readers learned. "It meets a great need. . . . It opens opportunities to those who probably have not been able to afford a college course in home training. Too long we have educated our girls away from the home. Many are qualified to take their place in the business world. Too few are qualified to feed their families for health efficiency. It was a step in the right direction when the Indiana State Board of Agriculture gave to the womanhood of the State this splendid opportunity of ten days' training in homemaking." The School lost its name after '75, the 53rd year of the school; by '76, it was known merely as the Girls State Fair School. Nearly all of the original focus had fled

decades earlier.

In 1923, the fifth annual Indiana State Fair School of Home Economics August 27-September 7 required girls to wear a cadet blue uniform of chambray, everfast suiting, linen, or any other cotton material, with white collar and cuffs. Wives, mothers, or daughters ages sixteen to twenty-six, upon arriving in Indianapolis, hopped a streetcar going to the Fairgrounds. Dr. Schweitzer gave more health lectures; three moving picture shows were featured, along with home decoration, music, and literature lectures.

The 1926 State Fair School of Home Economics boasted girls representing each Indiana county. (A later report claimed eighty-nine arrived from seventy-four counties.) The Board hoped that the eighth annual School graduates, Indiana's future homemakers, would have "a larger vision of homemaking and recognize it as woman's greatest profession."

Five gas ranges purchased from Chambers Manufacturing Company of Shelbyville for the school kitchen set the Board back $423.21.

Edith Skeel of Sandborn won the $100 Marott Scholarship to Purdue; Margaret Hurt, Thorntown, took the $100 *Indianapolis Star* Scholarship to Purdue; Nellie Terry, Ladoga, claimed Marott's $50 Purdue scholarship; Helen Johnson of Monrovia and Opal Barton of Boonville both won Terre Haute State Normal's $50 scholarship prize; Louise Jessup, Carthage, won $50 to attend the Muncie State Normal School.

That year's three honor girls to return in '27, were Olive Caywood, Bainbridge; Lucille Elrod, Coatesville; Dorothea White, Indianapolis.

At the 1935 Home Economics school 168 young women from seventy-seven counties learned how better to perform their duties. Lectures discussed

health, teeth, book reviews, feet and shoes, interior decorating, cheese, laundry, sewing, Girl Scouts, and diet.

Seven scholarships totalling $490 were offered by Central Normal College in Danville, Schlosser Brothers for Purdue, Richmond's Earlham College, Franklin College, Terre Haute's Indiana State Teachers' College, and Indiana University.

By 1936, enrollment had increased to 158 from 82 counties, and ten scholarships totalling $796 were awarded to "outstanding Educational Institutions"; 205 applied for the '37 school. A total of 8,150 meals costing 11-1/4 cents each were served in '36.

Honor Girls returning from 1935's school were Ida Ray of Franklin, who went on to become the third woman member to the Board; Mary Elizabeth Wein, Lafayette; Lois Drake, Sullivan County; Mary Bulliett, Corydon; Dixie Lee Wilson, Boonville; and Ruth Magner, Orange County.

Thirteen girls attending 1951's Twenty-ninth Indiana State Fair Girls' School of Home Economics (three were selected from each county to attend the school) received "Honor Girl" special awards; the Board paid their expenses to return for the '52 Centennial Fair. The girls (and their counties) were: Kathryn Connelly, Grant; Jackie Steward, Putnam; Virginia Murphy, Marion; Patsy Leevey, Tippecanoe; Emily Neese, Madison; Mary Lou Wilking, Lawrence; Lorene McCormick, Knox; Lois Fisher, Shelby; Alice Graves, Monroe; Sally Martin, Posey; Anita Boone, Boone; Ruth Berry, Clark county. Margarett McColl, White County, earned the Special Honor Award.

The Home Economics School enrollees baked four thousand cookies that Fair. On Sunday, they paraded from the School to the Coliseum Church Service to hear the speaker and assist in conducting services.

On the Model Home

ON JANUARY 8, 1918, Indiana State Board of Agriculture President Leonard B. Clore of Franklin suggested securing a "proper" legislative appropriation to build and furnish several rooms in a "model sanitary farmer's house.

"Imagine somewhere within the State Fair Grounds a farmer's house of modern plan, possessing every sanitary feature of lighting, heating, ventilating, sewage disposal, storage and care of food, etc." Printed plans could be distributed to Fairgoers.

Eighteen years later, the Model Farm Home, built with Works Progress Administration labor, was open day and night from nine until ten during the 1936 State Fair. Twenty-three firms contributed to the modern five-room house. Late in 1943, Board director Levi Moore disclosed, "you will never find blue prints . . . we picked a sheet out of some home magazine." Estimates placed the number of visitors at one thousand per hour.

Later plans for a model farm barn in 1937, a silo, and a "regular farm section" around the home were postponed, then never effected. However, by that year, L.S. Ayres & Company decorated the entire home, "depicting an up-to-date idea of interior decorating."

In March 1937, the suggestion arose that 1937-1941 Fair Manager Harry G. Templeton should live at the model home, so that "during his leisure hours, he can devote considerable time to saving the Fair Board a lot of money." Lt. Governor Henry F. Schricker and his family lived there each of the months from October to July, 1937-1940.

"My father did not want to move to Indianapolis," his daughter Margaret Robbins recalled in 1992. "But he felt that by being there [at the Fairgrounds] he could keep a better eye on things."

L.S. Ayres re-painted the interior walls every year, which created problems for Mrs. Schricker when curtain-hanging time came after the Fair.

Republicans called it "Honeymoon Cottage" during Schricker's residence. When 1941 Fair Manager Paul S. Dunn lived there it gained the name "Fair Manager's Love Nest." The Board also apparently picked up Dunn's coal bill and bought him a car. Board member/Senator John Bright Webb, a Democrat, called the home "damned."

The Model Home, which L.S. Ayres still regularly decorated, wasn't initially made available in 1942 to new secretary-manager Guy Cantwell (1927's Board president), then not at all, since the War Department took it over for the duration of World War II, along with most of the Fairgrounds.

Orval C. Pratt, who took over as secretary-manager in February 1945, was voted out of the Model Home on July 12, 1946, at Lt. Governor Richard T. James' and Governor Ralph F. Gates' request. Secretary Ruel Steele, his wife, and two children were authorized to move in.

"He will only be there at the most two and one-half years," James claimed, "as he is now attending Law School four nights a week and will be completed in two and one-half years. He will be there only through the balance of Governor Gates' administration."

What was the Board to say – No? Poor Pratt moved into an apartment. Six months later the Board, having "heard" about it, upped Pratt's salary $60 to cover his costs.

Eventually, almost every Board secretary/manager stayed at the residence. Today, the Model Home is the Hospitality House for special Fairgrounds guests.

◆◆◆

The Model Farm Home was open day and night from nine until ten during the 1936 State Fair.

Twenty-three firms contributed to the modern five-roomer. Estimates counted visitors at one thousand per hour.

L.S. Ayres & Company decorated the living room and the porch/breakfast nook.

"On Better Babies"

THE STATE FAIR of 1920 bore the "Better Babies Contest," a new department "which proved to be a great success." It was a contest by physical examination.

Indiana Board of Agriculture President Samuel Joseph Miller of Indianapolis called it "great because it took on the interests of the people in every walk of life and from every part of the state and ... it developed to the mothers ... knowledge and information that they could not have bought for $100 from a reputable physician in the state. [The Board] paid liberal prizes and [the mothers] were kept from expense while attending the State Fair." Miller correctly forecast that the contest, which cost the Board $709.88, would grow to "mammoth proportions."

Dr. Ada E. Schweitzer of the State Board of Health's Child Hygiene Division directed and managed the first year's program. She called the new contest "a school of education in eugenics."

Dr. James C. Carter, a children's disease specialist, along with Dr. John W. Carmack and Dr. B.J. Larkin, "three of the most noted men in diseases and treatment of children's diseases that could be found," examined the tiny Fairgoers, many of whom are still around.

The Board of Health's 1920 State Year Book report categorized the "Defects of Children by Systems and Organs," disclosing 123 physical defects – general oral and teeth defects: 13 cases; eye defects: 4 cases; ear defects: 1 case; enlarged tonsils: 24 cases; probable adenoids problems: 1 case; other defects in head, face, and neck: 1 case; enlarged glands: 13 cases; bone defects of chest and back: 2 cases; heart problems: 2 cases; lung problems: 3 cases; abdomen abnormalities: 6 cases; genital defects: 10 cases; defects in the extremities: 7 cases; posture problems: none; problems with coordination of muscles and nerves: none; apparent disorders in nutrition: 1 case; and miscellaneous problems: 35 cases.

The contest was "no longer an experiment," Dr. Schweitzer said in 1921. "Why shouldn't a state which has the best corn and the best stock have the best babies?" She credited Board Secretary Charles F. Kennedy with the idea.

Designed for children ages one to three years, the contest in 1921 offered classes for twins and triplets. City children were examined on Monday, rural ones on Tuesday, and the twins and triplets on Wednesday.

Scoring was based on a thousand-point scale – "the combined score for the height and weight, the mental tests and the complete physical examinations, and every score was carried out three and four decimal places to avoid error."

In 1921, the scores ranged from 942.2 to 999.7. Scores in '22 were impressive: two-hundred and ninety-five out of three-hundred and twelve entered tallied 990 and above; twenty-one were 999 and over; one was 999.875 (a twin).

"The Indiana better baby will soon be the typical Indiana baby," Schweitzer wrote for 1922's *State Year Book*. That year, the contest slogan was "Every Day Is Baby Day, but State Fair week is Better Babies' week. Then the Indiana Better Baby leads them all."

Crowds peer through the Baby Contest windows at Indiana's Better Babies in 1929. This building, just west of today's Hook's Historic Drug Store, was razed in 1968.

Children play in 1930 at the fenced and shaded Mother-Baby rest park between the Better Babies Building and the Manufacturers' Building.

Schweitzer outlined Better Baby qualifications in '22: healthy parents; instruction and care of mother by a physician; a mother free from overwork or worry; a diet of "mother's milk" with a gradual weaning by the end of the first year; regular hours for meals, bath, and sleep; water to drink between meals; undisturbed sleep in a dark room with a constant current of cool, fresh air; clothing that does not restrict; gentle play with quiet laughter; a part of each fine day out of doors; daily exposure to sunlight, indoors or out, with the eyes protected; comfort and the avoidance of extremes of heat or cold; a happy home; regular "checking up" by a physician; protection from kissers with germs, fingers poking for teeth, showing off, bounding and high tossing, unsuitable food, too frequent feeding, pacifiers, dirt, discord, loud voices and nagging, movies, and jazz.

The 1923 Better Babies Contest was one of the Fair's most popular features, attracting nearly nine hundred mothers "with as many infants, and the

talented corps of managers and examining physicians made the contest of much value to the mothers for the upbringing of their children."

One baby in '23 scored 999.92813. That year, Schweitzer recommended devising "... some method of scoring which would make some allowance for familial and racial types ... most parents are really more interested in the physical health of their children than they are in actual scores ...."

J.E. Oliver of Oliver Chilled Plow Works in South Bend was credited with assistance in erecting the (lesser) Better Babies Building for non-contest examinations and baby care demonstrations. The Oliver Chilled Plow Building roof was moved between the Manufacturers' and Woman's Buildings, and the resulting pavilion hosted the infants' contest.

A special $10,000 appropriation built the first Better Babies Building in 1924.

Dr. Schweitzer provided a Baby Contest and Baby Building Clinic report

Designed for children ages one to three, the Better Babies Contest offered classes for twins and triplets beginning in 1921. City children were examined on Monday, rural ones on Tuesday, and the twins and triplets on Wednesday.

Rules for the Runabout Better Baby in 1927 recommended long hours of sleep, dispelling fears, instilling religion, increasing imagination, mid-afternoon rest, etiquette, and teaching caution.

on January 29, 1926: in 1921, 127 contest, and 101 non-contest babies were examined; in 1922, totals were 314 and 42; in 1923, 652 and 88; in 1924, 748 and 267; and in 1925, 885 and 302.

A day nursery had been instituted. Two psychologists administered mental tests. Better Babies Building visitors in '25 totalled 25,542. The 1926 contest had 1,200 entries.

By 1927, a new Better Baby Contest Building (for the Better Baby Contest, Baby Center Demonstration, and Baby Health Club), a Red Cross Building, and Administration Building remodeling made the Fair "the most modern and best to be found in the Union."

The *State Year Book* recorded that "the annually growing baby contest continued to be held in the Woman's Building until 1927, when a new contest building was completed just west of the Better Babies Building."

Sixteen hundred babies were entered in the 1928 Better Baby Contest. The September 6 *Indianapolis Star* reported "thirty babies an hour is the rate of examination."

Doctor Schweitzer presented a plan on October 25, 1928, for a thirty-five by seventy foot fenced and shaded Mother-Baby rest park between the Better Baby Building and the Woman's Building. She got it.

In the 1932 contest, Jack Edward Schleicher scored highest, nine-hundred and ninety-eight and two-hundred and twenty-four thousandths, among twelve- to twenty-four month-old city boys. Patricia Jane Hinkle, competing in the twelve- to twenty-four-month-old class, scored 998.79063.

"In the past decade," the Board of Health commented for the 1932 *State Year Book*, "parents have been urged to protect babies from smallpox and diphtheria before one year of age, an age when they are not well able to resist these diseases. The contest histories showed only a few protected from smallpox and only about twelve percent from diphtheria."

Doctors observed numerous cases of thumb sucking, "which result in deformities of the mouth . . . . [M]any parents fail to realize the importance of keeping the baby's teeth clean."

Bye-bye Baby Contest in 1933. Annual Board costs had reached $2,000, and the State Board of Health had discontinued its Child Hygiene Department.

Late in June 1933, Boardmen learned that the Board of Health planned to put on "a real health show" featuring its different bureaus and allied organizations. Another tradition began that year.

T.A. Stewart wrote and asked whether he could cash a $3 Baby Contest premium check payable to Jack Pullen. Check number 14,379 was dated September 21, 1928. The Board took care of it.

A far, far cry from the first one, the Baby Contest, open to babies from three months to three-year-old toddlers and sponsored by Indiana Farm Bureau, was inaugurated at the 1984 Fair. Prizes were awarded to "Mr. and Miss Congeniality," and best costume, and that's the

Phyllis Marian Greer, none-too-pleased daughter of Mr. and Mrs. Dorcey Greer of Indianapolis, is weighed during the 1930 Better Baby Contest.

extent of examination any of the babies received.

Today, Hook's Historic Drug Store opens its doors to thousands every year. Perhaps one or two visitors were there when it was a Better Baby Building many years ago, too ago to remember.

Unidentified Better Babies from 1929 look more like "Little Rascals" – perhaps a reader will recognize her/himself and contact the Fairgrounds.

In 1929 a trail of dolls led Baby Contest visitors along a poster path describing the schedule for the "Six Stages of Baby's Sun Bath" from March through August. Cautions against thumb-sucking, exercise advice, cod liver oil recommendations, and an approved shoes display rounded out the exhibit.

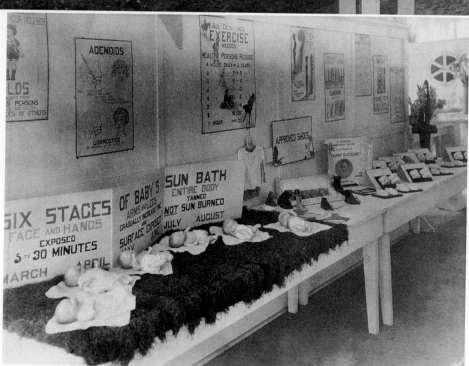

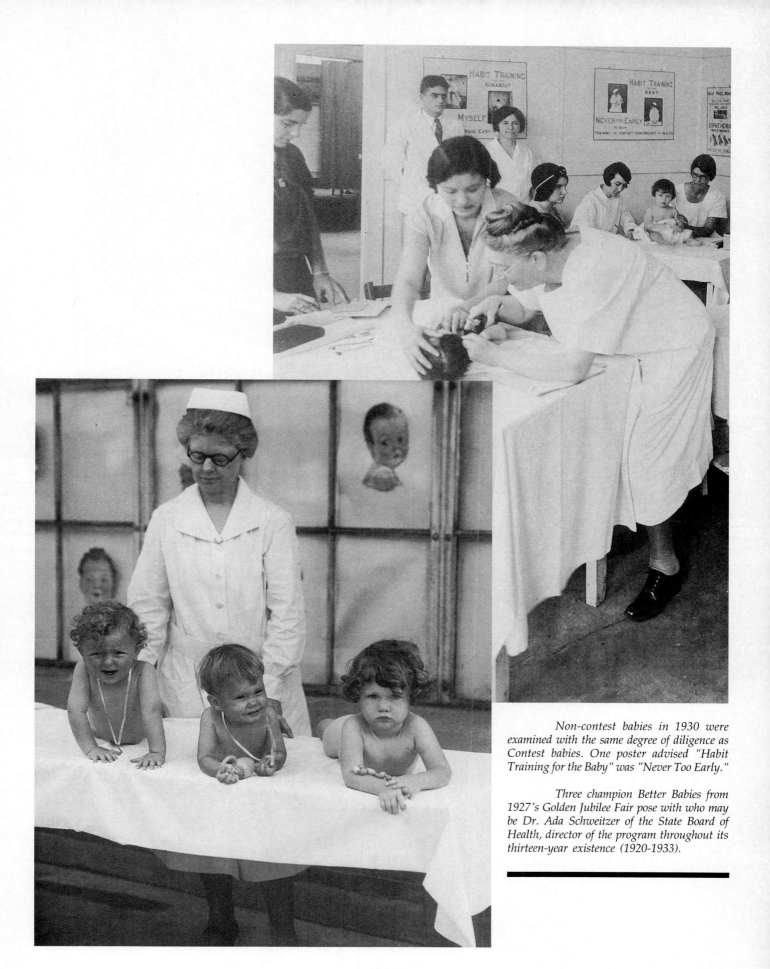

Non-contest babies in 1930 were examined with the same degree of diligence as Contest babies. One poster advised "Habit Training for the Baby" was "Never Too Early."

Three champion Better Babies from 1927's Golden Jubilee Fair pose with who may be Dr. Ada Schweitzer of the State Board of Health, director of the program throughout its thirteen-year existence (1920-1933).

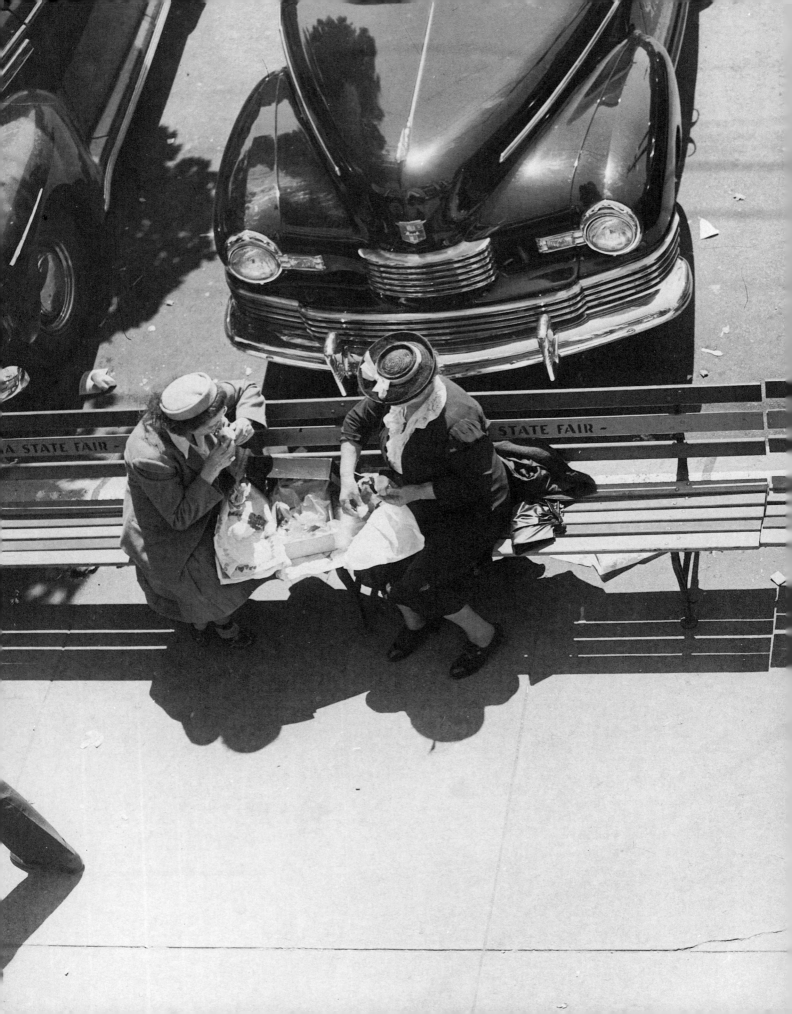

❖The Hoosier Scene

*From showcasing
the latest medical
technology to recreating
a pharmacy from
Indiana's past,
the Fair is more than
our biggest celebration.
Gathering material
from past, present, and
future, the Fair
is a microcosm
of Indiana and
its links to the world
around it.*

DURING the periods the Fairgrounds served as a military camp it was an integral part of the struggles gripping the entire world. The Fair has also mirrored the concerns of its visitors during less trying times in history. The state of education, revolutions in the field of communications, and how to maintain law and order have all been features or concerns of the Fair. This ability to anticipate and reveal what is on the minds of Hoosiers has allowed the Fair to survive and thrive during the transition from the agrarian to the industrial.

By 1877, "with 3,792 miles of railroads . . . the state boasted the largest rail mileage in the U.S. and there was an additional 1,000 miles of road surveyed or in the process of construction."

Traveling to the 1891 Fair was much easier than getting to the first one. Fifteen railroads centered at Indianapolis, with many connecting lines. Passengers rode "at the usual excursion rates," while Citizens Street Railway Company street cars charged a five-cent fare each way. A right of way agreement allowed Citizens' cars directly onto the Fairgrounds.

Monon Railroad on the west and Lake Erie & Western to the east provided "ample siding and platforms for handling passengers" at the new Fairgrounds in 1892. Easy livestock and machinery unloading saved exhibitors "much annoyance and expense."

Citizens' double track electric cars ushered visitors directly to the new Fairgrounds, and in 1897 passengers debarked at the Grandstand. An advertising card touted "Special Rates on all Roads in Indiana. Excursion Trains on all Indianapolis Lines. Street Cars running to Center of Park. No Dust! No Waiting."

In 1907, Indianapolis was "the second largest railway center in the Union, and the largest center of interurban electric roads."

As more and more technology invaded everyday life, many Fair visitors could still remember the "good old days." Writers for the state Conservation Department's June 1950 "Outdoor Indiana" recalled the Fairgrounds "of the horse and buggy days – the gas light days. Four-wheeled street cars known as dinkies galloped their routes out historic College Avenue, Central Avenue and Bellefontaine Street, the latter at that time boasting four rails in the street. All converged on what is now Fairfield Avenue and, up a mud street where water often covered the rails and the ties showed plainly, clanged their way to the Fair.

"The automobile was just making its initial appearance on the city streets but it was rather tough going 'way out to the Fairgrounds and many an unwary or overconfident horseless carriage operator was mired down and pulled out by a couple of horses hitched to a wagon."

Growing hordes of automobile arrivals led the 1917 Board to levy a fifty-cent charge on each as it entered the grounds. The fee entitled the owner to take his "machine" into the Fairgrounds, and "carrie[d] with it the privilege of having it parked by the management." The parking tickets had claim checks attached.

"The plan," President Leonard B. Clore noted, "was effectual by diverting these away from the crowd and into the parking place, where with careful systematized placing, the thousands of cars were handled so that any car could be reclaimed and placed into immediate use at any minute, of any hour of the day."

Many visitors arrived at 1937's Fair by Indiana Railroad System interurban, paying only 1-1/2 cents per mile for a round trip ticket. The transportation network could boast "not a single passenger fatality on interurban lines last year." Five interurban lines radiated 750 total miles from Indianapolis throughout the state.

One hundred sixty electric trains, "an average of seven for every hour," arrived or departed the downtown Indianapolis Traction Terminal every twenty-four hours. The high speed trains served Indianapolis, Louisville, Fort Wayne, Peru, Richmond, Terre Haute, "and all intermediate points." Fair visitors paid "special low excursion rates." Trains from the north dropped off passengers mere blocks from the Fairgrounds. Street cars destined for the Fairgrounds picked up where the interurban left off.

"[I]ncreasingly large numbers of fair visitors have been riding the electric trains in preference to driving their own autos. Among the chief reasons are the freedom from road traffic and parking problems . . . . [L]ate in 1931 a million dollars worth of new high speed cars, capable of traveling 70 miles an hour or more were put in service between Indianapolis, Louisville and Fort Wayne. Many . . . have luxuriously furnished observation lounge compartments[.]

"The large system of high speed electric interurban railway lines is peculiar to Indiana. It forms one of the largest electric railway networks in the country, and is typically Hoosier. It is known throughout the country."

Indianapolis Railways street cars left every five minutes in 1938 on the "Illinois-Fairgrounds" line. For "seven cents cash or four tokens for twenty-five cents," Fairgoers boarded downtown at Illinois Street and headed home from the stop east of the main entrance. Travel time was "from twenty-three to twenty-five minutes depending on the density of the traffic." The route ran north from downtown on Illinois Street to 34th Street, east at 34th to Fairfield Avenue, north-east on Fairfield to Coliseum Street, and north into the Fairgrounds.

"Although all of its interurban railway lines have been abandoned within the last few years," Indiana Railroad System offered "substitute modern truck and bus service over substantially the same routes formerly served by the traction cars. The deluxe safety coaches operated by this company connect Indianapolis with Fort Wayne, Terre Haute, Kokomo, Peru, Muncie and many intermediate points, affording a fast and convenient service for State Fair visitors[.]"

Where Did You Stay During the Fair?

FAIRGOERS planning more than a day at the Fair needed a place to stay. Early on, local homes and hotels welcomed visitors. Few ventured beyond a day's visit until "night attractions" partially cured the problem. The Fair became many farmers' vacations; they stayed right on the grounds. And livestock exhibitors slept with their prize animals.

Mrs. R.M. Irwin proposed building a miniature golf course in March 1930 across the south end of Mechanical Field, south of the Swine Barn.

Boardmen initially rejected, then okayed the deal, charging $1,200 a year for the 60-by-200 foot east-west strip just west of the Shell filling station along Maple Lane Boulevard. The day the contract was signed, the city park board got into the act, enacting a resolution prohibiting a golf course within five hundred feet of a boulevard.

Back went Barker and the Irwins, who looked elsewhere, paced off distances, finally deciding, with park board approval, on land east of the Fairgrounds and 250 feet north of the Fall Creek bridge. Rent was halved, and the Board furnished flood-lights and water – it became the Tented City Golf Course.

One of the largest Tented City turnouts came during the 1946 "Victory" Fair. Tented City operator Lyndes L. Latimer reported that 1,753 Fairgoers in 350 groups camped that Fair. Not once had a theft been reported in his twelve years.

Former president Louis Demberger announced in '49 that getting rid of Tented City in '48 had been a mistake. "It seemed as though we had been operating this at a loss, but the people who used this are willing to pay more for it."

President Homer Schuman blamed a former publicist for spreading the wrong word (actually, the Board vote spelled the campers' knell). Anyone could still pitch a tent; only tent rental was out. Dumping manure there hadn't helped market the site, either.

The rare Fairgoer took a room in the Fairgrounds Hotel, originally built in the early 1900s. Back in '23, the hotel was relocated and expanded; it featured a new basement kitchen and twenty upstairs sleeping rooms.

Time caught up to the Hotel in June 1965: "once a landmark and later described . . . 'as an eyesore,'" it was torn down in June 1965, *Indianapolis News* informed. The two-story stucco just inside the Fall Creek Parkway entrance required "excessive" costs for improvements demanded by the state fire marshal and the Indiana State Board of Health.

"We have no plans . . . to replace it," said Board President Oscar T. Blank. Negotiations with private developers for a modern motel at 38th Street and Fall Creek were tabled until after the Board reorganization later in the year. The investor group had offered $25,000 a year; instead, the site became a parking lot, a "crying need" at the Fairgrounds.

◆◆◆

Race horse owners and livestock exhibitors lodged at the Fairgrounds Hotel for forty years. Army Air Force officers used it as their officer's club during the World War II occupation.

Manager Vivien Hill used naughty matchbook covers to advertise "a good place to sleep."

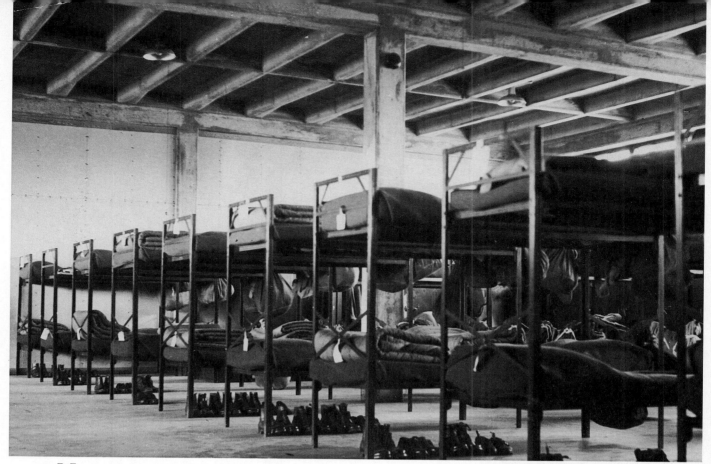

NOT only have the Fairgrounds served state and nation through tough times of peace, when drought and depression took their own toll; the Fairgrounds have also taken the lead in times of armed conflict. Considered a constant in a changing world, the Fair nevertheless has stepped forward for war's greater call. Troops occupied the Fairgrounds four times, and the Fair has been canceled twice. The Civil War ruined 1861 Fair plans.

The American Civil War spanned April 12, 1861, when Fort Sumter was fired upon, until the April 9, 1865, Appomattox Court House meeting between the Union's Ulysses S. Grant and the Confederacy's Robert E. Lee.

All State Fair preparations were called off May 16, 1861, although the Board agreed that if, later on, the "condition of the country is so changed for the better as to make it expedient and admissable," Fair preparations would resume. Many in the land thought the struggle would be a short lark.

Beginning April 20, Indiana volunteers were inducted, then quartered at

---

Air Corps instructors' bunks filled a floor in the 4-H Girls' Dorm.

the Fairgrounds, which became Camp Morton after Civil War Governor Oliver P. Morton. Fairgrounds buildings soon housed five thousand soldiers. The army also occupied State Board offices in the old State House.

The grounds also provided sufficient area for drilling the volunteer army of farmers, shopkeepers, drummers, boys, and mechanics.

The occupation was a disastrous, irretrievable setback for pioneering Board of Agriculture work in all areas of its agricultural and scientific toil. No premium records exist for several early Fairs, "in consequence of the loss of papers, incident to the military occupancy . . . ," according to the 1875 *Agricultural Report*.

Before the troops arrived, "everything was in prime order, general thrift and cleanliness prevailed, but alas, the foul destroyer, war, and the general carnage and ruin consequent thereon, and occasioned by the open rebellion and treachery of a portion of the States, to overthrow the best government ever instituted among men, our beautiful fair ground, the offspring of an increasing importance of fostering the agricultural and mechanical interests of our beloved State, fell a victim, as have other interests, to the ruthless hands of those who seem-

Indiana War Fair

ingly take a pleasure in carelessly destroying everything that does not exactly meet with their views."

Answering Abraham Lincoln's call to stop "this rebellion, with which the country has been cursed," volunteers came pouring into the capital ". . . nearly one thousand per day for at least a week; the State had not tents or other camp conveniences . . . [so] the Governor [was] compelled to make some speedy arrangements for the reception of our brave volunteers."

Contacted by telegraph, the Executive Committee voted unanimously to pose no objections to the occupation, "*provided sufficient guarantees are given that the property or timber shall not be damaged*" (italics in original). A guarantee was drawn up for the signatures of Governor Oliver P. Morton and other officials, but "by the multiplicity of other duties, and the great rush of business . . . and for other reasons unknown . . . the said guarantee was never signed."

In the onslaught of the encampment, the grounds were severely damaged, and all previous improvements were nearly destroyed. Many trees were peeled and killed. The bluegrass sod's "green mantle of rich verdure" was ravaged. "Good judges" estimated $15,000 insufficient to repair the destruction.

Boardmen acknowledged the grounds belonged to Indiana, somewhat justifying the wrong occasioned by the occupation. Yet they argued that the Legislature had, by special act, created the State Board of Agriculture "for specific purposes, with certain powers and privileges guaranteed to them," which included holding real estate and exclusive use of a room in the State House.

"But whether right or wrong, legal or otherwise, the State Board surrendered use of the fair grounds in an hour of our country's peril . . . when no other accommodations . . . could be had . . . saving the State at least an immediate expense of $10,000."

Estimates from as early as 1861 stated that at least $5,000 was needed to begin the long trek back to the grounds' former gracious beauty. Agriculture's champions doubted whether "under all these embarrassing circumstances" they could resume their "former usefulness" at Camp Morton until the damage was repaired by Legislative or other means.

Early in 1862, Camp Morton was surrounded with "stout oak palisade" and turned into a Confederate prisoner-of-war camp. By the war's end, 15,000 prisoners had been interned on the grounds; July 1864 saw a peak of about 5,000 rebel soldiers under guard. Many died under the most horrible conditions: exposure, malnutrition, and sickness.

A map in a September 1891 *Century Illustrated Monthly Magazine* compiled "from sketches by several persons who were on duty in the camp while the prisoners were there," shows nine hospital buildings, three hospital tents, a dozen barracks, a baseball grounds, and the creek called "The Potomac." A guard line cut the grounds nearly in half. Colonel Richard Owen was commandant.

Board halls and stalls, "not being of a size or character required at a rendezvous or prison . . . (were) torn down or so changed, as no longer to answer the purposes of the Board." Deep ditches surrounding the grounds, on guard against prisoner tunneling, needed filling to restore the grounds to their "original beauty and convenience." Macadamized military roads traversing the grounds would be leveled.

Three hundred ten forest trees, less than one-third the original number,

remained. Half of those still standing were dead. "Competent judges" estimated the dead trees would average 1-1/2 cords of wood each, "worth near three dollars per cord."

The Board recovered a fireproof safe valued at $200, two dozen lamps, as many axes, that many spades, twelve picks, six shovels, and assorted stamps, presses, and books.

Greater still was the loss of knowledge. The Board's State House room, which once held specimens "collected during the geological reconnaissance of the State, by the late Professor Owen, State Geologist," was emptied. "Numerous specimens" of grain, seeds, wool, fibrous plants, "and many other interesting and

valuable articles, besides a considerable number of books, which would have formed the nucleus of a cabinet and library" were missing. Books, reports, and essays were scattered; most were lost. At the outbreak of hostilities, many of the geological specimens were "hastily jumbled into boxes" and consigned to the State House cellar, "where they still remain." Sadly, "some of the larger and most interesting specimens occupy the be-fouled niches of the front portico of the building, and others are wholly destroyed."

Nearly four years later, Board President Ambrose Dudley Hamrick reported no payment of the $5,189.20 claim against the "General Government," and he had no indication when it would be paid.

Despite the economic disaster of the century's second Black Friday, Secretary Fielding Beeler insisted that 1869 would "long be remembered as one of unparalleled prosperity to the whole country. Just at the close of a bloody internal war, unprecedented in the annals of history in the loss of life, [and] cost to the nation, . . .the whole energy of the people seems to have recuperated."

It was a hard time, however, for trade. "The present stringency in the

money market is chargeable to the unequal balance as between home products and foreign importations," Beeler wrote. "As a people, we consume too much from abroad, and produce not enough at home." Despite Reconstruction's repercussions, the Fair of 1869 was eminently successful; the Board considered it the most successful one ever in the State, "or in the Northwest."

◆◆◆

INDIANA'S State Fairgrounds saw action again during the Spanish-American War. In 1898, Camp Mount, named for Governor James A. Mount, located at the Fairgrounds. The Indiana National Guard mobilized there before shipping off to fight in the Spanish American War.

In a breath, Spain declared war on the United States on April 24, whereupon Congress voted on April 25 to retroactively declare war as of April 21. The war was halted by protocol August 12 when Spain agreed to give Cuba independence, cede Puerto Rico and Guam to the U.S., and allow the American occupation of the Philippines.

It was the nation's shortest war, and Indiana was ready. The 1895 state legislature created the National Guard out of the Indiana Legion. Insufficient funds canceled 1897's encampment, according to the 1938 *Guard Yearbook* at the Office of the Military History Project Director, Military Department of Indiana.

"[T]he result was that on the outbreak of war with Spain, the Indiana Guard was prepared to take the field before that of any other state." Ironically though, not one Indiana National Guardsman saw combat. Nearly all got no farther than Fernandino, Florida, about a mile from the train station.

Mount heard from the War Department "at 6:15 on the evening of April 25." His orders were to provide an Indiana complement of four infantry regiments and two light artillery batteries. Mount promptly ordered all Guardsmen to report to Brigadier General Will J. McKee at the Fairgrounds. The response was so great that "Indiana alone could have supplied the entire number of men called for." Governor Mount "publicly stated [that]. . . he thought it best for all whose domestic affairs at all hindered their enlisting to step aside and let others take their places."

Frankfort's company, under Captain Allen's command, was the first to reach the Fairgrounds on April 26. More arrived every hour, quickly exceeding the number of tents available for shelter. Many Guardsmen were quartered in the Fairgrounds barns and buildings. Everyone had reported by that evening, and Camp Mount acquired its name.

War's death threats spurred haste in matters of matrimony. One Guardsman couldn't wait for war's end before marrying his sweetheart. On Sunday, May 8, Private Leroy Thompson, of Company L, Kokomo, second regiment, married Delia Wilson, also of Kokomo, with Chaplain Carstensen officiating, according to *Indiana Woman* magazine. A veterinary surgeon, Thompson was "one of the best horsemen in the brigade." He was given Sunday night honeymoon leave, and ordered to report back at noon Monday.

Lieutenant W.T. May of the regular Army's Fifteenth Infantry mustered the 157th Indiana Volunteer Infantry Regiment, which became part of the Army's Third Regiment, the first ready for service. May was appointed lieutenant colonel. (The 157th got its name through picking up where Civil War regiment numbering left off, which itself picked up where the Mexican War had left off.)

On May 15, the troops marched from the Fairgrounds to Union Station, taking the train to Camp George H. Thomas in Chickamauga Park, Georgia. Detraining at six on Tuesday morning six miles from camp, they marched to a "dreary routine of camp life without a break." They were quartered there until May 30, when orders sent them to Port Tampa City, Florida. "The order was naturally received with delight by soldiers who were fed up with inactivity."

June 1, camp was struck. The 157th regiment reached Tampa on June 3 "shortly after noon," where it was attached to the Third Brigade, "a provisional division of the Fourth Army Corps." Rumors spread of battle in Cuba. The Third Brigade received orders at one point to ship out, only to hear countermanding orders at the last minute. The 27th Battery was the only Indiana unit actually sent into enemy territory during the war. Shipped to Puerto Rico, Indiana Guardsmen were on the brink of battle when word arrived that the Spanish had surrendered.

The 160th and 161st Infantry were ordered to Cuba with the army of occupation. The 161st Indiana Infantry resulted from the War Department's second call on May 25 for another quota. Companies from Jeffersonville, Columbus, Richmond, Shelbyville, Hammond, Monticello, Mount Vernon, Madison, Lawrenceburg, New Castle, Rushville, and Michigan City were ordered to report to Camp Mount. Captains Jacob Porter and John J. Buckner, both of Indianapolis, raised two "independent colored companies" and a regiment of "white volunteers."

Orders sent the Indiana soldiers home on August 30; they reached Camp Mount on September 2. Eight days later, everyone got a thirty-day furlough, except the 27th battery, which got sixty. On October 10, the regiment re-assembled at

INDIANA UNIVERSITY R.O.T.C. BUILDS MEN
AND HELPS SAFEGUARD THE NATION

the Fairgrounds and remained there until November 1, when the men were mustered out.

Nineteen died from disease and accident while in federal service. A hospital "adjacent to the regimental lines at Camp Mount" was established August 30 to care for the returning volunteers. "Tentage, flooring, blankets, sheets, pillows, cots, ticks, straw, cooking apparatus and all other necessary equipment for field hospital purposes," were delivered for the effort.

Mount also ordered the Surgeon General, Colonel Orange S. Runnels, to acquire "medicines, nurses, delicacies, nourishment" and "ample preparations for every want of these brave men . . . prostrate with disease[.]" Runnels wrote to Mount from the "State Hospital, Camp Mount" on October 5 to report that 269 Guardsmen had received "every service . . . that intelligent affection and skill could suggest . . . with a mortality of four." At

that point, twelve soldiers were still sick in bed.

Now Runnels wondered what his orders were. Mount responded two days later: Runnels was to stay at the hospital and "spare no pains or cost needed for the comfort and care of our sick soldiers." By that point, the weather was turning cold, so the hospital moved to the "commodious 'Administration Building' . . . adjacent to Camp Mount, whither the sick men were removed on October 9." The building was heated to aid the men's recovery.

Patriotic Board Executive Committeemen offered free use of the grounds even before Mount issued his call. Troops stayed in camp throughout the summer and during the 1898 Fair. "Considerable" damage was wreaked upon nearly forty buildings and barns; the south, east, and street car entrances; the fence, seven water closets, thirty shade trees, and "miscellaneous." Repair estimates tallied $9,037.50

Indiana University R.O.T.C. crowded a lot of water-cooled firepower into this exhibit from the early 1920s. Weapons, equipment, and training photographs told the recruitment message.

with claims lingering unresolved through 1905.

◆◆◆

◆ 144 ◆

Mobile Army men and machines paraded in this crowded 1940 State Fair Main Street scene heading west. The "new" coliseum is at the right.

BY THE TIME the 1917 Fair opened, the United States had been at war with Germany since April 6.

"Any wife, or mother" accompanied by children of the soldiers encamped on the Fairgrounds was admitted free at the north gate. Soldiers in uniform were also admitted free at the pass gate during the entire week. Troops paraded each afternoon in an exhibition drill on the infield across from the Grandstand.

The "War to End All Wars" was in its final year when the 66th annual meeting convened in January 1918 in State House Room 12. "We are just beginning to realize . . . how important it is that every acre of ground in our state be made to produce the largest possible amount of food product," Governor James P.

Goodrich told the Delegate Board. "[I]mportant as the work of the men at the front is . . . feeding these men . . . is of supreme importance[.] [I]t is more necessary that we perfect and increase our material resources here at home . . . without them the armies would be helpless[.] France and England and our allies in this great war, are looking to the United States not only to furnish the money, to furnish the men, but far more, they are looking to us to furnish food . . . ."

Iowa's Governor Harding had visited Indiana recently with his conservation fact-finding committee. Harding told Governor Goodrich that when his group "asked the National Council of Defense at Washington [to] what states in the Union they should go to get the information, they were told, 'Go to Indiana. Indiana is in a class by itself. Go to Indiana.'"

The "Hoosier Fair" of 1918 was a "big training camp for food producers." Premium awards recognized bread made

from war flour. Bread, cakes, pies, and war-time confections were made of flour substitutes or flour combinations. All entries made from ingredients other than war flour were eliminated from the prize-winning classes.

"[O]ur food supply has assumed such a serious aspect that we must watch every channel to see that all lines of activity conform to national necessity," warned Federal food administrator Dr. Harry Barnard in a letter to all county and state fairs.

"Feature the war preparations . . . appetizing foods prepared in conformity with the substitute requirements of the U.S. food administration . . . the full educational force of your fair will be thrown on the side of our national welfare and you will have to your credit . . . a valuable patriotic service."

Displays from the Committee on Public Information filled two railroad cars. One contained captured "Hun" war material: shells, guns, "other up-to-date munitions of war," and "late plans of air ships."

After the Fair, the Board agreed to turn the Coliseum, the Brick Horse Barn, and other buildings over to the Army for "the Vocational work or the convoy detachments" until the Great War ended, but not beyond June 30, 1919. Armistice Day came on November 11, 1918, with the Treaty of Versailles following.

Devastating peace ruined American farmers, laboring under the "old rules." Caught in the backlash of post-war surpluses, their economic back was broken seven years before the Stock Market Crash in '29. Back at the Fairgrounds, a post-evacuation grounds report disclosed that the buildings needed "considerable repair."

Great Depression cash-hard times demanded creativity to keep the gates busy when the 1931 Fair opened. Few Fairgoers jingled surplus fifty-cent pieces and quarter dollars to fund State Fair trips, especially farmers, for whom the bottom had fallen out years earlier. A novel way to induce Ma and Pa to load the kids and Grandma into the truck was required.

An August 27 *Danville Gazette* report alerted farmers, "Bushel Of Wheat Will Open Portals – State Fair Association Offers Novel Method of Gaining Admission To Grounds – BUT GO TO NORTH-EAST GATE – As Cash Customers Will Be Crowding Other Entrances.

"One bushel of wheat will be accepted for admission to the Indiana State Fair on . . . Farmers Day . . .as [fifty-cent] payment for one adult admission, one bushel will admit an automobile and one-half bushel will admit a child under twelve . . . .

"Indiana farmers have more wheat than they know what to do with . . . money is scarce . . . the State Fair is of such value to the visitors, especially from rural communities, that the loss is warranted.

"It is the first instance of a State Fair Board reverting to barter for admission, and the result is expected to be widespread." Publicity Director Levi Moore called it "a good publicity stunt." Wheat admissions ultimately totalled $200.78. Trucks hauled away the grain, and the farmers kept their bags and baskets.

Despite Europe's second World War and Edward R. Murrow's anxiously awaited reports from bomb-torn London, the Board reluctantly rented the Coliseum for an America First rally set for May 29, 1941. Board member/Senator John Bright Webb voted against the move, as he considered "this fellow [apparently Montana Senator Burton Kendall Wheeler] as an appeaser of the worst sort."

Fellow Boardman E. Curtis White agreed: "[I]f England falls, we will be in a worse war than we have ever dreamed of . . . [America First is] lending aid and comfort to our enemy." He certainly believed in free speech, "but in a critical time like this it is different." America First, claiming to represent "three million of our young men," later asked to pass out literature during the Fair. They were turned down.

Three months and a day after a successful Indiana State Fair featuring a harness racing meet which *Life* magazine called the "biggest in attendance" ended, the Pacific Fleet was ambushed in Pearl Harbor.

1943 Many may remember war-time steel pennies. Board Finance Committeemen decided May 17 to charge flat amounts for Coliseum events, since "the last month or so there has been a shortage of (copper) pennies."

Again, the Fairgrounds served its nation. Board Finance Committeemen heard in March 1942 of a letter that Governor Henry F. Schricker had received from the Army Air Corps. The fly boys wanted the Fairgrounds. Boardman E. Curtis White, who felt the Fair was "an educational institution just the same as any of our colleges," wanted to keep the 4-H functions intact. "If there is anything to keep the minds of the youngsters off the war, it is the 4-H Club."

An occupation wouldn't be simple. Twelve to fourteen hundred cars were in depot storage in the Agricultural and Poultry Buildings, the Saddle Horse and Draft Horse Barns, and the Swine Barn.

Indiana was going to be the "arsenal of the nation," Schricker informed the Board," . . . because we are centrally located."

Already, Illinois and Ohio had given up their fairgrounds; now Indiana was needed. "The three places are necessary in the set up . . . to take care of the supply of air corp demand," Captain Shields from the War Department, Division of Ohio River Engineers, told Board members.

President J.B. Cummins didn't like the idea one bit. ". . [T]hey do not know what [the fair] means to the state. [It] puts out more education in one week than any university does in any one week . . . [W]e owe it to our boys and girls out in our districts to have this Fair." But World War II was bigger than the Indiana State Fair.

"When I say that we want the entire Fairgrounds," Shields said, "I mean everything within the fence on the four sides and between the two railroads." Some buildings would house the soldiers and their officers, while others would store material for "certain air corps units."

"We regret that we have to ask for this sacrifice, but it is necessary," Shields said. "[T]he industries from the west coast have been moved steadily inward . . . the coast line is going to catch a lot of trouble. Your part will be to give up certain 'niceties' such as the State Fairs."

"Thus the Fair Board and the state turned over to the Air Force the finest fair plant in the United States for the duration and are assured that it is the best of all the fair plants for their purpose and needs as well," said the 1942 *State Year Book*.

On June 1, after weeks of discussing whether or not to convene an abbreviated 4-H Club Fair, Webb observed sadly, "I think it has got to the point that we can have very little to do with what happens. I think the livestock and agricultural industry in the United States is a forgotten industry . . . when this thing is over it is going to be a different world."

Of course there were imposed shortages other than gas and tire rationing, but for Indiana the loss of the annual State Fair seemed more devastating to many Hoosiers, especially livestock breeders who depended on the Fair as a showcase and business opportunity.

From 1942 to 1945, the U.S. Army Air Corps used Fairgrounds buildings for specialized training and for storage and shipping of vitally needed parts for the air war.

One of five state fairgrounds leased by the Air Corps, after a period of development the Fairgrounds became the Fifth Service Command's 836th Army Air Force Specialized Depot. Only the Coliseum and Saddle Horse Barn remained in the Board's civilian hands. The War Department lease began April 1, 1942, and was designed to end "one year from the date upon which the present National Emergency is declared to no longer exist." The U.S. Government paid the Fair Board $1 for rent for the three year period.

There was no Indiana State Fair in '42. Hitler and Tojo's war cancelled an idea to have corn, flower, peach, apple, tomato, and bee queens. With no State Fair, 4-H programs were devastated – there was simply little reason to try anymore. That sobering reality led the board to convene "streamlined" 4-H Club Fairs from 1943 to 1945.

Captain Henry E. Harris arrived at the Fairgrounds April 1, 1942, and assumed command. Colonel F.D. Lynch began his command April 28; an infield area was cleared for his plane. Harris took over as the executive supply and operations officer. By March 17, 1943, Lynch was transferred and Colonel Raymond R. Brown assumed command. First Lt. Maurice L. Campbell was named Depot Supply Officer, relieving Harris, then a major, who handled other duties. Brown got his transfer orders on July 8, 1943, and Lt. Colonel R. Walter Evans took command.

An Air Depot Training Station was set up May 20, 1942, at the Fairgrounds, and troop detachments were trained at the Turret and Bombsight School and Armament Training School, according to "unclassified" microfilm records.

Morris Coffman, a nineteen-year-old Civil Service instructor, taught enlisted men how to maintain airborne gun turrets. Coffman's assignment was the all-electric General Electric turret. "Most had .50-caliber guns," Coffman said. "We turned out a class every six to eight weeks." Other types of turrets included Consolidated, Sperry, and Martin. Coffman's turret ultimately was attached to Northrop P61 Black Widow night fighters and the top-secret B29 Superfortresses. One hundred fresh G.I.s came in each week for training at eight-week schools, according to John Trimble, a turret instructor.

The Fairgrounds general storage Depot handled supply items, "the volume of which increased to such an extent during the latter part of 1942 that personnel and available facilities were under considerable stress to cope with the existing situation." The rush overwhelmed storage resources. As many as 160 rail cars clogged the tracks; charges for detaining

the cars were "excessive." In 1944, an estimated thirty railcars arrived daily.

Every kind of Army Air Force property was sent for storage. Much was obsolete. Twenty carloads of World War I balloon equipment carried markings from "many of the principal cities of this Country as well as Hawaii. Many items still in containers carried markings 'RUSH – DEADLINE DATE NOV. 18, 1918.'" Because of Army Air Force regulations, however, none of the ancient and out-of-date equipment could be "disposed of" until January 1944.

On April 16, 1943, the Depot was redesignated as the 4th Army Air Force Storage Depot. By the end of May, when the United Nations Depot 13 located at 219 W. South Street was absorbed, the Depot at the Fairgrounds was handling Class 02-I Allison engine parts.

"Specialized Depots had not as yet come into being . . . Depot No. 13 was one of the first Depots to specialize in handling one class. During June 1942, Brigadier General C.P. Kane, then Colonel, and Chief of the United Nations Branch, discontinued the handling . . . [of] any class except 02-I. This was the beginning of the existing Specialized Depot program, and the soundness and practicality of this method of operation was later proved." Captain Harold P. Kehoe

John Trimble (right) and a G.I. buddy relax at their bunks in the 4-H Girls' Dorm in 1943.

was made Depot Supply Officer; Campbell became Assistant Depot Supply Officer.

Then on August 7, 1943, the Fairgrounds acquired title 836th AAF Specialized Depot. Class 02-H (Pratt & Whitney engine parts), at 711 Sand Street, and Class 08-D (Wright engine parts), at 3000 Shelby Street, were absorbed. "Tens of thousands of barrels" filled Fairgrounds buildings; there were acres filled with jeeps, known in military lingo as "special purpose vehicles."

Overcrowding led to outdoor storage of some maintenance parts. Depot carpenters eventually built roller conveyor systems which "greatly expedited the flow of supplies" from the freight cars. The system was so efficient that the May 1944 issue of *Plane Facts* ran an article about it titled "Handymen Descend on Warehouses."

Ultimately, the 836th became "the primary source of supply of engine maintenance parts for most of the first-line fighters and bombers." By October 1943, a new Allison engine was due, available space was crowded, and more was needed. Three "larger buildings" lacked walls or

world. Planes flew engine parts direct . . . to every war theater. Planes came here from Italy, North Africa and Europe to obtain vital and critical parts.

"A B-24 bomber, grounded in a lonely South Pacific atoll, could not take to the air because of lack of one tiny carburetor part. A plane flew directly from Indianapolis to the grounded bomber.

"At one time it was estimated there was more than $1,000,000,000 in aircraft parts stored mountain high at the fair grounds. The Wright contract alone amounted to more than $500,000,000. The entire spare parts output of the Allison Division of General Motors Corporation, the entire parts output of the Ford Motor Company, the Studebaker Corporation and Curtiss-Wright Corporation, most of the spare engine parts for Pratt & Whitney engines, came to Indianapolis.

"All the replacement carburetors the Army owned were stored here. During the peak, more than six hundred orders a day were being filled in all the way from single items to carload lots. There were 2,685 employees. [The paper later reported 2,586 was the total.]"

Now, "expensive, precision parts, made with so much skill and care, parts which may have cost $75 to $100 each" were destined for the scrap heap, "junk for $3.75 a ton." One cause for such waste was that the aircraft engines were obsolete "before they even could be installed." The parts had little civilian use, "for the engines were built for speed and high efficiency – too costly for commercial use."

Mrs. Rosemary Jones, a Fairgrounds civilian expediter living at 6264 Central Avenue, purchased 1,000 five-inch diameter, eighth-inch thick airport spotlight lenses for $3 from the War Assets Corporation in February.

"Among household items that might possibly be fabricated from the plate glass circles, Mrs. Jones theorizes, are picture frames, book-ends and drapery holders . . . A friend bought a dozen with the idea of converting them into powderboxes," the *Indianapolis Times* reported on February 27, 1946.

The *Star* reported March 13 "almost everything was sold as junk. Most of it brought less than $40 a ton. The auction netted approximately $400,000 in cash.

"[The] biggest juiciest item which was sold as junk was 100,000 pounds of silver-plated scrap, some of it consisting

of nearly 1/8 inch of silver on heavy aircraft engine bearings." It sold for less than $165,000. All scrap purchasers signed an oath that none of the parts would be used "for the purpose for which they originally were manufactured."

"'It was an expensive war!' one officer said the night of the auction. 'We would have saved the taxpayers money if we could have pushed the whole business into the lake or into a big hole in the ground. The government spent much more money in trying to find buyers, advertising for bids, marketing and shipping the material, than it realized on the sale.'

"There'll be no lowering of the flag – for the flag was shipped last week . . . and the 100-foot steel flagpole was sawed down and shipped, too. The officers and men will be gone. The last meal will be served at noon today [March 13] in the officers' mess . . .[T]he officers' club will become a hotel. At midnight the guard detail at the gates will salute each other and go home, leaving the gates open. You won't have to have a military pass any more."

The last piece of government equipment to leave the Fairgrounds was a fire truck which had stood guard four years. It was reassigned to the Veterans' Administration hospital in Marion.

◆◆◆

◆◆ **Remember these dates? VE Day was May 8, 1945; VJ Day was August 15, 1945.**

1954 Secretary-manager Kenneth Blackwell served as the administrative vice chairman of the Red Cross Civil Defense Medical Treatment Station 17, Emergency Welfare District 2B – headquartered at the Administration Building, 1200 East Maple Road.

A December 28 personnel file, which listed 148 medical treatment stations, described the first practice plans for "Operation Beehive," an exercise to be implemented the following February 15. "Beehive," the first county-wide exercise

for Red Cross medical treatment station workers, convened at the Indiana University Theatre.

Attached to the personnel list was "RED CROSS FUNCTIONS * MARION COUNTY CIVIL DEFENSE MEDICAL TREATMENT STATIONS AND EMERGENCY WELFARE CENTERS," which outlined what to do under emergency attack. It was Red Fear.

The revised Statement No. 1 of September 1954 opened with the dire remark, "In an emergency attack anywhere in Marion County, there will be a great number of casualties, all occurring in a matter of seconds."

Non-professional "auxiliary" aid from the civilian population was critical to the treatment and casualty station plan, as "there are not enough doctors, graduate nurses and other professional personnel to take care by themselves of more than a limited number of casualties."

By the time of the preparation report, only enough doctors and nurses to staff 105 stations had been enlisted. No medical supplies or equipment had been stored at any of the sites. Some medical supplies were stockpiled, and drugstores were asked to inventory "a more than normal supply of certain medicines."

The Indiana State Civil Defense gave estimated casualty levels expected if and when a "nominal type of atomic bomb, namely, 20,000 tons TNT equivalent, such as was used at Hiroshima and Nagasaki" was ever dropped in central Indiana. A daytime raid on downtown Indianapolis would yield devastating results on the 376,000-member "affected population." An attack with warning would produce 83,625 deaths and 52,545 "living" casualties, leaving 239,830 uninjured. A daytime attack without warning would kill 108,505, injure 79,720, sparing 187,775 from injury. Nothing was said about the homeless and starving.

Equally precise night-time attack statistics on the capital city's downtown were less gruesome, with an estimated affected population of 256,500 people. With a warning of an attack, 13,500 would die, 23,900 would merely suffer, and 219,100 would be left uninjured. Without warning, 24,920 would die, 46,755 would be injured, and only 184,825 would remain uninjured.

"Larger A-bombs and the hydrogen bomb would be destructive over larger areas, probably resulting in more

casualties. Authorities say that an adequate Civil Defense system will cut the number of casualties in half."

The casualty stations had the job of providing emergency welfare services which were categorized into food and clothing, population registrations (names, addresses, extent of injuries), spiritual guidance from "spiritual captains and other pastors" and "in some instances, recreation facilities, especially for children."

Naturally a civil emergency could result from tornadoes, floods, fires, and industrial explosions, but in Indiana everyone was used to that.

Prize livestock, harness and auto races, and high school marching bands shared Grandstand attention with parades of armed might well into the Sixties. Mock combats enthralled fans. Veterans and Military Day in 1962 focused on an Indiana National Guard demonstration showing the weapons, equipment, firepower, and maneuverability of the modern infantry division. The nation was still comparatively uninvolved in Vietnam, although President Kennedy had said our advisors would fire back if fired upon.

Four years later, in a sad reflection of the "police action" in Southeast Asia, widows were eligible for both junior and senior divisions of the 1966 Homemaker of the Year show.

Indiana National Guardsmen check "casualties" in this late 1960s Grandstand demonstration of modern warfare.

Art Rice Held an Eighty-Six Year Part-Time Job

ARTHUR RICE, a long-time Fair employee, first came to the Fairgrounds in 1901 at the age of seventeen. Born November 3, 1884, he died on October 11, 1990, less than a month short of his 107th birthday. He worked on the Fairgrounds off and on for, oh, about eighty-six years. Literally.

Rice remembered watching buggies and digging dry wells for outdoor "facilities." In the early days, there was no Midway; only a ferris wheel and merry-go-round. Fairgoers brought box lunches and dined on the lawns. He remembered using mules and three horses to grade the Track of Champions.

Each summer Rice and others cleaned the Agriculture and Arts Building walls since the white frame edifice where the Agriculture-Horticulture Building now stands was a favorite pigeon roost. One of Rice's biggest jobs was dipping 1,200 wooden chairs into a tank of yellow ochre. Another big job was shoveling manure into the one-horse (mule, actually) spring wagon.

Rice remembered when a small Italian airplane hit a flagstaff atop a barn and landed in the Infield. He remembered when the Fairgrounds included acres of wheat and corn. "The center field was planted with wheat, and there were 156 acres of corn planted on the northeast section.... The rest was a forest, except for the main stretch along the south road." People often picnicked in the Fairgrounds woods during the early Fairs.

Former grounds superintendent Jess Stuckey recalled Rice telling about a road house where a fast-food restaurant now stands. The grounds crewmen would get drunk at the road house, stumble back to sleep in the Fairgrounds' "north woods," awake the next morning, and go back to work.

After digging the dry wells, Rice stayed on as a washroom attendant, he recalled in an August 1973 *Indianapolis Star* article. "We made about 15 cents an hour in tips, working a 10-hour day. That was better than the $9 a week we were paid for clean-up."

Arthur Rice (right) and Arthur E. Lunte discuss their many years of work at the State Fairgrounds, as they inspect a 1906 Cadillac on display at the 1975 Indianapolis Auto Show.

During a July 1934 Finance and Advisory Committee meeting, "it was taken by consent that the Board pay the colored people who take care of the toilets and allow no tips." Toilet porters and matrons were paid on a no-tip basis in 1937. Restroom help was warned again in February 1940 not to shine shoes or to take tips.

Bedding stored in the wooden Administration Building's rafters was brought out for cleaning as the Fair approached. Anyone on business there negotiated dirt or mud, since 38th Street and "Fairground Road" weren't paved. "All the buildings were wood, with wooden sheds to house cattle, sheep and swine. The choice display tents were those in the recessed area under the old Coliseum.

"Church groups offered refreshments at stands. Games of chance, concerts by quartets and 'test your strength' booths vied for attention with balloon ascensions, a demonstration of 'high-speed gasoline tricycle' motorcycles ...." Rice also remembered the hotel, where owners of "high-class" horses stayed while on business.

Night-time lighting hurdles were tackled aggressively. Display areas glowed in gas torch light. Once, when days of rain created problems, Rice poured gasoline from milk cans onto the muddy ground. Set afire, the ground was dry enough to use after the blaze died down.

And those supply trips downtown? "I'd hitch up old Charley, a race horse, to the wagon and head downtown ... I had to hold a loose rein because if he felt one tug, he'd take off fast. It took us all day to get down to Vancamp's or Vonnegut's on Maryland Street and back to the fairgrounds."

◆◆◆

Fodder Feeding Won't Make Race Horses . . . STICK TO WHEELER'S — West End of Grand Stand!

As Close as Your Phone

THE STATE FAIR has never failed to showcase useful inventions to an appreciative public. After Alexander Graham Bell invented the telephone on June 2, 1875 (patent #174,465, on March 7, 1876), it was only natural that two phones were installed in Camp Morton's Exposition Building for public viewing at the 1877 Fair. The first Indianapolis telephone exchange, called Bells Telephone Company, opened in 1878 or 1879 in a building at 117 East Washington Street.

By 1882, the Gilliland Private Telephone, located at the "head of Massachusetts Avenue, Indianapolis," claimed that it "operates without a magnet, gives and receives messages through the same stationary tube. Its capacity is about two miles." Interesting?

By 1956, calls reached the Fairgrounds by dialing WA 3-3431.

◆◆◆

Telephone technology has been a regular feature at the Fair since the first display of the convenience in 1877, only two years after its invention by Alexander Graham Bell. By 1938, eighty telephones awaited visitors.

EIGHTY TELEPHONES
For Your Use at the Fairgrounds

The Indiana Bell Telephone Company welcomes you to the Indiana State Fair and hopes that your visit proves enjoyable and entertaining. Telephones have been provided throughout the grounds for your convenience in 60 handy locations. In addition, there are 20 telephones available at a special Telephone Station in the Grand Stand. An operator is in charge ready to assist you in placing calls.

 If you are a visitor from another city and wish to get in touch with home during your stay in Indianapolis, remember that Long Distance is quick, dependable and economical. Lowest rates on out-of-town calls are in effect after 7 every evening and all day every Sunday.

Radio and Television: A Hoosier Roundup

INDIANA STATE Fairgoers discovered radio's potential and saw their first television years before the first local station broadcast. Manufacturers and retailers demonstrated and sold the new technology that would change the world. Pioneering radio men were quick to offer their services at unheard-of prices and the Board of Agriculture promptly embraced mass communications' potential.

WFBM Broadcasting Station of Merchants Heat and Light Company let 1926 Boardmen know that "if they were approached by anybody . . . for broadcasting they would be very glad . . . arrangements [were necessary] to get material into WFBM either through the Western Union or Bell Telephone Company." There was no charge.

In 1928, the Board paid WKBF Radio (later, WIRE, then WXTZ, now WFXF) $274 to broadcast a half hour twice every day of the Fair, at midday and early evening from a room above the old Administration Building Publicity Office. (Indianapolis' first radio station, WKBF went on the air in 1923.) WLS of Chicago broadcast four or more hours daily from the Women's Building at no charge.

Radio station WFBM aired daily during 1943's War Central noon hour. WOWO came for a day, and WISH, WHAS, and WBAA, along with Cincinnati's WLW, brought their programs. Thirteen radio stations aired from the Fair that year. The *Indianapolis News, Times,* and *Star* covered the event but refrained from picture taking since the process required silver, which was needed for the war effort.

In 1946, Purdue student Wayne Rothgeb and his friend Gordon Graham originated the first noon farm show on radio station WBAA from the Purdue Building. To open the show, they recorded a barker selling fish cakes and apple sauce. In return for a daily plug, the two and their boss drank free coffee for the week. Rothgeb went on to become farm director of WKJV-TV in Fort Wayne.

◆◆◆

ON THE LAST day of January 1946, the biggest thing in Indiana radio history was offered on whatever terms the Board wanted. Harry Smythe of Fort Wayne's 10,000-watt WOWO, along with WIBC's Ed Mason, Ken Chapman of WISH, and *Indianapolis Star* publisher Eugene Pulliam, offered a 165-station statewide publicity and entertainment broadcast.

The proposed all-Hoosier radio show would reach an estimated 3,427,000 listeners. Already, eighty-three various "artists" had been lined up to appear at the Fair during the 2-1/2 hour Hoosier Radio Round-Up continuous broadcast.

Each station had a farm program, Smythe claimed. Combined, the advance publicity was worth "five, six or seven thousand dollars." Mason claimed it was the first time in history for the undertaking, planned for Saturday night, August 31.

"[Y]ou are getting and will get the greatest advertising means that has ever been offered," Smythe boasted July 12. Each participating radio station would save "duplicate billings" and send them to each Board member marked "paid in full." The deal really sought to convince the very traditional State Fair Board that radio advertising was a better buy than the newspaper equivalent. A log book similar to a newspaper's scrapbook would show radio was a greater medium, Smythe claimed. "The radio will well surpass in dollars and cents that which has ever been done before by the newspaper."

Despite rumors, Smythe vowed to "absolutely deliver" Olsen and Johnson, Herb Shriner, and Singing Sam. "I have the word that Hoagy Carmichael is coming, but not in writing," WOWO's man claimed. "He is foxy, but I am quite sure he will be here."

Other acts scheduled to appear: the Doctors of Harmony from WRTC, Elkhart; Fred "Grandad" Campbell of WKMO, Kokomo; the Tennessee Drifters with Gil & Johnny from WJOB, Hammond; Country Cousin Chickie, Emmy Lou, Little Jimmy, and the Delmar Brothers from WIBC, Indianapolis; and the 35-member Elks Chanters from WBOW, Terre Haute. WOWO provided the Hoosier Hop and the ABC Network performers.

Already 103 performers were lined up from all corners of Indiana. (Some apparently weren't talented enough to make the grade, however, and Olsen & Johnson's act ran twenty-five minutes longer than expected). Smythe claimed ABC would carry the show for an hour "coast to coast" on 195 stations.

Something went wrong with the 1948 Hoosier Radio Round-Up when amateurs appeared on a network broadcast. The following January, Indiana Broadcasters Association president Bruce McConnel told the Board, "I don't think we should put on a broadcast with local talent. Frankly, I was sick about the show last year."

◆◆◆

The Fairgrounds Radio Center

THE RADIO Center was the first post-war building, erected in 1947 across Main Street from the Swine Barn at the site where 4-H'ers formerly exhibited swine.

The Radio Center originally featured twelve radio studios on the second floor (although they almost were dormitories) and the paddock on the ground floor, with forty-four stalls and Speed Department director and veterinarian offices. Sports and entertainment stars visited the building, now known as the Communications Building. Visitors sat in studio audiences or watched through hall windows.

The building was considered a wise move. Speed Director A.G. Norrick observed, "Everybody knows that the Grand Circuit racing we have here during the Fair is the best money producer we

The W.H. Rodebeck Company, statewide distributors of Victor electric products, shows its wares at the Fair, including a line of movie projectors and cameras, phonographs, and microphones.

have. Three-fourths of our Grandstand is sold out solid way ahead of the Fair.

"The Grand Circuit says we should have a paddock. Instead of having to come out of barns all over the grounds, the horses are stabled before the race in one central place next to the Grandstand, and they are under guard before the race; there is provision for a saliva test.

"If we are going to make progress in Grand Circuit racing, and make this one of the biggest centers of Grand Circuit racing in the country, we ought to have a paddock. And that's saying nothing about your radio rooms, Levi (Moore)."

Since the building wasn't completed by Fair time, radio stations took spots on the Grandstand's second floor. Ed Mason of *Indianapolis News'* WIBC, along with the entire Indiana broadcasting community, was wild about the Radio Center. ". . . [T]here is no place in the United States like your new broadcasting studios in the paddock," Mason volunteered in 1948.

"I have been asked about it by important radio officials in other states. It is one of the finest things in the United States. Every broadcaster will tell you the same thing."

There were now forty-four radio stations in the state, counting the FM outlets, up from thirty the year before. Of these stations, thirty planned to broadcast sometime during Fair week.

WLS planned on broadcasting

from the new north side Machinery Field location, a factor Publicity men considered "a drawing card." WHAS figured on bringing in Herbie Koch and his organ in the Coliseum, a repeat of '47.

The Radio Center dedication was slated for Saturday, September 4, from 3:30-4 p.m. "Every effort is being made to have at least one national network carry the program," Publicity's Louis Culp reported. "We are trying to get the presidents of the four networks and FCC." The Fair Board and Indiana Broadcasters Association were also slated to appear on the program. Wow! The entire deal cost $300.

1948 That accursed blight, progress, raised a stink during the May 13 Board meeting. Armond Gemmer and Culp of the Publicity Department reported that RCA and Admiral Radio had complained the day before, "considerably disturbed about the television proposition we have with Block's.

"It is their wish that we keep all television off the grounds," Gemmer said. "There is no station around here and you couldn't pick up a television broadcast in

enough last year, but now that television is really here, people will believe that they can pick it up any time or any place."

Gemmer recommended giving "a picture of what television holds in the future. We don't have television out here on a commercial basis. It is strictly for an educational purpose."

"It might in some way be connected with the fight between the *News* and *Star* for the third television permit in Indianapolis," offered Karolyn Holloway.

Gemmer believed "probably two television stations" would be operating in Indianapolis by the time the '49 Fair rolled around. "Those men yesterday wanted us to ban all television from the grounds this year, but I hope the Board will ignore their request," Gemmer urged.

Three days before the 1949 Fair opened, the Board rejected television's offer of free coverage during the Fair.

"Some of the Radio people . . . want to televise the Fair and Races," Roger Wolcott announced. "I told them they couldn't come in unless they had the approval of the whole Board."

"My thinking along that line," responded Gilman C. Stewart, "because television is so new and because of the effect it might have on our Fair, I would be hesitant in entertaining this idea."

"The Speed department should have something to say about this as it would involve the races," President Homer E. Schuman commented.

Speed Superintendent L. Orville Miller had "thought about it considerably." As he understood the proposition, the new medium would televise harness races' beginning and end, "and one could see this part of it better from a television set than those people sitting in the Grandstand. I don't want to be obstreperous or backward and I know television is a coming thing, but I am just wondering if it would hurt the sale of our tickets. If the public knew they could see the races at home if it were a hot day or looked like rain, it might hurt our attendance," Miller declared.

"Up home," Earl J. Bailey chimed in, "where some of the folks have television sets they invite in a group of people to

this locality. They are going on the theory that a demonstration out here leads people to believe that television is here and they can pick it up any time they want to."

Certainly no fears of newer technology displacing them entered into RCA and Admiral's minds. "They believe unscrupulous salesmen will come in and sell television sets to people who have seen television work at the Fair and believe that it will work for them."

As early as 1939, Fair visitors had experienced the wonders of television technology at a WLS exhibit. Approximately

38,754 visitors paid a dime to see the display.

"At the present time," Gemmer noted, "it would take thousands of dollars, too, for any home radio in this territory to receive television broadcasts."

Gemmer had told the radio companies there wasn't much chance the Board would cancel its plan to have Block's at the Fair.

"They agreed that there was no bad reaction from WIRE's television exhibit last year," Gemmer said, "but they said that television had not advanced

Fair visitors watch the announcer during a live radio broadcast from the Fairgrounds' Radio Center on station WIRE.

see the show, and if there are very many of those sets around here it might hurt us."

"I don't know about that," Wolcott responded, "but there are a lot of small folks who would be seeing this show and it might educate them as far as the races are concerned."

After discussion of costs for the platforms, cables, and wires, Bailey remarked, "If you let them come in free it would set a precedent and they might want to come in free again next year."

Although a motion and second called for approval for television, the tube was voted down for the 1949 Fair.

1949 *Prairie Farmer* magazine rented office space at the Paddock (upstairs, actually, in the Radio Center) by the time January rolled around. The magazine, established in 1841, stayed through its December 21, 1963, edition, calling itself *Indiana Edition, Prairie Farmer.* By its next edition (January 4, 1964; location now at 1308 N. Meridian St., Indianapolis, until 1976), the venerable farming magazine called itself *Indiana Prairie Farmer.*

1953 The *Indianapolis News* made its twenty-first "Hoosier Home Town" stop-off at "State Fair, Indiana." The photo essay showed the secretary-manager's home, originally constructed as "the governor's summer cottage."

"You easily could consider this Main Street . . . " the *News* claimed, "[I]t has so many of the components of a typical city main street. Many of the fair's principal buildings are located along the street which is broad, well-lighted and complete with a grass esplanade."

Electric power consumption equalled a town with 6,000 souls. The Coliseum ice machine, "if turned to commercial use," could generate 250 tons of ice. Parking space could accommodate 20,000 cars (12,000 on the Fairgrounds, 250 trucks and 4,000 cars south of 46th Street, and 5,000 cars across 42nd Street on thirteen acres belonging to the Deaf School).

Live Television! Big Fairgrounds Stars!

SOME VERY BIG events happened in the Radio Center. WTTV-Channel 4 set up shop and broadcast from the east end studios from October 1955 to mid-1957. "We had quite an uninhibited experience when we were here," veteran sportscaster Chuck Marlowe remembered in 1991.

At the time, Frank Edwards was news director. "Frank was one of the top newscasters – he was a commentator – best identified for his UFO books, including 'Stranger Than Science' and 'Strangest of All.' He was on the Jack Parr Show. General Curtis Lemay was one of his closest friends.

"Frank had a .250-3000 varmint rifle," Marlowe remembered. "He'd bring that up here occasionally and we'd see moles and muskrats across the inside of the track . . . we'd take pot shots at those muskrats and whatever during the winter months when they'd be out here kicking around in the Infield."

WTTV aired a Radio Center television and radio program; Edwards did the newscasts and Marlowe handled sports. Edwards had worked in India-

napolis, then moved up to network radio with Mutual Broadcasting in Washington, D.C., before returning for his first television assignment.

"We had the forerunner to American Bandstand here – 'Top 10 Dance Party,' produced by an agency, Victor & Richards, out of New York. We had many guests," recalled Marlowe.

"This is back in the days when the record companies used to come through and hype their records, right at the same time as payola, although we were never caught up in any of that. Capitol Records, Decca Records and others would bring their stars in as well as their records."

"Top 10" originally aired weekdays at 3:30 to 5 p.m. from the Radio Center. Area teens – up to 15 couples – danced to top songs in Studio A in the Radio Center's southeast corner.

Elvis Presley and Colonel Parker also visited Studio A. "We had the first television appearance that he made after signing with RCA when he was on his way to the Ed Sullivan Show," Marlowe said. "He sat there with about thirty Indianapolis high school kids, many of whom had no idea who he was.

"We sat on a sofa and talked for a little bit; every time I'd ask him a question, he'd turn over to the Colonel, the Colonel would nod his head and Elvis would turn around and answer. He'd never answer anything that the Colonel didn't say to answer."

But there's even more to this story. "The big pressing RCA had at the time – they brought it to me and had the sides marked A and B. And they said 'Play the A side.' It was a horrible record. Just absolutely horrible. About a week later they called back and asked what the public response was, and I replied, 'Lousy.'

"They said, 'What do you mean?' And I said, 'It's a horrible record.' And they asked, 'Which side are you playing?'

"'The A side, the side you marked.' The 'horrible' song was 'Mystery Train.'

"And they said, 'Oh, my Lord. Flip the record over.' We flipped the record over and it was 'Heartbreak Hotel'" – the number one song in 1956. About a week afterward RCA came out with a new pressing with "Heartbreak" on both sides. But this was after the Sullivan show.

Hollywood's top names also appeared in WTTV's Radio Center studio. Richard Widmark made one of his first television appearances on the show while in town promoting a movie. "Widmark stood over in the studio on the northeast corner of the building with his back to the door and wouldn't talk to anyone, absolutely no one, until the program was on the air. We thought he was a snob. It turned out he was so scared – he had never appeared on live television before. He apologized."

Stan Kenton was on the show many times, Marlowe recalled. "He did the sock hop with us one time. We rolled in a piano at his request one time and he played fifteen minutes, including his 'Intermission Riff.' Back in those days, musicians were not allowed to do that, but he did it because he was so big and powerful."

Marlowe also hosted a boxing show called "Champions in the Making" from a boxing arena set up in Radio Center's east end hallway. "One of the first bouts that I ever did was a 16-year-old boy out of Louisville, against an Indianapolis PAL Club opponent – and he knocked him silly. He came back the next week and knocked the next guy silly – and we used to comment at the time that Cassius Clay would probably become a very good boxer."

1960 Harry Andrews, WIBC farm service director, "sounded off" in the *Indiana State Fair News'* May 2 edition about why

Cigar securely clamped, shirt rumpled, a bemused newspaperman studies his fishbowl "scoop" at the end of the day.

the Fair was so successful: "Undoubtedly because the backbone of the Fair – agriculture – has not been overlooked or shortchanged by the members of the Fair Board or the working management. The State Fair is an institution . . . it reflects rural Indiana."

Fair On The Air

THE FAIR went on the air in 1984 with electronic media coverage stretching throughout the state. A fifty-four radio station news network transmitted four daily updates. Radio station WIRE fed the five-minute newscasts from its on-site remote center to its Indianapolis base for simultaneous release via ground lines to the network's stations.

WTTV brought hour-long specials to Indiana TV audiences about the Queen Pageant, the High School Marching Band Contest Finals, the Fox Stake, and the 4-H Spotlite Sale. The shows were fed to Fort Wayne, Evansville, South Bend,

and Terre Haute. The network lasted through the 1988 Fair.

The Fair's Press Department also produced three mini-capsule daily news briefs; the 2-1/2 minute segments were transmitted statewide via satellite.

1991 More than two hundred twelve television and radio stations covered the Fair, counting networks. More than one hundred daily and weekly newspapers, magazines, and national trade journals covered and reported the Fair. Nearly seven hundred media staffers worked the Fair.

◆◆◆

Good for What Ails You

Nurses from Riley Hospital and the Nursing School of Indiana University demonstrate the proper way to make a bed in a hospital setting.

MEDICAL technology – particularly artificial limbs in the dawning days of the Fair – were popular with Fair crowds. Rarely, however, would State Fair standards allow patent medicine vendors on the grounds. Considered preposterous, even dangerous back then, those balms, extracts, and remedies nevertheless "cured" multitudes.

The National Surgical Institute, founded in 1860 and headquartered in Indianapolis, with branches in Atlanta and San Francisco, advertised its services in 1874: "Treatment of All Cases of Surgery, Chronic Diseases, Deformities; Piles, Fistula, Female Diseases &c." Medicine, readers learned, was "Born in Ignorance, Cradled in Superstition, Matured in Ecotism."

The American Specific Company, Box 15, Indianapolis, hawked ZOZORA BALM CONES in an 1888 Fair flyer: "We want every lady in the United States that is afflicted with any of the ills that women are heir to . . . to send for our confidential circular."

The cones were guaranteed to "cure you . . . [O]ver one hundred years ago, this wonderful panacea was discovered. We could and can give you the testimonials of over 1,000 women from every quarter of the globe.

"[At] $1.00 per box, neatly packed and sent by mail . . . you can be your own doctor. Remember this! If you are afflicted listen to us." The cones were sold "only C.O.D., by mail, or lady agents."

The Robert Long Hospital provided an innovation and service "without stint or cost" to the Fair in 1917: a physician and a nurse were "constantly on hand to minister to sick and disabled,

treating nearly 40 cases during the week."

In 1926, the Red Cross protested that its burden of caring for Fair visitors had grown onerous after seven years. "The work has grown and has been carried on under a great deal of a handicap," Red Cross' Dr. Fortune complained. "At times, it has been a very serious question whether the Red Cross should undertake to do the work under such a great handicap."

The Red Cross asked to be included in the Board's building plans. During the 1926 Fair, the Red Cross doctor and his assistants averaged 100 "more

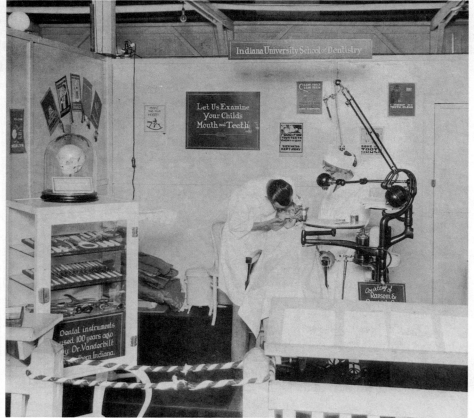

or less serious" cases daily at no charge at its hospital and first aid station.

"What we really need there is a building with the proper water facilities, proper toilet facilities, a place that will be a proper place for sick and injured people," Dr. Fortune said.

The Red Cross ministered to 634 patients "in addition to 187 redressings." Two hundred thirty cases were Indianapolis residents, 331 came from beyond the capital city, while sixty-five were from "18 or 20 neighboring states . . . a building like the baby building would suit our needs," reported Dr. Wagner of the Red Cross.

During one of Dodson's World's Fair Coliseum performances in 1930, a rider fell from her horse, fracturing her shoulder. Taken to the Red Cross hospital, the injured performer discovered no doctor in the house, although six physicians apparently were on the grounds. The Board promptly informed the Red Cross that if it wasn't going to stay on the job, replacements would be found.

In another accident that year, a Women's Building visitor crossed a re-

American Red Cross workers take a break from the Fairtime medical rush to be photographed in front of their building and ambulance in 1937.

The Indiana University School of Dentistry displayed dental tools and techniques from the past and the present.

Hook's Drugstores in 1966 established an old-time pharmacy at the Fairgrounds in the building that had once housed the Better Babies contest. Today it displays balms, tonics, and cure-alls from the early days as well as an 1875 working soda fountain.

straining rope and stepped on a ladder, causing a shelf of canned goods to fall on her. The accident was the woman's fault, according to Women's Building director Thomas Grant.

Interesting medical advice was offered in "Gas and Water Works Handbook," 10th edition, published by the Pittsburgh Equitable Meter Company for 1930-32. In case of lightning strikes, first aid called for dashing cold water on the victim. Mad dog or snake bites required sucking the wound and cauterizing with caustic or a white-hot iron, or cutting out adjoining parts with a sharp knife. There were two tests for death: one, "hold mirror to mouth. If living, moisture will gather." Secondly, "push pin into flesh, if dead the hole will remain, if alive it will close up."

Secretary-Treasurer E.J. Barker almost lost his free Boy Scout help ushering the Coliseum in 1931 when he sought a "nominal fee" for a May 16 Scout program. The Board ended up giving the Scouts free Fairgrounds rent and a free tent during the Fair; and they told Barker to get in touch with the Scouts' Captain Francis O. Belzer "and have him understand that we want the Boy Scouts at the Fair." A $250 donation was thrown in to sweeten the deal.

Belzer announced in June the Scouts wanted to discontinue ushering, and instead asked free admission on Thursday, to be designated Scout Day. Belzer proposed Scout service for the Red Cross, along with messenger and errand duties, and that's what they did.

Belzer founded the Crossroads of America Scout Band as a drum and bugle corps in 1917; the organization, the oldest and largest in America, celebrated its Diamond Jubilee in 1992.

The Scouts had been highly praised for Fair-time service in January 1918 when outgoing President Leonard B. Clore proclaimed, "Ah! These are the little men whose services were in evidence from early dawn to late at night, and turn when you [would], four, five or more of these boys were ready as messengers, first aid, and a long list of services which came gratis, so that ... our hats are off and our gates ever open."

Anyone selling patent medicines, remedies, and "quack doctors" were prohibited from the 1938 Fair. Mr. Roach, the man with the barber concession for the past seventeen-eighteen years, was informed he had to comply with state law.

The "Gothic style" Emergency Service Building, constructed during 1952-53, originally housed grounds and Indiana State Police (about 50), city police (about 300 to direct traffic outside the fair), doctors, nurses, and ambulances. The top floor housed a modern restaurant, serving diners either cafeteria-style or by waitress. Publicity called it one of the largest in the state; it featured advance payment "to a new high of more than 1,000 meals per hour."

The Service Building Red Cross staff treated 100 abrasions, 93 blisters, 110 colds, 142 headaches, and 110 stomach aches that first year of its operation. The Red Cross operated an emergency hospital at the Service Building, with a twenty-four-hour staff of doctors and nurses. From this command center, parking for more than 12,000 cars on the Fairgrounds was controlled by a staff of 500. The fire department was on duty at all times with ten firemen and two trucks.

In 1966, Hook Drug Stores recognized Indiana's Sesquicentennial in a marvelous way when it transformed the Board of Health Building into the Hook's Historic Drug Store. The nineteenth century drugstore and pharmacy museum sought to preserve the history of Indiana pharmacies and curiosities from patent medicine's heyday.

The store was built around massive antique and ornately carved wall fixtures with matching counters built in 1852 for Cambridge City druggist Samuel H. Hoshour. Purchased from Richard Grigsby of Cambridge City, the fixtures were used by his father as recently as 1961.

A nationally known tourist attraction, the store contains pharmacy and drugstore antiques, and features a vintage (and working) 1875 soda fountain and an automatic piano (colloquially, a nickelodeon). The piano, Seeburg Model K, was made by the Seeburg Company of Chicago, circa 1920. It has a piano and mandolin rail and a set of violin pipes.

1977 The Red Cross treated 1,634 cases, ranging from delivering a baby to soothing blisters. Doctors and nurses donated their time.

1991 The Red Cross treated 1,130 insect stings, compared to 41 the year before.

Farm Bureau Firsts

AGRICULTURAL and livestock associations and county societies wholeheartedly lent support to their State Fair, then were joined by farming's most powerful forces during the 1920s.

At the first post-World War II Fair in 1946, the Indiana Farm Bureau Cooperative Association looked back on its role with "the Community: Shortly after the first World War, the business of agriculture went into a slump that proved to be a forerunner to the national depression. During this period, the country learned that the farmer's economic welfare is of basic importance to the business done in his community. One of the main reasons for agricultural conditions during that period, was that the farmer was buying at high prices and selling for low. To remedy this situation, he and his neighbors organized their own purchasing co-op."

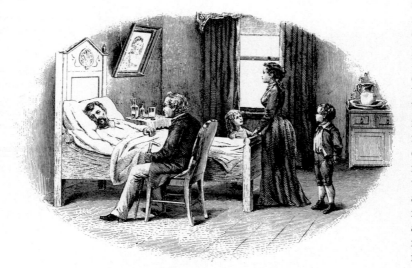

Indiana Farm Bureau's 1950 premium list advertisement said much about that Fair: "More than 100,000 Indiana Farm Bureau families . . . welcome Hoosierland's biggest farm show . . . back for another exhibit of the best Indiana farm products [.]

"Display tables and show rings at the Fair offer many educational opportunities to older folk and rural young people, who have had a large part in making the State Fair the success that it is today.

"The many State Fair activities bring the picture of Indiana farm and urban production into clear focus and [draw] Hoosiers closer together as they strive to solve the economic problems of the state. Youth are prepared and trained for future leadership in their communities."

One hundred thousand members strong, the Indiana Farm Bureau chose the Centennial Fair in 1952 to announce, "We've Come A Long Way."

"Since the Morrill Act [U.S. Senator Justin Smith Morrill] was passed in 1862 during Lincoln's Administration, Land Grant Colleges have sprung up all over the United States to lead the way to improved farming and a higher living standard for farm people . . . . [F]ood has become more plentiful and relatively less expensive.

"One hour of average factory labor in 1951 would buy 10 loaves of bread; while in 1929 that wage bought only 6.4 loaves. Farm [mechanization], improved methods, soil conservation, and voluntary farm organizations have strengthened our nation through increased production . . . truly a wonder-working century."

Something really big happened in the Cattle Barn in March 1969 – the Golden Anniversary of Indiana Farm Bu-

More than 10,500 Indiana Farm Bureau members dined in the Cattle Barn during their 1969 Golden Anniversary celebration. Three hundred forty servers worked twenty food lines; everyone was served in forty minutes. Each paid $1 for the no-frills dining affair.

reau. The *Muncie Star*'s sports editor Bob Barnet wrote, "There were more than 10,000 of them, and they parked their cars and climbed down from the chartered buses and moved slowly through the spring sunshine into the huge State Fair Coliseum.

"The faces of the men were reddened by wind and sun, but the faces were scrubbed and the shoes were shined and the women looked as if they really could bake a cherry pie . . . not the kind that comes out of a box.

"They looked like working people . . . ." And they were. They were the

ones who labored to make Indiana great and they were here to celebrate.

They sang "The Star Spangled Banner," repeated "The Pledge of Allegiance," ate dinner, then listened to fellow Hoosier Clifford M. Hardin, the secretary of agriculture; Purdue Dean Earl Butz; and finally crooner Eddy Arnold.

More than 10,500 people were served the evening meal through twenty food lines in forty minutes, according to Barnet. Three hundred forty served and the operation went so well that the Indiana Board of Health filmed it, with plans to use the film for training, Barnet wrote. The entire affair cost each Farm Bureau member $1.

The record number of people served indoors at a single sitting, 13,383, or 5.4 miles worth, happened seven years later, March 17, 1976, in the Cattle Barn for a golden anniversary gathering of the Indiana Farm Bureau Cooperative. The previous world's record was set by Chicago's McCormick Place in 1971 when 10,158 were served.

The meal was served in fifty-three minutes at $3.21 a plate. The event earned the Fairgrounds a temporary berth in the *Guinness Book of Records*.

◆◆◆

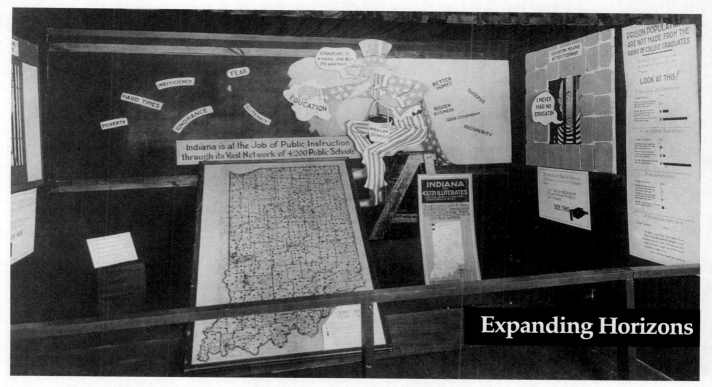

Expanding Horizons

An educational display from 1931 reveals the literacy rate in Indiana and the probable life of crime that lies ahead for those who can't read.

In front of the 1934 Old Fashion School House, the original group of students pose in their authentic costumes.

EDUCATING Indiana's youth has always been a vital purpose of the State Fair. A week at the Fair was considered superior to a week at any university. Some Hoosiers may remember attending the Fair *with* their school as an official field trip.

1834 Indiana's educational system owes much to farmers – and to one in particular. John Beard, a "plain, simple-hearted" Montgomery County farmer, ensured a permanent Indiana common school fund in 1834 when the Indiana legislature established a state bank, according to Marion County's Judge C.H. Test, a member of 1878's "Committee of Arrangements and Reception for a Meeting of the Pioneers of Indiana."

Beard was credited with an amendment to the act establishing the state bank; once a sinking fund had paid the state's loan, "the residue of said fund . . . [was] appropriated [as a permanent fund] to the cause of common school education."

"His name should be precious to every boy and girl who enjoys the benefits of our common schools," Test declared during Pioneer Convention opening ceremonies at the State Fair. Test's father had settled in Indiana territory sometime in 1810.

1855 President (Major General) Joseph Orr's suggestion of moving the sheep pen and putting up another tent for "young men's work" in 1855 was "an excellent idea, and one characteristic of the taste and judgment of that officer."

1856 During the March 4 afternoon session, Governor James A. Wright favored dividing a special $1,000 State appropriation into classes "for young ladies and young gentlemen" from Indiana. Premium amounts were fixed at the next meeting.

A new 100-foot-long Young Men's Department hall "after the manner and style of the other halls" was built for that Fair.

1878 Indiana School of Art pupils exhibiting their work were allowed four admission tickets to the Fair. The Board extended special thanks to "institutions for the education of the deaf and dumb and the blind, the Purdue University, and a number of the city and country public schools" for educational exhibits.

The exhibits, requested by the Board, were "highly instructive and interesting to thousands of visitors . . . who have thus, for the first time, been enabled to acquaint themselves with their modes of instruction."

The Indiana Institution for the Education of the Blind had "perhaps the most attractive exhibit by any one organization, consisting, in addition to other educational and industrial productions, of musical and other entertainments by the pupils."

1880 "The trust reposing in us is no sinecure," President William Henry Ragan told the Board soon after his 1880 election. "To aid, to encourage, to build up, to educate, should be our motto."

1888 Woman's State Fair Association president Mrs. A.M. Noe had no doubt that "there is no better method of awakening an interest among the children than having a children's department . . . A few years ago, the first [children's department]

exhibit of fossils was made. It was a wonderful incentive . . . it is an educator . . . ."

1898 Governor James A. Mount read from a letter dated the previous December from Purdue University President James Henry Smart; president from 1883 to 1900, Smart wrote, "I believe that a great deal of the education of our children in the country, in school and out, has a tendency to make them dissatisfied with their surroundings, and unduly fosters in their minds a desire to seek their fortunes in the large commercial centers."

1908 Purdue Professor W.C. Latta addressed the Board on "Elementary Agriculture" at the January 7 evening session. Professor E.J. Allen, from the Indianapolis Manual Training School, discussed "Manual Training." Professor Fassett A. Cotton, the superintendent of Public Instruction of Indiana, talked about "Progress of Industrial Education."

1925 "Your Board has been doing a remarkable work . . . A few years ago the

The Schoolmaster, Mr. Cravens from Indiana University, teaches geography to his students at the old-time school where 1934 Fair visitors could watch instruction modeled after yesteryear.

Visitors could walk through the Modern School at the 1934 State Fair to experience current teaching methods and materials.

State Fair was simply a place for horse racing and amusement," Governor Emmett F. Branch told the annual conference and delegate meeting on January 7, "but, today, our State Fair has become one of the great educational institutions of the state . . . educating the boys and the girls on the farm . . . bringing contentment to them in a way that has never been before.

"It is educating the public and bringing the city and the rural districts together, as no other agency could possibly do."

Secretary-Treasurer E.J. Barker agreed. "Aside from our livestock and agriculture exhibits, Indiana has set a standard for other fairs along the lines of a Boys Camp and Girls School; thus we are striving to educate the Boy and Girl along lines that will cause them to remain on the farm."

1929 Charges of favoritism came to Board light on June 19. Muncie's "Ball Brothers College" called it "un-fair that we give Purdue and I.U. everything," Barker said, "and then we charge them and Terre Haute for exhibit space when they are a State institution and

Staff at Work at Fair Grounds

Ernest T. Pyle, editor, John E. Stempel, Beulah Radcliffe, Katherine Cleary, Mary Ann Thornton, Herman Myers.

an educational institution the same as these others."

Ball Brothers' representative had asserted his loyal support of the Board, including legislative support, but swore the college would not return "as long as we let other schools in free. That is his position."

Barker agreed Ball Brothers' argument had its points, but "there is the other side. If they take space and occupy it in the Manufacturer's Building, they are taking space that is salable."

The secretary-treasurer was against giving up the spaces, each worth $160, at no cost. Instead, he suggested free tent space or meeting them half way in the Manufacturer's Building. "I wouldn't give them the entire space in the building as we furnish at our expense the booth equip-

---

The curious and seekers of learning sought out Indiana University's exhibit building west of the Women's Building. Indiana Daily Student was published every day beginning in 1922 from its headquarters to the right.

Ernest T. "Ernie" Pyle was the State Fair edition's first editor.

ment, janitorial service, etc." The Board approved Barker's recommendation.

Ball Brothers College had been founded April 4, 1918, as the "Eastern Division of Indiana State Normal School." Its first name change, to Ball Teachers College, came in 1922. Seven years later it was again changed to Ball State Teachers College. The fourth oldest state university finally adopted Ball State University as its name on February 8, 1965, but it was never officially known as Ball Brothers College.

In an early bit of '30 business, President Ulysses C. Brouse and his fellows approved giving the two teachers' colleges, "the one at Muncie and one at Terre Haute," free space at the Fair as long as it was "purely educational" and "attractive for the Fair."

1930 The Fair's one big feature "which has rapidly developed and is of paramount educational value," was Boys' and Girls' 4-H Club work. "This work has trebled in recent years," Barker pointed out. "It is about to crowd out our adult classes in some departments."

1932 An Indiana University Building was needed to adequately house I.U. exhibits, outgoing Board President Guy Cantwell said in January 1928.

Finally in 1932, the Indiana University Exhibit Building, specifically built not to obstruct Grandstand fans' view of the track, opened; dedication ceremonies began at 1:30 p.m. on Tuesday, September 6. Fairgoers sat in the 800-seat auditorium, equipped for motion pictures and stage shows.

The building's first-year program featured talking pictures, concert music, instrumental and vocal solos, and scientific demonstrations. The Millersville Eastern Star Building had been razed to make room for I.U.

Purdue's Dean John Harrison Skinner didn't want I.U.'s building to get a heating plant and withheld support for the building until funding was obtained. He had not been reticent in a May 14 letter complaining about a Purdue Building roof leak (a new roof was needed).

Meanwhile, I.U.'s Director of Publicity Frank R. Elliott was so pleased with the Board that he threw in an extra day of B-town band music.

Thanks to the state's oldest university and an enterprising student journalist, the State Fair had acquired its own

daily newspaper in 1922.

Ernest Taylor "Ernie" Pyle, columnist and war correspondent who died in 1945 covering the Pacific War, is credited with convincing Indiana University officials to publish the summer edition of the *Indiana Daily Student* on the Fairgrounds during the 1922 Fair. The tradition lasted through 1955.

Pyle edited the first Fair edition. Eight-page press runs of 12,000 to 15,000 copies were distributed free every morning.

The effort was "one of the outstanding features of the Indiana University exhibit," the *Student* later reported. The "seven-column affair . . . contained news of the fair and publicity matter concerning the University. It was supported by Bloomington advertisers . . . ."

Reporting and editing were based at the I.U. headquarters at the Fairgrounds. Then the copy reached Bloomington by messenger or was called in by telephone. Production and printing stayed in Bloomington.

Arbutus, the university yearbook, claimed "Fair officials have asked the University to publish the *Daily Student* on the fair grounds again next fall as the official State Fair paper."

The paper's newsroom moved to the Indiana University Building in the

In their 1934 display, the McGuffey Club sports the dress worn in the early days of their McGuffey Reader.

1930s; in 1949 it was "the only such enterprise on a fairgrounds in the country[.]"

1932 Perhaps it was Indiana Farm Bureau's new quarters in the new Grandstand that prompted the *Hoosier Farmer* journalist to write, "It has been said that the Indiana State Fair is the greatest educational institution in Indiana."

The Fair, in Governor Harry J. Leslie's opinion, was "the grandest thing I can think of, for our youngsters to give them an idea of other persons and know other people. I want you to encourage the children."

The Fair was the children's "plaything," Leslie noted. Without fairs, children would fail. "Encourage these youngsters in all of this 4-H club work. In America, we like competition . . . I want you to give them a chance to be American . . . ."

1934 An important press notice was read to the Board on February 9. Superintendent of Public Instruction Floyd McMurray intended to immediately release news that the 1934-35 school year

schools could report that one in six could read and only one in nine could write. Back then, only one in sixteen had ever studied arithmetic, one in one hundred had studied geography, and only one in 145 had ever studied grammar.

The Board invited all to come see the "Century of Progress," proud of "INDIANA, the state in the union whose educational system DID NOT BOW TO THE DEPRESSION, the doors of whose schools remained open, whose torch of liberty and enlightenment did NOT GO OUT . . . ."

1936 Even without new 4-H Club buildings, the Fairgrounds were hailed as the "world's most beautiful exposition grounds," hosting "a fair devoted to the advancement of Indiana people featuring Agriculture, Education, Industry and Entertainment."

Did someone say Education? This Fair, Hoosiers visited the log school of 100 years earlier, the frame school "of 50 years hence," and the modern school of 1936. Inside the 80-by-120 foot education exhibit building, a visitor could find school supply exhibits, books and school equipment, and doll and miniature airplane building contests, "which also proved most interesting to many thousands last year." More than 300,000 had visited the 1935 Educational Exhibit.

Fairgoers learned that "Indiana has always maintained a high standard in Education which was exemplified by the Educational exhibit . . . 'Progress of Education in Indiana.'"

1937 Near the schools, McGuffeyites put up a building where they exhibited antiques, old-fashioned clothes and household furnishings, and old school books.

The Educational Building was "the only building in America for public education on a fair grounds," Fair manager James L. Beattey told the Board early in the year. Indeed, Superintendent of Public Instruction Floyd McMurray declared Wednesday, already designated as Educational Day, as the first day of

would begin officially at the Fair "as a result of action taken recently by the Indiana State Board of Education."

Wednesday, September 5, already had been chosen "Education Day." Any student attending the Fair that day would be excused from school. Although it did not become part of the Fair's official name, the words "and educational exposition" were used in connection with that year's advertising.

An 1834 log school house was built for the "Century of Progress in Indiana Education" exhibit; a portable modern school house "failed to materialize" until 1935. A high school teacher was hired to coordinate the effort.

Indianapolis Technical and Greenfield high schools and Marion County Schools sponsored the log school activities. The McGuffeyites presented their programs "of early Indiana social life."

Over at the new four-room brick, concrete, and stone modern school, one fully appointed room hosted the modern curriculum. A $1,000 appropriation covered building costs, "as some of this amount will be returned in the sale of space to school equipment manufacturers," Lt. Governor M. Clifford Townsend said in June.

Both buildings were sited west of the Red Cross Building and south of the new Conservation Department game pens.

School was in session every day of the Fair; the McGuffeyite organization conducted class in the log school. The teacher used books and materials from that historic time. Pupils dressed as they would a century earlier.

The "Century of Progress" exhibit wasn't complete without a hobbies display and the parade of champions in "standard educational contests" – oratorical, Latin, and band. It was a great success.

The Board considered the hobby display vital: "HOBBIES represent a wise use of leisure time, while CRIME with all its sinister possibilities is often the result of an UNWISE USE of leisure time."

A special insert in that year's premium list recalled a sad fact about Indiana of a century hence, when typical township

Indiana's most prominent teacher's colleges, Indiana State Normal College (Indiana State University in Terre Haute) and Ball Teachers College (Ball State University in Muncie), display their programs at the 1927 State Fair.

school in Indiana, "and if children attend the Fair, they are counted present at school."

School buses again were released to bring tomorrow's leaders to the Fair. "Several hundred" buses brought children to the Fair in '34; "several thousand" were counted in '35.

1939 The "Junior Educational Activities Buildings" joined the Fairgrounds building roster. A three-building complex, the Exhibit Hall, Girls School, and Boys Dorm have since hosted thousands of 4-H'ers. Two of the buildings, although unfinished due to strikes and labor disputes, were occupied during the Fair. The boys were housed in the Girls' Dormitory east end.

Fifty thousand 4-H Clubbers, Boy and Girl Scouts, Catholic Youth Organization members, and others listened as Governor M. Clifford Townsend gave the Opening Day dedication address. "Short speeches were made by representatives of various patriotic educational societies of Indiana," *State Year Book* readers learned.

Thousands toured the buildings where more than 700 youngsters were housed. Then on First Evening, Boy Scouts put on a camp fire program before a packed Grandstand.

1944 Cancelling the State Fair 4-H finals this year had been far too great a wartime sacrifice, President Paul Gayland Moffett pointed out in January.

"Reports came from leaders in all parts of the state that interest in many 4-H Club projects immediately subsided and many were not brought to a successful completion. It was then realized that the state fair had been the pinnacle of educational events in Indiana's rural life. This mistake was rectified."

Board Secretary-Manager Guy Cantwell, with more than three decades of Board and Delegate service, knew what he was talking about when he told delegates, "Years ago in Indiana, and over the nation as well, our educational system received sharp criticism from agriculture – then known as 'farmers'– because their youth were educated away from the farm

in all directions." Rural youth had developed "an inferiority complex" as a result.

"Life other than farming looked down upon the farm boy and girl," Cantwell recounted. "The farm parents educated their children to escape the farm drudgery where they did favor education at all.

"Realizing this, farm people agitated for a change in the educational objectives in our common school objectives. The terms 'clodhoppers' and 'hayseeds' were common. 'Livestock man or breeder' carried more respect but was still not tops. An educated man was superior even if an underpaid teacher or clerk. Farming did not require brains and 'any fool' could farm. We here can recall those attitudes," Cantwell told listeners.

Farmers distrusted Purdue until it located farm laboratories throughout the state. "Soon a program for the training of farm youth was broadened to include more than money – to give a well-rounded program that would build successful farm men and women."

"This," Cantwell said, "is the origin and scope of the 4-H Club." The State Fair had first recognized 4-H Club activity in 1922, "by placing premiums on motion of E.J. Barker in the fair budget."

Cantwell recounted two 4-H milestones: the first Indiana corn show was in 1905, and 4-H Club work began "about 1910." Club work at the Fair had increased "steadily until in 1941 club entries were 60 percent of all the entries." It was for this reason that even World War II would never again call a halt to 4-H.

According to Cantwell, the 60,000 youth enrolled in 4-H "did better work and completed more projects because the Club fair was held. They will do better work next year." Sadly though, "most of our farm youth who are gone to war will not return to the farms."

1947 "It is their State Fair," outgoing President Otto Lawrence Reddish pointed out in January. "It belongs to the people of Indiana. Humans love Fairs and the object and purpose of Fairs is to serve and help humanity. The anticipation of going to the Fair rings deep in the youthful heart and is a lasting memory. And to the farm youth, whom we classify as the backbone of our State Fair – they are the real foundation of

any Fair – it is part of their education to attend a Fair or to exhibit and compete in one. To the grown-ups, a Fair is a valuable short-course in the study of those matters in which they are chiefly interested, plus the entertainment, sociability and pleasure which only Fairs can give."

1957 In the Fair program, Governor Harold W. Handley told Fairgoers, "The Indiana State Fair is truly education in action. In fact, the Fairgrounds has been referred to as the 'state's largest classroom.'"

The Fair began inviting teachers to visit the "classroom" that year on Teachers' Day. That practice continued into 1960 when one school superintendent from each county was invited to attend.

1965 William E. Wilson, State Superintendent of Public Instruction, decreed "inasmuch as Wednesday, September 1, is also considered Education Day, students entered in this contest may attend the State Fair on this day without being counted absent from school."

1976 The Fair hosted two young European women as part of an international 4-H sponsored program designed "to promote world peace and global understanding." Magdalena Stehli of Switzerland and Edith Brummerhoff of West Germany also had toured the nation after their arrival in

the country in May. After a two-month stay in Washington State, each stayed with three different Indiana families before returning home in October. (Indiana was one of the first states to participate in the International 4-H Youth Exchange program.)

1985 A new 4-H sale joined the roll call at the Fair this year. The 4-H Rabbit Highlight Sale, premiering as an adjunct to the Spotlite Sale of 4-H Champions, initially featured champion and reserve champion pens of three rabbits.

Both sales later were developed to include more participants; both "scholarship award ceremonies" are designed solely for the 4-H'er. Ninety percent of all auction proceeds go directly to the 4-H champion exhibitor. The remaining ten percent is divided equally and donated to the 4-H Foundation and the State Fair Scholarship Fund.

The Spotlite and Highlight Sale participants generally apply their proceeds toward college education or as an investment back into their agricultural operations.

1991 By the final year of the Fairgrounds' first century, 206,497 Indiana youth were enrolled in 4-H; fully thirty-four percent came from the larger suburbs and cities of Indiana. As it entered its eightieth year, the program offered more than fifty activity options.

FROM THE START, an event as great as the State Fair attracted more humanity than could be counted in most Hoosier burgs and hamlets. Odds and averages guaranteed that rogues rode in from the wilds along with the farmers. Alcohol and gambling generally elicited the greatest and most frequent outcry from without and within. State Fair lawmen with police powers patrolled the grounds, maintaining order and guarding against trespassers.

Every premium competitor at the first Indiana State Fair knew "a strong and efficient police" force patrolled "day and night." Awarding committees and "strangers from other states" registered at "committee of reception" headquarters at the Capitol.

1858 A breach in the exemplary behavior expected of every State Fair exhibitor had consequences. Police removed anyone "threatening violence" against judging committeemen from the judging ring.

1859 Miscreants from outside Society's respect suffered different consequences. Superintendent James L. Bradley made the pickpocket's life miserable at the New Albany State Fair. "He has made his detective arrangements in this regard perfect," the *New Albany Daily Ledger* reported. "Visitors, however, had better look after their own valuables themselves, as much as possible, without distracting their attention from the show."

Even officials were not immune. Someone picked Union County Board member W.H. Bennett's pockets of $36, all he had, according to the town's *Daily Tribune.*

One thief caught stealing a sponge cake claimed he hadn't eaten in two days. The *Ledger* disclosed that the miscreant "pretended to sob most piteously, but nary a tear was seen to fall. He is undoubtedly a thief of the lowest grade."

In another case, "a belligerent showman was lodged in jail for misconduct, and will have his trial before the Mayor[.]"

1864 Long-overdue, the issue of a corn crop premium withheld in 1860 from Marion County's Ellis R. Lake came before the Board on January 7, 1864. A two-man committee was appointed to settle the matter by February 23's meeting.

They discovered "by an examination of the affidavits on file . . . submitted by Mr. Lake, October seventeenth 1860, it appears that the corn crop in question was harvested from the fifth to the tenth of October, 1860, and specimens were exhibited at the State Fair following.

"[T]he corn was required to be weighed and harvested in December, allowing sixty-eight pounds to the bushel. But the corn having been weighed in the fore part of October, and no evidence being before your committee in reference to the number of pounds estimated to the bushel, the corn being green and heavy at that season of the year, fully two months before it should have been weighed, or could have been accurately estimated, your committee can readily perceive how one acre of land can be made to produce two hundred and sixty-three bushels.

"[T]he award to Mr. Lake and others in the class of field crops . . . were not legal, and, therefore, not binding upon the Board, for the following reasons: 'The gathering to be done and corn weighed during the month of December and reported to the January meeting of the Board. Entries to be made and specimens exhibited at the fair . . . two hundred and sixty-three bushels of corn, in fair weight, were never grown upon one acre of ground in a single season.'"

The committee recommended that Lake's application for the premium should be "indefinitely postponed."

1865 Exhibitors traveling any great distance to the 1865 State Fair in far away Fort Wayne came by rail. They came from all over to win; many lost before leaving the depot.

By Bessie Keeran Roberts' 1960 account in "Fort Wayne's Family Album," many were picked clean by pickpockets, especially those arriving by train. Those who won may have needed their prize to pay the train fare home.

"When a train arrived, several would jump into the car and begin picking pockets. As fast as they had finished with a man, they would chalk a cross on his coat, so that the 'boys' would waste no time on him." By the end of the Fair, discarded wallets filled a bushel basket.

1867 State Boardmen were haunted by the aftereffects of procrastination when President Ambrose Dudley Hamrick brought up the "Lake premium" again during the January 9 afternoon Delegate Board session.

Former president Stearns Fisher "now re-called a distinct recollection of the whole transaction, and . . . contrary to the rules for the . . . Awarding Committees, they had made the award at the time of the fair, instead of recommending and referring the matter to the State Board, at their January meeting, and was clearly of the opinion that the Board were not bound by the illegal action of the Awarding Committee."

Board member Joseph Poole of Attica "differed – that as Mr. Lake had presented the required affidavits of the crop, and the awards had been made, the Board was bound and should pay, although he had no doubt that fraud had been perpetrated."

One Agricultural Department judge had "no positive information concerning it, but thought two hundred and sixty-three bushels of corn to the acre, a large crop."

Poole moved to pay Lake. Others opposed it. The entire matter was referred to the full Board.

Despite Muncie Board member Dr. John C. Helm's argument that "there appeared there was fraud – the quantity per acre being greater than ever was or could be grown upon an acre of ground," the Board on January 11 appointed a three-member investigating committee to decide whether Lake's premium should be paid.

On March 6, the committee was authorized to compromise "with the parties upon the best terms possible." The following morning, Lake agreed to $50 as full payment. Nearly seven years had passed.

1869 Competition was open to penal supply manufacturers. B.F. Haugh & Company, Indianapolis, won a silver medal in 1869 for its iron prison, with no argument from the judges. The men were "dumfounded at the inventive genius of the age, and found, upon inspection that this Iron Prison was a perfect man-holder, or trap, inside of which we did not care to be, and awarded the premium and departed."

1871 "A part of the expense of night police might be disposed with by making shutters to your hall doors and locking them at night," President James D. "Blue Jean" Williams advised the Board on January 3.

Stout watchmen maintained a sturdy, if not questionable, patrol. Fair policeman A. Hinchman was reimbursed $12.50 to cover a fine and costs, "as assessed against him by the City of Indianapolis," for assault and battery while "in the discharge of his duty as policeman, during the Fair."

1872 There were insidious evils at the Indiana State Fair as well. Honorary Board member General Solomon Meredith lambasted railroads, fast horses, and cattle premiums at the annual meeting.

"He spoke in strong terms of the disparity between the premiums on horses and those on thoroughbred cattle . . . . [A]gricultural societies in this State of-

fered no inducement to promote the introduction and breeding of thoroughbreds. We were to-day retrograding, and could show less fine cattle in the State than ten years ago.

"He deprecated the system of offering large premiums for fast horses, and encouraging a propensity toward field sports and gambling. He was particularly severe upon the practice of permitting pools to be sold within the Fair Grounds. He also animadverted in strong language upon the grasping spi-rit of the great railroad monopolies which had absorbed our local railroad lines, and now refuse to offer fair terms to persons having stock to ship to State and other Fairs."

In a somewhat milder manner,

former President Hamrick believed that if the iron horse men "were approached in the proper spirit, favorable terms could easily be obtained." Poole agreed.

1880 Punishment was harsh and often lengthy. During the afternoon session on February 17, Board President William Henry Ragan called for leniency for John Marvel. The hapless exhibitor had been banned forever from premium competition in 1874 "on account of some informalities and indiscretion," as well as "conduct unbecoming a gentleman and an exhibitor," in "Corn, Tomatoes and General Collection of Farm Products."

Marvel "had been punished severely, was now penitent, and requested to be again allowed the privilege" of State Fair premium competition. He was forgiven.

1885 Manufacturing transgressions against the state outside the Fair confines concerned Board President Robert Mitchell enough that he warned in January 1885 of "a species of fraud being extensively practiced upon the farmers of our State . . . [with] articles manufactured in the penitentiaries . . . ."

Mitchell wanted them "branded as such." Tennessee especially was "flooding" Indiana with convict-manufactured wagons.

"Now is it right that purchasers should thus be imposed upon? If that wagon was required by law to be branded as penitentiary made, the purchaser who buys it would do so with a full knowledge that it was made by convict labor, and of course [is] an inferior article."

"The law ought also to apply to boots and shoes, stoves, and all other articles made by convict labor. I repeat, brand them as 'penitentiary made.'"

1888 $1.75 in counterfeit money appeared in the Woman's Department.

1897 Board members and delegates joined on January 5 to demand convening legislators to amend the Canada thistle ban to include bull thistle, wild lettuce, teasle, jimson, "and other obnoxious and injurious weeds that are so rapidly spreading over the farms and highways of our State."

1900 On the last day of the Fair, a Mr. Cotton was dismissed "on account of his having been active in causing the arrest of several persons who had paid for privileges for giving shows on the Fair Grounds."

1913 The Board protested to Marion County Commissioners on January 7 against a liquor license transfer to "the saloon known as the Scanlon Place" on 38th Street. Late in June, the Board joined with state Senator Linton Cox in resisting the application made by William Roedocker. Yet a third time, the Board in September approved continued resistance against the application.

 Scanlon Place may have been the roadhouse where Fairgrounds laborers reputedly drank at night.

1914 The services of the police, a justice of the peace, constables, and their meals cost the Board $1,001.80. The next year, city police and detectives cost $858.09, while the duties of a justice of the peace, a prosecuting attorney, and several constables cost $279.50.

1918 President Leonard B. Clore awkwardly thanked "ten to forty-five of the city's best officers and patrolmen, besides a liberal assignment from the Plainclothes Department . . . . [I]t is a pleasant memory, however, that it evidently was a case of the presence of the army foisting features in the face of the Outlaw, if such these were, so that person and property were secure." Soldiers, ready and waiting to ship "over there" encamped on the grounds throughout the Fair.

1921 Widespread rumors of gambling in Fairgrounds buildings led the Executive Committee on April 5 to order first-year Superintendent Forest Neal to put "a stop to all gambling or crap shooting . . . and if need be . . . have the parties participating arrested."

1927 The presence of the devil's drink was suspicioned at the Fair, so in February Board vice president Levi P. Moore recommended hiring a plain-clothes de-

Police officers take a moment to pose with their dates at the Indiana State Fair.

tective to investigate liquor sales and drinking at the Fairgrounds. All employees and horsemen were informed in March that drinking and gambling weren't permitted; the actual hiring of the detective didn't occur until after October 25.

 A man caught stealing a rabbit was barred from exhibiting at the Fair, but forgery really hurt Johnson County Calf Club exhibitor Carlos Canary. Canary showed up Saturday morning after the Fair to claim his $12 premium, only to discover someone else had obtained the statement the night before, forged his name, and made off with the money.

 "It has hurt club work in Johnson County because of different boys being accused," Secretary-Treasurer E.J. Barker asserted. A $12 check was sent to Master Canary in January, and an investigation was dropped.

1929 "Certain practices in the Horse Department" were delicately discussed at great length on January 9, in the afternoon before and following Board elections and reorganization. An Executive and Finance Committee's recommendation asserted that "after careful investigation of certain practices . . . subject to criticism, [we] believe that there have been some irregularities . . . . [T]hese matters [must] be cleared up in such a way that they cannot happen again in any department."

 Executive and Finance Committeemen already had learned that "similar conditions existed previous to this time in more than one department[.]"

 Still, there was no overt insinuation that Board member Roy Graham of

Franklin had awarded premiums to his family. Then the controversy hit the papers. Graham went public, claiming the Board had "vindicated" him. A month later, former President Roscoe Conkling Jenkins made a motion that Graham "was not vindicated . . . ." His motion carried.

 Former president Guy Cantwell suggested Graham resign "for the best interests of the Board." He got his second. At the vote, ten favored the resignation, two opposed it.

 Barker turned to a *Franklin Star* article "with big headlines:" "PERSONAL ENMITY IS BACK OF ATTACK, WAS STATEMENT OF GRAHAM. State Fair Board Member Says Vote of Confidence Followed Charges that personal enmity for him prompted the malicious charges launched against him . . . by R.C. Jenkins and E.J. Barker, and that a vote of confidence was given him . . . ."

 Graham testified in the article that Barker had turned on him after he offered friendly advice on ". . . a certain matter [what it was, no one told] that concerned him very much and made a bitter enemy by so doing."

 Graham, for the record, apparently had opposed Jenkins' bid to regain the Board presidency.

 Graham claimed Barker resented his advice and became his enemy. "I have been guilty of no crooked work as has been charged in the statement given to the newspapers by Jenkins and Barker and I will not resign. I do not intend to allow two vindictive enemies to paint me as a criminal without striking back," Graham said, calling for a full investigation.

Graham had awarded "unearned prizes to his father and brother," Jenkins and Barker charged in the *Indianapolis Star*. "Graham's accusers, led by R.C. Jenkins of Orleans, charged that last year Graham gave [his father and brother] fifteen prizes for horses which never were judged by authorized judges."

According to Barker, $215 in "unauthorized awards" had gone to Graham & Son (Graham's father and brother) in 1927 and $359 in 1928.

"The alleged unearned prizes were discovered accidentally, Mr. Barker said.

"Graham told board members that he had been following a practice established long ago of awarding prizes to classes which were unable to get into the Coliseum for judging. This resulted from lack of time to exhibit all classes properly, he said, and when the exhibition 'ran late,' the classes near the end of each day's exhibits were judged by the board member in charge of the horse exhibition."

Both years, the unfortunate Grahams were last in line, left patiently standing until Roy brought their prizes.

Barker had alerted other Board members of Graham's deeds after his discovery. He threatened immediate resignation if the Board failed to support him for blowing the whistle on his superior. Cantwell, for one, was convinced Barker had acted "in all good faith in giving this material . . . and with only great reluctance." He believed Barker deserved "full exoneration."

Board member S.W. Taylor of Boonville believed Graham's horses' "act . . . nothing compared to this article. This article . . . is a worse charge against the man than the charge of his giving his father and brother the premiums."

"You aren't doing anything but bluffing him," President Edwin D. Logsdon commented, suggesting a motion to ask Graham to refund the money if the others were indeed serious. The Board could get the money back if they thought Graham had stolen it, "or was the cause of someone else to steal it."

Passing resolutions "don't get you any place," Logsdon pointed out. Graham's actions weren't dishonest, Cantwell said. Graham simply let his relatives "pick off this money."

Purdue Dean John Harrison Skinner was embarrassed by the entire escapade. "During the agricultural conference, when we had a large number of people from all over the State, I do not know how many men, but quite a large number, must have been a dozen anyway . . . came and sort of poked fun at me and asked, 'What about the Board of Agriculture?'"

Graham was henceforth kept away from horses and placed in charge of

Parking and Police in 1929-32. He was voted out in '33 on the second ballot.

On Friday of the 1929 Fair, with only one day remaining, Horse Department director J.E. Green of Muncie "was satisfied that there was crookedness and inefficiency" in his department. One judge had admitted he was in over his head.

"One man is not capable and the other admitted he would not give a fair decision," Green said. Green asked for and received the privilege of changing judges that night.

"I am mighty pleased with the

way the fair is operated now," Governor Harry G. Leslie said in November. "One of my great hobbies is that I am not very much in favor of graft. You know that there is no evidence of it out there. That is why I am pleased."

1931
In late July, the Board learned of massive theft. Sixteen tons of manure had been stolen!

"We have sold the manure on the fair grounds to the State Farm," reported Barker, "and last year, we received over $2,500 for it [Ohio Mushroom Company also bought some]. Someone has been stealing it and Mr. [Forest] Neal can tell you about it."

Neal claimed "a Mr. Arthur had contracted with Mr. Treeter to haul the manure and Mr. Schultz had advised the boys who hauled the manure that they could go in the fair grounds and get it and they should pay no attention to the men who were there. The boys hauled the manure to Fort Harrison and loaded it on cars and shipped to a man in Chicago."

From there, the steamy trail had grown cold. Neal said he knew sixteen tons had been taken. "It was agreed to have Mr. Neal and the Secretary to try to collect for the sixteen tons."

1932
In September Barker disclosed he had learned of "questionable practices being carried on," including liquor handling and prostitution. The Board asked to be told about it when such cases occurred.

1933
Boardman and former State Representative Charles Y. Foster of Carmel wasn't someone to mess with, as his gatemen would bear out. Following the '33 Fair, a man named Sam Lyness brought suit against the Board, claiming he had been "abused and beaten" by one of the gatemen.

Foster described the case: "Mr. Lyness with two women came to one of the gates at the street car entrance with a horseman's ticket and tried to get all three through on the one ticket . . . Lyness forced his way in and was caught by Mr. Doan, our gateman, and put out. Mr. Lyness then went around to the east gate and Mr. Doan beat him there and kept him out. I invited Mr. Doan to come eat dinner with me for faithful performance of his duty."

Lyness, through his attorney, claimed he was injured "so that he has been compelled to use a cane since." The Board took no action.

1934 Prohibition was out (the year before), the Depression was on, and draft beer was sold from three stands in 1934; the Grandstand throng drank it bottled. Walter Long of Lebanon picked up the retail beer concession. Sterling Brewery of Evansville, Kamm's of Mishawaka, and Patrick Henry of Marion won the wholesale beer bid.

The Indiana State Police showed up in force in '34, the second year in the force's history. Director of Public Safety Al Feeney traded year round police protection in exchange for a new command base. Troopers stayed in the barracks formerly housing Indiana National Guardsmen. In another security measure, 140 locks were installed throughout the Fairgrounds.

1935 Only Indiana beer was sold at this Fair, and the Board made the vendors pay for the Federal license. No draft beer was sold in the Grandstand.

All that drinking and such riled the womenfolk. Mrs. Letta B. Clift, president, and Mrs. Ross Campbell, secretary, of the Hancock County Women's Christian Temperance Union wrote July 12, protesting "the sale of intoxicating liquors upon the grounds of our State Fair . . . We offer this protest, not only in behalf of exhibitors, who desire the same standards of clean and wholesome social conditions upon the grounds, as they maintain within the fields of their own splendid exhibits, but also, as a protection to the youth, who visit our State Fair."

The following February, Stoney Creek Township residents of Randolph County sent a resolution protesting the sale of beer, "light wines," or intoxicating liquors. "It was taken by consent to place same on file."

1937 Once furtively swigged in the barns, beer now sold openly consumed better judgment in a heavy-handed episode. A reportedly drunken Fairgrounds policeman "took a swipe at [a boy without

a ticket in the Cattle Barn] with his billy, hit the side of his face and ran the boy off the grounds." An investigation discovered the boy was a cattle handler, "had a perfect right to be there," and the owner just hadn't given him his ticket yet. The flatfoot was summarily dismissed.

In another incident, a draft horse exhibitor took off his coat (to which his arena button was attached), stepped away from it to speak with a groom, and when he sought to return, a policeman accosted him. "Due to the action of the policeman," the exhibitor ordered his horses from the ring after the first day of the show. The copper had "threatened to blackjack and

arrest him."

Luckily, Dean Skinner was there to safeguard everyone's morals, if not their skulls. In November he complained about a drawing at the *Indianapolis Star* tent during the past Fair. "It has not only been objectionable by Purdue [which he embodied], but objectionable to members of the Board [none of whom had spoken up]. It should have attention."

1939 Mr. Clack and Mr. Wagner of the Laymen's Civic Legion, a group of self-

appointed guardians of citizenry morals, appeared March 9, after a year of releasing accusations to the press concerning lewd shows at the Midway, Fair-time gambling, and alcohol sales.

Wagner was not there "to make any violent protest or to censure anybody, but merely to call attention to something we felt shouldn't be going on . . . as a part of the program."

While the Board and Indiana "take a great deal of interest in the 4-H Clubs . . . serving as host to a large number of school children . . . some of those [Midway] attractions were not exactly elevating and perhaps would give a decidedly wrong impression to adolescent people. . . . [P]erhaps [Johnny J. Jones Shows] has slipped in a few attractions that might attract a few extra dimes to his coffers."

The Laymen's only interest was "obtaining that high standard" the Board was always talking about, according to Wagner.

Board member/Senator E. Curtis White pointed to "many" resolutions that the Church Federation of Indianapolis had passed "not knowing the situation apparently." One resolution had accused the Board of permitting gambling.

White "happen[ed] to know" Lt. Governor Henry Schricker in '37 or '38 had said "some book makers [were] trying to operate. He sent down orders positively for them to decease. They covered up a little and continued," leading Schricker to threaten bringing in State Police to throw the bookies out.

The bookies had actually approached the Board, asking permission to run their operation. "We absolutely turned it down," White told the two accusers. "Yet, these statements were made apparently without any investigation, and thousands of our Indiana people believe there was gambling out there."

Concerning "suggestive or lewd shows" at the Midway, White claimed that other than one show several years earlier which was closed "immediately," there had been no complaints.

White claimed to have seen shows "ten times worse" at the Indiana

Theater or Lyric Theater "where every school child goes." Promising to work with churchmen, he reminded the Laymen that the Board had sponsored "this 4-H movement."

Schricker then stepped up to the plate: "Now, we remember a time . . . days before Prohibition days, when bootleggers were posted in every barn and on the grounds and were actually selling bootleg liquor. We gathered up whiskey bottles by the load after the Fair was over . . . .

"The last Fairs I had anything to do with," Schricker stated, "I defy any man to say they saw a drunk on the grounds." State Police were under orders to arrest "any man that had any sign of intoxication.

"We did sell beer at the stands. People wanted beer. There was no harm I could see for a man to sit down and eat a sandwich and drink a bottle of beer." Schricker claimed false accusations published early in 1938 "left a very bad taste and certainly was unfair to the Board."

Then Schricker counter-accused: "Your association plastered our Board time and again in the public press here saying we were selling liquor." He charged the churchmen's quest was founded on less than saintly causes. "Certainly it was all done, not to hurt the Fair so much, but to plaster the Governor of Indiana, and to hit him you hit the Board of Agriculture. That is the actual fact of the thing."

Now Schricker focused on the gambling accusations. "We don't allow gambling. The only one we had . . . if you call it that – was the bingo game. We did have that corn game . . . we got $1,000 for that, but it was run on a high order . . .

"We can do away with that bingo game . . . and still have a Fair, but it seems to me they ought to start and do away with it in the churches in Indianapolis before they start on the Fair Ground." The Board did without bingo in '39, although the game had earned $1,500 the year before.

The only other possible form of gambling at the Fair, Schricker said, was "the fellow that guessed your weight."

White urged the church association to use its influence "that you don't allow these reports . . . almost apparently political – to continue, because on this Board it is just evenly divided, eight Democrats and eight Republicans . . . ."

Although Wagner admitted he hadn't visited the Midway in '38, "one of the shows . . . was one of some colored people who were appearing practically nude. Now, what it was, I don't know, or what sort of an act it was, or anything of the sort.

"Anyway," Wagner smugly concluded, "we have accomplished our purpose and perhaps you have."

1940 Mrs. Carter and Mrs. Henman of the Women's Christian Temperance Union complained in June about drunkenness during the Fair.

"I am here to see if we could not keep liquor off the Fairgrounds," Mrs. Carter said. "All over the State they plead with me, farmers and everyone. They said it is an educational place and should not have liquor. It is not just the W.C.T.U. asking for this. In the country they say they do not want it on the Fairgrounds."

She had "especially" seen drunkenness "at a certain place" in the Manufacturers' Building.

"Before we allowed beer to be sold on the Fairgrounds, everyone who came there had a bottle on his hip," E.C. White told the two crusaders. "I believe we have eliminated 95 percent of the drunkenness . . . . [Children] see it everywhere, not just on the Fairgrounds. When you cater to the public, you just cannot go contrary to their wishes. If our children saw it only on the Fairgrounds, it would be different."

"Naturally . . . it's better . . . and you're getting Extra Goodness!" – Hoff-Brau ale and beer was sold exclusively at the 1940 Fair. Another vice found at that Fair: "Three in a Row" Reno and basketball north of the Women's Building. Cliff Thomas of the Riverside Amusement Park operated the concession.

1946 Before the Fair, Secretary-Manager Orval C. Pratt reported "many demands" to sell whiskey for one night in the Manufacturers' Building as opposed to "bootlegging it in." Board consent ruled out whiskey altogether.

Boardwoman Karolyn Holloway asked, "Aren't you going to have fewer beer permits since the law [not] to sell intoxicating beverages to minors is in effect?"

Former President Ulysses C. Brouse, "thinking about our coming generation," was against beer at the Fairgrounds.

The following day, Director Francis M. Overstreet observed, "in the past, anyone who wanted beer paid for their space and paid their license fee and a little additional. We had twenty-seven."

"Off hand it seems like twenty would be enough," Lieutenant Governor Richard T. James observed.

"What are we going to do about this law that prohibits minors?" Board man Charles R. Morris asked. He suggested putting up "No Minors" signs. A firm decision, if reached, was not recorded.

Area youth vandalizing the Fairgrounds were "the meanest I ever saw," Secretary Pratt reported on October 24. Even with State Police cooperation, the kids were breaking windows and jimmying locks.

1948 "Frankly," draft horse breeder Charles J. Lynn said in January, "we would not like to have the saddle horse group in with us."

Twice the year before, he claimed, "at midnight, the police had to be called on to stop disturbances, as some of the stalls had been converted into drinking parlors. We do not like to mix our boys in with this type of caretakers."

Lynn, vice president at Eli Lilly, called them "drunken orgies" occurring on the Fair's first two nights in a complaint letter to Boardman Roger Wolcott.

"There are some who think the day of the draft horse is through, but this is not true. When cheap farm prices return, I believe that we will see a lot of people go back to draft horses as a cheap means of farm power."

A member of Indiana Draft Horse & Mule Breeder Association, Lynn bred prize Berkshire hogs, Polled Shorthorn cattle, and Percheron draft horses at his Lynnwood Farm in Carmel.

1954 Frank A. White's column "The Hoosier Day" in the July 28 *Greensburg News* and *Lebanon Reporter* reported, "The Indiana State Fair Board has torn down the brick, steel and concrete redoubt on the grounds that served as a post for Indiana State Police.

"This stronghold was erected in the hectic days of John Dillinger, notorious bank bandit. Al G. Feeney, then Indiana State Police superintendent [1933-35], was the guiding light of this 'model state police fortification' and discussed its features in detail often with this reporter.

"Feeney, later mayor of Indianapolis, feared the bandit gangs, such as that of Dillinger, or Brady, might some night seize a state police post, use the radio, and issue false orders. Upon his insistence, and with contributions from business concerns to supplement state appropriations, he built the fairgrounds post until it would have withstood a siege of trench mortars and aerial bombing."

Stangely, no one remembers it.

State Fair security officers deliver change for 1954 ticket takers.

(Counterclockwise from upper left) Franklin Delano Roosevelt; Lum and Abner; Lula Belle; Captain Kangaroo; Johnny Cash; (l-r) Dick Lugar, Bob Hope, and Governor Whitcomb

(Counterclockwise from upper left) 1959 State Fair Queen Carol Parks of Crawfordsville and her court; Rosemary Clooney; Tennessee Ernie Ford; Nat King Cole; Morris the Cat; Sandi Patti; Jimmy Durante; Red Skelton; Pat Boone

(Counterclockwise from upper left) Dale Evans and Roy Rogers; (l-r) Donna Douglas, Max Baer Jr., 1963 State Fair Queen Sharon Lou Schregg of Rensselaer, and Irene Ryan; Tom Jones; the Oak Ridge Boys; Lyle Waggoner; Anita Bryant; Jim Nabors; (l-r) Dan Blocker and Lorne Greene; Lawrence Welk; Bob Horton

◆ 188 ◆

(Counterclockwise from upper left) Sonny Bono; the Fifth Dimension; William Shatner; Earl Butz; Kenny Rogers and Dottie West; John Denver; Reba McEntire; Otis Bowen; David Cassidy

◆ 189 ◆

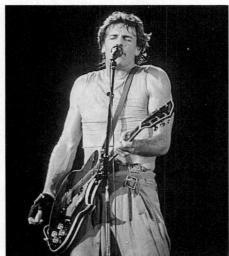

(Clockwise from upper left) The Jacksons with 1973 State Fair Queen Elizabeth Ann Buening of Huntingburg; Governor Orr and his dog; Hank Williams Jr.; Neil Young; Mark Patrick and future sweater; John Mellencamp (inset); Dolly Parton; Willie Nelson; Bruce Springsteen

The Sport of Kings

IN 1852, Copperbottom, a roan gelding, "one of the western country's best pacers," made it to the speed ring at the first Indiana State Fair. The race track was a mere furlong in circumference. No premiums were awarded for speed alone.

Barring rain-outs, harness horses have trotted or paced in half-mile or mile races at every State Fair since then.

1856 Twenty dollars were offered for the fastest trotting horse, but the State Board "prudently required that not more than four minutes should be consumed in trotting a mile."

1859 A delegate's resolution in January called for a report "in regard to the expediency of abolishing racing at our State Fairs." A compromise that kept the races also forbade purses of any size: "[T]he encouragement in raising and training gaited horses, viz: pacing, racking and trotting – by offering liberal premiums at our State Fairs is not only right and in accordance with the spirit of the law . . . but should be continued by the State Board.

"At the same time the awarding of premiums to the man whose horse can make his mile in less than four minutes, the time settling the question as to premiums, is not only impolitic, immoral and unwise, but it is against the best interests of the whole agricultural interest of the

State, and . . . [we] recommend that the State Board abolish all premiums on horses for speed."

1860 In January the Board resolved "that it is improper to award premiums to horses for speed alone, without taking into consideration other qualities. [It has never been the custom of the State Board of Agriculture to favor speed in horses over other qualities. That is to say, speed alone has never been the test]" (brackets in the original).

"Speed" soon described the department in charge of horse racing. For a century, until the Sixties, horse racing was managed by the "Speed" director.

1866 In the first Fair back at Camp Morton, harness horses raced on a new track for $20 gold purses offered to each divisional winner.

1869 In January, a heated debate over fast horses, gambling, and the advisability of offering premiums for speed alone took several days to resolve until Boardmen finally decided that "it would not be wise to abolish these [trotting and pacing] rings altogether."

They also decided that it was up to the Board to set racing rules "as will exclude from the management of such rings all persons not known to the Board

A packed Grandstand throng cheers while jockeys guide their steeds in a running race sometime before the horseless carriage era.

as reliable citizens of Indiana or sister States."

Trotting and pacing horses were judged "with reference to form, size, style, speed, action and endurance." The best time, 2:25, earned Rushville's James Wilson $100 for his pacer. The fastest trotter, owned by Payne & Powell of Henderson, Kentucky, turned in a 2:38 time, a second faster than the $100 first premium recipient, Isaac B. Loder of Rushville. Loder's double trotting team entry took the $50 first premium.

1871 Two new pacing and trotting speed classes were established on the last morning of the Fair. The fastest pacer, with no better than a 2:50 time "in public," and the fastest trotter, who had never beaten three minutes, raced for $75 first premiums, $50 second premiums, and $25 third premiums.

Race provisions required entry fees based on ten percent of premiums offered, with seven-horse minimums in each class. Indianapolis entries dominated the pacers: J.T. Berry's horse won, James Hackney's took second, H.C. Campbell's came in third. In the trotting class, Louisville's George Dorsey took first,

A "Hot-Foot Row" racehorse stable scene from September 1912. Millard Sanders' Barn A is in the foreground.

In 1960, Speed Department Director Ed McNamara honored driver/breeder Walter McCord with a gold lifetime pass to State Fair races. McCord's horse Walter McKlyo was the first horse to win a race on the Track of Champions.

followed by W.T. Ball of Middletown and August Clinton of Raleigh.

The "Roaring Grand" Circuit was born that year when track representatives met in Cleveland with Colonel William Edwards. Competition officially began in 1873.

1872 "Soon after dinner time the amphitheater, and the space on each side of the track . . . was packed by a dense throng of people, on foot and in carriages, drawn thither . . . by the report that some fast horses on the Trotting Park Course would be entered. [T]he first . . . was the pacing race . . . five started, but all interest was centered in 'Copper Bottom,' who won the $800 pacing purse at the lower course in the morning, and 'Hoosier Tom,' an entry for the same purse." Copper Bottom won the first and third heats; Hoosier Tom took the second. "Copper's best time was 2:21, the fastest ever made on that track."

A bay trotter, "driven by John [W.] Browning, and said to be owned by a Mr. Nesbit, took two straight heats, his best in 2:27. As in the other race, the interest centered around two horses, the one mentioned and the gray horse 'Unknown.' The latter gave John a hard tussle for the first place, but the little bay stepped away from him nicely, never making a break in the race," winning $150. Browning, from Indianapolis, claimed $300 in the eighty-two entry Horse Sweepstakes with the best trotting gelding, taking three straight heats "by neck only" in 2:47, 2:45, and 2:46.

A "very interesting" double team race saw winning heats of 2:55 and 3:03; the winners belonged to Glydden (alternately spelled Gliddon and Glidden) & Williams of Raleigh. The Raleigh men's trotting stallion won two heats, in 2:44 and 2:45, to take $100.

The pacing stallion race was "a very close and interesting affair, between T. Dickerson's horse, from Versailles, and John Edwards' from Monrovia, who kept almost side by side during the two heats, but Dickerson's animal [winning $100] managed to come in, about a neck ahead, both times, in 2:37 and 2:38 . . .[T]hree other horses. . . came in just after every one forgot that more than two were engaged."

1875 Race fans on Wednesday and Thursday of the Exposition's second week were favored with a $3,500 "Free for All Trot" and an $800 running race. Third week races offered a four-trot card, with a $1,500-purse "free for all." National rules governed the events.

1876 In the "Fast Ring," Monarch Jr. won the $120 trotting stallion three-minute race, turning in a 2:51 mile time for owner W.J. Walworth of Kokomo. The 2:30 open pacing victory, worth another $120, went to Bay Sally for bringing Laurel's J.A. Gosnell the 2:24-1/2 win. Captain Stone, owned by Daniel Burge of Cincinnati, won the race open to all trotters "that have never beaten 2:40" with a 2:37-1/2 time.

1878 Somehow, entry fees weren't paid for the 2:35 Free-for-All Trot, and the Board called off the $350 purse race. James S. Wade, Edinburgh, and Rushville's J.P. Fairley, however, put up 20 percent of the fee and released the Board from a third-place payment, so that their horses Roger Hanson and Hero might race. Wade's Hero took the $200 first prize; Fairley's Roger Hanson claimed the $100 second prize.

Roger Hanson also came in second in the 2:40 trotters class, taking $45

Fans crowd both sides of the Fairgrounds' mile track at the end of a harness race sometime during the early 'teens. The automobiles have steering wheels on the righthand side. A penciled caption on the reverse, "View of track and paddock . . . where Grand Circuit stars will meet," leads the historian to surmise it's 1911, when the Roaring Grand came to Indianapolis.

A placard on the judges' stand proclaims Minor Heir's 1:58-1/2 world record time, set in 1910. The banner strung on the scaffolding at the left insists "Dare Devil Schreyer," scheduled for a 4 p.m. dive, was the "most sensational and highest paid performer on earth."

behind the $90 prize-winning Lady McD, owned by M.A. McDonald. In the 2:30 or less open pace, Horace Greeley, owned by Seymour's Asa Woodmansee, won the $75 first-place prize. Bay Sallie took the $35 second for James Wilson of Rushville. Lum Nave, Covington, took a $15 third place with Little Ed.

1880 Owners of the four pacers known as the "Big Four" were offered $500 for a September 29 exhibition. The "Big Four" were Sleepy Tom, Mattie Hunter, Rowdy Boy, and Lucy, who first put pacers "on the map and [who] made themselves for several seasons the biggest drawing cards on the Grand Circuit," according to *The*

American Trotter (John Hervey; Coward McCann Inc., 1947).

But the Big Four didn't appear at the Fair. Instead Mr. Loftus and Mr. Chancy brought a double horseback standing race each day for $150. One pacing race offered a $25 purse.

1881
General Superintendent Fielding Beeler had discovered in the past year "a great desire among the horsemen who patronize our track to have some improvements and changes made . . . I leased the dwelling and track to Mr. Webster Beymer for $150 for the year, he to make the proposed improvements at his expense, and I to pay engineering expense."

Beeler explained that Beymer "coated the track with manure, plowed the same under and placed the track in first-class condition, and so far as I have learned the horsemen have been well pleased. A prominent one has assured me that it is not excelled, in some respects equaled, by any half mile track in the West."

1882
Speed Department premiums paid $1,805 for running, pacing, and trotting races. "Some of the trotting and pacing was very good," Superintendent William A. Banks wrote, "but not what it should be, and I am sorry . . . that nearly every race had to be made up on the day of the race, and not filled according to rule . . . [S]ome plan should be adopted to prevent the necessity of sham races."

The top purse for speed, $200, went to Mr. Maxwell with Lady Elgin in the Free-for-All Trot. Billy G, belonging to George Grimes of Rockville, won $75 in the 2:35 pace. W. Fields of Washington, Illinois, brought Judge Samuel to win $100 in the Three-Minute Trot. Buck Dickerson of Greensburg won $80 with Jim Ervin in the 2:37 trot race. S.J. St. Clair of Indianapolis won $120 with Radclift in the four-year-old and over Running Race.

The Free-for-All Pace victory and $160 went to T.J. Dewey's Charlie H. Connersville's W.A. Hanson took $125 with Lady Elgin in the 2:30 Trot. The consolation race paid only $40 to winner S.J. St. Clair with his horse, Leaveridge. Ben Davis, Indianapolis, brought horses which took third in the Free-for-All Pace and second in the 2:30 Trot.

1886
Olla Podrida's March 20 "About Town" column in *Western Sportsman and Live Stock News* gossiped, "as usual about this time of the year there is a great deal of talk in regard to putting the tracks in shape. When it comes to talk, this city [Indianapolis] can lead them all . . . in regards to a mile track, 'nothing but talk.'

"There are enough owners of good horses in this city to form a Gentlemen's Driving club," Podrida wrote. "[T]here are men who keep their horses for recreation that could put the fair grounds track in very good order and find a much better place to speed their horses than on our bad streets.

"[Fairgrounds superintendent] Mr. H. Stout has leased the Exposition track to W.H. Pritchard and he will at once put the track in first class order. Horsemen that are thinking of sending their stock to other tracks should call on him before doing so."

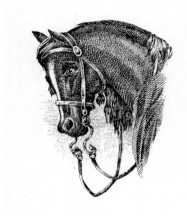

Incorporated and published in Indianapolis beginning in 1877, *The Western Horseman and Live Stock News* is the oldest and largest turf publication devoted to the trotting and pacing horse. The magazine changed its name in 1891 to *The Western Horseman*, again in 1917 to *Horseman*, and to *The Horseman and Fair World* in 1926. The publication moved to Lexington in 1955.

1888
Although Indianapolis Mayor Caleb S. Denny congratulated the Board on their purchase of twenty more acres, he doubted "the wisdom."

"[I] had hoped to see you sell your old grounds, if possible, and buy new ones near the line of the Belt Railroad, as I briefly expressed myself last year." He supposed the new acreage was part of a plan to build a mile race-course.

"[W]e all know that (horse racing) has become so indissolubly connected with the other features of these annual exhibitions that it is folly to talk about divorcing the two. The people would not tolerate it."

Denny was "advised" that the grounds' half-mile track would be abandoned "and another of the same circumference built further north," if the Board indeed planned to stay there permanently.

He cautioned the Delegate assembly to think twice before spending their money at Camp Morton. To his thinking, the Board could sell both parcels of property "for a handsome profit." Denny wanted the Board out of town.

"Indeed, I suppose the fifty-six acres, after removing all the material on and around it, could readily be sold for more than enough to buy seventy or eighty acres near the Belt Railroad and fit it up for fair purposes, including a mile track. I fear," Denny advised, "the best sites were not examined by your committee a year ago." A site further north would do well.

Without that critical mile track, "you can not induce the owners of fast horses of the country to come here," Indianapolis' top citizen counseled. "With one, you can, and thereby almost double your receipts." Not only would more trotting association revenues fill Board coffers, but Indianapolis would benefit as well.

"[A]nother effort ought to be made to secure a new location, where stock will not have to be driven or hauled two miles by exhibitors, and where the greatest attraction . . . can be provided by giving exhibitions of speed on a mile track."

The Mayor just didn't want cattle herded through the best part of town.

1892
"Indianapolis will become one of the greatest trotting and pacing horse centers in the country," *Western Horseman* predicted on January 1 in heralding the move of the Fairgrounds to its current location, then known as Voss Farm.

Already, "it is understood that some individual or association will lease the track, and at least two big race meetings will be given annually."

It was "pretty well understood" that John S. Lackey, "the world renowned combination sale conductor, of Cambridge City, Ind., will transfer his base of operations here, and already rumors of new stock farms to be started, or brought here, are numerous. . . . No point that has been so long neglected, furnishes one-half the facilities for the trotting and pacing horse business, as does the vicinity of Indianapolis."

Horseman subscriber C.W. Claybourne, laid up with the grippe, nevertheless felt well enough in January 15's edition to advocate building "the record-making track for the United States . . . Indianapolis can be made the banner horse city for harness horses in the United States. Geographically speaking, we are in the center of our great nation."

That month, outgoing Speed Department Superintendent Evan H. Peed reported that Fort Wayne and Cambridge City convened race meetings the same week as 1891's Fair, "giving much larger purses and having good mile tracks."

The Voss Farm purchase forever ended that hindrance. January hadn't ended before new Speed Department Superintendent Hiriam B. Howland remarked, "We will have a track that shall be a credit to the new order of things, and it must be the best in the world."

Horsemen wasted no time in scheduling races. The Indiana Horse-Breeders' Association scheduled its annual meeting August 30-September 2, "over the new Mile Track." It hadn't even been built yet.

Bates House guaranteed a $300 yearling trot stake; *Western Horseman* offered a $400 purse for 2:40 pacers; Liveryman's $500 Guaranteed Stake drew four-year-old trotters eligible to the 2:30 class; the $500 Grand Hotel Guaranteed Purse was for 2:25 pacers.

In the May 13 edition of *Western Horseman*, an unnamed correspondent from Independence, Iowa, knew ". . . the national game of baseball is well patronized in the large cities, but by a class of people now the votaries of such gambling contrivances as the pool box.

"Why should not a race track in . . . Indianapolis . . . receive as large a patronage? Because at the present time the English method of racing to saddle at the uncivilized gait of the runaway horse has a first mortgage upon all cities of upwards of 100,000 population . . . .

"Indianapolis may become a leading turf center of civilized speed, but . . . different methods must be pursued than those which now prevail at the race tracks. If . . . the *Indianapolis Sentinel* and the *Journal* could be induced to favor the

turf upon which the people's race horse the sulky-carriage [performs] . . . in preference [to] the turf of the gamblers' race horse, the runner, the people of Indianapolis may have an opportunity of witnessing as many racing contests of legitimate speed as now take place in the smaller cities."

Horsemen in 1892 called the new regulation mile track reaching into the north woods "second to none." Completed on July 19, the "Track of Champions" required 17,000 yards of soil hauled twenty-five miles. Within twenty-four hours, the track hosted its first speed trial – Silvertail, "driven by a lady, went the fastest mile of his life – 2:07 – and would have gone at least two seconds faster but

for a break," reported Speed Department Superintendent Howland.

An ad in *Western Horseman* on September 16 shouted: "The Indiana State Fair! The Banner Meeting . . . With the Choicest Lot of Horses that ever answered the Starters' Bell in Indiana . . . see some of the Records Smashed Over the Newest and Fastest Track in the Union."

September 23's *Western Horseman* agreed everything on September 20 was "in perfect order and nothing could be added that would improve the track, except that it was a little soft at the surface. The need of a drenching rain was apparent and the track would be superior to any in the State." Walter McKlyo was the first horse to win a race on the mile track; in 1960, driver/breeder Walter McCord was honored with a gold lifetime pass to races at the Fair.

Western Horseman's September 30 edition reported "a good speed program was on the card for the afternoon [the 23rd], and the vast audience enjoyed it as only lovers of America's greatest sport."

In the three-year-old trot, "ten youngsters came out for the heat and four horses were drawn. Nellie S. took first position at the turn and was not bothered during the heat. Merry Maid wanted second place and fought hard for it, but was unsuccessful."

There were six heats that day; Ethel B. was the eventual victor, winning the last three heats.

". . . Billy Boice was thrown out of a 'bike' by Ayers rearing up with him just before the 2:37 trot. He was not hurt much . . . Alabama, the chestnut daughter of McCurdy's Hambletonian, is one of the safest of her class, she makes no mistakes and never fails when called upon to increase her speed. She is a born trotter or George G. Fuller is a master reinsman. The writer thinks both figure to some extent."

1893 The Indianapolis Driving Club was allowed to use the Fairgrounds during the first week of September for its fall speed meeting. In November, a Board committee met with the club to "adjust differences existing as to claims for rents due to the Driving Club [which apparently sub-let its contract] for use of the track by the foot-ball teams of the Indiana universities."

1895 The Track of Champions claimed its first world record during eleven Speed races when Robert J., a gelding driven by E.F. "Pop" Geers, paced a mile in 2:02-1/2. The record was short-lived, however, since Geers took Robert J. south to Terre Haute two weeks later and shaved off another second.

In the best three of five 2:13 Trot Special, $2,005 went to Rensselaer Wilkes, a bay horse, for three winning heats of 2:11-1/2, 2:15-1/4 and 2:15-1/4.

1896 The Grand Circuit made its first Indiana appearance, stopping in Indianapolis and Fort Wayne. The September 14-19 Fair offered a $4,000 purse; on closing day all Speed races were called off "on account of rain." Although the series returned to Fort Wayne in 1897 and 1898, it didn't visit Indianapolis again until 1911, and then not again until 1926.

1897 Two days before the Fair, 1,200 one-dollar reserved Grandstand seats were set aside for enthusiasts to cheer Joe Patchen and Star Pointer on Friday and Saturday. The three-heat race between the "mighty and invincible" Star Pointer and "the equally great and much admired" Joe Patchen was billed as "The Battle of the Kings."

The track gained a world's record and "a plethoric purse" of $3,000. The heat times were 2:04-3/4, 2:03, then 2:01 in the third heat raced on Saturday. Star Pointer won the first and third heats.

Great as he was, Joe Patchen's greatest contribution to the sport was his son Dan Patch, undisputedly the greatest horse of the dawning days of the twentieth century.

The Speed Department recorded 331 entries, "and it is an incontrovertible fact, a matter of history now, that we had the greatest list of entries, numbers and quality considered, ever gotten together at any race meeting." Twelve races paid $7,400 in total purses.

"Two in Three" races were conducted, with no race longer than four heats. In case of a tie, the judges settled "on the summary."

Monte Cristo, a bay gelding, earned $250 for taking a second in the 2:30 trot's first heat, then two first places. His top time was 2:22-1/4. The best time came in the Free-for-All Pace with Lotta Loraine, a bay mare, pacing the mile in 2:09 and 2:09-1/4 heats.

"The conditions were most unfavorable for the trial," Speed Department Superintendent Marc S. Claypool reported. "The fields of starters were large, and at no time were we able to use the entire track, on account of rain, so that we are unable to judge fairly of the merits of shorter races." He suggested "Three in Five" races for the next Fair, with no more than five heats.

1898 President Charles B. Harris wanted a half-mile track built around the Speed Barns. "Such a track will cost nothing to keep up and will save working the mile track until September 1 of each year."

"Continuous" and "incessant" rain prevented any Speed contests, which was tragic, since entries came from "many of the best stables" and were the "best horses now on the trotting and pacing courses."

1899 The fastest time, 2:06, came in the first heat of the $800 Free-for-All Pace. Indiana, a black gelding, led all three heats.

1902 Late in April, the Board considered whether to build a half-mile race and training track inside the mile track, but deferred any decision until after the "State Militia" held its May 12-19 encampment. The new track contract was approved on June 2.

During the Fair, the best time, 2:06, came in the third heat of the 2:08 Pace. The Bishop, a black gelding, won all three heats, claiming $450.

Coast Marie, a black filly pacer, won the last three heats of the $1,000 Kentucky Stock Farm Expectation Purse; her best time, 2:20, came in the third heat. In the $5,000-purse trotting division, the best time, 2:14-1/2, came in the second heat, honors going to the black colt Pat Henry.

1903 A whopping $1,000 was appropriated for the Western Horseman State (sic) Race. The Board opened the stakes for two- and three-year-old trotting and pacing colts bred in Indiana. They also set up 2:13 and 2:24 trots, and 2:08 and 2:20 pace stakes, each offering a $1,500 purse.

The Indianapolis Racing Association contracted for two race meetings

The northside race horse barns were found just beyond the track's northwest side. The Indiana School for the Deaf insisted that the Board tear them down in 1905.

annually of four to six days each, with a five-year option. No "lewd, immoral or illegal acts" were allowed. Although the association had exclusive rights, a provision allowed the Retail Grocers' Association races and one-day picnics.

A fence was built to line the half-mile track that spring, and lofts were constructed in five of the horse stables south of the main track.

Rain beginning on the second day canceled four days of mile track races. However, "to entertain the people," four races were arranged on the half-mile track. Each offering a $400 purse, the races were set up for 2:12, 2:20, and 2:25 trotters, with a 2:17 pacer class. The best times came in the three pace heats: 2:16, 2:15-1/4, and 2:14-1/4. Black Pet, a black mare, won all three.

1904 "The half-mile track has fully demonstrated its value, and it will have still greater worth if the Board will place it in such condition that it can be used as a wet weather track," President John L. Thompson advised.

◆◆◆

The Great Dan Patch

ON A CHILLY and rainy day in 1905, a crowd of 30,000 gathered just to see whether the legendary horse Dan Patch would set the Fair's first two-minute mile on a rain-soaked track. An estimated 5,000 had camped overnight on the track, and police threatened to call the entire thing off.

Although Dan Patch set a new track record of 2:00-1/2, the first athlete to endorse a product still failed to break the two-minute barrier.

Five years into his career, Dan Patch already endorsed an entire society's products: Dan Patch cigars and chewing tobacco; Dan Patch sleds; Dan Patch washing machines; a coaster wagon, a hobby horse, scarves, pillows, sweaters; there was even a dance called the Dan Patch two-step. Thousands of "genuine" Dan Patch horseshoes were sold. Fans visited him outside Minneapolis on the Dan Patch Railroad, some seeking to pluck hairs from his tail.

Foaled in 1896, the famed mahogany bay pacer was barely into his Grand Circuit career when everyone called him unbeatable; no one would bet against him. From then on, Dan Patch raced in speed exhibitions against time.

Dan Patch was an accident, of sorts. *Esquire* claimed that Oxford storekeeper Dan Messner winked at an 1894 sale and found himself owner of a broken down nag named Zelica. Over in Illinois, former world record holder Joe Patchen was standing stud. Zelica had a decent pedigree.

For $150, come March 1896, Zelica foaled a friendly colt Messner named after himself and the sire. Messner didn't think Dan Patch had a chance of winning on a race track when he turned him over to Johnny Wattles for training.

One of the trademarks of Dan Patch was his crooked left hock. Wattles discovered this while training the horse. When the spokes were kicked from the

Driver H.C. Hersey and Dan Patch. The "king of his kind," Dan Patch never lost a race during his career; other horsemen refused to race against him, forcing the famed pacer to race against time.

left wheels of two sulkies in a row, Wattles realized the crooked hock made Dan Patch throw wide in full stride. From then on, the horse pulled sulkies with axles lengthened eight inches.

Dan Patch was four years old before his first race, and then it was a mere 2:35 match against two local horses at Boswell and witnessed by neighbors. Dan Patch won.

People started noticing the invincible pacer at Indiana county fair tracks that year. The next spring in Lafayette, Dan Patch was boxed in and lost the first heat in a race favoring Milo S. But "The Patch" won the second in 2:16, then won the third and fourth heats as well. In his career, Dan Patch lost only one other heat and never lost a race.

Not long afterward, C.F. Sturgis of Buffalo, New York, paid Messner $20,000, and Dan Patch went on the Grand Circuit. By late 1902, he won eighteen races. On April 29, 1902, Dan Patch became the second horse to pace a mile under two minutes at 1:59-1/2. Star Pointer held the record, with 1:59-1/4, set in 1897.

By now, no one would race against Dan Patch. Past Board President Marc S. Claypool boasted in 1902 how Indiana's "horse interests . . . have for many years played a prominent part throughout the racing world . . . It is for Indiana's glory to produce the only, the unbeaten, the unconquered, the king of his kind, 'Dan Patch.'"

In December 1902, Marion Willis Savage of Minneapolis, International Stock Food Company tycoon, purchased Dan Patch for $60,000 and set about promoting his feed. "It was a brand-new advertising technique," Roscoe Macy wrote in February 1947's *Esquire*.

Dan Patch trained on the only indoor half-mile track in the world, according to USTA's *Hoof Beats* magazine. Steam-heated, electrically lit, Savage's 130-box stall stable had 1,400 windows. During his exhibition years, Dan Patch and his four white-clad grooms traveled in a private white railcar.

In 1905, the same year "The Patch" failed to pace a mile under two minutes in Indianapolis, he did it at Lexington, in 1:55-1/4. Racing officials refused to recognize Dan Patch's fastest time, in an exhibition behind a dirt shield, when a 1906 Minnesota State Fair crowd estimated at 93,000 watched him pace a mile in 1:55. Fifty years elapsed before the time was bested, according to *Hoof Beats*.

Seventy-three Dan Patch miles averaged a time of 1:59-1/2; fourteen averaged 1:56-1/2.

He came up lame after a Los Angeles exhibition mile in 1909, and Savage retired him to stud. Undefeated and the holder of nine world's records, on July 11, 1916, Dan Patch died from a heart condition, following a reported overfeeding. Told of the death while hospitalized for minor surgery, Savage himself died a day later.

◆◆◆

1907 The Board had sought "for years" to attract trainers "for the entire season," but inadequate year-round boarding accommodations deterred this effort. By January 1907, the grounds residence had been converted into a hotel for horsemen. Managed correctly, in President H.L. Nowlin's opinion, the hotel could be "first class."

When the Fair failed to attract the Grand Circuit, *Horseman Magazine* sponsored futurities for three-year-old trotters and pacers — known then as the Western Horseman Stake — offering a $2,100 purse. Today, both Horseman Futurities are the oldest continuously raced events of their kind in the nation.

Bettie Brent, a black filly owned by H.M. Stambaugh of Youngstown, Ohio, won both Horseman pace heats, the first in 2:17, the second in 2:12-1/4. Four days later in the $4,100 trot, Kentucky Todd, a black colt owned by Cruickston Park Farm in Galt, Ontario, won the first heat in 2:10-1/2, and the second in 2:09.

The best time was recorded in the first heat of the $2,000 purse 2:11 Stake Pace — Laura Bellini, a brown mare owned by A. McDonald of Boston, paced the mile in 2:05-1/2.

1909 For a special attraction, the Board approved a race between Dan Patch and Minor Heir, "the two great pacing stallions . . . provided that any reasonable arrangement can be made . . . ."

1910 M.W. Savage brought Lady Maud C., Hedgewood Boy, George Gano, and Minor Heir, his "aggregation of great pacers," for exhibition.

Minor Heir finally broke the track's two-minute barrier that year. The eight-year-old pacer handled the mile in a 1:59 time trial, then racing against time four days later knocked off another half-second. The track record stood for twenty-eight years.

Indiana State Fair Grounds

Dan Patch drinking out of a cement tank built of Universal Portland Cement.

1918

Five running races on the mile track, including the "Indiana Derby," greeted Opening Day visitors. *The Hub of the Universe* claimed, "it has often been said that there was no such thing possible as combining in one race meeting running and harness contests . . . (but) the Indiana State Fair has two tracks, both of which are always in prime condition."

A derby represented "the highest type of racing and the crowning event of any race meeting no matter in what country it is held," according to *The Hub*. After those races, each afternoon the half-mile track hosted three running events, "each one a contest for a reward of real value."

Both Horseman Futurities moved four meets to Columbus, Ohio, and then four to Syracuse, New York. One industry expert speculates the move was precipitated by horseman dissatisfaction about Indianapolis track conditions or accommodations, or possibly because the Grand Circuit, which convened each January, shuttled some races from track to track depending upon financial inducement.

1920

Single G, the "sensational Hoosier pacer" with a 1:59-1/2 record, wintered in the Allen Brothers' stable. Ed Allen drove and trained the horse.

Allen brought Single G to the Fairgrounds from Iowa in 1918. The champion raced through its twenty-sixth year, clinching 262 heat victories in 436 starts, an historic record which still stands. Born on April 4, 1910, in Centerville, Single G died on December 6, 1940.

Pacing horse breeder Frank P. Fox grew tired of his yearlings selling at lower prices than trotters, so in 1927 he sponsored the Fox Stake for two-year-old pacers; it became the most prestigious race of its kind.

The Fair saw three great Single G races. The one in 1918, a match race where two-minute star William lost on a "slightly off" track, attracted three train-loads of Cambridge City residents, practically the entire town. Single G was timed at 2:01-1/2, 2:03-1/4, and 2:01-3/4. He lost a race the next year in a split-heat decision to Miss Harris M.

1922

"Pop" Geers, "one of the most celebrated reinsmen in the history of American turf," visited the Fair. Geers drove the eight-year-old bay pacer Sanardo to a 1:59-1/2 record in a September 5 time trial.

Through Indianapolis business guarantees, the Speed Department program gained new $2,000 and $3,000 stake purses for the trotters and the pacers; entries totalled about 140 "of the best horses of the country."

Stake guarantors included the Indianapolis Chamber of Commerce, 2:09 trot, $3,000; the English Hotel, 2:05 pace, $3,000; L.S. Ayres & Co., 2:18 trot, $2,000; the Severin Hotel, 2:11 pace, $2,000; Schloss Brothers Clothiers, 2:12 trot, $2,000; and E.J. Robinson, free-for-all pace, $2,000.

1925

The Horseman Futurities, the races attracting "the best three-year-old trotters and pacers in the world," were purchased in January for $2,000. Back for the first time since 1917, in the trotting division alone, there were "six or eight of the best starters in the world."

The Board joined the Grand Circuit later that year; they still belonged to American Trotting Association.

Grandstand crowds cheered the 2:04 Pluto Water Trot Stake and the L.S. Ayres $5,000 2:10 Trot Stake.

The Governor Stake, a 2:18 trot, offered a $1,000 purse. Silver Flash Gas sponsored a $5,000 pace; Marott Shoe Company put up $1,000 for three-year-old pacers. Schloss Brothers Clothiers, Stegemeier Cafeteria, and the Severin Hotel sponsored other races. After the Fair, advertising touted the track's training merits.

1926

In January, Will Gahagan of *Horseman & Fair World* told the Board Frank Fox would back "a two-year-old pacing stake in the early closing events in the amount of $1,000." This event became known the world over as the Fox Stake.

Fairgrounds horsemen announced on March 25 that the body of Peter the Great would be disinterred at Laurel Hall Farm, and they wanted it buried at the Fairgrounds, where they would erect a $2,000-$3,000 monument. The issue was referred to the full Board and never mentioned again for twenty-four years.

◆◆◆

"**I** HAVE sponsored what they call 'Fox Two-Year-Old Pacing Stake,'" pacing horse breeder Frank P. Fox told the Board in January 1927. "It looks like the stake will be worth $10,000 to $13,000.

"This stake will sell for $2,000. There are eighty-nine entries paid up now. There probably will be fifteen go[ing] to the post. The guarantee is a purse of $5,000 but it will probably be from $10,000 to $13,000."

By several accounts, Fox, an oil-man, farmer, and former race driver minus part of a leg, had grown tired of seeing his pacer yearlings sell at lower prices than trotters. So, he offered his own race.

The Board, never suspecting what the future held for this "Fox Stake," took the matter "under advisement" and then accepted it at Fox's asking price. The first purse, $14,887.63, was the richest ever for two-year-old pacers.

Red Pluto, housed in Septimus F. "Sep" Palin's Fairgrounds training stable, won the first heat of the inaugural

---

The Grandstand crowd on its feet in this close Fox Stake finish from 1963. Ralph Baldwin drove Race Time to the victory, claiming the silver punch bowl seen in the foreground.

race, breaking the world's record for two-year-olds – perfect for the Fair's Diamond Jubilee celebration. Red Pluto already had set a trial record of 2:05-3/4, becoming the fastest two-year-old pacer in history.

The son of Peter Pluto, Red Pluto won in 2:06, never once yielding the lead. The second-place finisher was more than two lengths behind. Fox's own horse, Bin McKlyo, lost a tire in a first-turn accident.

In the second heat, Palin trailed Abbe Guy to the halfway mark, then caught up, after momentarily breaking stride, to win with a time of 2:08-1/4.

Today, the Fox Stake is the oldest, most prestigious harness race of its kind for two-year-old pacers. Injured in an accident, Fox sold his namesake race to the *Horseman* for one dollar. He died April 19, 1931.

◆◆◆

1927 Harry Stokes drove Hollywood Jacqueline to the Horseman Futurity pace's best time, at 2:03-3/4. Silver Flash Gas was back with its Pace Stake, as was the L.S. Ayres Trot Stake. The Senator Farm also offered a pace stake. A whopping purse of $51,500 was put up for harness racing, and the Grandstand was packed.

The Diamond Jubilee Fair launched the track's golden years as a major training site and, beginning in 1929, home of a prestigious annual auction, the Speed Sale. Fifty horsemen trained at the Fairgrounds.

The nation's oldest colt racing association formed that year. The Indiana Trotting & Pacing Horse Association was incorporated on May 12; incorporators were J.E. Green, Fox, Abriam Boyd, Fairgrounds blacksmith Clarence Cole, well-known presiding judge and starter Horace Greeley Winings, Sep Palin, and Max J. Kennedy.

1928 The Board had the chance to bid on the Hambletonian, but because of Grandstand inadequacies, they turned it down. Frank Fox's proposition for a $10,000 stake for three-year-old pacers was demurred for the same reason.

1930 The Mile Track of Champions was lit for the first time. (This information is counter to another "first lighting" claim fifteen years earlier. The lighting was sold soon after the first year.)

The Fox Stake offered a $12,000 purse; overall, Speed Department awards reached $56,000. Harness and running races were scheduled each evening on the "well-lighted track," followed by the Gordon Fireworks Company's "Hawaiian Nights."

Sep Palin's second Speed Sale on November 11-13 catalogued 296 Standardbreds; Board policy charged nothing, although they stipulated that Palin had to pay for a watchman.

1931 State Representative Charles J. Allardt appeared on January 29 to discuss his bill to license horse racing and legalize pari-mutuel wagering, with fees going to the Board. The Board promptly declared, "we are not authors of this bill, were not consulted about it, didn't know anything about it then and don't know much about it yet."

The next day, a formal resolution against the bill reminded doubters that "the Board is primarily educational in the development of Agriculture and allied industries and the provisions of the bill are not in harmony . . . [T]he Indiana Board of Agriculture is not interested and does not wish to be involved."

Horseman & Fair World publisher Fred Terry offered the three Horseman "Stakes" (three-year-old pace and trot and the two-year-old trot Futurities) and the Fox Stake for a purse of $4,500, or $500

Grand Circuit racers in 1957 line up behind the mobile starting gate. Although the Fair Board vehemently resisted at first, by the early 1940s, the gate assumed its place alongside other innovations which help reduce race times and pre-start crashes.

less than the year before, provided he received payment of $5,500 in 1932, if the printed financial report showed a profit in 1931. Purses paid in 1930 came to $22,347.88, he reminded Board members.

Hedging, the Board was concerned about its six-day, $49,500 purse. The Boardmen argued which association rules would govern the meet. Terry offered, as he had the year before, to pay for the four futurities to race under the American Trotting Association rules. The Board adopted ATA rules a month later.

A new brick, steel, and concrete Grandstand made a second year of night races an even greater attraction, but the day races "proved the best that were ever witnessed in Indiana." Three world's records and five records for the year were set.

"It was the best racing ever seen here, and 26 heats were made at an average of 2:02-1/5, with the fastest heat at 1:59," according to a Board report in the *State Year Book*.

1932 Eighteen months after the last Board discussion of pari-mutuel betting, a Mr. Fields of American Turf Association of Louisville proposed another pari-mutuel plan. If a pari-mutuel bill passed in Indiana, the racing group would rent the Fairgrounds "for thirty or forty days together or divided, for a running horse race meet."

Fields wanted an appointed racing commission to handle licensing with a fee of "not less than $1,500 per day." According to his plan, the state Board of

Education and the Board of Agriculture would split proceeds.

American Turf operated tracks at Latonia, Churchill Downs, Lexington, Chicago's Washington Park and Lincoln Field, and Chicago's Hawthorn track, and was willing, if such a bill passed, to enter into a lease agreement. Offering a "nominal sum" for such a contract to show his good faith, Fields proposed to pay $500 per day rental.

The Board chose to defer action until a January 5, 1933, meeting, but the subject never came up.

Whether to rent the grounds and Grandstand for a fireworks pageant during two weeks in June was deferred for thirty days in a January 30, 1933, decision while Boardmen awaited the outcome of the pari-mutuel bill before the General Assembly. If the pari-mutuel bill passed, fireworks would conflict with racing dates.

But no bill passed, and all bets were off. The Indiana legislature took nearly fifty years to pass a pari-mutuel racing law.

Grand Circuit purses reached a total of $50,150, with $27,050 paid for day races on September 3, and day and night action on September 5-9. Walt T. Britenfield drove two-year-old Logan Scott to the Fox Stake's fastest victory, with a time of 2:02.

The Horseman Futurity three-year-old trot offered an $8,000 purse; its pacing adjunct offered half. William Caton, driving The Marchioness, turned in 2:02, fastest ever in the trot's history.

The Horseman Futurity two-year-old trot offered $3,000.

Harness and saddle stakes were down from the year before, although the Board's *State Year Book* account proclaimed "the race program was the best seen in the United States and twenty-six more horses actually raced here than at any meeting held in 1932."

That year, for the second time, Grand Circuit stewards scheduled Syracuse concurrently with Indianapolis for the upcoming season. Syracuse, the first fair admitted to the Grand Circuit, had split the showing in 1930. The Board threatened not to convene Roaring Grand races in a feint to end the conflict. None felt the Grand Circuit would call the bluff.

Whether to pay $4,500 for the Horseman Futurities and the Fox Stake was deferred until the January 5 meeting. Boardmen discussed $3,500 before adjourning.

1933 The Board came to regret its Grand Circuit cancellation threat. Secretary-Treasurer E.J. Barker announced January 30 that he had written to Grand Circuit secretary Will Gahagan, asking why Syracuse had been allowed to buy the Horseman and Fox Stakes.

Barker had also called Gahagan, only to learn that *Horseman & Fair World's* Terry had informed him "Indianapolis was not going to belong to the Grand Circuit. It was the understanding if Syracuse was given the same dates as Indianapolis, (the Board) was not to buy any stakes."

Sep Palin's Stable was found near the track's second turn in this 1936 Speed Barn scene which old-timers claim is little changed from today.

Barker suggested Syracuse take dates the week after Indiana, "and according to a recent letter they are giving consideration to the change . . . ."

But there was no Fox Stake at the 1933 or 1934 Indiana State Fair. Both meets went to Syracuse, along with the Horseman Futurities, not to return until 1935. The Syracuse Fox meets paid the lowest purses in the history of the race.

Deep into the Depression, Speed Barn stall rentals were past due, and horses were stabled at the Fairgrounds in declining numbers. Known for shodding Dan Patch and Single G, blacksmith Clarence Cole received rent reduction for his shop at the east racing stables from $20 to $12. The widow and son of Mr. Lee, the other blacksmith, with a north side shop only half the size of Cole's, paid $10.

Yet once again, Indiana boasted the nation's best race program. Twenty-six harness races, with 209 starters, averaged eight horses to a race. Iowa followed with the next greatest number of starters in a week, a distant 135.

Six days of harness purses dropped to $15,620.53. Several races were set for half-mile horses. Scheduled races included the 2:10 Early Closing Pace, The Mayor's Early Closing (2:15 trot), and the Governor's Early Closer (2:15 pace).

L.S. Ayres offered a $1,500 purse for the 2:10 Early Closing Trot. Cedar Hill Stock Farm's 2:22 three-year-old trotter class offered a $700 purse. Hotel Lockerbie put up $1,000 for an Early Closing 2:05 pace, but there weren't enough entries so it was changed to a 2:07 pace offering a $800 purse.

1935 Right after Everett Samuel Priddy, a 1931 and 1933 Democratic state representative from Warren, took over as president on January 9, the Board legislative committee drafted a pari-mutuel bill for introduction to the House of Representatives.

Ten days later, Fair Manager Dick Heller told the Board that another bill actually introduced called for an across-the-board 1-1/2 percent state fee on all pari-mutuel monies and had no license fee. A provision allowed county and State Fair harness pari-mutuels "at a cost of $25 per day."

The Public Morals Committee and the House of Representatives were holding off the vote until the Board came up with its own version. But Boardmen opted to sit back and support legislative committee amendments.

By February, the Board's $100,000 annual mil tax appropriation hadn't arrived, and the pari-mutuel bill hadn't yet passed. The Board was concerned about meeting the new Grandstand bond issue. Heller warned of a State Fair "in receivership." The money had to come from somewhere, so the Speed Department's $3,000 budget increase was cut.

Speed director Charles R. Morris balked, arguing "there is not a thing about the State Fair that produces as much revenue as the grandstand when you have good races." He got $2,000 back.

◆◆ **Colonel E.J. Baker of St. Charles, Illinois, paid $900 for a snow white yearling gelding at Palin's Indianapolis Speed Sale in 1933, then promptly put the trotter under Palin's tutelage at the Fairgrounds.**

Greyhound would make a name for himself.

Greyhound with Sep Palin driving was a major drawing card during the Great Depression. The Fair Board once offered Palin $5,000 if Greyhound beat the world's record time of 1:56-3/4 – but the event was rained out.

The pari-mutuel bill was defeated in the House. "There apparently [was] a general wave of feeling through the state" that horse race betting was still out of the question. Thanks were extended to both political parties for their assistance, and Board members/State Senators John Bright Webb and E. Curtis White.

American Trotting Horse Association still governed the Fair's races; a new fence went up along the inside and outside of the track, but a January '35 Speed Department Barn report revealed only four out of twenty stables on the east and north sides were fit to stable horses.

The Saturday card lined up three $300 races for half-mile and Indiana horses. As director Frank J. Claypool explained, the races developed Standardbred breeding opportunities in Indiana; "it creates an interest throughout the state."

But the horses got off to a slow start. Only two entries in one race and a mere three in another led to their cancellation on a rainy Labor Day Monday, although 77,687 paying customers still attended. Heavy rains then forced a total wash-out of the races, but not before Calumet Fingo turned in 2:09-1/2 in the Horseman Futurity's slowest time in eleven years – and not before Sep Palin drove Greyhound to a dismal 2:05 in the rain-delayed Horseman Futurity Three-Year-Old Trot.

1936 Indiana Trotting and Pacing Horse Association convened a spring meet in June before Lexington's meet. Heller received a telegram in January from "all of the leading race horse drivers wintering in Florida" – Palin, Tom Berry, and Fred Egan – asking for the privilege of the meet. They were successful.

The State Fair harness racing's purse dropped to $39,300. The Fox Stake offered only $10,000. The Governor's 2:16 trot and The Mayor's 2:16 pace both offered $1,200. And again, the Grand Circuit had scheduled Syracuse for the same dates.

Palin brought off another Indianapolis Speed Sale which proved portentous to the sport. Carmel businessman Leo C. McNamara, Sr. visited November 10 and bought the first horse auctioned – Hal Dale.

The stallion's third offspring, Adios, was auctioned off at a $2,000 top price at the October 1941 Speed Sale. That horse went on to set seven world pacing records, including the '42 Fox Stake at Saratoga. Adios eventually became the "prepotent pacing sire of the 1950s and early 1960s."

An Adios son, Bullet Hanover, won the '59 Fox in its fastest time, 1:57 – more than two seconds faster than the record. Adios' son Bret Hanover took the '64 Fox victory.

Today, 98 percent of all pacers trace their pedigrees to the horse Mr. McNamara bought so many years ago.

1937 The track was resurfaced for the first time since 1910. Outgoing Fair Manager James L. Beattey considered it "just a question of time until [the track] will be the finest training grounds in America." Two new Speed Barns were built.

Despite the era, Boardmen weren't shy about offering harness racing exhibition money, in this instance, for Greyhound and the European champion Muscletone. In August, Sep Palin asked the Board by wire whether the Fair would pay $15,000 for an international match race. A counter offer of $12,500 was made, "providing the race is two out of three heats."

Twelve days before the Fair opened, the Board learned Muscletone

wouldn't be ready to race "in this country until October 8 or later." By September 2, however, the Board learned the match race would be in Illinois.

Just before the Fair, *Horseman & Fair World*'s Fred Terry offered the 1938 Horseman Futurities and Fox Stake for $4,500, plus $500 in magazine advertising.

A Board counter offer of $4,750 was refused, since Terry already had been offered $4,500 for the Fox Stake alone. That news scared Finance and Advisory Committeemen enough that they accepted Terry's offer. Terry promised not to increase prices in the future; he only wanted "what they were sold for, years ago."

Another proposition, for a Single G exhibition race, priced at a mere $25, was turned down "since we have had him for the last four or five years."

Opening morning, Sep Palin was offered $2,500 if he drove Greyhound on September 10 to a new track record and $5,000 if the horse lowered the world's record. The world's record for trotters, set in a 1922 time trial by Peter Manning, was 1:56-3/4. The deal included daily Grandstand appearances.

Radio station WIRE agreed to broadcast the effort; the two-hour afternoon broadcast, beginning at 2:45 p.m., involved thirty-nine radio stations which had "laid everything aside." But if it

Bullet Hanover with John F. Simpson Sr. driving set a Fox Stake record in 1959 with a 1:57 time. The following year Simpson drove the pacer to a Horseman Futurity victory.

rained Friday, the deal was off. And it rained.

What to do? Publicity Director Levi Moore asked every Board member to his office "to say something over the broadcast." And since it was raining, leaky roofs were discussed. Greyhound moved on to Lexington and knocked three-quarters of a second off the record.

1938 Another big harness racing record was made when Her Ladyship set a new pacing time of 1:57-1/2. The record remained untouched for thirty-seven years. This year's $47,200 Grand Circuit Race program featured pace and trot events for half-mile track horses, a $5,000 Horseman Futurity trot (the pace paid only $1,839), $8,000 for the new Horseman Stake for two-year-old trotters, and $10,000 for the Fox Stake.

H.M. "Doc" Parshall drove Blackstone to a 2:05 Fox victory, fully three seconds slower than 1932's Logan Scott victory, and only a second faster than Red Pluto's victory way back in 1927. Peter Astra took the first Horseman Stake victory, turning in 2:05-1/4. Parshall drove.

The Claypool Hotel, L.S. Ayres, Cedar Hill Stock Farm, and Hook Drug Company each sponsored a race. The Lady Drivers' Race for 2:10 (2:20) trotters offered $500 from Lexington's Walnut Hall Farm.

On September 6, Grandstand throngs watched Greyhound in an exhibition race against his 1:56 world's record time. Sep Palin drove the steel gray gelding to 1:56-3/4, a track trotting record which stood until 1969 when Nevele Pride broke it in 1:54-4/5. (Twenty years later, Peace Corps broke Nevele Pride's record in 1:54-1/5.) Palin took a $2,500 prize. Three-quarters of a second faster and he would have pocketed $2,500 more.

1939 Auto racing propositions received in January were turned down because the cars tore up the track, which wasn't banked properly anyway. As Board man Phares L. White pointed out, "we are building up one of the finest tracks for racing and training in the United States. Let's keep to that idea."

In a unique September 5 matchup, Greyhound hitched with Rosalind, the World Champion mare, set a world

Her Ladyship, driven by H.M. "Doc" Parshall sometime in the 1930s. The horse set a world's pacing record of 1:57-1/2 in 1938; it still stood thirty-seven years later.

trotting record of 1:58-1/4. Palin drove. Greyhound also set a 4:06 world record in a two-mile trial on September 19.

The United States Trotting Association was formed this year in a merger of three eastern associations. The Board still belonged to the American Trotting Association, but soon joined USTA.

1940 In January, Speed Department Superintendent Harrie Jones and Sep Palin urged the Board to approve a Grand Circuit meet during the last week in June. Both hailed the opportunity to boost county and State Fair horsemen; since all proceeds would go to charity, they asked for free rent. Trotting Horse Club of America and Grand Circuit Stewards fully supported the plan and were offering $25,000.

The Board gave no response at first. Finally, they accepted the offer, but only under distrustful conditions which

treated the entire event as a profit-making enterprise.

But the Grand Circuit nearly didn't make it to the Fairgrounds that year. A barrier – a rudimentary starting gate in the form of a wire or rope, the precursor of the modern starting gate – was the cause. Speed Department Director Charles Morris disclosed in February "an effort from some source to use barriers in starting harness races."

He can be blamed for the Board's obstinacy. In Morris' opinion, with the right kind of starters and judges who knew horses, "the races will be conducted according to rules, and you will have better racing."

Harrie Jones and Leo McNamara, a co-founder of USTA, tried to reason with the Finance Committee in May. McNamara claimed that the barrier "increased fairness, decreased scoring, and regained the public." Most fairs were using it that year, he said. No one, however, told the Indiana Board of Agriculture how to run harness races.

"I have not reached the point yet where I am willing to submit to Hitler tactics," Morris maintained. He and the Board stood on published race conditions, and the Grand Circuit would have to go by Indiana's rules.

"If they cannot do that," Morris declared, "we will withdraw our membership from the Grand Circuit." He recommended a telegram threatening that sentiment.

"We might lose a few horses, and we might gain several," Morris argued. "Whenever they have ironclad rules, I am ready to stop." A $15 preliminary USTA membership was approved in the same breath.

When June 3 rolled around, Morris was somewhat less truculent. "It seems that when we decided not to use the barrier it caused quite a little confusion."

Finance Committeemen had "met and talked it over, and McNamara was here, and they decided that we would go ahead" as originally planned. A telegram to that effect was sent to Grand Circuit's New York headquarters.

But "before any answer was received here," the Circuit "put out an Associated Press dispatch over the country that we had withdrawn from the Grand

Delvin Miller drove Blackhawk to the 1940 Fox Stake victory in 2:03-1/4. Miller went on to claim four Fox victories.

Circuit and that they were going to try to get another track to take over the race.

"I think the Grand Circuit needs us worse than we need the Grand Circuit," Morris stoutly defended.

McNamara wanted the Board to okay the barrier, and Morris' softened tone indicated he was now willing.

McNamara told the Board on that June day, "I never would have got into this if I did not think I had a contract satisfactory to the Board." He had arranged for meet underwriting, and made other contracts, including two Fair-time stake races he thought were squared with the Board. By now, 167 owners and 302 horses were entered, and the Junior League had sold two-thirds of the Grandstand's box seats for opening day. "I think it is arousing a lot of interest for your fall meeting," McNamara declared.

So "after further discussion," it was moved and seconded to allow the barrier for the June meet "if the Board sees fit."

When information reached Board "ears" June 14 that bookies planned to set up shop during the meet, all agreed "we want the Indiana statutes complied with."

At that Fair, the Governor's Stake, a 2:14 trot, offered a $1,200 purse. A 2:14 pace was called the Lieutenant Governor's Stake. Since McNamara had sponsored two $2,500 stakes, and the Board had misunderstood his intentions, his money went to those stakes.

In late August, Fred Terry reported "quite a lot of trouble" keeping the Horseman Futurities and Fox Stake in Indiana. A mile track under construction at DuQuoin, Illinois, was bidding more for the races. The Board promptly heeded the warning and committed for the '41-'43 races, with an option for the next two.

Come Fairtime, $58,700 for the purses was offered. Hook Drug's three-year-old pace stake was for horses eligible to the 2:15 class.

Twenty-seven-year-old Delvin Miller, driving Blackhawk, won his first of four Fox Stake victories at a time when "few young men were coming into a sport which was thought to be dying," according to notes retired *Indianapolis News* sports writer Vic Rensberger left behind. "Soon the starting gate, pari-mutuel betting and night racing were to make harness racing the world's fastest growing sport and Del, along with many others, millionaires."

1941 *Life* magazine called the Fair's harness races the biggest in attendance this year. Earlier, Morris declared "[Grand Circuit stewards] all recognize the fact that Indiana has the best race meeting in the United States and we will continue to have good races."

Bill Gallon won with Lee Smith driving in the fastest Horseman Futurity three-year-old trot in the race's history at 2:01.

Rensberger watched what happens when harness races haven't a starting gate during the sixteen-horse Fox Stake. The horse Eddie D. unseated Palin and circled the track twice before he was caught. Delaying the race half an hour, Eddie D. finished twelfth and seventh.

1942 All Fair contracts, except for Fred Terry's stakes, were immediately cancelled when the Army Air Corps occupied the Fairgrounds. As Terry pointed

A runaway Adios Cleo after a spectacular four-horse tangle on the backstretch during the second heat of the 1961 Horseman Futurity for three-year-old pacers.

out, "the two-year-old fillies have to be raced this year."

There was no other place in the nation where Terry wanted to see the races. But that wasn't possible, and the Fox Stake, the Horseman Stake, and the Horseman Futurities convened at the year-old Saratoga Raceway. Late November action approved subsidizing the stakes to ensure their return after the war.

1943 With a $5,000 bid, Greenville, Ohio, won the right to host the 1943, 1944 and 1945 Horseman Stake, the Horseman Futurities, and the Fox Stake. It was an arrangement both the Board and Fred Terry found entirely satisfactory. Saratoga wanted them back, but offered only $4,000.

1944 Despite World War II, the Board's valuable racing stakes were main-

tained, since they "fill our afternoon grandstand with a paying public," President Paul G. Moffett told Board delegates in January.

"[W]hen they return to us our afternoon grandstand will be filled by spectators who revel in the grand sport of kings," Secretary-Manager Guy Cantwell agreed.

1945 A November 6 *Indianapolis Star* article declared that the track required eight inches of dirt before the 1946 harness racing could begin. Nothing had been done to repair it for more than three years.

1946 The Grand Circuit returned on September 2-6. Some Grand Circuit horses visited Terre Haute in 1944 and 1945, but Leo McNamara, "Indianapolis harness racing authority," secured the Fairgrounds dates at the track stewards' meeting early in December 1945.

For 1946, Speed's A.G. "Fred" Norrick proposed a $97,700-purse program, including the sorely missed stake races. The Board's outlay was roughly $14,000 higher than their contribution in 1941.

Norrick proposed four races each day, with three half-milers on Saturday, naming one race "Governor's Stake," another "Commissioner of Agriculture," and a third titled after the Board. The highest purses were an estimated $20,000 for the Fox Stake, "the most valuable event ever raced by two-year-old pacers," according to *Horseman & Fair World*, and for the Horseman Stake.

The weather was fine throughout the races. Thomas Berry drove Poplar Byrd to the Fox's biggest purse victory, $20,585. Berry's fastest time tied a record of 2:02, set 'way back in 1932 by Logan Scott.

Horseman hailed the meet: "[T]he enforced vacation of four years seemed to be a build up for the most successful fair and race meeting in the history of the city. Never before have such crowds attended, averaging over 100,000 per day with a sellout in the big grandstand hours before the start of the Grand Circuit program."

"The mile track at the fair grounds . . . always a favorite with trainers as a place to prepare a stable for the campaign, is even better than ever, and many stables are there for the winter. The

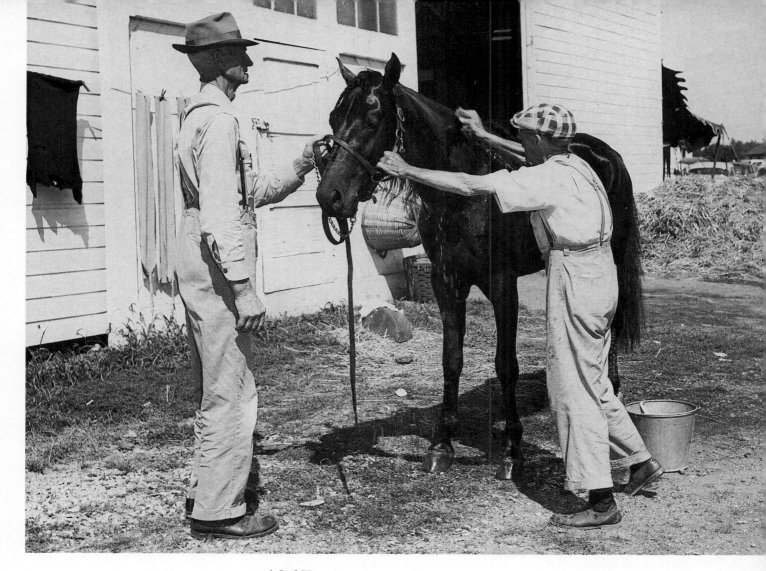

good old Hoosier state has always been a center of the breeding, training and racing of the harness horse and the return of the state fair track to active use has stimulated the sport to the highest point in its history."

A paddock was needed. Speed Director Norrick recommended a location east of the Grandstand. A record 192 horses had been entered for races, "in the neighborhood of 44 more" than ever before.

The "Nation's Leading Training Center" at "The Crossroads of America" already offered every possible reason to locate there: a half-mile wet weather training track; completely repaired and modern barns; a blacksmith shop; a harness supply and repair store; miles of cinder jog paths; a plant "second to none for proper training of campaigning stables"; a great mile track newly re-soiled; hotel and restaurant accommodations; continuous maintenance – all in the heart of Indianapolis, with street car service.

1947 Pari-mutuel harness racing hadn't come up for a long time when a January 16 National Horsemen Association letter was considered. The association was conducting a legislative campaign "favoring and doing much" to get a pari-mutuel bill passed.

"This bill was considered and was very highly favored at the Annual Conference of your County and District Fairs, January 7th, at the Lincoln Hotel . . .[I]t is our intention to go forward with this movement . . . which we feel will be very beneficial to the Fair Associations, and as you know, will be beneficial to all taxpayers which are burdened to the utmost . . . ."

The letter sought $25; a statement was enclosed. The Board turned down the request.

The Hoosier Futurities asked to race at the '47 Fair, Board members learned. Each of the four stakes needed $2,000 from the Board; the Board countered with $1,500.

Groom Tom Foley of Akin, South Carolina, washes down Mr. Borden while James McDonald of Canton, New York, looks on in this 1954 Fairgrounds Speed Barn scene. Parker Whiting of Fort Wayne owned the horse.

Secretary-Manager Orval Pratt obtained Board approval March 25 to serve as secretary to Sep Palin's November Speed Sale. The affiliation led to his resignation two years later.

"It would be an asset to the Fair Board to have a Speed Sale of national scope here on the grounds," Pratt informed his Board.

President Moffett thought well of the idea, "because we can develop this through the cooperation of the Board to be one of the biggest race horse centers in the country."

Speed Department Director Norrick got into the act on May 16 when he obtained the Board's okay to partner with Palin for Speed Sale exclusives.

Film star Charles Coburn and his pacer Rush Hour following the horse's 1950 State Fair two-heat victory in the $3,000 Hoosier Stake. Jake Rodman drove.

1948 Harness racing purses totalled $134,000; the largest-ever field of horses was set to vie for the big cash prizes. The Fair had joined the Grand Circuit's Big Five the year before. The over-three-year-old series of trot and pace events involved the Fair, Springfield, Milwaukee, DuQuoin, and Delaware, Ohio. The series lasted five short years.

Sep Palin convened a three-day Speed Sale during the last week of October. The sale grossed $300,000.

1949 Orval Pratt wasn't at the January 6 meeting; perhaps he was intentionally absent. The night before, the *Indianapolis News* claimed, "Mr. [Louis] Demberger said the Board probably would investigate a recent horse sale conducted at the Cattle Barn under the joint sponsorship of Mr. Pratt and Mr. Sep Palin, Indianapolis horseman."

Demberger read from the article, "In another place here, it says: 'Some certain member expects to ask an investigation of the Speed Sale affair.' I did not make these statements, nor have I at any time made such a statement to any newspaper." Perhaps he had commented "off the record." Beyond Boardroom closed doors, someone knew Pratt was acting independently.

Further complicating matters, Pratt and Palin had leased the Cattle Barn late in the year for the Indianapolis Speed Sale, right on top of Coliseum Corporation's lease on the big "parking garage."

Speed Department Superintendent L. Orville Miller worried over "considerable publicity" about the Board's practice of renting an already-leased Cattle Barn. It was a relief when Palin agreed to hold off until the Board straightened things out.

Pratt's affiliation with Palin was a sore spot; so was the fact that he operated PDQ Stables at the Fairgrounds. Pratt was re-hired, but only after the Board mandated that secretary-managers and grounds superintendents could not participate in "any other activities of any remuneration or profit on the Indiana State Fairgrounds while in our employ."

Pratt resigned on March 1 in a dispute over salary differences and charges that he co-sponsored a Speed Sale without Board permission. The *Indianapolis News* reported that Pratt had "been under fire since November . . . it was further charged that he used the Coliseum without approval from the Coliseum Corporation, holder of leases on both the Coliseum and the Cattle Barn."

In a February 4 letter to Boardman Homer M. Schuman, Pratt insisted that he had "worked for the inter-

A fast field of horses on their way to the wire during 1954 racing action.

est of the Board and tried to do a good job." But when the Republican-dominated Board decreased his salary from $7,200 to $5,100, Pratt, also a Republican, quit.

The 1950 Hambletonian was up for bids, and Palin wanted the Board to try for "the race of races of harness horses. Indiana has the best accommodations." Palin was confident 100,000 would watch a Hambletonian meet at Indianapolis. "I think it would be the most wonderful thing that ever happened to the Indiana State Fair if we could get it."

Sold on a three-year contract, the race would cost the Board $9,000 to $10,000. Purses were running at $60,000. DuQuoin, Illinois, wanted the race "very badly," Speed Superintendent Miller said. "DuQuoin certainly does not have the facilities that we do, but I imagine it will go to the high bidder." Miller considered it "the chance of a lifetime."

That chance had been turned down in '28. But the "Hambone" slipped

through Indiana's hands forever. Good Time Park in Goshen, New York, won the bid, and kept the Hambletonian through 1956.

The stake wasn't in the cards for Indiana, anyway – the following July, then-Board president Kenneth Blackwell told his fellows that Leo McNamara had said, "if we had offered $1,000 more, we still wouldn't have gotten the Hambletonian stake."

"If we lose the two stakes we get from Bob Terry, we might just as well admit we haven't got a racing program," Miller replied. "Another thing, the New York State Fair is really going to give us some competition . . . a lot of stables are splitting their members. They bring their colts here and give their mature horses to New York."

"The Great Dan Patch," a Hollywood movie about the immortal pacer, premiered . Starring Gail Russell, Dennis O'Keefe, Ruth Warrick, Charlotte Green-

wood, and Henry Hull, the film concentrated on Dan Patch's life in Indiana.

Actually, the movie revolved around a chemist (O'Keefe), his wife (Warrick), and a trainer's daughter (Russell). Dan Patch had no speaking part and played a relatively minor role. Visalia Abbe, with a best time of 2:08-2/5, was cast to portray Dan Patch.

In mid-June, Boardman Roger Wolcott announced that the movie premiere was set for July 20, with a Grandstand showing. The movie men also wanted to present a Dan Patch trophy to the winner of a September 3 all-Indiana race, but they didn't do it.

Six-day race purses totaling $146,256 set a new world's record. Vaudeville acts were featured between Grand Circuit harness races.

A packed Grandstand and infield crowd is on its feet at the conclusion of a harness race from a half century ago.

Sep Palin in his later years in this photo from the 1947 Harrisburg (Pennsylvania) Sale.

SENTIMENTAL tradition tried on a macabre set of colors in 1950 when the Single G Memorial Association sought hallowed ground for horse bones. Twenty-four years after their first request, horsemen asked again to bury their dead. The 1926 campaign to inter Peter the Great at the Fairgrounds had been ignored. Now, Bert C. West, Single G Memorial Association secretary, and on *Horseman & Fair World*'s staff, offered a more tempting proposition.

Single G fans had been conducting a nationwide fund-raising drive to disinter Single G from his unmarked grave near Tipton. They planned "the most fitting monument possible," West wrote July 29. Formed that spring, the society thought the Fairgrounds posed the "most fitting" burial ground and monument site, a Mecca where "thousands" would flock for a viewing. They also wanted to bring the remains of Peter the Great from Laurel Hall Farm.

"This would easily be one of the greatest projects ever staged by the sport," West believed. He certainly must have been correct.

West and associates proposed burying the bones of "the greatest pacer of all times" on one side of the free-act platform, and doing the same with Peter the Great, "the greatest trotting stallion," on the other side. Then there could be two winners' circles.

With "correct landscaping," the two gravesite winners' circles would assuredly be "one of the most colorful" anywhere. The monuments would be bronze tablets set into granite. Project funds already existed; the American Legion, which owned the old Laurel Hall Farm, would cooperate. Speed Department Superintendent Miller was all for it. Wolcott didn't care, although he warned, "if you are not careful, you will have a horse burial ground." A response was deferred until after the Fair.

This time, horsemen didn't wait nearly a quarter century to press for an answer. *Horseman & Fair World*'s Bob Terry and Dr. S.M. Cotton from Gold-smith showed up on November 21. Terry claimed a memorial winners' circle would add value to the racing program. He proposed a location between the Grandstand stage and the band stage.

Already, several hundred dollars in donations from nationally prominent figures and "average horsemen" had been raised through *Horseman*, USTA, and *Canadian Sportsman* efforts.

Yet another letter was read into the record: "Single G was bred, owned and raced by Mr. William B. Barefoot, of Cambridge City, Indiana. For fourteen years, Single G raced throughout the United States and Canada, and when he retired he joined the Indiana stallion ranks and became equally famous. On December 6, 1940, he passed away on the Float

---

Single G, "the greatest pacer of all time," driven by Fairgrounds horseman Ed Allen. Born in 1910, the horse claimed 262 heat victories in 436 starts, an historic record which still stands.

were removed and 16,000 yards of rock-free clay replaced them. Twelve inches of old clay were removed from the turns and filled in with fourteen inches of new clay. Four inches of clay were added to the straight-away.

1961 "In regard to the questionnaire you sent us pertaining to a pari-mutuel bill . . . the Fair Board . . . felt it advisable not to have a statement from the State Fair that might be influential to some of the county fairs," Secretary-Manager Earl J. Bailey wrote on January 19 to *Muncie Star* farm writer Bob Barnet, secretary-treasurer of the Indiana Association of County & District Fairs.

Eleven county fairs had voted earlier to ask lawmakers to support a pari-mutuel bill in 1961. Three voted against it; four abstained. The leading Fair, the only one with a mile track, dared not comment for political reasons.

Fair crowds cheered during five days of racing, featuring county fair winners, an eleven-entry Horseman Stake, two Breeders Filly Pace races, and two Walnut Hall Stud Filly Trots.

USTA rated the Track of Champions at 2:02-2/5 against a norm of 2:05 for a standard mile track.

Rain split the Fox Stake into a two-day race. George Sholty drove Coffee Break to a 1:58-1/5 win in a thirteen-horse field, claiming the winner's share of the $55,635.33 purse in the second fastest Fox.

After the Fair, Ed McNamara worried that the Board wouldn't continue harness racing support after his term ended. Joe Quinn, who had seen the Hoosier Hundred become "recognized as second only" to the Indianapolis 500, was taking over track events.

McNamara wrote to fellow Board members, ". . . Grand Circuit Harness Racing during the great Indiana State Fair is truly a tradition. Excepting the war years of 1942-45 . . . Grand Circuit Harness Racing has been raced at the Indiana State Fair consecutively since 1913!!! It's not easy to discount or disregard a half century of tradition, is it?"

MONEY to these events, something which had never been done before!

"Consequently, $4,000 was added to Horseman Futurity #50; the following year $6,000 was added to Horseman Futurity #51; and now for the Horseman Futurity #52, the Indiana State Fair Board has committed to ADD $10,000 to the amounts paid in by the horsemen."

McNamara pointed out that in 1956 the Board added $2,000 to the Horseman Stake #20 for two-year-old trotters, and $2,000 to the "world famous" Fox Stake #31.

The Board hadn't stopped there; they added $4,000 to the two-year-old "classics." Then for the kicker: when June rolled around, opening yearling entries for Horseman Stake #22 and Fox Stake #33, the Fair would double the added money for both events to $4,000 for each.

"[T]he Indiana State Fair Board has just finished a complete re-surfacing of the mile track with a high compression clay material in an effort to give the horse-

men the best and fastest track possible. A new trailer-home park has just been completed with sanitary sewers, individual water outlets and adequate lighting – again for the horsemen.

"[W]e are doing our best in your behalf; to build good race tracks, to build big races and to operate a friendly race meeting, all of which will make your broodmares and their foals worth more money!"

1959 Bullet Hanover won the first heat of the Fox Stake at a time of 1:57, knocking a half-second off the twenty-year track record. In the second heat, Bullet Hanover won again with 1:59, setting the two-heat record for two-year-olds. The record stood until 1976 when Crash broke it in 1:55-3/5, with Billy Haughton driving to his third of four Fox victories.

1960 That fall Clay County clay was used to resurface the Track of Champions. Nearly 10,000 yards of rock and dirt

1962 A March 21 letter reached Professor Jerry M. Macklin of the 4-H Club Section at Purdue in response to his March 19 question concerning the risk of rain during the Fair.

"If I understand your query correctly," agricultural climatologist James Newman wrote, "you are asking – what is the risk of rain on any given day during the Fair. This we can answer rather precisely."

In a nine-point response, Newman predicted, "The risk that at least one day during the State Fair will receive .10 inch of rain or more is near 90 percent, for any two days during the fair [it] is near 75 percent, and for any three days it is near a 60 percent risk, four days at 30 percent, five days at 10 percent and seven days at less than 1 percent.

"The chance that no rain will occur during . . . [the Fair] is approximately 8 percent."

Earlier, in point three, Newman claimed a 80 percent risk of no rain in Indianapolis on any day of the Fair. In point two he figured only a 10 percent chance of half an inch of rain.

The nation's best trotters and pacers were set to vie for $280,000 in night race purses – a first for the decade. But five days of rain canceled the entire harness racing program, with the exception of two ITPHA heats. Climatologist Newman should have bet on that one.

Perhaps the rain was just as well. As President Royce wrote to *Indiana Farmer* that year, "the types of entertainment that appeal to people have certainly changed. Television has played an important part in this . . . horse racing used to be a major feature. We still have the best harness racing program in the United States bar none, and facilities second to none for holding these events. Still, attendance is disappointing.

"Interest in auto racing has supplanted interest in harness racing as evidenced by the fact that in five days of harness racing we grossed [a scribbled out] $38,000, while in one day of auto racing (the 1961 Hoosier Hundred) we grossed [a scribbled out] $105,000."

The Board had voted on August 2 to make a $40,000 added money bid for the 1964-66 Hambletonians. The effort was unsuccessful and DuQuoin kept the race that could have demanded anything it wanted from the track's one-mile oval on Wednesdays before Labor Day.

Randy Huntzinger shoes the three-year-old pacer filly Wico Mico's Queen in the Number 5 Barn in Jeff Edwards' Fairgrounds Stable in April 1992.

All other races would have been scheduled around "Hambletonian Day." Purse estimates for the five-day card exceeded $400,000. The Board promised "no auto racing . . . for at least thirty days prior . . . ." ("Ninety days" was scribbled out of a draft.)

Indianapolis Times sports editor Jim Smith wrote that day about what led Ed McNamara to spearhead a drive to secure the Hambletonian:

"Money Isn't the Answer – Oddly enough, and much to McNamara's disgust, Indiana was never mentioned.

'Say, what are we, a bunch of step-children. . . .'

"McNamara was informed that it had been the opinion of the USTA and the Hambletonian Society (based on rumors) that the Indiana State Fair was going to give up harness racing . . . ."

"Money is not the answer to getting the race! Indiana has an excellent chance of getting the race for a number of reasons. One, it meets all the requirements of the Society, that it be raced on a mile track, and in the daytime. Second, Indianapolis is ideally situated . . . and has more than enough facilities to accommodate the harness horse folk, and the fans."

"This much is certain. Indiana has to have the Hambletonian in 1964. If they don't, there is an excellent chance the sport will die here."

If some other track plucked up the "Hambone," Indiana would be left "with a second rate card that would get little or no support.

"In the past year, when the Indiana State Fair was running the week after the Hambletonian, horses that competed in it ran [trotted, actually] here in the Horseman Futurity, the oldest consecutively raced harness event in the country."

Smith disclosed that the Horseman would be "leased" to another track, "possibly for $10,000."

A revenue yields and economic effect study on pari-mutuel betting for thoroughbreds in Indiana was completed in October 1962 by Robert J. Pitchell, a former director of governmental research at Indiana University. He predicted $24,332,000 in total direct annual economic impact on the state, based on five new tracks costing a total of $25,000,000.

On another harness front, after the Brazil Area Ministerial Association wrote opposing "the fact" that pari-mutuel races would become part of the Fair, Secretary-Manager Bailey replied that although Indiana Association of District and County Fairs "went on record as advocating to the legislature pari-mutuel betting . . . this, however, is not a program of the Indiana State Fair, and of course the legislature would have to enact such a law . . . This I do not foresee in the immediate future."

1963 Secretary-Manager Hal L. Royce responded in June to a May letter from Ohio's director of agriculture asking about pari-mutuel racing:

"For the past three or four sessions of the Indiana General Assembly a bill legalizing pari-mutuel betting at certain specified locations . . . has been introduced . . . fostered by . . . Indiana Trotting and Pacing Horse Association, and seemingly meets with less favor at each session. The bill this year failed to be reported out of committee.

"[T]he popularity of harness racing in Indiana is seemingly declining year by year . . . [W]e offer as good a harness racing program . . . as can be found, with facilities second to none, and yet each year witness a decline in the numbers attending.

"[W]atching the horses race is a side issue any more; rather, most of those in attendance at the more popular tracks go for the privilege of placing a small wager."

Meanwhile, the harness racing community worried about Board developments.

"Ever since your appointment of Joe Quinn as master of auto publicity to the Board of your State Fair, there have been persistent rumors that the Grand Circuit harness racing program will end on Labor Day," Grand Circuit president Octave Blake wrote on October 9 to Governor Matthew Welsh. "The Indiana State Fair has been a fixture on the Grand Circuit for many years now, and the horsemen, both in Indiana and throughout the United States, have great faith that the Fair Board will do the right thing."

If the rumors Blake had heard were true, conflicts with the Hambletonian would preclude "some great horses" from making it to the Fair. . . . I do hope that you will appoint a Speed Secretary who knows horses and horsemen."

Welsh told Royce to draft a reply. ". . . I have appointed Mr. Joe Quinn to succeed Mr. Ed McNamara . . . but it does not necessarily follow that he will be the director of the 'Speed' Department."

Of course, Fair department appointments were made by the Board president. Who would be in charge of harness racing wouldn't be determined until the annual Board reorganization.

"[T]hese assignments are made after due and careful consideration of the experience and aptitude on the part of

Bret Hanover, with Frank Ervin driving, set a 1:55 world pacing record in a heat of the 1965 Horseman Futurity, only to lose to Adios Vic's identical time in the final heat. The horse paced the Fox Stake's fastest second half in 1964 – :58-1/5.

the individual board members . . .," Royce wrote for Welsh.

When the Board reorganized, and when McNamara left, there was no more Speed Department; only Racing, and Quinn was in charge.

A year earlier, when the Hambletonian had been up for bid, Welsh/Royce wrote, "there was some possibility that it might not return to DuQuoin . . . permit[ting] us to close our harness racing program on Labor Day [Wednesday, September 9, would be selected as the final day of the Fair, not in conflict with the Grand Circuit; Quinn scheduled the State Fair Century Race at 8 that evening after the last harness race.]

"[O]ur board is quite conscious of the conflicts involved. . . . [T]here is no attitude . . . to in any way embarrass harness racing, even though we have been somewhat disappointed the past several years in the public's acceptance of same."

Quinn saw fit to write on December 2 to Blake: "[I]t is one fervor[ed] wish that you may . . . offer suggestions to us which will greatly enhance the future of the Great Hoosier Exposition."

Not only would harness racing be scheduled over four days near the end of the Fair, but "it would be well to try a program under the lights on Tuesday night," Quinn wrote. "What do you think of that?"

Quinn informed Blake he had indeed been named director of racing, which included horses and cars.

"Although my name has been rather frequently mentioned in conjunction with auto racing, I did have the pleasure of bringing harness racing to life in Terre Haute, Indiana, after a lapse of thirty-three years since Axel, Nancy Hanks, Robert J and the Harvester made marks at the old kite-shaped track."

1964 "... (Joe) Quinn wants to SHOW

Hoosier harness race enthusiasts he can WIN a PLACE in their hearts at the Indiana State Fair," a top-of-the-page January 9 *Indianapolis Times* story laughed.

"Quinn wants to sell pictures of fans' favorite horses – for $2 each. Several Fair Board members (and possibly the attorney general's office) say the feeling is mutuel – pari-mutuel.

"Quinn's $2 pictures would be sold before each race at 'picture booths' under the Fairground grandstand. Each picture would bear a number corresponding to a number of a horse in the race.

"'Then when the race is over,' Quinn said with a straight face, 'pictures of the winners would suddenly become valuable since that was a good horse. We'd then be willing to buy back pictures of the winning horse at – oh, say $5, $6 or maybe $8 or so.'

"'Of course, pictures of those horses that lost would be of no value to us and we wouldn't be willing to pay a cent for them.'

"Quinn likened his plan to one practiced more than 25 years ago at a dog track in southern Indiana. At that track, bettors – uhh, rather, dog fanciers – bought 'shares' in the dogs before each race.

"After the race the winner became more valuable and the track management was more than glad to pay a premium to buy back the share. Shareholders in losing dogs were stuck with their worthless shares.

"'[H]arness horse racing once was a big thing in this state. But the breeding and selling of horses was just incidental to the feed, silks, sulkies, trucks to haul horses, and other such businesses. Now most of the old big breeders of harness horses have moved out, creating a terrific economic loss,' Quinn said. 'It's time we stopped this outflow of money from the state.'

"'Why, up at one Chicago track, I have figures that show that 64 percent of the autos parked there during races are from Indiana. And that Hoosier money is going to Illinois,' Quinn said.

"Quinn said if his 'picture' plan is approved and it pays off, it would offer good evidence of strong backing for passage of a pari-mutuel bill in the 1965 Legislature." But the picture never came together.

Drivers line up their horses in a practice start behind the gate before the State Fair crowds show up in this scene from the 1950s.

World Record Pride

Trainer-driver Stanley Dancer steered four-year-old Nevele Pride to a 1:54-4/5 world's record in an August 1969 time trial, breaking Greyhound's 1938 record.

IT WAS the first year for Sunday racing in 1969 and the first time for a Sunday Fox Stake. George Sholty drove Truluck to 1:57-4/5, still four-fifths of a second slower than Bullet Hanover's 1959 record, but second-fastest all the same.

Then, trainer-driver Stanley Dancer steered four-year-old Nevele Pride to a 1:54-4/5 world's record in a time trial that day, August 31, breaking Greyhound's 1938 record.

The bay trotter was "an irascible animal," according to *Hoof Beats*, "given to kicking, biting and striking, but his redeeming features included perfect behavior on the racetrack and speed that stole the breath of fans and horsemen alike."

Nevele Pride's feat made national news, and it might never have happened but for the efforts of Ted Ketcham,

a track conditioning expert from Minnesota. According to a columnist for the Salisbury, Maryland, *Daily Times*, Ketcham "worked (an) impossible mile race strip into perfect condition . . .

"This historic mile at the Hoosier Capital . . . was of course and as it should have been . . . given worldwide headlines. . . . In the background . . . was one individual whose work made possible the mile . . . ."

Ketcham fixed a Track of Champions rumored to be in "terrible condition." *Hoof Beats* claimed Dancer had threatened to call off the trial if the Fair Board failed to "make vast improvements in the fairgrounds oval at the 11th hour."

"The track had been the subject of considerable concern as late as Saturday afternoon," *Harness Horse* editor Les Ford wrote. The Century stock car race, a

National Championship motorcycle race, and Kochman's Hell Drivers had torn the track into "deplorable shape."

"Pounded and scarred during the week prior . . . and subjected twice daily during the harness racing meet to the abuses of an automobile hell-driving show, the ancient mile track was proclaimed by most of the horsemen . . . as perhaps the most unlikely strip of dirt anywhere over which to make an assault on a World's Record . . . ."

Tractor lights circled the track that night, seen "as late or early as 4 a.m." By Sunday morning, Ketcham had miraculously transformed the track. Dancer called it "perfect . . . every bit as good as last year."

Ketcham had resuscitated the track, Nevele Pride did his part, and some said they heard Greyhound's ghost kicking in his old stall at Palin's stable that night.

A month later, $3,000,000 led Nevele Pride off to stud, but not before he set another world's record at Saratoga a week later just as a thunderstorm struck, with 1:56-4/5, the fastest time ever trotted or paced on a half-mile track.

Nevele Pride was in his third consecutive year as Harness Horse of the Year. He had won fifty-seven of sixty-seven career races, earned $871,738 and retired as the fastest two-year-old, three-year-old, and aged trotter of all time on mile and half-mile tracks.

◆◆◆

1972 Fair officials announced a "Hat Trick Series" federation involving the Indiana State Fair, the DuQuoin State Fair, and the Illinois State Fair – all sites for Grand Circuit harness racing. The added money stakes series was thought to be the incentive to attract outstanding East and West Coast and Chicago-area horses. Under the plan, each track would add $400 each year to each of six stakes events. To win the money, a horse would win at all three tracks in the same racing season. Indiana Hat Trick races included the $35,000 Horseman Stake; Hoosier Futurity filly trot and filly pace; $35,000 Horseman Futurities; and the $70,000 Fox Stake.

Two free-for-alls, the "Single G Pace" and a trot, were included in a change allowing Indiana owners to bring their top performers home from the raceways for Hoosier audience appearances.

Ricci Reenie Time, with a 1:57-2/5 best time, won the Fox Stake without finishing first in either heat. First-heat winner Faraway Bay was slower, with 1:57-4/5, then was set back for breaking stride in the second heat.

1973 "World Championship Racing" moved Opening Day events to daytime only instead of afternoon and night heats. For the first time, the Fair offered the "Pride of Indiana," its own five-race series of two- and three-year-old colt stakes, "open to the world," replacing ITPHA's former sponsorship.

The Single G Free-For-All Pace was made an early closer and was raced on Fox Stake Day. The Fox field divided into two elimination heats, and for the first time offered a $100,000 purse.

Another big change was the four-race "Indiana Night" designed for Hoosiers unable to afford to breed or buy a stakes colt, but who wanted to race horses at their State Fair.

State Fair harness racing saw another first: Richard G. Lugar, then-mayor of Indianapolis, presented the first Mayor's Trophy (in a long time) at the conclusion of the Horseman Futurity trot. The feature event was filmed and later televised statewide, the first Indiana State

Fair standardbred event ever televised statewide. And Lugar? The Indianapolis Mayor went to Washington next year. Coincidence?

1975 Two hundred fifty tandem truck-loads of Clay County clay, each carrying twenty tons, were hauled onto the Track of Champions. Four million pounds were dumped on each turn; the resurfacing cost, $22,000.

Indiana was one of few state fair-grounds to have both a mile and a half-mile track. The smaller all-weather track was a special limestone. (Wild geese in the Infield have been coaxed from the half-mile with grain when they stubbornly block horses' paths.)

The Track of Champions was ranked the fourth fastest mile oval in the nation. In forty-seven Fox Stakes there had been only one rain-out. A Fox Stake film was offered to service clubs, and for the first time the world's richest two-year-old pacing event was televised in four Indiana cities and Louisville, Kentucky.

The 79th Review Futurity for three-year-old filly trotters, rained out at the Illinois State Fair, was raced in Indianapolis.

1976 The (Lyla) "Crickett Reel Memorial" for three-year-old filly pacers was inaugurated in honor of the late Harness Department office manager who died in an auto crash the previous winter after leaving to work for USTA. The Indiana Trotting and Pacing Stakes leaders stabled in the "Hoosier (Walton) Barn." Racing

memorabilia from the days when Indiana was known as "the land of pacers" was displayed. The Single G Society was the Hoosier Barn host.

Crash set a new record of 1:55-3/5, in the Golden Anniversary $105,721 Fox Stake, televised statewide the second year in a row.

Filly divisions of the Horseman Futurity Trot and the Horseman Futurity Pace were established.

1977 More two-minute miles burned up the Track of Champions than any other in Indiana harness history, among them the Fox Stake, the Hoosier Futurity two-year-old colt pace, and both Horseman Futurities. The Horseman Stake was a mere fifth of a second over two minutes. (The next year, Courtly broke two minutes with 1:59.)

1982 A new world speed record for two-year-old trotting geldings was set during the racing season. More than 100 harness horses trained at the Fairgrounds during the winter season.

1983 Rambling Willie retired at age thirteen. Rambling Willie had trained at Indiana county fair tracks before becoming his era's all-time leading moneywinner. He earned more than $2 million; his longevity was attributed to his owner's practice of tithing winnings to the church.

1984 Marauder, driven by Dick Richardson Jr., set a new record of 1:53-4/5 in the final heat of the 58th Fox Stake, knocking 3/5 of a second off the 1981 record. The two-year-old pacer equalled CrossCurrent's track record set in 1983 as a three-year-old.

1987 In the Fox Stake, Albert Albert, in 1:52-4/5, tied the world record for a pacing two-year-old, set by Nihilator at the Meadowlands on August 16, 1984. The Fox Stake saw a record number of entries and a record-breaking purse of $222,155.

1988 Albert Albert set a new three-year-old pace record of 1:52-1/5 in the Horseman Futurity. Chris Boring drove.

Beach Walker, paced by Thomas Haughton (Billy's son), claimed the Fox Stake first heat victory with a 1:53-3/5 time, winning $48,146. Guru, an Indiana-owned horse with Jim Curran driving, won the Fox's second heat in 1:54-3/5, claiming $45,655.

The twelve-horse field might have been bigger if the Yonkers Raceway had not scheduled a $600,000 pari-mutuel for the night before the Fox Stake.

Custom Metals' "Race for the Gold" offered $1,000 in gold coins divided between the fastest Indiana trotters and pacers. Guru took $500, and the trotter gold was divided between Ornery Cuss, Hot Dog Rocky, and Gin Miss, all with 2:00-3/5 times.

1989 Righthand Man set a world record time, 1:52-1/5, in the first heat of the 63rd Fox Stake's second division.

Heather and Lace, a three-year-old filly, won both heats of the 80th Horseman Futurity, including a second heat time of 1:53-3/5, breaking a 1985 track record and making her the fastest

Marauder, driven by Dick Richardson Jr., set a new record of 1:53-4/5 in the final heat of 1984's 58th Fox Stake, knocking 3/5 of a second off the 1981 record. The two-year-old pacer equalled CrossCurrent's track record set as a three-year-old in 1983.

three-year-old filly ever on the Track of Champions.

Charmher, a two-year-old pacing filly, won both heats of the 53rd Hoosier Futurity with a new stake record of 1:56-1/5.

Peace Corps won the first elimination heat in the 80th Horseman Futurity Trot in 1:54-1/5, breaking Nevele Pride's 1969 trotting track record. Peace Corps, of course, broke the stake record and set the Grand Circuit season mark for three-year-old trotting fillies.

Atlantic, a two-year-old trotting filly, set a new stake record of 1:58-1/5 in the first heat of the 53rd Hoosier Futurity.

Drawing Board raced the fastest mile ever on the Track of Champions, 1:51-4/5, during the 80th Horseman Futurity pace, breaking the year-old record set by Albert Albert.

Indiana gained its first pari-mutuel law that year when Governor Evan Bayh signed the measure May 9. The law created a governor-appointed racing commission charged with deciding rules and regulations, and licensing track operators. The next step for pari-mutuel betting would be finding a track location.

1990 Deal Direct, a Canadian two-year-old pacer, set a new world's record, 1:51-4/5, during the 64th Fox Stake, with the fastest mile ever by a two-year-old pacer. He also tied for the fastest pace on the Track of Champions regardless of age. Deal Direct also set a world's record for two heats.

1991 The offspring of Indiana's best Standardbred stallions continued to benefit from specially funded Indiana Sires Stake races for two- and three-year-old trotters and pacers during the Fair.

Two-year-old horses sired by Indiana stallions have raced the Sires Stakes every Fair since 1980, except 1982. Three-year-olds have raced at the Fairgrounds since 1988.

A Stallion Registry was created in 1975 by Indiana Standardbred Board of Regulations in a move designed to develop a better quality breed. Special monies are allotted each year to fund Sires Stakes racing.

Honcho Hanover tied the 1:54 stake record in the Hoosier Futurity 55 Colt and Gelding pace first heat. Stubby B set the new 1:53-2/5 stake record in the second heat.

Pensive set a new stake record, 1:54-4/5, in the first division of Hoosier Futurity 55 Filly Pace. Signita claimed the second division in 1:56-2/5. In the final, Signita won in 1:54-2/5, setting another stake record.

Crabby Yankee won the first heat of Horseman Futurity 82 three-year-old

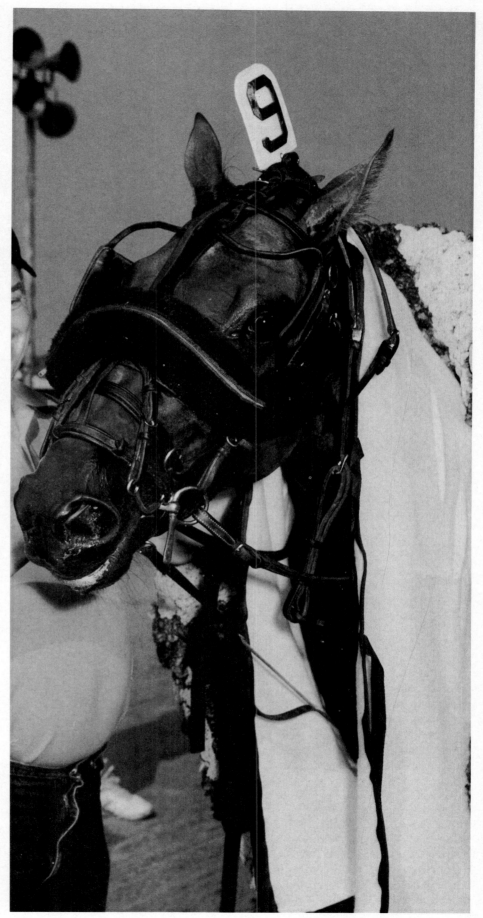

Deal Direct, a Canadian two-year-old pacer, set a new world's record, 1:51-4/5, during the 1990 Fox Stake, with the fastest mile ever by a two-year-old pacer. He also tied for the fastest pace on the Track of Champions regardless of age, and set a world's record for two heats.

Open Pace in 1:53. Interpretor won the second heat in 1:51-4/5, tying Drawing Board's stake record.

Safely Kept won both heats of the 65th Fox Stake, in 1:52-4/5 and 1:53-2/5; the purse was $60,643 of the $121,286 total.

The five-day purse totalled $584,326 for all races: ITPHA, Overnights, Hoosier Futurities, Horseman Stake, Horseman Futurities, Fox Stake. All told, 274 horses raced.

During the Fair, the Indiana State Fair Commission issued "requests for proposals" from private developers interested in opening a pari-mutuel track at the Fairgrounds.

The plan had legislative and Governor Evan Bayh's support. A pari-mutuel track could be "blended into the Fairgrounds," Indiana State Fair Commission Chairman Donald Tanselle said.

A paying track could provide critically needed funds, estimated at $47 million, to restore the aging Fairgrounds.

(A group of twenty Taiwanese businessmen interested in the track as a pari-mutuel investment toured in October.)

"How serious is Carmel real estate developer and horse owner Paul E. Estridge Sr. about building a pari-mutuel horse track in Indiana?" asked the *Indianapolis Star*'s "Behind Closed Doors."

"Serious enough to risk a half-million dollars in 'development costs.' The whopping expenditure came to light last week in Estridge's proposal to the State Fairgrounds Commission to build a pari-mutuel track at the fairgrounds.

"The inch-thick document shows that Estridge's firm, Sagamore Park Group, already has hired a prominent track design firm from Philadelphia, Ewing Cole Cherry, plus a racing consultant, attorney, banker, lobbyist and accountant."

Equally in the running, Lafayette-based Pegasus Group also had a plan to develop the Track of Champions in connection with Churchill Downs

Icarus Lobell won a heat in the 1981 Fox Stake in 1:54.2.

in Louisville, Kentucky. At press time, no resolution had been reached, although Sagamore dropped out in May 1992.

1992 House Enrolled Act 1050 became Indiana's first (developer-palatable) pari-mutuel law when Governor Evan Bayh signed it into law February 26.

Grand Circuit dates fall outside the Fair for the first time, on August 27-29. Crowds greater than those which once thronged old Grand Stands are expected to cheer on the nation's oldest continuously held Grand Circuit races.

◆◆◆

Diehard harness fans take their seats before the races begin in this bleacher scene from 1954.

A.J. Foyt and crew members carefully guide a Ford engine block from a car in 1974.

MOTOR-powered speed contests are nearly as old as the Fairgrounds itself. The old Board of Agriculture approved automobile races as early as 1900, and such events began in earnest years before the Indianapolis Motor Speedway was built. In fact, an old Fairgrounds racing program claims car owner Carl Fisher, dissatisfied in 1908 with the Fairgrounds "horse" track, banded together with other wealthy car owners and built the Speedway. But there were time trials before then, and they made history as well.

1903 The world's first one-minute automotive mile was recorded late in June at the Fairgrounds track. Barney Oldfield drove Henry Ford's red 999 Arrow "Red Devil" car around the dirt mile. United States Auto Club historian Donald Davidson confirms this remarkable record, as does "Ford: The Dust and The Glory" by Leo Levine.

1915 From the *Mooresville Times'* "Sports Mirror," dated August 29, 1990: "The Indiana State Fair, originator of many exposition ideas, will offer a new one [in 1915] . . . night racing on the mile track. Ten speed demons in up-to-date racing creations are under contract to give contests for the first time in motor history on an illuminated track."

The International Motor Contest Association and the Board teamed evenly to produce the races – three events, on Friday night, Saturday afternoon, then that night during the Fair. As part of the deal, the Board joined IMCA. A $50 check issued on September 3 bought five shares in the new company, now America's oldest auto racing sanctioning body.

1917 The Oldfield-DePalma Race was held August 4. Three match races between 1915 Indianapolis '500' winner Ralph DePalma and Barney Oldfield had

been called off because of rain on July 14. Since DePalma never raced on Sunday, the race was postponed until the following Tuesday, and it rained again. Oldfield ultimately won all three races, billed as the "World Dirt Championship."

1918 The Board and IMCA promoter John Alex "The Maker of Champions" Sloan worked out a fifty-fifty plan for automobile races on the closing day of the Fair during a February 9 evening meeting at the Denison Hotel. When Sloan died in 1937, he was running more races than all other U.S. promoters combined, according to IMCA.

1919 This year Howard "Howdy" Wilcox won the Indianapolis 500, aver-

aging 88.050 mph with a Peugeot. He challenged all the dirt drivers on the last day of the September 1-6 Fair, recalled retired newspaperman Richard Jackson of Greencastle. "He brought his Indy racer, but it was too big and the corners were too sharp for him. He couldn't get his big Speedway racer around the curves and the dirt track drivers beat him all to . . .

"I don't think he was all that shamed," Jackson remembers. "He ended up in the middle of the pack."

1921 Auto races wrapped up Fair entertainment on September 10, with Paul B. Franklin of Indianapolis promoting under the AAA Racing Association auspices. Franklin brought in six race cars and six AAA professional drivers in six events, in a fifty-fifty gross receipts deal. The agreement also held that "no other automobile race meet, speed trial or contest between automobiles or an automobile and aeroplane will be allowed" without Franklin's consent.

In April, Executive Committeemen had decided to have no other races that year since "the automobile races at the Speedway are on the 30th day of May and the automobile races at the Fair are on the 10th day of September [and] will fill the patrons of Indianapolis and of the fair with all of the racing that they will care to have happen for this year[.]"

1926 Although the International Motor Contest Association offered to pro-

Henry Ford's 999 "Red Devil" car clocked the Fairgrounds' — and the world's — first one-minute automotive mile in June 1903. Barney Oldfield drove.

Howard "Howdy" Wilcox challenged the Fairgrounds dirt track drivers after winning the 1919 Indianapolis 500. He and his big Peugeot were beat "all to . . .," according to one witness.

Barney Oldfield and his trademark cigar. Oldfield won all three 1917 "World Dirt Championship" match races against 1915 Indianapolis 500 winner Ralph DePalma.

duce the opening and closing day dirt track auto races, Western Vaudeville Company staged them on the final Saturday of the Fair, September 11. The deal called for fourteen cars, four to six races, auto polo, and auto push ball.

1928 H.G. Clark of the American Open Racing Association of Springfield, Illinois, brought in afternoon open competition auto races, instead of hippodrome style in the Coliseum, on Saturday, September 8. Five events were promised, with the final race between the twelve fastest cars remaining from elimination heats. Clark offered a purse "to be not less than $2,500 and $1,000 if the world's one mile oval dirt track record is lowered."

1931 Over the July 4th weekend black race drivers tore up the track and themselves in the Golden Glory Sweepstakes.

Nineteen-year-old Robert Boone, fifth great-grandson of Squire Boone (Daniel's brother), was there: "They had a terrific wreck in the first lap," Boone recalled. "Charlie Wiggins, an Indianapolis Red Cab mechanic, won. There was his brother Lawrence, Wilbur Gaines and Jim Jeffries, also from Chicago, Bill Blackburn, Jimmie Jordan, and 'Wild Bill' Carson from Chicago."

Jeffries drove a Frontenac built in the late '20s by Arthur, Louis and Gaston Chevrolet, the 1920 Indianapolis 500 winner, at 410 West 10th Street in Indianapolis, according to Boone.

"There was a circuit," Boone remembered. "Evansville, Walnut Gardens near Camby, and Winchester."

Boone, who had lived at 16th and College, was a former Fairgrounds "racer" himself. "Sometimes we'd bring in our jalopies onto the Fairgrounds after dark and tear around the track."

The Golden Glory was a fifty-mile race, offering a $50 purse, according to Paul Prange of Indianapolis. "That was a lot of money back then."

Prange remembered the crash well. "They all piled up on the third turn in the first lap. Dust was everywhere. All were injured. It was a terrible mess."

The Golden Glory was a fringe operation not affiliated with any sanctioning body, according to old-time promoter Harry Speyer Jr. of Indianapolis.

"Jeffries was a quite a performer – no one could beat him," according to Speyer. "He was a hell of a driver. And there was a pretty good crowd at the race."

Like Boone, Speyer also remembered racing with his friends at night on the track, with the police in hot pursuit.

1935 Racing promoter George Lyons met with the Finance and Advisory Committee on March 25 to discuss the midget auto races he staged in the Coliseum every Wednesday night. The Wednesday before had seen a crowd "of about 3,500." Admission ranged from fifty-five cents to $1.10.

The Coliseum races were run in heats, and heat winners advanced to the final. All drivers were Indianapolis 500 milers, each with four years of dirt track racing experience; eight cars made a good race.

Veteran 500 driver Duke Nalon recalled driving in the Coliseum races. "Charlie Stewart, a former Oldsmobile dealer, had two cars, with engines designed by Charley Boleker. Barney Oldfield's cousin Lee also drove in the Coliseum.

"Paul Russo (another Indy 500 driver) and I were teamed together in those years. We drove for a man called Colonel Bridges, an inventor of glass-blowing machines in Muncie." Other drivers included locals Harry McQuinn and Les Adair.

"Back in those days we were on a winter-time circuit," Nalon recalled in 1991, "driving at Chicago, Detroit, Indianapolis and St. Louis three or four nights a week."

The Coliseum track had a tanbark surface. "It wasn't too bad, but it was completely different," Nalon said.

1940 Championship auto racing appeared to be dying in 1940, Harry Speyer Jr. recalled. He, Russell Fortune Jr., and William Devore, an Indianapolis 500 driver, appeared before the Board about a race on Sunday, September 15. Bowman Elder, who married Fortune's sister, was in on the deal as well. They already had obtained a sanction from AAA for a hundred-mile championship race.

Although the Board had passed an earlier resolution banning racing after an earlier promoter failed to pay the purse, they relented, but only if $1,000 was paid in advance.

Fortune was involved with thoroughbred horse racing practically his entire life, according to his son Russell III, himself unaware his father also dabbled in auto racing.

Speyer claims Art Sims (see below) appeared with him before the Board. "We got the Board to reverse themselves. We had to post a big bond and do work

The First Annual 100 Mile Speedway Race, [grou]nds, Aug. 2, 1924, Indianapolis Ind.

COPYRIGHTED BY PATTON

on the track. The purse had to be put into escrow."

Ultimately, $100,000 was required before any auto race hit the track again. Expensive AAA sanction requirements made it far too dear.

"Among the group of us, we questioned the prudence of coming up with $100,000 to put on the race," Speyer said. "We finally decided not to run it ourselves. It was an expensive proposition. We were out to promote auto racing, not make money."

The race, a sprint-type program with Speedway cars, was a financial success, he said. "The turn-out was about 25,000." But the expensive sanction requirements of the State Board and AAA were too great a cash outlay for Speyer and Sims, so *Indianapolis Star* sports editor Blaine "Blondie" Patton, promoter Lou Moore, and Sportsman's Club owner Jim Hussey promoted the race, as Speyer remembered.

"The only reason we didn't run it, was we didn't want to run the risk involved." Speyer didn't recall who won.

1941 Permission was granted for auto races on September 14. Promoters Lou Moore, Dick Miller, and Blondie Patton told the Board that the Indianapolis Auto Racing Association-sponsored event would be modeled after AAA-sanctioned races. Moore, third-place finisher in 1933's

"500" promoted at the Fortville midget track in the Forties, and owned Mauri Rose's winning Brickyard car.

Six short races of championship cars in a sprint format totaled 65 miles. Duke Nalon won the feature, a twenty-five lap final. Nalon drove for Mannix Brothers Garage at 34th and Illinois Streets in Indianapolis.

Boardmen learned T.E. "Pop" Myers, general manager at Indianapolis Motor Speedway while Eddie Rickenbacker owned it, was enthusiastic about the proposition "because the drivers have to make money during the winter months."

1946 An historic Board decision on August 21, would change the face of American auto racing forever.

Dick Miller, general manager of the Indianapolis Auto Racing Association, staged a September 15 auto race. His letter to the Board had a $1,000 check attached to influence the Boardmen's decision.

"Mr. Miller asked in his letter for the Board to watch the reaction and the effects of a 100-mile championship race with the thought that it might be made a permanent part of the Fair in the future, developing into a very successful revenue producer for the Fair," reported a Board meeting transcript. Miller offered to cooperate with the Board in the future.

All the drivers and nearly every spectator are black in this rare scene from the Fairgrounds' earliest known hundred-mile race, dating to August 2, 1924. Black historians and a review of newspapers from that time turned up no additional information.

Rex Mays, driving his Bowes Seal Fast Special, won that 100-mile AAA race. One day its descendent would be known as the Hoosier Hundred, the most prestigious championship dirt car event of all time.

But Indianapolis driver Al Putnam died in an accident between Turns 3 and 4 when his maroon race car, the (Fred) Palmer Special, hit the concrete at the bridge tunnel during a practice run. A September 15 Associated Press story filed from Indianapolis detailed part of the tragedy: "Putnam, research engineer for L.G.S. Spring Clutch company here, was making his third warm-up circuit of the one-mile dirt track when his car skidded and crashed into a concrete abutment of an overpass. The steering column pierced his chest."

The accident scared the Board. According to long-time *Indianapolis Star* sports editor Jep Cadou, former governor Henry F. Schricker, who would return to the state's top office from '49-'53, swore cars would never again race on the track as long as he was governor. That was true.

A dusty conclusion to the September 10, 1927, championship race on Auto Race Day. Only five cars started the twenty-five mile feature. A man named Schneider won, followed in by Fred Lecklider and Mack Dillman.

Barney Oldfield, clad in farmer's overhauls, takes the checkered flag at the 1933 "World Tractor Championship" race during the Fair. Oldfield's Allis Chalmers set a world tractor speed record of 39 mph.

In a remarkable September 17 letter to Board member Paul G. Moffett of Indianapolis, secretary-manager Orval C. Pratt (1945-1949) asked, "How did you enjoy the races yesterday? They certainly featured some fast and fancy driving." He made no reference to Putnam's death.

1948 In March, Arthur Sims of Tulsa and Harry Speyer Jr. of Indianapolis told the Board that the Circle City's Russell Fortune Jr. wanted to promote an auto race. They got the go-ahead.

Sims, Oklahoma oil millionaire Harry A. Chapman's mechanic, was "a plodding, deliberate kind of guy," according to Joe Collins, long-time Indianapolis racing fan.

A month later, Boardman Francis M. Overstreet of Columbus asked his fellows, "What are we going to do about automobile racing on the track this fall?"

"We will have a lot of trouble with the horse fellows if we allow automobile racing on the track," Secretary-Manager Pratt responded. "Horse racing pays as much during the course of the year as one auto race would make." So the Board voted against auto racing that year.

That afternoon, Mr. Neiman and Mr. Baker of the Indianapolis Motorcycle Club sought the Board's permission to stage an August 8 American Motorcyclist Association-sanctioned motorcycle race. They crashed.

Later that year, the Disabled American Veterans were turned down when they proposed to bring their 100-mile Championship Midget Race to the track on October 2-3. Although the DAV promised to restore the track, and even though DAV's Howard Watts pointed out that midgets didn't tear up the track like the thrill show's Hell Drivers did, the Board wouldn't budge.

Auto racing would return to the Fairgrounds, when a very patient man named Roger Wolcott joined the Board.

1949 A Mr. Palmer, Mr. Wixler, and (John or Earl) Townsend asked on February 10 to put on a 100-mile race in September after the Fair. Although State Fair leaders had no intention of allowing this, they extended "the courtesy of letting them appear before the Board."

Townsend had "no doubt but what this race would be a success, as in 1946 when a race like this was held here, it was very successful. The finest drivers in the country would appear here and every one would be proud of having it here." Proper arrangements were promised.

Karolyn Holloway, the Board's first female member, was concerned about the "publicity" after Putnam's death. "We do not feel the public would like for us to have such a race again here."

Townsend couldn't agree. "Only three men have been killed in the United States in the last four years in this type race." There often were horse racing fatalities, he pointed out.

After lunch, the racing discussion was on again. Wolcott moved to

Rex Mays won the 1946 Indianapolis Auto Racing Association 100-mile race driving the Bowes Seal Fast Special. He died after a 1949 Delmar Speedway crash that threw him from his car onto the track where he was run over by the other drivers.

rescind the auto racing ban. Phares L. White of Oxford seconded.

Speed Department Superintendent L. Orville Miller of Elkhart knew the horsemen wouldn't like it, and said so.

Board president Homer E. Schuman, Columbia City, warned, "We had a kick here that, if we continued on with this, the Fox Stake might be abolished."

But there were very few horses on the Fairgrounds after the Fair, the date when the Palmer family wanted to convene the race.

Almost two weeks later, Townsend and Palmers Senior and Junior returned to find out what was on the Board's collective mind. They needed an answer soon in order to get on American Auto Association's schedule; September 18 had tentatively been assigned to them.

In 1953, the second year of American Motorcyclist Association racing at the Fair, finalists await their trophies: (l-r) #1 Bobby Hill, third place; #98 Joe Leonard, second place; and #25 Everett Brashear, winner. Hill won the '52 National.

Townsend suggested a $2,500 guarantee and 15 percent of the gate. A "conservative" Board profit was estimated at $4,000. A three-year contract was requested.

Indianapolis Motor Speedway president Wilbur Shaw (500 winner in '37, '39, and '40) sent a letter vote of confidence. "I think that is a problem that should be discussed very thoroughly," Schuman said. "[W]e are obligated to the horsemen to keep a good track for them and we do not want to jeopardize losing any assets with regard to horse racing."

Schuman promised that the Board would discuss auto racing "later on in the day and will telephone you to let you know our decision." That wasn't entirely true, since the decision was reached almost immediately.

Miller reminded his fellows that *Horseman & Fair World* publisher Bob

Terry, who sold the stake races, had been offered more money to take them elsewhere. Terry was against auto races on the track.

After a few more minutes of discussion, Wolcott withdrew his motion to have auto racing. Pratt phoned in the bad news.

On November 18, Wolcott again brought up hundred-mile auto racing. He was looking for a date sometime between the Fair and the upcoming International Dairy Exposition.

Miller was against it. "You can't have a horse racing program and an auto racing program on the same track," he said.

But by mid-December Miller was willing to go along with the proposition. Bob Terry had no problem with auto racing if the Fair was extended an additional day. But the length of the Fair was kept to nine days.

1950
After losing their bid to hold the historic Hambletonian race for three-year-old trotters, State Fair Board members grew apprehensive about the status of the precious Horseman Futurity races they considered theirs.

There was also a concern that the track, resurfaced in '46, wasn't quite in shape.

That was Wolcott's cue. "Now, if we just had a good automobile race on this track right after the Fair, it would more than pay for resurfacing the track to Bob Terry's specifications," Wolcott remarked.

Joe Leonard of San Jose, California, *"the flying knight of the dirt tracks,"* set an eight-mile National Championship record, 5:56.8, in 1954 on the Fairgrounds' dirt mile. In 1969, the four-time AMA Champion raced against five-time USAC Champion A.J. Foyt on a three-lap course around hay bales. Leonard won by a length.

Three weeks later, Secretary-Manager Kenneth J. Blackwell read into the record a July 9, 1950, *Indianapolis Times* opinion article penned by Art Wright:

"If race fans REALLY want to see championship big car racing at the Fairgrounds they probably can make it possible for this year – by writing their views to Kenneth J. Blackwell . . . ONE: That a majority of the Fair Board members have no objections to auto races at the Fairgrounds. TWO: That the horse men are NOT against auto races at the Fairgrounds. . . . [K]eep those letters going to Mr. Blackwell if you WANT races there."

Blackwell also had a letter from M.K. Essig, secretary of the Mid-West Quarter Horse Breeders Association, read into the record: "[Art] Wright spoke of the campaign that is on to try to influence the State Fair Board to permit the use of the very fine horse track for the running of automobile races. This track was originally built for horses and has established a reputation the nation over both for the quality of the track and the quality of the horses that our State Fair races draw. Our State Fair track and the one at Albany, Indiana, which is a running track, are about the only two tracks left in Indiana that automobile racing hasn't taken over at least part time. Automobile racing will take the life out of a race track.

". . . I happen to know that our Association would do most anything to be able to put on a running horse meet at this fine track. This meet could be for both quarter horses and thoroughbreds . . . . If racing for running horses were permitted on this track, the races could be filled with Hoosier entries, but, if automobile racing were to be held to get high class cars, it would be necessary to go outside the state for at least three-fourths of the entries."

Essig could not know that the Hoosier Hundred would one day attract a high percentage of nationally known race drivers based in Indiana.

The tireless efforts of Roger Gould Wolcott led to the race known today as the Hoosier Hundred. Once second in importance only to the Indianapolis 500, the Hoosier Hundred quickly became the world's top dirt track race. Wolcott and race director Joseph Quinn, with the help of Indianapolis Motor Speedway owner Tony Hulman and track president Wilbur Shaw, scheduled the first race for September 18, 1953, but rain delayed it until September 26.

1953 Years in delivery, the Hoosier Hundred emerged thanks to Roger Gould Wolcott, chairman of the Board racing committee, and race director Joseph L. Quinn, Jr. Then nothing more than an American Automobile Association "100-Mile National Championship Race," the Hundred quickly became the world's top dirt track race, attracting crowds of up to nearly 30,000.

Wolcott of Indianapolis (Board appointee, July 1948 to November 11, 1953) was a former Republican state senator (1943-47), and one of the first American fliers in World War I France.

His grandfather Oliver Wolcott founded the town of Wolcott in 1861 and started a grain business which eventually grew to the point where he reportedly built the largest corn crib in the world, capable of holding 45,000 bushels of corn.

Quinn and Wolcott finally had convinced the Fair Board to promote the 100-mile auto race quickly named "Hoosier Hundred." With the help of Indianapolis Motor Speedway owner Tony Hulman and track president Wilbur Shaw, they were able to schedule the first race for September 18, 1953.

Early on, many thought the 1946 100-miler where Al Putnam died was the first Hoosier Hundred, but this auto racing tradition actually began in 1953. Long before that, black race drivers had convened for "The First Annual 100 Mile Spee[d]way Race" July 2, 1924.

The first Hoosier date was a wash-out, and the event was delayed until Saturday, September 26. Auto racing history waited a week, then Bob Sweikert drove home first in the closest finish in racing history, with Manuel Ayulo, Johnny Parsons, and Don Freeland breathing down his tailpipe.

Shaw told *Indianapolis Star* sports editor Jep Cadou that it was "the greatest auto race I ever saw." World class auto racing had come to the Fairgrounds.

"As a man who is not sure the automobile is here to stay, may I suggest we keep our tracks free of automobiles . . . . [W]hy not try to work out a few running horse meets?"

1952 The Centennial Fair's final day, September 6, was "Radio and Motorcycle Day," with 75 miles of American Motorcyclist Association racing. Bobby Hill of Columbus, Ohio, won the five-mile National astride his Indian motorcycle.

It was the first of many AMA dirt track championship races at the Fair, two years before the advent of the AMA Grand National Series. AMA returned in '53 and '54, then came to stay beginning in '69, with the exception of '87.

But that first AMA year, the Board "was not too enthused over the prospect and left the impression that it was just another day at the fair, in fact, closing day when everyone packed up to go home," according to the October 1952 edition of *American Motorcycling*," the sport was on trial."

After the race, "the lukewarm fair board turned into hot water. On a radio program live from the track after the race, President Earl J. Bailey of Lowell told his listening audience that it was one of the finest, best organized events he had ever seen and hoped that the boys would be back next year. "The reaction of the large crowd was proven . . . the answer was probably heard in South Bend."

The time gap between Sweikert and Freeland was a mere eight-tenths of a second. Ayulo, the fastest qualifier, finished in second place, a scant tenth of a second behind Sweikert. Sweikert was driving a rebuilt car which had crashed the week before in Syracuse, Cadou recalled in 1991. "That same car won the first four Hoosiers."

Seventy-three police officers were detailed to handle the race crowd. More than 18,000 fans reportedly watched; the purse was $24,674. (Official records less enthusiastically claim that only 13,066 came for the event.)

The top drivers made the Hoosier Hundred a club of sorts; the winners became an Indianapolis 500 "Who's Who": Eddie Sachs, Rodger Ward, A.J. Foyt, Parnelli Jones, Mario Andretti, and Al Unser.

But the first and as yet unnamed Hoosier Hundred had to fight to exist when it met resistance from an entirely different racing community.

In "Battle for Customers – Fair Board Faces Suit Over Auto Race," in the July 19 *Indianapolis Times*, Jim Smith

alerted readers that "The 16th Street Speedway is going to sue the Indiana State Fair Board for bucking private enterprise." [Now long gone, 16th Street Speedway was across from Indianapolis 500 Motor Speedway.]

Randall "Rags" Mitchell, Indianapolis Midget Speedway's general manager, told the *Times*, "It is not our desire to keep big car racing out of Indianapolis. Quite the contrary, we would like to see the race run here, for it will help racing. However, we do not want to see it run at our expense. We do not believe the Fair Board has any business in auto racing."

Mitchell feared that if the Board was allowed to pull off this one, "there would be nothing to keep them from building a quarter-mile track and running us out of business." Mitchell wanted a permanent injunction. He must have forgotten that the Fairgrounds had allowed auto races as early as 1900.

If plans for the Hoosier Hundred went ahead, the midget race would be cancelled, Mitchell said. "It mark[ed] the first time in the history of the [American Automobile Association's] two cham-

Bob Sweikert, seen here in 1955 after clinching the Hoosier Hundred pole position, won the first Hoosier in the closest finish in racing history, with Manuel Ayulo, Johnny Parson, and Don Freeland breathing down his tailpipe. Wilbur Shaw told Indianapolis Star Sports editor Jep Cadou that it was "the greatest auto race I ever saw."

pionships [that] sanctions have been granted in the same town on the same day," reporter Smith wrote.

Notified of the pending suit, Governor George N. Craig responded: "I am not in favor of the state or any of its agencies bucking private enterprise. But as far as the 100-mile race is concerned there isn't a thing I can do about it.

"The Fair Board is an autonomous group over which the state has no control in spite of the fact it is subsidized by three mills of the taxpayers' money. The Lieutenant Governor and myself, along with Dean Harry J. Reed of the Purdue School of Agriculture are ex-officio members of the board and have one vote. In addition I appoint five members to the board. But we don't by any

◆◆ ROGER Wolcott, no longer a Board member, but still coordinating the Hoosier Hundred, died on November 1, 1958, of a coronary occlusion while driving his Mercedes-Benz; saddened Board members in 1959 authorized a search for a perpetual trophy. They directed Tony Hulman and Joseph Quinn, Jr. to locate something suitable.

They found it among a collection of museum pieces in a New York silver shop. Their discovery, the George III Irish silver cup and cover, bearing the arms of St. George, was created by William Ward in Dublin, Ireland in 1805. Standing 16-3/4 inches tall on a five-inch silver and ebony pedestal, the irreplaceable Wolcott Cup is 19-1/2 inches in circumference, and features an intricate pattern of engraving. Hoosier Hundred winners historically were awarded a replica of the Wolcott Cup. Their names dating to 1953 are engraved into the base of the 187-year-old work of art.

stretch of the imagination control the actions of the board."

The remaining eleven members were appointed by farm organizations; "virtually all of them are members of the Farm Bureau, one of the most powerful organizations in the state.

"Notification of the suit probably will come as quite a shock to the Fair Board which meets Wednesday [July 22]."

Planning for a crowd of 15,000 for the Hoosier Hundred, the Board figured on breaking even on a $50,000 gate gross. "Earlier figures had shown a potential loss of nearly $10,000."

Secretary-Manager Blackwell had no comment on how the Board would react to the suit. "Asked how he would vote if he had one, Mr. Blackwell said, 'I would rather not say. But I do know how I voted when I was a fair board member and the subject came up.'

"'How?' Mr. Blackwell was asked.

"'I'd rather not say,' he replied." No matter, the threatened suit was just that – a threat.

The following year, "Rags" was at it again. The lead paragraph in an untraceable newspaper clipping buried among old files reported that "a suit was filed in Superior Court 1 today by the 16th Street Speedway asking that the Hoosier 100-mile automobile race . . . be stopped." The Board and Secretary-Manager Blackwell were co-defendants in the suit. Apparently, the Speedway had a midget race scheduled the same day.

"An AAA-sanctioned 100-mile race was held at the fairgrounds last September," according to the article. "Fair records show receipts totaling $71,373, and expenses of $74,106, a loss of $2,733.

"The injunction asks further that the Fair Board be restrained and enjoined from using any of the taxpayers' money in building or engaging in, or construction pertaining to conducting of the Hoosier 100 . . . ." The Speedway wanted the injunction "made permanent." That never happened.

Soon after the 1954 Indianapolis 500, sports editor Cadou in his "Cadou Calls 'Em" column warned, "If Randall Mitchell wants to stay in the big-time auto racing business, he should withdraw his silly injunction suit against the Indiana State Fair Board at once."

According to Cadou, the AAA had warned Mitchell it would withdraw all of his sanctions for midget events if he

went ahead with court action. Mitchell also promoted SAFE stock car events.

"[W]e think speed fans will hold him personally responsible [if Mitchell's suit sinks the Hoosier] and stay away from his programs in droves if he robs them of a chance to see the 500-mile race drivers in an outstanding dirt-track race.

"Last year, when Mitchell merely threatened court action, petitions were being circulated in gas stations, taverns and other business places along West 16th Street condemning it.

"The Fair Board spent $15,000 last year for a modern guard rail to protect the drivers and spectators. If there are no further auto races there, the investment will be a dead loss. There is every reason to believe the fair board would make a handsome profit out of this year's race as well as gratify our host of speed fans."

Deeply concerned with safety, Wolcott had overseen steel hub rail construction around the track's inside, both turns, and the backstretch. A concrete retaining wall went up outside the front stretch. The pit area faced the Grandstand from inside the track. Four sets of electric warning signal lights were installed for the drivers' sake.

Judge John Niblack dissolved Mitchell's injunction, according to Cadou. "Niblack didn't agree with him and threw it out of court."

Allen Crowe (left) gave the '62 Hoosier Hundred crowd a scare when he lost his left rear wheel coming out of turn four in lap 58. Out of control, his car went into "a slow roll-over" (top) serious enough "to render Crowe unconscious." Crowe was killed in the June 2, 1963, USAC sprint car race in New Bremen, Ohio.

Racing rivals (bottom) #98 Parnelli Jones and #1 A.J. Foyt struggle for the lead in the 1961 Hoosier Hundred.

The "Big Car" race, now actually called the AAA Hoosier Hundred, returned the second time on September 18, 1954. A crowd estimated at 19,000 [corrected to 17,876] saw Jimmy Bryan win the second race in the same car that Sweikert had driven the year before.

1954 After the Fair, motorcyclists clashed on September 11 for an 8-mile National Championship title following 75 miles of heat racing. Joe Leonard of San Jose, California, "the flying knight of the dirt tracks," set a new record, 5:56.8, trimming 3.78 seconds from a fourteen-year-old record.

1958 Edgar C. McNamara, an appointed Board director from Indianapolis in charge of the Speed Department, was unable to attend the September 23 Board meeting; he was attending his father Leo, sick in bed in Lexington. In his letter of that day, he asked the Board to approve several recommendations and offered an explanation: "You are all aware, I feel certain, of the criticism showered upon the condition of the race track for the Hoosier Hundred. May I tell you here and now that the race track was near perfect for the harness races; and the establishment of a new track racing record, plus the many other fast miles attest to this fact. May I further state that in my personal opinion, Mr. Ralph Wilfong, the

Astronaut Frank Borman presented the Virgil "Gus" Grissom bronze memorial winner's trophy to 1969 Century race winner Don White.

Don White, in this '61 action shot, won the Century in '66, '67, '69, '70, and '75. He was USAC stock car champion in '63.

Norm Nelson in the #2 Plymouth (left) and Tiny Lund in the #10 Ford head into the first turn during '65 Century New Car Race action. A.J. Foyt, driving a Ford, won that year – his third win in a row – with the race's fastest speed to-date – 83.401 mph.

Bruce Walkup in car #27 slides through turn 3 in front of Mario Andretti during '67 Hoosier Hundred action.

Dirt flying everywhere, Don Branson in #7 leads Rodger Ward (#3) and A.J. Foyt (#1) through turn 3 during the '62 Hoosier Hundred. Parnelli Jones won.

Gary Bettenhausen, who failed to make it to the feature, relaxes before the '66 Hoosier Hundred.

Mario Andretti with his STP Special in 1970 while thousands await the start of the first of four consecutive Hoosier Hundreds won by Al Unser. Vince Granatelli was the mechanic.

Going through a corner, #18 John Rutherford waves to the crowd in the 1973 Hoosier Hundred.

Al Unser early on in the 1971 Hoosier Hundred, his second win in a row. The race sponsors presented "Big Al" with a gigantic bologna following his victory.

Jackie Howerton, fastest qualifier in 1974, led all one hundred laps before claiming his Hoosier Hundred victory. Howerton averaged 87.590 mph, the slowest speed since 1965's race.

Parnelli Jones was polesitter when he won the 1962 Hoosier Hundred in one hour, six minutes, and thirteen seconds.

Rodger Ward took the 1959 Hoosier Hundred victory. Fastest qualifier, Ward turned in a then-respectable 98.442 mph.

contractor who resurfaced the track, did a fine job."

Eddie Sachs, winning the sixth Hundred in the red and silver #44 car, "looked like he'd been in a prize fight," according to Jep Cadou. "It was a bad load of dirt – it had rocks in it." Sachs managed to pocket $8,990 of the $32,760 purse with an average rock-dodging speed of 92.142 mph, the fastest yet.

A.J. Foyt made his first Hoosier Hundred appearance that year. Foyt, who ended up winning the great race six times was "just glad to make it. I was driving for Dean Van Lines then and I was just happy to make the show." It's doubtful whether Foyt's record for the longest streak of starts will ever be matched – nineteen in a row from 1958 to 1976.

"There were, and still are, rocks of all sizes on the race track which must be removed," McNamara wrote. "These rocks which have caused all the trouble were not, in my opinion, hauled onto the race track by Mr. Wilfong; rather, they have been here for some years."

Since the Hoosier, McNamara and race director Joe Quinn had spent "many hours" figuring "a way out." In McNamara's opinion, the track could be "made suitable" for both forms of racing, but it would take money. Money for that was needed to satisfy United States Auto Club that "ours is a 'safe' track."

He wanted track responsibility placed in Wilfong's hands. If a favorable decision could be reached at the September 29 meeting, Wilfong would have "the advantage of weather which he did not have last year."

1962 The Board scheduled a new auto race this year: the USAC 100-Mile Stock Car "Century" Race. On the Fair's final evening, September 5, fast qualifier Paul Goldsmith won the 9 p.m. "flying start" feature driving his red '62 Pontiac #1, averaging 71.768 mph. Don White finished in second a lap behind, and John Rostek chased in third. Eddie Sachs came in fourth.

Goldsmith, the 1961 USAC Stock Car champion, drove against the likes of teammate A.J. Foyt; Indianapolis' Rodger Ward, yet another teammate; and Indiana drivers including Dick Paswater, Roy Atkinson, Dave Whitcomb, and Whitey Johnson.

Foyt "ran right on Goldsmith's tail" for nearly seventy-eight miles be-

fore a plugged radiator forced him out. The fastest qualifier at 84.706 mph, Goldsmith had led the entire hundred miles.

"That Pontiac of mine is really a going machine," Goldsmith told *Indianapolis Times* sports editor Jim Smith.

Parnelli Jones in Number 98 won the 1962 Hoosier Hundred with a 90.604 mph average speed in one hour, six minutes, and thirteen seconds, never relinquishing the lead. Also the fast lap qualifier, Jones clocked 100.505 mph.

The tenth Hoosier had drawn the biggest crowd ever, 27,815, and paid a record $43,775 purse.

Allen Crowe, second to last in the starting line-up, gave the crowd a scare when he lost his left rear wheel coming out of turn four in lap 58. Out of control, Crowe's car went into "a slow roll-over" serious enough "to render Crowe unconscious," according to John Robert's account in *Auto Sports*.

The car's right rear wheel spun the car "around crazily with an eerie sound coming from the screaming engine. A sudden flash fire from the spilled oil engulfed the car but the alert fire crew handled the situation promptly and Allen's injuries were held down to minor burns of one hand and severe muscular pain."

Nearly a year later, Crowe was dead at age 34, killed in the June 2 USAC sprint car race in New Bremen, Ohio.

1963 A.J. Foyt won the second State Fair Century stock car race, driving a '63 Ford an average speed of 74.691 mph, undoubtedly one of the slowest times of his career. Foyt was fast qualifier, turning

in 83.799 mph. Gary Bettenhausen finished second; John Rostek followed him. Foyt won the Century again in 1964, 1965, 1968, and 1969. Asked about them in 1991, "Super Tex" said he recalled winning the races, "but none really sticks out in my mind now."

1969 A.J. Foyt and Don White raced in the 100-mile Century New Stock Car race on the August 22 State Fair opening night, in front of 19,270 fans. White took the victory and accepted his award, the Virgil "Gus" Grissom award, made possible by Indiana Motor Truck Association, from Mrs. Betty Grissom and astronaut Colonel Frank Borman, the Apollo 8 moon mission commander.

Racing director Joseph L. Quinn, Jr. scheduled the Fairgrounds' first national championship motorcycle race for August 28, and motorcycle racing returned for the first Fair-time race since 1954, "despite fears of some that the event would attract gangs of hoodlum cyclists," according to a special State Fair release.

Larry Palmgren won the thirty-lap National Championship feature astride his #5 Triumph in front of a crowd of 10,002 fans. Feature polesitter, Palmgren led laps six to fourteen, then grabbed victory in the final lap. Governor Edgar D. Whitcomb presented the Raymond Firestone Trophy to the Freehold, New Jersey, cyclist.

Not content with a mere race, racing director Quinn put on a show when he lined up four-time AMA National Champion (and '54 Fairgrounds feature winner) Joe Leonard in a match race against mere five-time USAC National

Ramo Stott drove for Hartley Truck Parts in Muncie in 1977 when he won the ninth annual USAC Indiana Classic stock car race; he led the entire hundred-lap feature.

Champion A.J. Foyt. The two raced a three-lap course around hay bales on the main straightaway, and Leonard won by a length.

1972 There were a lot of motorized horsepower shows at the Fairgrounds this year.

The "Indianapolis Midget Spectacular," a twin 50-lap racing program May 26, held the same night as the "500 Festival Parade," was a first for midgets on the mile dirt oval and offered a guaranteed $9,000 purse against 40 percent of the gross gate receipts. As planned, forty-two cars started the first feature. Tom Bigelow won, averaging 90.994 mph in 32:58.15.

Chuck Arnold of Indianapolis flipped three times in the red-flagged second fifty after hitting Indianapolis' Billy Mehner, who had gone into a spin after losing a rear wheel. Pancho Carter sneaked in for the win in the final quarter lap.

The 6th 100-mile "Indiana Classic" returned to the Fairgrounds on June 17. The USAC stock car race hadn't run at the track since 1970; new Grandstand construction precluded racing in 1971.

Auto racing director Don Smith assured spectators a faster and safer race due to the installation of concrete retaining walls and double guard rails. "We should have less time under the caution light since we've made these improve-

A.J. Foyt watches '74 Hoosier Hundred action. He hadn't won since 1969 and never would again. His final Hoosier try came in 1976.

Billy Vukovich powers through turn 3 in this shot from the 1980 Hoosier Hundred. Vukovich started sixth in the race and finished in fourth.

ments." A modern caution light system also had been installed.

The improvements led officials to expect the Classic to last under an hour. In the past, the race suffered long delays due to the old style metal outside guards (removed in the spring of 1971 to make room for the new safety improvements); there were thirty-five yellow-light laps and a fifty-minute delay at the '70 Classic.

Don White, the driver with the most wins in Indiana State Fair stock car history, was there. He had chalked up six wins at the Fairgrounds: the Classic in '67 and '68 and the State Fair Century in '66, '67, '69, and '70. White was also the current State Fair stock speed record-holder, clocked at a one-lap mark of 91.349 sec-

Steve Chassey wades through flying corner muck in this 1981 Hoosier Hundred shot. Larry Rice of Brownsburg won, averaging 85.757 mph, the slowest time since 1965's race.

Steve Kinser of Bloomington grooves one of his champ dirt car's tires in this May 1981 scene before the inaugural Hulman Hundred. Kinser led every lap of the sixty-mile feature, claiming $9,150 from the $44,100 total purse.

onds and an average of 86.393 mph for the 100 miles.

Fifty of the nation's greatest names in racing showed up including Roger McCluskey, Al and Bobby Unser, Johnny Rutherford, Gordon Johncock, and Charlie Glotzbach.

The thirty fastest qualifiers vied for a $15,000 purse.

Jack Bowsher took champion's honors, 6-1/2 seconds ahead of White and McCluskey.

Al Unser won his third straight Hoosier Hundred on September 9 in 1:06.07, averaging 90.749 mph. At 104.926, Unser also was fastest qualifier with his #7 Viceroy, powered with A.J. Foyt's engine. Foyt engines powered the first four finishers.

The year before, USAC took the championship points off the race which once rivaled the Indianapolis 500 in purse

prizes. As a result, the car owners didn't buy championship dirt cars in the new and separate series, according to retired sports editor Jep Cadou. The top drivers lost interest.

1973 The "Hoosier Sprints" made its first mile oval appearance after a May 26 rain-out. The qualifications and the 15-lap semi-feature had been completed before the rain hit; the two 50-lap features wrapped up on June 8. Billy Shuman won the red and yellow flagged first race; Don Nordhorn took the double yellow second race. Billy Engelhart was fast qualifier: 34.67 seconds, at 103.836 mph.

USAC late model stock cars vied for the 100-mile feature trophy in the seventh annual "Indiana Classic" on Saturday night, June 23, after a rain-out. Ten Dodges, nine Fords, eight Chevrolets, two Plymouths, and one Chrysler came to race.

Fast qualifier Larry "Butch" Hartman drove his #75 Dodge past the checkered flag in 1 hour, 13 minutes, 48 seconds, averaging 81.301 mph. Butch won $3,530.

Then USAC midgets, in a pair of 50-lap races called the "Firecracker Fifties" (rained out June 17), were cancelled completely after the second rain date, July 4, again was rained out.

Topping off the rain, a tornado touched down at one end of the dirt oval just as practice was about to begin. Parts of the Fairgrounds were severely damaged.

The twelfth renewal of the Century new car race met Sunday, August 26, the last day of the Fair. Jack Bowsher took the four-yellow-flag feature victory in 1:10.59.59, averaging 84.517 mph in his Ford Torino in front of a crowd of 7,877.

Wrapping up the seven-program racing slate, the 21st Hoosier Hundred tore up the mile track on September 15. Nationally televised by ABC's "Wide World of Sports," the Hoosier, with engines starting at 2:10 p.m., was blacked out in the Indianapolis area. Al Unser chose that Hundred to clinch his fourth straight win in a Ford-powered Viceroy.

Greg Weld, the fastest qualifier, led the first eleven laps before Unser took over for the balance of the famed hundred-lapper.

1981 On May 2, the Hulman Hundred, the Fairgrounds' second Silver Crown race, took its first laps around the track. It was the first year for the USAC Silver Crown Series, an eleven-race schedule.

A series of short events added up to a hundred miles in the race named after Tony Hulman. Former race driver and current State Fair Board director of motor racing Bruce Walkup organized and promoted the four-event evening: two fifteen-lap qualifying races, a ten-lap semi-feature and a twenty-four car, sixty-mile feature open only to open cockpit, championship dirt track cars.

After leading every lap, Bloomington's Steve Kinser won that first race driving Gary Stanton and Bill King's Brake-O #75. Presented by American Fletcher National Bank, the first purse totalled $44,100. Kinser claimed $9,150 as his share.

A.J. Foyt stepped back into the Fairgrounds picture in 1991 when he and his associates leased the rights to the Hulman race and rebilled it as A.J. Foyt's Hulman Hundred, adding 40 miles to the feature. Nineteen-year-old Pittsboro resident Jeff Gordon won.

Foyt also took over the Hoosier Hundred. "Outside of winning Indy four times, I think winning the Hoosier Hundred six times is among my most memorable accomplishments in auto racing," Foyt said when the lease announcement was made.

Dirt track racing's richest event, the Hoosier Hundred, returned for its 29th battle with a new twist: USAC Silver Crown and Gold Crown drivers earned points towards championships. It was Indiana's first year as one of the dirt track races chosen to award Gold Crown points, which went toward USAC's national driving championship, and helped attract big-

name drivers to the "Track of Champions." The new conditions made the Hoosier race the fifth stop-off on the Gold Crown Series schedule, and seventh on the Silver. Fifty-nine cars were slated to race. Larry Rice of Brownsburg took the victory, leading from laps one to one hundred.

1985 The green flag dropped for the first time May 18 for the Hoosier Bobtail 100 on the Great American Truck Race series. That Saturday night, twenty-two 14,000-pound trucks reached speeds exceeding 100 mph on a track accustomed to horses, dirt cars, sprints, and motorcycles. Qualifications were followed by twin 20-lap eliminations before the feature race.

Participants in the GATR season opener battled in 1,200-horsepower diesel rigs for the Detroit Diesel Allison Cup and $40,000 in awards. Hoosier racers entered: Gary Grissom, Indianapolis; Phil "Jesse James" Ploughe, Brownsburg, in an '81 Chevy; 1982 Grand National Champion Luther Burton, Columbus; and, driving a '73 Kenworth, Robert Pfeffer, Brownsburg, who finished in the top ten six times during 1984's eight-race series.

Driving an '82 Ford for Anderson's S&S Truck Parts: twenty-year-old Shawna Robinson, who as a rookie won the 1984 Milwaukee 150, becoming "the first woman in history to win a major motorsports event on a North American speedway."

Grissom won the first heat with his '78 Ford; Robinson came in third. In the second heat, Burton triumphed behind the wheel of his '76 Kenworth, and Ploughe drove to eighth.

The honor for winning the only semi truck race in State Fairgrounds history went to Charlie Baker of New Oxford, Pennsylvania, driving truck #93, a 1975 GMC.

Tony Bettenhausen (top left), '51 and '58 National Driving Champion, finished eleventh in the '57 Hoosier, fifth in '58, fifteenth in '59, then second in '60.

Tony Bettenhausen, in the #2 car, and Jim Hurtubise in the #3 car, duel around turn 2 during the '60 Hoosier Hundred. Hurtubise finished twelfth.

Eddie Sachs (far left, second row) won the sixth Hoosier Hundred in '58 with a record average speed of 92.142 mph. He finished second in the '61 Indy 500.

Don Branson came in fourth in the '58 Hoosier Hundred, his best finish. The '64 USAC Sprint Championship winner died in a double fatality accident with Dick Atkins at Ascot Park, Los Angeles, in November 1966.

Jimmy Bryan (right) won the second Hoosier Hundred in '54 driving the same car Bob Sweikert drove the year before. The car eventually won the first four Hoosier Hundreds.

Cars lined up for the '56 Hoosier Hundred race.

And what happened to the Great American Truck Race series? There's no answer at headquarters.

Back-to-back Camel Pro Indy Mile motorcycle racing saw Ricky Graham pick up his second 25-lap feature win on the famed "Mile Oval," clocked at 14:49.235, beating the track record he set in 1980. The second Indy Mile victory went to Hank Scott, who won here twice in 1981 and once in 1978.

A multi-purpose scoreboard with an electronic message line for instant feedback and general information brought a new dimension to Grandstand motor and harness racing events. Two computer terminals operated the center section: one for the stage-operated scoreboard, the other for the message center operated from the Communications Building.

1985

Winged sprint cars made their first appearance in the World of Outlaws/Copenhagen-Skoal Shootout May 11 at the mile dirt track, ninth stop-off on the Stroh's Challenge Cup series. The one-lap track record to beat was 33.070 seconds, set by Eddie Leavitt in a wingless sprint in 1981. Sammy Swindell, who had won the Fairgrounds' first World of Outlaws race in 1979 in a wingless sprint, reprised his victory.

1987

A new lap record was set August 30 at the Fairgrounds mile track – 101.402 mph by Bob Keselowski of Rochester Hills, Michigan, in an '87 Monte Carlo at the "Indiana State Fair ARCA 100" stock car race.

It was the only Automobile Racing Club of America race at the Fairgrounds, and the first stock car race since 1977's 9th annual Indiana Classic.

Five drivers from the last Classic showed up, including winner and hundred-lap leader Ramo Stott; Ken Rowley, who came in sixth; Bob Brevak, seventh-place finisher; fifteenth-place finisher Steve Drake; and Keselowski, who trailed twentieth with a blown engine after finishing forty-six laps.

At the time, Butch Hartman held the stock car one-lap qualifying speed record, 94.364 mph, set August 24, 1975, during the State Fair Century. The fastest hundred-mile stock car race to date at the Fairgrounds, 88.801 mph, in 1:07.34.00, came that same race, courtesy of Don White in his Dodge #5.

Keselowski was forced out of the lead in the fifty-first lap with rear end problems, and Dean Roper of Fair Grove, Missouri, roared his '87 Grand Prix to victory six car lengths ahead of Bob Strait's '87 Monte Carlo. Roper claimed $4,950 from the $38,060 offered in prize, point, and contingency monies after leading laps 10-19 and 64-100.

1989

Jack Hewitt of Troy, Ohio, won the 37th Hoosier Hundred August 27, the final day of the Fair, becoming USAC's winningest driver in the Silver Crown Series with eleven career wins.

The only problem to surface was that no one had thought about where to park race fans arriving during the Fair – most of whom traditionally expected a Hoosier Hundred Infield berth. With parking spaces filled with regular Fairgoers, entire car and van loads were turned away.

1990

Pennsylvanian Gary Hieber may have won the 38th Hoosier Hundred and earned a $12,150 purse, but the racing crowd's champion August 11 was Indianapolis' own Andy Hillenburg, who led the first ninety-six laps.

A crowd estimated at nearly 8,000 was constantly on its feet near the end of the final race promoted by the Indiana State Fair Commission, especially when Hillenburg blew his right rear tire

on his Waterloo lap. Hillenburg managed to limp his car to a fourteenth-place finish to the roar of the extremely appreciative crowd.

Hieber took over the lead after Hillenburg's blow-out. At the finish, the crowd cheered when Hillenburg climbed from his car and walked over to shake the victor's hand.

"I could see on the last ten laps that (Hillenburg's) tire was pretty well worn," Hieber told reporters. "I guess Goodyear wears better than what he had on."

Nearly overcome by his defeat, Hillenburg told reporters, "I didn't feel it going until down the straightaway . . . I couldn't believe it . . . but it was[.]

"It was brand new," said Hillenburg, who started the famed 100-mile feature on the inside of row two. "We didn't have time to cure it with no hot laps.

"I think it was our race to lose," he said of the fifth round in the Valvoline/USAC Silver Crown championship series. Fifty-six cars had been entered in the historic event.

Hillenburg's share of the $61,000 total purse, the largest in eighteen years, was $10,387. Lap leader prizes totalled $10,000.

Jeff Swindell of Memphis, Tennessee, was fastest qualifier, scoring a 109.479 mph lap in 32.883 seconds, followed by Danny Milburn of Indianapolis. Swindell nevertheless was far slower than a year-old record by Rich Vogler at 114.635 mph around the Fairgrounds mile track.

The entire event was plagued by red and yellow flags. Perry Ferrell in car #91 flipped during the first non-qualifiers race.

A five-car accident involving Larry Rice, Chuck Gurney, Dave Burns, and Bob Cicconi in turn four yellow-flagged laps two through eight. None finished a lap in the 100-mile feature on the dirt mile oval.

A Jack Hewitt spin into the turn two wall brought out the yellow flag again for laps 20-21, followed by the red flag when Hewitt caught fire. A rear brake rotor broke and tore through the gas tank bladder bottom, and the resulting fuel leak ignited Hewitt's champ dirt car.

Firefighters quickly doused the flames, and Hewitt suffered only minor transfer burns. The driver from Troy, Ohio, who had won the last two Hoo-

The late Rich Vogler muscles through turn 1 early on during qualification for the 1990 Hulman Mile. He finished second behind Jack Hewitt.

Bubba Shobert won an AMA Camel Pro Indy Twin Mile victory in 1982 and 1983 riding a Harley-Davidson, then in 1986 took a Twin Mile win astride a Honda. Shobert holds the one-mile track record for one lap, 102.241 mph, or just over 35.2 seconds, set in 1985.

siers, was taken to Methodist Hospital in Indianapolis for treatment.

The restart on Lap 21 found Hillenburg leading, followed by Swindell; Bakersfield, Californian George Snider; Stan Fox of Janesville, Wisconsin; and Warren Mockler, Westfield, Indiana, in the next four spots. Fox hit the wall in turn four on the forty-second lap, losing his fourth-place position. Brent Kaeding of Campbell, California, had driveshaft problems and dropped out after seventy-eight miles.

The battle for the top three spots was closely waged for most of the race between Hillenburg, Swindell, and Snider from laps 11 through 66. By lap 67, Hieber moved into the third-place spot and the first-three line-up remained at Hillenburg, Swindell and Hieber until lap 79 when Hieber made his move into second position, bumping Swindell to third.

The game soon changed to Hillenburg, Hieber, and Jimmy Sills, of Placerville, California, when Swindell stalled in the backstretch on the eighty-third lap, and the one-two-three line-up remained until Hillenburg's ninety-sixth lap bout with the bad tire, and his force-down to the fourteenth-place finish of the remaining fourteen cars still running. Hillenburg limped on the rim for three more laps while the other thirteen left him vanquished, yet undefeated in the crowd's eyes.

After the dust settled, Sills came in second, and Wally Pankratz of Yorba Linda, California, followed him in. Snider settled for fourth, and nineteen-year-old Jeff Gordon of nearby Pittsboro, Indiana, took the fifth spot after starting from seventeenth place.

1991 Hoosier Hundred victory came relatively easy for World of Outlaws veteran Jeff Swindell. Swindell led eighty-two laps after a sixth-place start. He finished eight seconds ahead of second-place finisher Jimmy Sills.

"I just kind of rode around," he told fans and reporters. He pocketed a $19,800 purse, far short of Foyt's 1968 $22,659 record purse. Polesitter Jack Hewitt led the first eighteen miles before a burned piston shut out his chances for a fourth Hoosier win.

Two red flags went out, ruining any chance for a time or race speed log. Larry Rice turned upside down in the fourth turn during the feature's nineteenth lap. Three laps later Larry Hillerud did too, but in turn 3. Randy Bateman hit the turn 1 wall one-quarter of the way into the race. Roy Caruthers flipped during the non-qualifiers event; Steve Chassey flipped during qualifications.

Only a yellow flag went up when Danny Smith hit the wall in the front stretch during his twelfth lap.

Foyt spent time on the track days before the race, insisting that Fairgrounds' track men cut down the corner crowns that harness horses need, but which could have sent champ dirt cars into an airborne crash. He got what he wanted.

Bob Cicconi, a regular Hoosier Hundred and Hulman Hundred competitor, has six midget, a Silver Crown (at Indianapolis Raceway Park), and one sprint car win to his credit.

Jeff Gordon of Pittsboro, 1990 USAC midget champion, won the 1991 Hulman Hundred after a fourth-place starting berth.

Johnny Parson roars through the first turn at the 1990 Hulman Hundred. Oil pump problems forced him out on the thirty-fourth lap.

George Snider at the 1990 Hoosier Hundred, the only one held during the State Fair. Only A.J. Foyt has Snider beat in Hoosier starts. Although he has never won a Hoosier, in 1978 "Ziggy" was fastest qualifier.

❖ Indiana's Showplace

After the last midway barkers and prize-winning sheep have left, the Fair facilities aren't folded up and put away until next year. Conventions, attractions, and exhibitions the year round call the Fairgrounds home.

THE FAIRGROUNDS' location at the "Crossroads of America" is ideal for entertainment and the purposes of industry.

National expansion blessed the central state. Developments in transportation, population booms – especially after the Civil War – and the need for new land soon pushed the boundaries of "the West" further beyond the prairies. Indiana's centralized location in the country – nearly all land-based links funnelled through the state – and the siting of the capital in Indianapolis created the Fairgrounds' advantageous position.

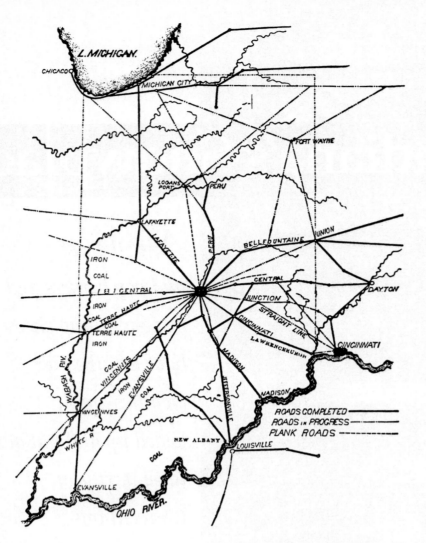

SETTLED in the heart of the midwest, by the late 1800s Indiana had become a center of transportation as well as a center of population.

Once ground was broken in the state, and the settlers established civilization out of the wilderness, Indiana journeyed towards its future as a national agricultural and industrial leader. From the beginning, the Indiana State Board of Agriculture touted Indiana's advantages.

Boardmen told everyone they knew that by 1870 Indianapolis was "the first inland city in the west" and was served by eleven railroads "running to all points of the compass." Within three years, Indianapolis called itself "the largest inland city in the United States," as three more trains joined the city's railroad system.

Indiana's location could not have been more strategic: ". . . between the great lakes on the north and the Ohio river on the south, and midway between the great oceans, in the direct line of travel from the wealthy commercial centers and manufacturing districts of the East, to the newly settled and rich agricultural and mining districts of the 'Great West,' having a climate and soil well adapted to the production of the most valuable grains, grasses, fruits, and live stock, with more miles of railroad and telegraph in operation than any other division of the globe in proportion to the population, her future importance seems clearly foreshadowed."

◆◆◆

While serving as ambassador in Berlin, capital of Prussia, former governor James A. Wright shared copies of the annual Agricultural Board reports with Baron Alexander von Humboldt, who couldn't restrain from writing a letter. It arrived in time for the January 1859 annual Board meeting.

Wright "honors me with his particular good will," the Baron wrote. "If I have deferred so long to offer the homage of my respectful acknowledgements . . . the delay was caused only by indisposition. The volumes . . . prove that at Indianapolis they know how to manage the interests of agriculture and industry with intelligent sagacity, and understand the improvement of natural resources."

A select committee of five promptly undertook the task of considering the February 25, 1859, letter. By the next morning, they resolved to frame the letter "in good taste" and hang it with a translation written by a "skilled penman" in the State Agricultural rooms. Humboldt was made an honorary Board member.

Friedrich Heinrich Baron Alexander von Humboldt, famed Prussian naturalist and explorer authored "The Cosmos." He discovered the decrease in the intensity of the earth's magnetic force from the poles to the Equator; he demonstrated the origin of igneous rock. The Humboldt Current, off South America's west coast, is named after him. Because the Baron died in 1859 it's doubtful whether he ever knew yet another accomplishment was a framed letter in the Board's office.

1866 The "Engines and Machinery/Leather and Leather Manufactures" judging committee found Indianapolis' Eagle Machine Works' portable saw mill and engine entry superior to that shown by Jonas W. Yeo of Richmond.

"In the trial . . . there was a great contrast . . . Eagle Machine Works, with ninety pounds of steam, cut seven planks, twelve and a half feet long and twenty inches wide each, in seven minutes, or at the rate of three thousand feet per hour. The second, with the same amount of steam, cut three planks of the same size, and from the same log, in three minutes, being something less than half the amount of the first. The first used the head-block of Owen, Lane & Dyer, by which one person could set the log; two persons were required for the other."

The worthy judges knew "any person who can appreciate the beautiful in machinery when in action, could see the great difference . . . the one seemed to execute its rapid work with an ease, indicating a greater capacity than was put forth; the other with over-strained labor, and an inability to continue it, and to the certain derangement of the engine."

For further validation, the committee quoted a windy sentence issued by "the most authoritative writer on the arts, Mr. [John] Ruskin." Ruskin, the noted English art critic, author, and social theorist, had after all, "stated truths as applicable to machinery as to living creatures, and a just appreciation of them will be a safe guide in the adaptation of power to machinery.

"'The right and true happiness of every creature, is in this very discharge of its functions, and in those efforts by which its strength and inherent energy are developed . . . in action, the calmness of trust and determination; in rest, the consciousness of duty accomplished and of victory won, and this repose and this felicity can take place as well in the midst of trial and tempest, as beside the waters of comfort; they perish only when the creature is either unfaithful to itself, or is afflicted by circumstances unnatural and malignant to its being, and for the contending with which it was neither fitted nor ordained.'

Quite a few washing machines were shown; the judges agreed "a washing machine, to be efficient, must possess a rubbing power. All but one acted by mere pressure only, most of them executing it by the pressure from rollers."

John Catt's washing machine demonstrated the Bourbon man's sagacity; it "acted with a rubbing power, which carried the article washed, forwards or backwards . . . between two wooden surfaces. The under one is formed of rollers and the upper of wood, pressed upon by the hand and held up to its place by a frame work. The objection to this machine, lies in the manner in which it may be used by a careless or reckless operator. It may be pressed so hard as to injure the articles washed. If a thick lining of India rubber were put upon it, this objection would be obviated."

(Manufactured by Jonas W. Yeo, Richmond, Indiana.)

Improved stump pullers, mailing machines, scales, and knitting machines were demonstrated and then recognized for their superiority.

1869 Master William M. Chase of Indianapolis took every first place in the "Painting, Drawings, &c. – Amateur's" List. He was judged best in fancy, portrait, animal, fruit, flower, and crayon painting.

The committee reviewing Indianapolis' Fairbanks & Company patent corset collection wanted the contrivances "classified as 'American poison' or 'consumption propagators,' and discarded by all true American women, as worse than a useless appendage, and highly injurious to health, as generally worn."

1871 Kimble, Aikman & Company, Indianapolis, claimed the $3 Domestic Implements premium for the best clothes wringer. Hildebrand & Fugate's rat trap caught a like amount.

Sinker, Davis & Company claimed fifty dollars and a silver medal for "best stationary engine, not less than twenty horse power, sufficient to run the machinery at the fair." The company won more silver for "best steam engine governor and valve."

Established at Indianapolis in 1850, the company incorporated in 1871 as Sinker, Davis & Co. Western Machine Works, with Thomas Davis as president and Alfred T. Sinker as secretary. Based at 101-149 South Pennsylvania Street, Sinker & Davis manufactured "Portable

and Stationary, Steam Engines and Boilers, Circular Saw Mills, and every description of Wood Working Machinery &c. &c. &c."

Pig iron and railroad iron vied for silver in the same section specimens of paper were judged. Iron didn't show, but Field, Locke & Company of Indianapolis won for the best wrapping paper.

1872 Hildebrand & Fugate, the Capital City, won with best hedge trimmer and sheep shearing implement. The company also had the best cross-cut saw, smoothing irons, meat cutter, knife sharpener, case of files, wrench, axe, and mattock.

A $25 special premium sought the best collection of rolled or hammered plate glass manufactured in America. Such glass already was being manufactured in New Albany and John B. Ford & Company of that city took the special premium and the silver medal for best collection of window glass and best polished plate glass.

Carriage and Wagon Hall was filled "largely" by Indianapolis' Shaw & Lippincott Manufacturing Company, "whose work, for its style and elegance, is fast winning for them a national reputation." Shaw & Lippincott had the best collection of carriages, wagons, and buggies, including the best two-seated carriage.

Indianapolis Wagon Works exhibited the farm wagon which hauled off the Cincinnati Exposition's blue ribbon (first) the week before.

The coveted Board diploma was awarded to Whitney Arms Company of New Haven, Connecticut, for its breech loading double-barrelled shotgun; G. Stevenson, Zionsville, for rubber nipples; Mrs. Adams of Coventry, England, for her lace needle work; and D.W. Haydock,

Indianapolis, for his "arrangements for teaching telegraphy."

1873 State Boardmen threw their arms open to European emigrants with a resolution to submit detailed information about the Hoosier state to the Vienna Exposition, "soon to assemble in one of the great European capitals."

They asked the Legislature to print, in German, English, and French, 30,000 copies of "the agricultural, mechanical, and mineral resources of Indiana, including its financial condition, its social advantages, its temperature, productions, and its adaptation to the various wants of the industrious emigrant from the Old World."

1880 Before the Fair, Grand Army of the Republic rented the grounds and buildings for $100. The G.A.R., formed in 1866 by honorably discharged Union army and navy veterans, lasted until 1949.

Lesser income came from an April 24 walking match on the track, the "Colored" Association's July 22 event, a July 30 Gun Club meeting, and the Colored Agricultural Society gathering on August 20.

1882 The national "Military and Knights Templar Encampment" hit Indianapolis July 1-6 in a massive competitive demonstration of military maneuvers at the Fairgrounds.

The Artillery Competitive Drill on July 1 was open to all U.S. artillery organizations, offering a $300 first prize for best "manual and mechanical movements . . . 'mount the carriage,' 'mount the piece' and firing two rounds of blank cartridges."

Each company in the July 3 Competitive Infantry Drill consisted of "three commissioned officers and not less than twenty-four men, . . . in conformity to Upton's Revised Infantry Tactics." Company captains were required to prove their men were actual members.

The July 4 "Free For All," open to all U.S. infantry companies, awarded $1,500 for the best-drilled militia organization in "the grandest military exhibition ever witnessed. [T]hat the award may be indisputably fair, the judges have been selected from officers of the United States Army [and] graduates of West Point."

"Free For All" competitors included McKeen Cadets, Terre Haute;

John Grate of Atwater, Ohio, a national commander of the Grand Army of the Republic, visited the 1946 Fair.

Company E, Asbury Cadets, Greencastle; Sherman Guards, Frankfort; Logan Greys, Logansport; Arcola Guards, Arcola; Indianapolis Light Infantry; and companies from Tennessee, Missouri, Louisiana, Arkansas, New York, Illinois, Washington D.C., Ohio, and Michigan.

The Grand Templar Exhibition Drill on July 5 was demonstrated by Raper Commandery No. 1 (Knights Templar) of Indianapolis, "winners of the second prize at the Triennial Conclave of the Grand Encampment of the United States at Cleveland, 1877, and of the first prize at [the] Grand Triennial Conclave at Chicago in 1880, and the holders of the champion banner of the United States."

Also participating: De Molay Commandery No. 12, of Louisville, Ky., "winners of the second prize at the Grand Conclave at Chicago, in 1880; holders of

the champion banner of Kentucky for 1882," and Louisville Commandery No. 1, "one of the best-drilled commanderies of Knights Templar in the United States." On the final day, Governor Albert G. Porter awarded the winners' prizes and the camp broke up.

1882 J.H. Clark & Co., Indianapolis, exhibited the Elbreg Reclining Chair: "The inclination of the back is regulated by a bar and ratchet, worked by the sitter without rising. The back can be brought nearly to the horizontal. It is well cushioned and very convenient for sick or lazy persons."

Flanner & Hommown of Indianapolis exhibited a "display of extravagantly fine burial caskets." S.L. Warner, also of the city, showed a "handsome line of burial cases to suit every demand . . . [T]here was an ornamented metallic case . . . secure against grave burglars . . . [T]he entire exhibit is of home manufacture."

The United States Encaustic Tile Company, Indianapolis, showed flooring and ornamental tiles "of a great variety . . . all made from material obtained chiefly in this State . . . [T]he manufacture of tiles for flooring purposes is a new industry in this country. The Indianapolis factory, erected in 1879, was the first attempt at the manufacture in the United States."

Professor A.W. Brayton, superintendent of "Geology, Natural History, Etc." remarked that Encaustic Tile's exhibit belonged "for its beauty . . . in the Department of Decorative Art . . . [S]ymmetrical architecture has been called frozen music, and . . . it may be said the encaustic tiles exhibited at the State Fair . . . are petrified beauty. It is crude Indiana clay etherealized and exalted by fire, form and color." In January 1884, the Board awarded the company a diploma, "this being a new industry in this State, and highly deserving of encouragement."

Oliphant Pedigo of Harrodsburg, Indiana, exhibited the Stone City Washing Machine examined by the "Special Merits of Unpremiumed Articles" committee. This device washed "by rubbing between two corrugated boards, one being cylindrical, and swinging against the other."

J. Yagerlenner of Nine Mile exhibited "a wire coil-[bed]spring with a top connection which holds every spring in its place[.]" Mixes' Bed Springs, exhibited by Indianapolis' T.B. McManis, featured wires "for a baby's cradle up to No. 8 wire for a bed for a person weighing three hundred pounds."

In "Hardware and Miscellaneous Articles," Taylor Brothers, Indianapolis, exhibited a railroad car coupling, "a device that would save great loss of life."

Indiana Wire Fence Company, Crawfordsville, exhibited a barbed wire machine capable of turning out 15,000 pounds of the product daily.

1886 Mechanical Department superintendents reported exhibitors from "every State save three," – thirty-eight at this time – "and applicants from several were

PORTABLE ENGINE.

Exhibited by SINKER & DAVIS, Indianapolis.

turned away for want of room." Carriages and wagons, buggies and sleighs, washing machines, and soap. All found in the Carriages and Wagons Department.

Board Secretary Alexander Heron later said the event had "assumed such a magnitude that we have been compelled to refuse entries . . . for want of space." Hoosier inventiveness and Mechanical showmanship were tops with 1,500 exhibits, compared with fourteen other major Fairs. Only Michigan came close, with 1,357. Indiana had 5,019 exhibits.

What sustained the Mechanical Department's claims of magnificence? Steam engines and separators; saw-mills, tile mills, and brick machines; apparatus connected with steam and other motors; hydraulic machines and force pumps of all kinds; hoisting, flour mill, and wood working machinery; evaporators, warming and ventilating apparatus; laundry and dairy machines; an "invincible" hatcher; a vegetable slicer; an automatic clutch; and aquariums; plus thousands more.

1887 The "Special Merits" report on the Grand Hall's second floor exhibits cited Flanner & Buchanan of Indianapolis, which "made a wonderfully attractive feature of the undertaking business without presenting any ghastly or gloomy features." The display had floral designs, "many of them bearing the insignia of the

different secret orders, a model of Crown Hill Cemetery viewed from the southeast, and a representation of the burial of Cock Robin, cleverly arranged with stuffed birds and suitable decorations and legends, true to the old nursery rhyme."

1888 "Well may this be called 'a new era,'" Heron stoutly claimed, "the future of which can only be conjectured." Scientists were "dumfounded" by recent inventions: the "dazzling electric light," hearing "the voice of friends from afar through the telephone," and, of course, natural gas.

1900 A July 4 thrill show at the Fairgrounds! A head-on crash of two locomotives! Crowds estimated at 35,000. The *Indianapolis News* reported: "The steam engines, both driven by obviously brave men [both jumped out], were backed apart on a special track to a distance of 4,000 feet and then raced wildly at a speed of 25 miles an hour to the point of impact.

"The crash sent the crowd into bedlam with some spectators firing pistols and others crying loudly. No one was injured.

"The streetcar company, however, was unable to handle the people going to the event, with a trip from downtown to the Fairgrounds taking three hours. People were forced to sit on the

tops of cars and several injuries were reported.

"A small riot occurred on one of the cars when the passengers became mutinous and demanded their money back." According to 1952's Fair program, "the conductor fled."

◆◆◆

PROMINENT Indianapolis attorney Merrill Moores had appeared May 1 "in the interest of the railroad association" to describe the kind of entertainment railroadmen wanted on Independence Day.

Moores left the meeting assured railroaders could rent the grounds on July 3 and 4 "for [the] head-on collision, horse races, bicycle races, automobile races, and other such amusements as the association desire[d] to give, not inconsistent with the laws of the State." The arrangement stipulated no intoxicating liquor "including hop ale," no gambling "includ-

ing pool selling," and $200 was to be paid before anything began.

1903 Non-awarded Indianapolis manufacturing exhibitors included International Motor Car, Fisher Automobile Company, and Earhart Motor Car Company. Twenty-six buggy and carriage manufacturers were there, with plenty of time before the introduction of the automobile into general use.

Among "Gas and Gasoline Engine" manufacturers were Neilman Machine Works of Evansville; Geiser Manufacturing, Indianapolis; Gemmer Manufacturing, Marion; Lambert Gas and Gasoline Engine, Anderson; and Reliable Machine, Anderson.

1904 Some of the Fair's Mechanical Department exhibitors were Brown Brothers, Nappanee; Dill Motor Power Pump, Danville; Farmers' Guide Publishing, Huntington (founded in 1836); Fort Wayne Wind Mill; Gaumer Engine, Marion; Flint & Walling, Kendallville; James & Meyer Buggy, Lawrenceburg;

The curious gathered in the aftermath of the Fairgrounds' great 1900 Independence Day Train Crash.

Knightstown Buggy; and Lincoln Carriage, Greensburg.

Companies exhibiting from Indianapolis included Acetylene Gas Light; J.I. Case Threshing Machine; Capital Gas Engine; H.T. Conde Implement; Enterprise Foundry and Fence; Everett Seed; Eastern Moline Plow; Fisher Automobile; Fairbanks, Morse & Co.; Gilbreath Seed; Gates-Osborne Carriage; Hearsey Vehicle; and Pope Motor Car.

1905 "Parke Davis & Company, through diligent application of their famous Kreso Disinfectant, contributed to the comforts of our patrons . . . and the healthfulness of stock . . . with the following results: (a) no disease reported among the animals; (b) comparative freedom of offensive odor from closets; (c) absence of flies and disagreeable smell in stock stables. . . .[S]incere thanks[.]"

1906 L.C. Munson Company was issued a medal for its "meritorious" lightning rod exhibit. (Indianapolis' David Munson showed the best lightning rods and points in 1857. Munson's lightning rods won several awards. One year he took a "Scientific Instruments" bronze medal. The same year he offered a special $3 premium for the best pair of ducks of any kind.)

1907 Automobiles claimed their own Mechanical classification for the first time. Gibson Automobile of Indianapolis was there, as was Frank N. Martindale of Knightstown, and the Cadillac Company of Detroit.

1908 The 32nd National Saengerfest, N.A.S.B., or in German, the "Saengerfest des Nord-Amerikanischen Saenger-Bundes," filled the Coliseum with singers June 17-21.

The singing festival inspired the State Board to equip the Coliseum, known as "Saengerfest Halle," with electric wiring and lamps. The Indianapolis Saengerfest Committee worked with the Board "in every way possible . . . to make satisfactory arrangements and contracts with the Light & Power Company to extend its service or trunk lines from 34th Street to the Coliseum Building."

1913 A letter from Indianapolis Automobile Trade Association convinced the Board to rent the Coliseum for a March 19-24 automobile show. Originally, the fee was set at $900 plus a charge for the electric current. When the association complained, the rate dropped to $700, plus electric, the auto men paying for their own janitors.

1916 The I.A.T.A. again secured the Coliseum and horse barn (except for Lon McDonald's aisle) for a February 28-March 4 show.

W.J. Galvin of Wilmington, Ohio, rented the Coliseum, and the brick horse barn, "except the south aisle, where Mr. Lon McDonald's horses are stabled," for a March horse sale.

Meanwhile, the Indiana National Guard 139th Field Artillery's Battery A used fifteen Brick Horse Barn stalls for battery and officer horses, and trained in the Coliseum.

Sears, Roebuck and Company of Chicago, whose catalog was an outhouse staple, drew a July protest from Indianapolis Board of Trade, the Merchants Association, and other local groups.

"These gentlemen were severally heard in the interest of their associations and after a discussion with members of the [executive] committee no action was taken."

1917 Because of last year's complaints from the business community, Sears-Roebuck and Montgomery-Ward, "Mail Order Houses from without the state," were declined exhibit space. Sears may not yet have acquired its David Bradley line of farm implements or part of the Fair's machinery exhibit dating as early as the 1880s.

"[I]t is planned that the board shall become a state institution, with broader powers and widened endeavor, and extend its fostering care throughout the whole domain of practical agriculture, co-ordinate with the theoretical and the experimental agricultural education, until all interests are brought into contact with its vital forces. To do this requires fundamental legislation along some lines, and a world of detail which must be the product of exchange of trained minds supported by a vision which peers far into the future."

1918 The Board's *Hub of the Universe* newspaper, published from 1918 to 1924, was so named because Indianapolis was the transportation hub of the nation, with twenty-six railroad and traction lines converging on the Hoosier capital.

1919 "Another means of convincing the people of our State and her law-mak-

ers of the necessity of improving the State Fair property would be to use for the public welfare this same property for twelve months in the year, thereby proving its economic value," Board president John Isenbarger remarked in January.

Before the month was up, a call came from the up-and-coming symbol of prosperity. John Orman, Mr. Snyder, Mr. Wiley, and "other representatives of the automobile interests" wanted an Automobile Exhibit Building. Indianapolis needed a big showroom befitting the auto manufacturing center status it enjoyed.

The building – "for the exhibition of Automobiles and accessories" – kept the Board busy that year. Completed

The Riley Hospital for Children Brace Shop exhibit during the 1920s. "Braces are Fundamental – In the treatment of children suffering from orthopedic deformities such as Bow Legs, Knock Knees, Club Feet, Curvature of the Spine, Infantile Paralysis, Etc." The light-colored brace below the main sign reads "Head Sling and Jury Mast (for Tuberculosis of Neck Bones – Take Weight of head off Spinal Column)" The brace next to it is a "Leather Jacket (for Curvature of Spine or Pott's Disease)."

in time for the 1919 Fair's automobile show, the Manufacturers' Building was soon declared "the greatest and most wonderful show pavilion on any Fair Ground in the United States." Many would-be exhibitors were turned away from the building "that promises to serve in the future so many demands and needs[.]" Automobile tradesmen promptly booked the building for spring and Fair shows. Each year more than $1 million in autos

were sold, promoters for the Home Show, later claimed.

♦♦♦

THE MANUFACTURERS' Building hosted the Indianapolis Chamber of Commerce's first Industrial Fair on October 10-15, 1921, in "the biggest achievement since the starting of track elevation," according to "Indianapolis First," a Chamber history. The *State Year Book* records 140,000 people came to see 383 "of the city's largest industrial enterprises."

Seven hundred eighty city-manufactured products, from acetylene gas to xylophones, were exhibited. Huge banners in downtown Indianapolis proclaimed the 'Made in Indianapolis' products exposition as "Industrial Indianapolis under one roof."

Board Secretary Charles F. Kennedy claimed he conceived the idea in 1920, originally as a "Made in Indiana" show, according to *Hub of the Universe*.

One Indianapolis manufacturer sold two train carloads of rope. "Another sold three mammoth machines," reported sales literature for another great show which opened the following year – the Home Show. "A lamp manufacturer had to stop booking actual orders. . . This is Exposition Capital." The event lasted into the 1930s.

The Fairgrounds Manufacturers' Building hosted the first Indianapolis Chamber of Commerce Industrial Fair in 1921. That first Fair boasted more than 400 exhibits and more than 100,000 visitors.

An obscured sign toward the left of the "New Exposition Building" (Cattle Barn) reads, "In This Building – Largest Exposition Building On One Floor in the Midwest – October 4 to 11 – The Second Indianapolis industrial EXPOSITION – Auspices Indianapolis Chamber of Commerce." Note the trolley car lines in the foreground.

The Goddess of Transportation welcomed new car buyers to numerous automobile shows. Indianapolis Auto Trades Association began showing new cars at the Fairgrounds early in 1916.

The 1916 State Fair Auto Show (this scene is from the Twenties) "which so well marks the march of mechanical achievement . . . was so vast that space was sought outside of the great pavilion . . . many exhibitors are said to have failed to see any other part of the Fair."

1921 The Board finally heated the Manufacturers'/Automobile Show Building, thus ensuring that it would become "an everyday plant for the use of this and kindred industries."

1922 Conceived by realtor and home builder J. Frank Cantwell and sponsored by the Indianapolis Real Estate Board, the Home Show made its first appearance on May 8-13 at the Manufacturers'/Automobile Show Building. (Cantwell called it "Exposition Hall.")

The first Home Show offered salesmen "A Selling Opportunity. The man who gets business these days is the man who goes after it. Selling in 1922 is no different . . . except that it takes a little

Announcing the
HOME COMPLETE
EXPOSITION

The cover of the first Home Show program, and the first home – fully built inside the Manufacturers' Building.

more pressure to complete the sale. People . . . are simply hesitating to buy, and the only way in which to sell merchandise is to find the point of contact – the selling opportunity."

The Fairgrounds provided the essential grand sales arena. Thousands would see the huge exhibit, millions by the nation's oldest Home Show's seventieth year in 1992. "The exhibitor whose floor sales do not give him profit enough to cover all his expenses will be the rare exception. . . ."

Letters were sent to "women in the home." The Real Estate Board knew "95 percent of the purchases for the home are made by women. . . . [B]uilding and home buying . . . without the wife is almost negligible."

Indianapolis public school teachers conducted a citywide essay contest, "Why One Should Own His Own Home in Indianapolis," for schoolchildren. Cards were handed out as kids left school for home and were also given to factory workers. Public speaking engagements, adhesive stickers for business stationery, and newspaper-ready fact sheets flooded the city. Streamers were hung across retail district streets. Billboards, posters, street car front boards, bank signs, and newspaper advertising, "the most powerful printed salesman of the present day," were employed.

"But the Big Punch – the thing that is going to bring the hundred thousand to the Exposition" was the giving away of "a ready-built five-room home." The best essayist was awarded the prefabricated portable home which today stands at 13th and Emerson Avenue.

The Home Show's marketing brochure touted its headquarters at the Manufacturers' Building as "easily accessible to automobile traffic and street cars. It is without question the biggest and best exposition building in Indiana."

1925 A February 17 letter from Indianapolis Commissioner of Buildings Francis F. Hamilton reminded State

◆ 270 ◆

Scenes from a Home Show of the Twenties. Shoppers saw the latest conveniences for every room in the home, from bathtubs to windows, to bedroom suites and curtains.

Boardmen, "Some time ago the City of Indianapolis passed an Ordinance extending the City Limits beyond the Fair Grounds."

Hamilton suggested that the Board "use your influence in getting an appropriation" to repair the Coliseum – "a fire trap" – and build a new grandstand to replace the old one which "we expect to condemn."

A later correspondence claimed the Coliseum's problem focused on "a lot of stoves underneath a wooden building." (By 1925, there were sixteen fire protection water hydrants on the Fairgrounds.)

Indianapolis Auto Trade Association's John Orman announced in February that his group wanted to hold "an immense bonfire" of old, used automobiles in the center of the race track. The old cars were "a menace on the streets; cars back of five years."

After the fire, the I.A.T.A. held a thirty-day used car sale in May. The cars' gas tanks were drained before being allowed into the Manufacturers' Building; none could be driven in.

1926 Indiana National Guard Adjutant General William H. Kershner told the Board March 25 that he needed a new place to stable the 139th Field Artillery

horses. He wanted a brick barn large enough to accommodate thirty horses.

The Guard proposed a 200-by-300 foot structure north of the feed barn at the Fairgrounds' northeast corner. Another acceptable location for the government-issued steeds was "the strip of ground between Fall Creek and the road." The full Board decided against the request on July 2.

By November, Kershner hadn't found deeding or leasing Fairgrounds land practical and asked the Board to spend $100 repairing an old horse barn. One better, the Board spent $200 at one of the northside barns. Monthly rental was kept at $40.

1927 Plans for "real service to the public by further use of the grounds aside from the fair are now being considered," Secretary-Treasurer E.J. Barker said. "These, we think will be of lasting service and real appreciation to the city of Indianapolis. . . ."

Barker wanted airplanes exhibited at the 1928 Fair. He had Orin Welch Aircraft Company, located in Anderson,

in mind. Board member Russell G. East believed that the Pennsylvania Railroad could be induced to exhibit a large passenger plane used in its new transatlantic airplane service. The Board encouraged him to contact railroad representatives. Barker ended up arranging for the display of three airplanes from the Hoosier Airplane Company on Lafayette Road in Indianapolis.

1928 The Indianapolis Automobile Trade Association shared Fair-time space in the Manufacturers' Building with Indianapolis Radio Dealers and Indianapolis Retail Furniture Dealers.

After the Fair, Barker rented 1,000 chairs for three weeks to an American Legion Post for a Tomlinson Hall marathon dance. The fee: 25 cents per chair, with a $1.40 breakage charge.

1929 The Guard was still stabling at the Fairgrounds when Colonel Henley requested barn and corral repairs and corral drainage. Henley bought the lumber; Superintendent Forest Neal's men

performed the labor and drained the corral.

In October, Sahara Grotto, a fraternal organization, asked to use a building for Friday night maneuver drilling until mid-April, then more frequently until June. An estimated fifty-five to eighty members participated.

Also in October, when Mrs. Mercer with *Prairie Farmer* magazine asked for their statement supporting the paper's efforts to stop chicken stealing, the Board voted unanimously "that we endorse the efforts of the *Prairie Farmer* to make the identification, arrest, and punishment of chicken thieves more effective."

Fort Harrison personnel played pony polo in the Coliseum beginning November 1, at $150 per month for six months, "not to exceed two hours each Saturday night and Sunday afternoon."

A Mrs. Bailey received Board permission to build a horse training enclosure with new material at her own expense on the northwest corner "near the place she built last year."

Hogs from throughout America came to the National Swine Show, the

An elaborately decorated Auto Show in the Manufacturers' Building greeted new car buyers twice every year.

The price for this new Lincoln isn't far from the cost of a current economy car.

New Stutz cars attracted interest at the 1926 Auto Show. Fairgoers could see new cars three to four months before winter show exhibitions. "The success of the motor shows at the Hoosier exposition have been so successful that exhibitions are now annually staged at a number of other large fairs over the country," the Board of Agriculture reported in the late 'Teens.

first time ever in conjunction with any state fair. Six other locations in Ohio, Illinois, Missouri, and Iowa were found unsatisfactory before the decision that Indiana was best, if financial assistance was possible.

Barker recounted a herculean effort: "As it was the last day in the afternoon of the session of Legislature, it seemed next to impossible to think of getting an appropriation, but I talked to a few leaders in both the House and the Senate" and "so I prepared a bill and it was introduced at eight o'clock in the evening in the House and passed without a dissenting voice and went over to the Senate and in one hour and seven minutes" it "was ready for the Governor's signature."

A $10,000 appropriation covered premiums, judges, and other show expenses. A condition allowed legislators to approve the list of swine judges. Apparently, the General Assembly knew more about pigs in 1929.

After premium amounts were set, Swine Show committee members noted "the total classification for all breeds, including open classes, Fat Barrows, 4-H Pig Club [which, when originally overlooked, brought on Purdue reproaches], Futurity and Breed Special amounts to $23,743, which we believe is the largest amount of money ever offered at any swine show except a World's Fair.

"Indiana has one of the best equipped fair grounds in the United States and the very best of shipping facilities." Iowa alone sent twenty-three herds to the national show. Two hundred nine exhibitors competed. "It was the greatest swine show ever held in all history, bar none," said the *State Year Book*. "The wonderful swine pavilion was filled to capacity and over 400 head were housed under a tent."

Board member Russell G. East received Board approval in 1929 to help arrange an exhibit of the passenger plane which the Pennsylvania Railroad would use in soon-to-be inaugurated New York to San Francisco service.

The "Colored K. of P. Grand Lodge" gathered in a national encampment and convention on August 18-24, at the Coliseum and the grounds northeast of the racetrack.

Mrs. Fred Duesenberg and others who cared gathered October 11 in the "Automobile Building" (a.k.a. the Manufacturers' Building) for their annual card party to benefit Sunnyside, a charitable institution for tuberculosis patients.

Indianapolis Aircraft Association's W.A. McCurry came forward in March stating the Cattle Barn doors were neither wide nor high enough for the larger airplanes in its show. McCurry offered to pay for enlarging a door to 16-by-22 and then offered a two- or three-year contract to justify the change. A month later, costs had scared off the fliers' door project.

In July, Secretary-Treasurer Barker brought bad news: only $500 of the $2,000 rental had been paid at contract signing, a departure from policy. Then the show promoters "fell down," he said, and the show was taken over by "an organization of young men in Indianapolis under the leadership of Wallace

This swine barrow head adorns the Swine Barn; numerous Fairgrounds livestock barns carry similar decorations.

O. Lee and Mr. Hottel of Capitol Airport."

Unfortunately, the show failed to attract sufficient attendance, and Barker couldn't collect the $1,500 still owed – "to stop the show when it was being backed morally as a civic enterprise did not look like a wise thing to do." Even after deducting $500 from the bill, Barker was unable to collect, but he kept trying. (Sometime before 1930, Barker gave up.)

Barker disclosed on September 30, 1930, he hadn't learned his lesson about McCurry and "cow barn" rental. McCurry, also promoting the Indiana Industrial Exposition, had failed to pay that bill too. Only $200 of $2,500 had been received up to the time when exhibits began showing up. When Barker refused to open the doors without additional payment, McCurry produced $800 more.

A "where's my money?" call after the Exposition opened discovered McCurry sick in bed and "Mr. Clancy, an attorney, and Dr. Hewitt" on their way over to the State House to "discuss" what McCurry still owed.

When the doctor and Clancy arrived, consultation determined that another $500 could be paid. A poor financial diagnosis argued insufficient booth space sales. Accommodating and civic-minded as always, the Committee agreed to let the show open as planned.

1930 "The Nation's Home Show" had become "an INSTITUTION . . . unrivaled attention and its influence is state wide. Indianapolis is the center of a web of railroad, interurban, and paved roads. Indianapolis merchants enjoy the patronage of a 2,500,000 population within a 75 mile radius. COME TO INDIANAPOLIS! Sell your product to these millions who represent the largest percentage of home owning people in the world. Indianapolis, center of the nation; center of population; center of home building and home owning."

"Each year . . . there is designed, built and displayed a full sized Master Model Home. This home is the exposition's most outstanding feature . . . in truth a master model home, of master design, and master materials. After the exposition this home is transplanted to a select Indianapolis neighborhood and sold . . . generally to someone who has spoken for it during the show."

Curtiss-Wright Service of Indiana and Curtiss-Wright Exhibition Corporation furnished old-time planes, gliders, and modern aircraft on Aviation and Auto Race Day.

Their Captain Cook and Mr. Pickens described a grand spectacle: a two-hour pageant of aerial progress with fourteen planes (including the Mystery Ship, 300-Mile Ship, two Curtiss pushers, and a Ford Tri-Motor), flying stunts, V-formation flying, outside loops, a girl flier, and multiple parachute jumps.

Crowds could witness a refueling demonstration with the St. Louis Robin, three men in a race of jumping balloons, balloons bursting, and an eight-plane air race radio-directed by a man sitting in the Grandstand. For the evening

"Join the Aviation School of the Junior Chamber of Commerce," proclaimed this float in 1927.

The Fairgrounds hosted the Indiana State Guernsey Sale following the 1932 Fair. Guernseys, "the herd improver," were – at least to the breed's producers – "the quality quantity breed."

show, two planes "battled" fireworks, "cutting loose with a trail of fire." An air queen was crowned.

Concern over a "ringer" led Secretary-Treasurer Barker to suggest adding a Horseshoe Pitching Department rule barring "Jimmie" Risk from further participation "on the grounds of his being a professional."

So why not take Risk? "Main Street Indiana" columnist Fred D. Cavinder of the *Indianapolis Star* discloses that "[o]ne of the most unusal Hoosier sportsmen ever was Jimmie Risk of Monticello, boy wonder of horseshoe pitchers in the 1920s. . . . One of only a few men to earn a living tossing horseshoes, Risk traveled by horse and buggy in the early days, doing shows for $10 at blacksmith shops and country stores."

Risk toured with Roy Rogers and Gene Autry, and entertained World War II and Korean War troops. A Risk-tossed horseshoe could flick the ash from a cigar forty feet distant. Winner of eleven Indiana titles, he could light a match with the first pitch and extinguish it with the second. He tossed a few shoes for Harry S. Truman.

According to Barker, horse shoe hustlers had no business at the Fair, but no action was taken.

1931 Six years after official warnings, three years after a dozen small fires in one Fair week, and two years after the city's Board of Safety comdemned the old Grandstand, a new one replaced it.

Shortridge High School's Parent-Teacher Association put on a benefit card party on April 23, with proceeds providing student financial aid and scholarships for those who would never become leaders without help. Proceeds from a dance that same night bought new band uniforms and musical instruments.

There was some real Depression dickering during a mid-April afternoon meeting after the PTA's Mrs. Losey had already secured free rent and 700 chairs. The Indianapolis Athletic Club had donated 400 chairs, but Mrs. Losey needed 1,400 more.

Barker offered them at 5 cents each, whereupon Mrs. Losey claimed she could get them downtown for 4-1/2 cents each, "and while she would like to get [them] at the Fair Grounds," she had to save all she could. The difference came to $7. The Board reconsidered. Former president U.C. Brouse then moved for 4 cents, and the deal was done.

1932 Although the Fair had long been called the "Show Window" of Indiana agriculture, E.J. Barker believed "its scope should be broader and should bear the name of the Indiana State Fair and Exposition.

"We should encourage all kinds of industry. I hope to see the 1932 fair carry with it an 'Industrial Exposition' second to none ever held in the middle west, and this Industrial section of the fair [is to] be composed entirely of Indi-

ana-made products." He was certain of statewide manufacturing cooperation.

That first-time event in the Manufacturers' Building, the "Indiana State Fair and Pageant of Industry," gloried in "everything from vases to motor trucks."

1933 "There is not enough (Manufacturers' Building and Mechanical Field) space sold or prospects to even start a show [for the exposition]," Secretary-Treasurer Barker scoffed in late July. Only 7 out of 124 twenty-by-twenty foot Manufacturers' Building spaces had been sold.

Governor Paul V. McNutt's man, J.D. Hull, blamed it on economic conditions, stuffiness in the Manufacturers' Building, and exhibitors faced with high prices. The Board finally cut exhibit space prices in half and made electricity concessions. Lieutenant Governor M. Clifford Townsend promised to "make the sale" for sixty spaces to the Electric League of Indianapolis. When the Fair came, only half of the spaces had been sold. Apparently, a capacity crowd hadn't been lined up for four years.

Baseball fans could learn where to buy their Babe Ruth underwear at the 1933 McLoughlin (underwear and pajamas) Manufacturing exhibit, part of Kokomo's display in the Manufacturers' Building.

"You're there with a Crosley," Fairgoers learned in 1927. Fine furniture as well as a quality radio, the Crosley brought baseball, football, "big fights" political conventions, opera, and jazz to every household able to afford one.

Kimball offered everyone a fine piano from "factory to home." In the background in this Manufacturers' Building scene, Los Angeles County exhibited its tourism merits in the waning days of the Roaring Twenties.

INDIANA'S FIRST POLICE TRAINING SCHOOL. JULY 1935.

INDIANA State Police convened their first recruit school, spanning five weeks, at the Fairgrounds beginning on July 5, 1935. The recruits slept on rock-hard Army cots in a room above the Horse Barn; sixty-one graduated from that first class.

"An old Army master sergeant was our drill sergeant," recalled Herman Freed, one of the first graduates and the first superintendent of the State Police Training Academy. Recruits marched to the Fairgrounds hotel and back for their meals. "It was the greasiest place I'd ever seen," Freed remembered. There always was a waiting line at the latrines.

Classes were conducted in the old Indiana University Building west of the Women's Building. Chairs without arms forced the recruits to take notes in their laps. "It was hot," Freed recalled. "You can't imagine how hot it was." Buildings didn't even have screens on the windows, he said.

Five State Police transmitting/receiving stations went up around the state beginning in October the year before; one was at the Fairgrounds. All five were operational by May 1935.

1935 Despite the dismal exposition show two Fairs earlier, sales were up considerably for the 1935 Fair and exposition. "One company in the machinery field sold machinery to one person amounting to over $17,000," the Board reported in the *State Year Book*. "This prob-

ably was due to the fact that the condition of the farmer during the last two years has been improved and he is now purchasing new machinery for his farm."

The Manufacturers' Building contained the most exhibits ever in its history. Exhibitors there claimed more sales and more leads than ever before.

1937 Linco Gas Company won approval to stage an evening airplane show featuring stunts, skywriting, and a take-off from atop an auto. The promotion included erecting two "attractive" twenty-foot Linco signs in front of the Grandstand. The company also sweetened the offer by agreeing to take aerial photographs of the Fair.

"The Indiana State Fair has been considered to be a one week's show but practically every week in the year, various expositions, attractions, conventions such as Auto, Food, Funeral Director, Dog, Poultry, and Home Shows; Rodeos, Midget Auto Races, Dances and Parties, Livestock Sales, etc. have rented the buildings."

But the Board could be persuaded to turn away good money, if the appropriate threats were made. In April, Fair Manager Harry Templeton disclosed the Coliseum had been rented for an April 15 to May 5 Roller Derby schedule. By May, a fall contract had been signed.

But Roller Derby was unwelcome competition. During the November 5 Board meeting, six protesters in-

Members of the first Indiana State Police Training School take a break in 1935 for a class picture in the Indiana University Building. Herman Freed, first executive director of the Indiana Law Enforcement Academy, is in the third row, far left. Frank A. Jessup, ISP superintendent from 1953-7, is in the third row, sixth from the left. Paul Minneman, in the fourth row, second from the right, the first trooper killed in the line of duty, was shot in a gun battle with the Brady Gang. His death prompted Indiana legislators to pass ISP's first pension legislation. Ray Dixon, second row, second from left, was shot and killed in a gun battle with the infamous Easton Brothers Gang. Others which Herman Freed recognizes in this photo are: 1961-63 superintendent John J. Barton, Paul Wilhelm, Edward Buchanan, Delvice Masterson, Mark Nelson, Robert Clevenger, Price Cox, Abe Taylor, Cliff Ward, and Max Branch.

Indiana State Police mantained its headquarters and safety exhibit for many years in a now-gone building just west of what now is Hook's Historic Drug Store.

cluding Harry Martin and Marc Wolf of the Theatre Owners Association showed up to complain. Explaining that 422 theatres belonged to their association, Carpenter protested the Fairgrounds' theatrical productions, "especially the 'Roller Derby.'"

According to Carpenter, "the people coming in from outside the State are directly affecting the theatre industry

about 22 to 25 percent" during Roller Derby meets. Theatre owners objected to "carnival entertainment," he said, asking that "such types" as the Roller Derby be denied use of the Fairgrounds.

Theatres paid taxes, and Wolf offered a list to prove it. The theatre owners weren't opposed to industrial and auto shows and the like, "only to entertainment directly in opposition to their theatres." They felt Roller Derby and "such attractions should not be held in federal, state or municipally owned buildings."

There was leverage behind the demand. Bair reminded Boardmen they had paid only $500 for statewide advance publicity motion pictures promoting the Fair. It was a special deal which should have cost, under regular advertising rates, $5,000, he claimed. Bair went so far as to suggest, "If you don't want to pay the $500, take it up with the Board [of Theatre Owners] and I think it can be done without charge." Theatre owners would even be glad to place cards in their lobbies advertising the Fair, if they got their way.

Purdue Dean John Harrison Skinner promptly moved to bar "any shows of this character 'Roller Derby'" and to work out a deal to limit such continuous shows from lasting beyond a week. Then he withdrew that motion and submitted another, which carried, to ban Roller Derby in 1938. That year there was no Fairgrounds Roller Derby, and motion picture houses didn't charge to show State Fair reels.

Senator/Board member E. Curtis White later commented, "I see where this Roller Derby is coming again to Butler. I think they should not be allowed to operate during the Fair. Last year it certainly hurt our night shows." Publicity Director Levi Moore disclosed that "the Theater Owners came across, and we will not have to pay the $500 as before."

1939 Sonja Henie and her spectacular ice show graced the Coliseum grand opening. Arthur M. Wirtz of Chicago Stadium, who brought in Henie, the Indianapolis Capitals hockey team, and the Coliseum's ice floor, wanted to "open this building with a bang." He was confident Henie could do it "with her great name and drawing power."

Long-time WRTV-Channel 6 news anchor Howard Caldwell recalled Henie's ice show rehearsals and performances. "This was the base for her shows," he said. "She looked like a little doll."

Henie kept her show at the Coliseum until a falling out with Wirtz; she formed her own show the following year on a portable rink at Butler's Fieldhouse, according to historian Herb Schwomeyer. "She was a really atrocious personality . . . swore profanely . . . a very nasty woman . . . a beautiful nasty woman." Henie, "the Greatest Star of Them All," was still at the Coliseum, though, in November 1949, "In Person – Not A Picture."

Horse shows for show horses are as old as the Fairgrounds. The Night Horse Show, with its beginning in the old Coliseum, soon took on $50,000 in purses and national prominence after the new Coliseum opened in '39. Prominent celebrities and orchestras regularly complemented the event. The shows grew and evolved into separate events.

1941 The Stokowski All Youth Orchestra performed at a June 10 fund-raiser

Sonja Henie's "Hollywood Ice Revue" cast seen during Coliseum practice sometime during 1948. Henie readied every season's show from the Coliseum.

at the Coliseum for the Indiana State Symphony Society. The Society's Franklin Miner provided two reasons for choosing the Coliseum: capacity and to test whether the youth orchestra would work out for summer symphonies. The Youth Orchestra had been playing the national networks for four years; Stokowski was considered "the greatest man on acoustics and would be a good test for the Coliseum."

The youth orchestra was named for Leopold Stokowski, the highly dramatic conductor of the Philadelphia Orchestra (1912-1936). After leaving that organization, Stokowski conducted other famous orchestras for brief periods, and in 1962 founded the American Symphony Orchestra.

Show horseman Wallace O. Lee argued that it was necessary "to maintain the cultural things of life . . . such a thing advertises our state in a very fine way throughout the world." The Indianapolis Junior Chamber of Commerce co-sponsored the orchestral event.

1945 Shortridge High School convened commencement exercises on June 13 in the Coliseum. Other schools were offered the same rental deal as Shortridge: $200.

1946 None of the manufacturers had any new machinery in the first year after the war, and labor strikes had complicated matters. Instead, they went out into their territories, rented back what they had sold and showed that. New machinery remained scarce well into 1948.

1947 "We don't sell things at the Fair," Deere Plow's Charles Moreland contended after the Mechanical Field was moved to the Fairgrounds' north side. "We are in the wholesale business and every cent we spend is charged to advertising." Moreland borrowed his equipment "from every farmer . . . I had it there – secondhand, but it was there."

International Harvester's Jack Callahan claimed Babson Milking Machine Company reported "between 3,300 and 3,600" fewer attendance at its new northside exhibit berth. Babson considered itself fortunate however, because the Fair's nearby helicopter attraction drew a crowd. (The Board scheme to increase attendance by exhibiting a helicopter worked, but the machinery people considered it a hazard.)

Buyers and breeders gather in this scene from the old Draft Horse Barn where the East Pavilion now Stands. Only the west end of the old Barn still remains.

The Coliseum Corporation booked the Roy Rogers Rodeo. "I think a Roy Rogers' Rodeo is strictly in a class by itself and is one of the biggest shows," Coliseum manager Dick Miller announced in late '46. "I, myself, think he is a better showman than Gene Autry."

The Funeral Directors' exposition and convention in the Manufacturers' Building, a regular since the Twenties, collected a $1,000 rental.

The Mid-West Sports & Boat Show's archery concession was responsible for forty-one broken window lights. The Manufacturers' Building show was co-sponsored by *Indianapolis News* and William H. Pfau the promoter. Whatever the *News* made on the show was donated to its charities.

1948 The Indiana Draft Horse Breeders Association Sale made its first showing in the spring of '48, with somewhat less than 100 head sold. With no more than half a dozen such sales in the nation in the last years of the 20th century, the sale was considered the "granddaddy of 'em all," according to show managers.

Immaculate Heart of Mary Church rented the Coliseum for $500 on May 29, for the CBS Radio show "Give and Take." The church's Father Sahm took exception with the price, since "True or False," a radio charity benefit for American Cancer Society, paid only $250. True as the claim was, the Board didn't budge.

1949 The Watchtower Society, the "religious organization that believes in noncombatant[s]," rented the Manufacturers' Building in July. Since the group donated twenty-five percent of the meals served during its event, rendering impossible any accurate picture on concessions, the

Board charged them twice the normal amount.

Rentals between May and June: Baptist Youth in the 4-H Buildings; city garbage truck storage in the "Agri-Hort" Building; a Lionel Hampton Band gig in the Manufacturers' Building; a horse show and cattle sale in the Coliseum and Cattle Barn.

Indiana Motor Truck Association's James Nicholas secured Board permission to use the Cattle Barn in late July for its fleet safety rodeo contest. "This Rodeo . . . is a contest to pick the best truck driver in the State," Nicholas said. The winner went on to the national contest in New Jersey. Equipment dealers furnished new equipment. Contest trucks had never been driven, the truckers' secretary-manager said.

The new car show attracted buyers in the 1950s when cars were still big, heavy status symbols of American motoring freedom.

Buicks, Lincolns, Cadillacs, and Fords filled the Manufacturers' Building.

The International Dairy Exposition

HOME OF
INTERNATIONAL
DAIRY EXPOSITION

1. COLISEUM—Seats 10,500 persons; where daytime judging and night entertainment will take place.

2. DAIRY CATTLE BARN—4½ acres under one roof; stall space for 2,000 head of cattle.

3. MANUFACTURERS BUILDING—Housing exhibits keyed to show the dairy cattle farmer how to make more money.

4. YOUTH BUILDING—Rooms and dormitory space for 900 FFA and 4-H Club boys and girls.

5. PARKING AREAS—Stone, gravel and hard-surface space unlimited.

6. SADDLE HORSE BARN—Where dairy cattle sales will be held; also additional stall spaces for cattle, if necessary.

7. GRAND STAND—For afternoon entertainment.

8. WOMEN'S BUILDING — Checkroom, cafeteria, and additional housing facilities.

9. SWINE ARENA — Additional housing facilities for 200 persons in dormitories.

10. HOTEL—Housing facilities.

11. PURDUE EXHIBIT BUILDING—Special exhibit on dairy cattle production.

12. INDIANA UNIVERSITY BUILDER —Continuous entertainment furnished Farm Film Foundation.

13. AGRICULTURAL BUILDING—Festival of Dairy and Related Foods—first of its kind in U. S.

14. DRAFT HORSE BARN—Dormitory space for 200 persons; also additional space for cattle.

15. RAILROAD SIDING — Facilities for loading and unloading cattle.

16. RADIO CENTER — Facilities for the-grounds radio broadcasts.

The International Dairy Exposition lasted three short years at the Fairgrounds before bankruptcy disaster. The event required every building, rivalling the State Fair in scope.

Imperator Smithson Ivanhoe, the 1950 Grand Champion Ayrshire bull owned by Curtiss Candy Company.

AS EARLY as January 1948, discussion confirmed what many Fair Board members already knew: the Fairgrounds was the only place in the nation with facilities capable of staging so huge an event as the International Dairy Exposition. The Cattle Barn was considered one of the best show places in the country. The dairy people called the Manufacturers' Building "one of the most modern in the middle west, especially constructed for exhibits of dairy, feed, barn, and industrial exhibits."

The Youth Buildings were "the most modern in the country." Transportation? No problem. The Fairgrounds was considered "the logical place" to host the national dairymen.

Dairy breeders had met in 1946 with the Indiana State Chamber of Commerce with "a definite plan of action. . . . Indianapolis . . . was a natural permanent home site for dairy cattle shows[.] [A]lmost equidistant from every great dairying region in this country and Canada . . . Indianapolis, only 85 miles from the center of U.S. population, is a city accustomed to handling crowds and making visitors comfortable through its 40 hotels with 10,000 rooms available, its daily incoming 125 trains and 600 buses, and its six airfields. To this was added the magnificent availabilities at the Indiana State Fair Grounds, combining ample exhibition space, hotel facilities on the Grounds, and two railroad sidings for loading and unloading cattle. Yes – this was certainly the logical place."

A mid-April 1948 meeting of Indiana Chamber of Commerce, Indiana Farm Bureau, and International Dairy Exposition men considered whether the Fairgrounds contained facilities adequate to be the permanent host of the Exposition, as well as of the 4-H and the FFA Congresses. At least 40,000 visitors were anticipated, but nearly 200,000 visited each of the first two expositions. The first attracted more than 1,500 open class entries.

The event used the Cattle Barn, the Coliseum, the Manufacturers' and Youth Buildings, the Draft Horse and Swine Barn dormitories, the Agricultural and Indiana University Buildings, the Women's Building cafeteria, the Radio Center's broadcasting facilities, railroad sidings, the cashier's room, and office space in the Administration Building. Rent was $10,000 cash, plus out-of-pocket expenses.

Diana Bartlemay of Richmond, the 1966 Fair Queen, welcomed Manufacturers' Building visitors to the RCA exhibit.

New cars fill the 4-1/2 acre Cattle Barn during the Fairgrounds' heyday as an auto storage depot. Three hundred cars were stored in the Barn at one point in the Fifties.

1949 The Manufacturers' Building opened with exhibits "pertaining to the farm and home and the latest in automobiles[.] [M]any automobile manufacturers strive to show their latest models at the Indiana State Fair for the first time."

1951 In October, "The Festival of Dairy and Related Foods" beckoned women to the Third International Dairy Exposition – the "World's Fair of the Dairy Industry." Nationally recognized authorities welcomed listeners.

The "Festival," the first show of its kind in the United States, convened in the Agricultural Building.

A Monon Railroad siding southwest of the Youth Buildings allowed easy loading and unloading of cattle.

Nightly Coliseum entertainment brought audiences the likes of the Bokara Troupe teeterboard acrobats; aerialist Ethel D'Arcy; comic unicyclist Jacques Gordon; the Hannefords, "celebrated bareback riders with the Giant Percherons"; Staples World Championship Rodeo; the Cathalas, who juggled hoops while perched atop rolling balls; Kinko the Human Pretzel; and much more. Ford Division, Ford Motor Car Company offered gold, silver, and bronze emblems to 4-H and FFA exhibitors in the Junior Show.

"The exposition . . . annually brought some of the finest dairy cattle in America to the State Fairgrounds for exhibition and judging," according to newspaper information circulated by the Indianapolis Association of Credit Men's Service.

Then the bubble burst: on November 13, the Exposition declared itself bankrupt. The Fairgrounds stood in line with eighty-six other creditors holding claims totalling $60,092.65.

1952 Kingan & Company, the "King of Fine Foods," supplied all meats used at the Fair. RCA Victor, with four manufacturing plants in Indiana alone, exhibited in the Manufacturers' Building. The century-old Studebaker Corporation sold "the sleek and spirited beauty of the excitingly styled '52 Studebaker Starliner."

Fairgrounds action took a breath after the Fair and then returned for twenty October days of Hollywood Ice Revue, "the world's greatest ice show," starring Barbara Ann Scott. Along with Scott: Carol Lynne, Skippy Baxter, Andra McLaughlin, Freddy Trenkler, The Bruises, and Michael Kirby.

Nationally prominent, the Winter Club of Indianapolis sponsored the 1952 Olympic Trials.

1957 Following the 1957 Fair, three hundred '58 Chevrolets, Fords, and Oldsmobiles stored in the Cattle Barn awaited public introduction, reported the *Indianapolis News* farm editor Frank Salzarulo. The barn served as a zone depot for Oldsmobile. Later, the figure jumped to 700 and included '58 Edsels, Chryslers, Nashes, and Buicks.

Salzarulo called it "one of the lucrative building rental contracts on the Fairgrounds." Storage charges were twenty-five cents per day for all cars except for Oldsmobiles. A special General Motors arrangement called for a storage fee of fifty cents per car per day and an additional $4 for a car inspection fee.

> ◆◆ The Indiana University Building hosted continuous Farm Film Foundation entertainment in 1951. And what films they were! Remember "Cheese Family Album," or "Telephone Cable Cuba"? Or "Welding Comes to the Farm," "Filbert Valleys," and "Give Me Liberty"?

1958 The beautiful Flower & Patio Show, a landscaping and gardening exposition not seen since Exposition days, opened in the Agriculture-Horticulture Building. It was a success from the start.

From 1959 to 1985, the show welcomed visitors in Exposition Hall. As with all living things, the show grew beyond those confines and moved to the four-and-a-half acre West Pavilion. "The (Christmas Gift &) Hobby Show was our first show," recalled founder Edward Schoenberger. "We thought there was a need for people to learn hobbies, and to express themselves through hobbies.

"Then we started the Flower Show with Gordon Milne, the *Indianapolis Star* garden editor – he knew there was a need." After touring the nation's other flower shows, Schoenberger and his wife Thelma started their own show. (Frits Loonsten Inc. and Maschmeyer's Nursery Inc., two exhibitors, are there today.)

The former Educational Building went International that year, with exhibits by Indiana's foreign trade partners. "We are now ready to include exhibits and visitors from the entire world," President John A. Craft proclaimed.

Premium list readers learned that "this new 'international look' will help create a better understanding of the world problems, and will open a new market for our exhibitors and also serve as a media for the exchange of cultures."

Preston Woolf, president of the Indianapolis Council on World Affairs, was given the credit for being the "guiding force" behind the "Tiny World's Fair." By 1959, the International Building attracted 40 exhibitors and 300,000 visitors.

1960 Many Indiana Manufacturers' Association members displayed their products in "their" building during the Fair. Business and Industry Day was observed on Labor Day. The Fair Board's "growing recognition of the importance of manufacturing in Indiana" led the IMA to announce building improvements. "IMA's emblem will be placed on the building near the main entrance."

The IMA reported a notorious visit to the Manufacturers' Building:

"The Turbocraft boat that Indiana Gear Works, Indianapolis, made for Nikita Khrushchev as a gift from President Eisenhower attracted considerable interest at the Fair, as did Indiana Gear's other Turbocraft boat, the only one in history to successfully navigate the Colorado and Salmon Rivers, . . . the fastest and most dangerous river to navigate in North America.

"Khrushchev's boat, which never did get wet, had rested on the front lawn of the U.S. Embassy in Moscow. It was not presented to the communist leader after he canceled Ike's visit to Russia [Gary Powers and his U-2 spy plane had been shot down over the Soviet Union on May 1]."

Estel Callahan, Board director of the Manufacturers' and International Buildings, and later secretary-manager, launched the boat from its Moscow resting place with an assist from Senator Homer E. Capehart.

The Board rented the Coliseum for a Billy Graham evangelistic crusade October 2-30. Two years earlier, the Board refused to reduce a $20,000 space rental for a rally that Oral Roberts, the "professed faith healer," wanted to pull off.

A Cold War hospital in boxes unwrapped at the Fairgrounds during May and June when the Indiana Department of Civil Defense set up for practice in the Girls' School Building. The pre-packaged hospital contained 200 beds, operating rooms and all the "necessary" instruments. One of twenty-five such units throughout the state, the hospital was on display for doctors, nurses, and others interested in how the nation would cope in case of the inevitable nuclear war.

For 1960's Fair, former secretary-manager Estel Callahan secured the Turbocraft boat that President Eisenhower almost gave to Khrushchev before that year's U-2 spy plane incident.

Convertibles, status symbols of the middle class, drew crowds during the 1960s Auto Shows.

A HALLOWEEN opening night explosion under the Coliseum's southeast box seats during the Holiday On Ice "Mardi Gras" finale killed 74 and injured nearly 500 out of the crowd of 4,327. A scant three minutes remained in the performance. The orchestra continued to play, according to one eyewitness.

It was one of Indianapolis' worst disasters. Many spectators were thrown to their deaths onto the ice or killed by concrete and wreckage in the first explosion. Fifty-four fell in the fiery crater, dying in fifty- to seventy-five-foot high flames after the second explosion.

What remained of the icy floor was turned into a temporary morgue as victims were pulled from the debris. Body 22A was the last to be removed.

The cause was horribly simple: propane leaking from a tank in an airtight, windowless concrete concession storeroom exploded below the stands when ignited by a heater used to warm and dry popcorn.

In the aftermath of the Hallween 1963 Coliseum explosion, the ice floor doubled as a morgue while workers sifted through tons of debris and wreckage searching for survivors.

By November 11, the *Indianapolis Star* reported "a freakish chain reaction of accidents" had caused the awful tragedy. The first detailed accident reconstruction had been completed. Ultimately, the Marion County Grand Jury issued a twenty-one-page report. Seven people were indicted for culpability on December 9, five for involuntary manslaughter, including Coliseum Corporation manager Melvin T. Ross. State Fire Marshal Ira J. Anderson and Indianapolis Fire Chief Arnold W. Phillips were indicted on misdemeanor charges.

During the first trial on July 7, 1965, witness Paul Sims of Carmel testified that "skaters had made a tour of the ice, coming into formation, when something let go, an explosion . . . there were objects, bodies flying."

(One victim recalled looking up at the Coliseum clock; the time was 10:55 – a newspaper account placed the time at 11:06 – a Civil Defense report puts the time at 11:04.)

By the Red Cross first-aid instructor's account published in the *Indianapolis Star*, an "immediate fire with a great flame [shot] toward the center of the ceiling, with a very pronounced hiss sounding like air coming out of a hose. The flame was in the middle, approxi-

The Coliseum Explosion

mately, of the gaping hole left by the explosion."

Sims saw "'human bodies burning' in the pit, from which a single torch of 'very hot white fire' shot 15 to 20 feet in the air."

Hell had come to the Fairgrounds.

1966 The International Building touted its world-wide links: "Europe – with plans for construction of a deepwater port at Burns Harbor on Lake Michigan, Indiana will have a new trade and travel link to Europe and Africa via the St. Lawrence Seaway; Asia – Indiana has close ties with the Far East. Hoosier industrial, agricultural and educational contacts can be found in virtually all sections of free Asia; South America – with her Ohio River ports and a sister state in Rio Grande Sul, Brazil, Indiana has a closeness to Latin America which is envied by other midwestern states."

International Building exhibits were jointly sponsored by the Fair Board and the Indianapolis Council of World

Lt. Governor Robert Rock shakes hands with Captain Narcumol Thirayothin of Thailand during the 1966 Fair while foreign officers from the Fort Benjamin Harrison Finance School gather for International Day reception activities in the International Building.

A scene from high up in the Coliseum of an Indianapolis Boat, Sport, & Travel Show before the event expanded to include several Fairgrounds buildings.

Affairs. Fourteen countries took part in exhibit planning.

1968 Sears & Roebuck brought an avant garde film starring Credence Clearwater Revival and O.C. Smith, featuring psychedelic photography and "groovy" fashions.

Small planes landed in the pre-Fair infield, and were then moved to the north side aviation exhibit through a special gate at the track's north side.

In a three-week post-Fair period ending November 17, the Coliseum hosted Henry Mancini and guest Jose Feliciano; fifteen Holiday on Ice performances attracted 92,716 and grossed $202,227.50; the Indiana Pacers lost to Houston, Minnesota, and Denver; and there were four days of public ice skating. The Christmas Gift and Hobby Show posted a record 117,634 attendance. The 1968 pre-Fair Western Horse Show boasted the largest Palomino show in the nation and was rated second biggest overall.

1970 The State Fair English Horse Show (with the George Freije Band and Earl Gregory at the console organ) was acclaimed the best 1970 horse show in the United States by the United Professional Horseman's Association, and received a Five-Star rating, the best possible, from *Horses* magazine.

Eli Lilly & Company was celebrating its ninetieth year when it exhibited in the International Building during the 1966 Fair.

New boats fill the West Pavilion (Cattle Barn) during the Indianapolis Boat, Sport, & Travel Show. Today the show attracts an estimated 200,000.

Seen at the 1971 Indiana Black Expo ribbon-cutting: (l-r) Indiana Sesquicentennial Commission's George S. Diener, Expo General Chairman James C. Cummings, Miss Indiana Black Expo, Beverly Thompson, Indianapolis Mayor Richard G. Lugar, and Associate General Chairman Reverend A.J. Brown.

Earlham College exhibited at the inaugural Indiana Black Expo, convened in Exposition Hall.

1971 The first Indiana Black Expo opened its doors June 19-20 in Exposition Hall. Miss Indiana Black Expo, Beverly Thompson of Indianapolis, reigned over the event which coincided with the 150th anniversary of Indianapolis.

General Chairman James C. Cummings Jr. called it "more than an exposition which graphically depicts the history of blacks in the state of Indiana . . . Black Expo '71 is a celebration, joined in by all black citizens . . . celebrating our progress, which is the result of the toil of generations of blacks and their determined fight for equality."

Expo sought "to cause both black and white citizens of Indiana to look back upon the history of blacks in the state of Indiana in an attempt to introduce a new level of sensitivity for the problems faced throughout the years by blacks."

American and National Basketball Association stars battled in the Martin Luther King Jr. basketball game. Proceeds benefitted the Southern Christian Leadership Conference recipients of the King Scholarship.

1972 Shrinedom celebrated its 100th year; the Shrine Hospital was fifty years old. A successful Shrine Night on August 25 at the Fair sent a $2,500 check to the Shrine burn unit in Cincinnati.

1974 The Indy Super Pull, the largest tractor pull ever staged on the North American continent, roared into the Coliseum February 1-3. It was the first national pull.

Tractors unlike any State Board of Agriculture member had ever seen pulled sleds east to west on an eighteen-inch, tightly packed clay surface that National Tractor Pulling Association officials and competitors later claimed was the finest ever constructed.

A smoke machine vented exhaust outdoors, leaving inside an enormously throaty din which shook the Coliseum and mauled eardrums. Pullers

The Seven Eleven Soul Food Spinoff drew fans to its booth with chances to win prizes.

Former Indiana Pacer Jerry Harkness, chairman of the Martin Luther King Jr. basketball game; Bill Russell, former coach of the Boston Celtics; and Black Expo General Chairman James C. Cummings watch Expo festivities.

Competitors at the Indy Super Pull came from throughout the nation in quest of the sport's greatest purses.

battled for a $50,000 purse in the event sponsored by the Fair Board and NTPA.

1975 The Indiana Flea Market, the state's largest regular event of its kind, opened for the first time.

The first Indiana State Fair Hunter and Jumper Show, formerly an adjunct to the English Horse Show, appeared; more than 300 competitors vied for prizes. Meanwhile, the English Show, with American Saddlebreds, Hackneys, Morgans, Arabians, and Tennessee Walkers, offered Shetland Futurities for the first time.

1977 An all-events Appaloosa regional meet was added to the Western Horse Show, billed as the second largest quarter horse show in the nation.

1978 Indy Super Pull offered a record $76,650 purse. More than 170 pullers from seventeen states and Canada were on hand. The biggest winner's check totalled $4,520.

1980 Indy Super Pull VII attracted an estimated crowd of 60,000 to see the nation's top drivers battling over $80,000, the largest purse in the world.

1981 The first six-figure championship in saddle horse history was offered at the Board's newly renamed 1981 All American Horse Classic – "Competition of Champions!" A $100,000 National Saddlebred Sweepstakes was split among three show divisions.

On top of the big money, three-gaited 15-Hand Saddlebred and Saddlebred "shown in hand" World titles were offered for the first time. More than 800 horses and ponies from thirty-five states and two foreign countries competed, including thirty-five World and National Champions.

The name change, from the English Horse Show, came after a State Fair steering committee recommended "an ex-

A young equestrienne talks with her friends in the Saddle Horse Barn before taking her turn at All American Horse Classic Competition.

Peruvian Paso Fino horses await their turn at competition in the West pavilion warmup ring.

citing, sports-oriented competition" intended to appeal to a public "unfamiliar or uninterested in 'horse shows.'" Unfortunately, the new direction was never really followed, and by the 1990s, scarcely 300 attended any one night of the Coliseum event, although the sweepstakes purses remained high.

1982 A purse of $100,000 was offered at Super Pull IX.

1983 A startling $117,000 purse was offered for Super Pull X.

1984 The Fairgrounds hosted five of the ten largest paid-admission events in the state. These events accounted for nearly two million of the four million people attending the Top Ten.

The Fairgrounds' top shows: first, the Indiana State Fair; fifth, the Indianapolis Boat Sport & Travel Show; seventh, the Indiana Flower & Patio Show; ninth, the Indianapolis Home Show; tenth, the Christmas Gift & Hobby Show.

What did the Fairgrounds mean financially to Marion and its surrounding counties each year? A whopping $50,934,528 in generated revenue, based on a formula by the Shreveport-Bossier Conventions & Tourist Bureau.

1986 A Human Power Vehicle Demonstration drew crowds to the Natural Resources Building; so did Indian artifacts and wild edibles, and a bicycle touring demonstration.

1988 This year's Western Horse Show ranked ninth in the nation for futurity payouts $46,747.80. The '88 National Appaloosa Horse Show was the largest equine show of one breed ever in Indiana. More than 1,100 registered Appaloosas from throughout the nation competed in 100 classes.

The centerpiece home at a recent Home Show, one of three built that year.

A J.I. Case salesman steers a bulky contraption few recognize as a harvester.

A showman with his "in-hand" American Saddlebred champion during All American Horse Classic competition.

1990 Fifty-one years after the first national swine show, the 1990 Lean Value Seven Breeds Swine Conference overflowed into the Sheep Barn. It was the first time Chester White, Duroc, Hampshire, Landrace, Poland, Spot, and Yorkshire swine – from twenty-two states – had ever gathered on such scale. Five hundred ninety-five boars, and open and bred gilts changed hands in the conference's $666,425 one-day sale.

After a low of 26,467 spectators the year before, the Super Pull was dropped in 1990.

1991 A national Bill of Rights tour stopped off in October at Exposition Hall; an estimated 28,000 viewed the historic document.

247 draft horses showed up for the Indiana Draft Horse Breeders Association Sale, including Percherons, Belgians, two Shires, and sixteen Suffolks. Although the first sale in 1948 was open only to people from Indiana and the surrounding states, by the '80s it had expanded to include the entire North American continent. A separate division called the North American Breeders Sale opened in 1991 to people who had bred and raised the horse they sold.

The National Pork Producers Council announced early in December that World Pork Expo would come to Indianapolis in 1994, capping two years of effort by the Fairgrounds staff working with the lieutenant governor's office, the City of Indianapolis, and Indianapolis Convention & Visitors Association.

1992 Revived as a leased event, Indy Super Pull, "America's Premier Pulling Event," offered a $57,000 purse for the nation's tractor pullers.

Jamie Donaldson
GEORGETOWN, KY.
UNRETOUCHED

INDIANA PACERS
ABA
CHAMPIONS
1969-70

INDIANA PACERS
EASTERN DIVISION
CHAMPIONS
1969-70

❖ Good Sports

*F*rom basketball
to ice skating
to bicycle racing,
no other location
in Indiana history
has offered —
and delivered —
the same degree
of athletic and sports
entertainment.

THE PACERS' winning seasons, Indiana's first world-title boxing match, the Indiana Wizards, Dick the Bruiser vs. Cowboy Bob Ellis – nearly all memory of these events is lost in the dust of forgotten times, but events of national and world importance made history at the Indiana State Fairgrounds.

Gruss vom Festplatz June '24. From Emma Killinger

29stes Bundesfest des Nord-Amerik. Turnerbundes, vom 18. bis 25. Juni 1905 in Indianapolis

By Courtesy and Copyright by W. H. Bass Photo Co., Indpls.

POST CARD

58752

1907 Manual Training and Shortridge High Schools, both of Indianapolis, asked on March 19 to use the grounds for a field meet and practice, but got no further than extracting the Board's promise to take the matter "under advisement." Twenty years later, Shortridge used the half-mile cinder track for training and the "inner field" for spring football practice.

1921 The Indianapolis Athletic Club brought amateur boxing to the Coliseum this year.

1924 An International Gymnastics Festival, "Das Neu-nundzwanzigste Turnfest Des Nordamerikanischen Turnerbundes," convened June 21-24, 1924, in perhaps the rarest of all Fairgrounds athletic ventures. Athletes performing calisthenics filled the Infield, where more than 300 ten-by-twelve foot white tents were neatly pitched. Foot racers dashed around the Track of Champions; wrestlers grappled; fencers sparred. It was the 29th annual gathering of the North American Gymnastic Union.

Gymnasts used the grounds free "subject to the rights of the horse trainers and persons having privilege contracts with the Board." A tent set aside for the California delegation offered cigars and magazines for athletes' free time after field practice. The Fine Arts Building housed "all the most modern gymnastic devices," including a "basket ball alley," the readers of the *Indianapolis Morning Star* learned. Athletes sprinted, jumped, performed dumbbell drills, and climbed.

"It is the principle of the German athletic societies to slight no form of gymnastic movement, and great proficiency has been attained by many of the members in the art of climbing." On the athletic field's north side, three poles connected by wooden bars thirty feet above the ground created a "climbing device" from which five ropes were appended. Climbers typically needed seven seconds to scale the thirty-foot height in "hand-over-hand style."

Two thousand Turners engaged in the festival climax, witnessed by 12,000 onlookers, "by far the largest crowd of spectators that ever witnessed a festival program." St. Louis' acme could claim a mere 8,000.

Crowd enthusiasm was overwhelming, according to the *Star*. "At times the applause was so great that men feared for the stability of the [Grandstand] structure."

U.S. Vice President Charles Warren Fairbanks personally congratulated Germany's nine-man delegation. "As if by instinct, the athletes from across the sea formed themselves in military position and their hands went to their caps . . . Gut Heil! Gut Heil! Gut Heil! burst from the thousands of German throats" after Fairbanks finished praising the Deutschland delegation.

White-bloused girls performed barbell and dumbbell exercises. Bands and drum and bugle corps played, "accompanied by groups of dancing girls in vari-colored costumes." Twenty-four girls of the Independent Turnverein of Indianapolis "engaged in a Spanish dance, which pleased the big audience immensely." Then 121 girls of Indianapolis' gymnastic societies, "attired in blue bloomers and blouses with red flowing ties" performed wand exercises. Pittsburgh's Central Turnverein girls demonstrated hoop exercises. The next day everyone went home.

◆◆◆

High School Basketball

STATE basketball sectional tourneys were fought at the old Coliseum from 1921 to 1924. The Coliseum, with a turf and tanbark arena, had a special platform built for the games, Richard W. Jackson, old-time Fairgrounds visitor, recalled. "Everybody could see. The seats were good." Sectionals always were a good place for girl watching and girl searching, according to Jackson, who attended Arsenal Technical High School.

Franklin High School, with Ernest B. "Griz" Wagner coaching, prevailed 35-22 over Anderson in the "Final Four" of the (1921) tenth annual Indiana High School Athletic Association State Final Basket Ball Tournament. A standing-room-only crowd filled the 7,200-seat Coliseum, which more typically hosted horse shows and livestock exhibitions. The Franklin team roster included: Carlyle Friddle, forward; John Gant, forward; Robert "Fuzzy" Vandivier, center; James "Ike" Ballard, guard; Harold Borden, guard; Harry King, guard; James Ross, forward; Hubert Davis, forward; and Charlton Williams, guard.

Spalding's Official Guide governed the March 18-19 event. All games were played in fifteen-minutes halves. Twenty-one was the first year for radio broadcasts of the final tournament, according to basketball historian Herb Schwomeyer's research.

Franklin repeated its victory – its third consecutive – the following March 17-18, again with Coach Wagner. The 26-15 win over Terre Haute Garfield went to: (full roster) Ross, forward; Davis, forward; Gant, forward; Friddle, now playing center; "Fuzzy" Vandivier now playing guard; and King, Williams, and Ballard, all in guard spots.

During March 16-17 finals in 1923, "The Alices" from Vincennes clinched the title in a 27-18 triumph over Muncie Central. John Adams coached Byron Harper, forward; Firman Wample, forward; John Wolfe, center; Raymond Allega, guard; Harold Mayo, guard; Reese Jones, guard; Loyal Duncan, substitute; and Edwin Prullage, substitute.

Martinsville, with Coach Glenn Curtis, took its turn in 1924 with a March

The Indiana High School Athletic Association (IHSAA) "Final Four" basketball games convened in the old Coliseum, the Cattle Barn, and then in the new Coliseum during World War II.

15 victory over Frankfort, 36-30. Martinsville's roster: Darrell Wright, forward; Robert Hine, forward; Hugh Brown, center; Warren Schnaiter, guard; Robert Schnaiter, guard; Stanley Byram, forward; Clarence Poling, forward; Walter Messmer, guard; Lester Reynolds, guard; and Raymond Ennis, guard.

Indianapolis sectionals and IHSAA state tournaments were settled in the "New Exposition" Building (the Cattle Barn) beginning in 1925. Frankfort's "Hot Dogs," with Everett Case coaching, claimed IHSAA's "top team" title on March 21 in a 34-20 victory over Kokomo. Basketball's founder Dr. James Naismith presented the "Final Four" and other IHSAA awards.

Fans ate at the Women's Building cafeteria near the Domestic Science

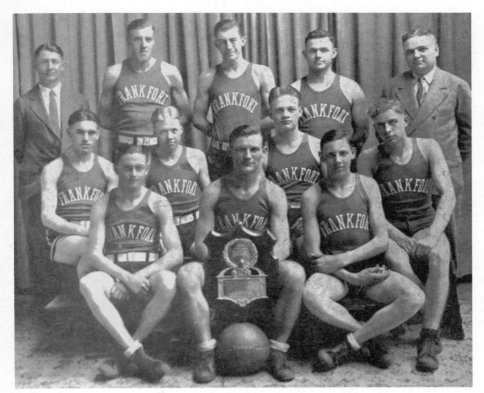

kitchen. When the Butler University "crowd" asked to use the Manufacturer's Building for basketball games, rates were set at $250 each game, provided Butler bear the costs for heat, lighting, gas, water, and other expenses.

IHSAA was charged $3,000 for the 1926 basketball tournament in the "Cow Barn." The group had shown a great profit, Board members learned. Secretary-Treasurer E.J. Barker reported that the IHSAA "seemed to be considerably agitated" over the increased price. Two years earlier the basketballers paid $1,000 for the Coliseum, and in 1925 they paid $2,000. They paid $3,000 again in 1927.

A major headache was that "tournaments often come at a very soft time... [A]utomobiles by thousands come in the fair grounds and [we] can not keep them on the drives, they go anywhere they can and tear up the grounds any way that seems to be easiest...

"Several articles appeared in the Indianapolis papers and one very criticizing article in the *Star* sent in from Franklin was a real 'stager,' at the Board of Agriculture," Barker reported.

Gene Thomas coached Marion High School's "Giants" to a 30-23 victory over Martinsville during 1926's March 19-20 finals. The "Giants" roster included: Glen Overman, forward; Everett Chapman, forward; Charles "Stretch" Murphy, center; Robert Chapman, guard; Karl Kilgore, guard; Zed Usher, forward; Stephen Johnson, forward; Homer Davidson, center; Edward Heck, guard; and Hal Chasey, guard.

Somehow, the Cattle Barn roof was damaged during the tournament. Billed for repairs, IHSAA wanted the Board to cover part of the costs, claiming others had damaged the barn as well. The Board left it up to Barker how best to settle the issue.

In the March 18-19, 1927, IHSAA basketball tournament Martinsville repeated its '24 victory, this time in a 26-23 win over Muncie Central; Curtis still coached the "Artesians." The team roster included: John Wooden, forward; Arnold Suddith, forward; George Eubank, center; Lester Reynolds, guard; Robert Lockhart, guard; William Neal, forward; Vincent Bisesi, guard; Virgil David, guard; Marshall Tackett, guard; and Charles Caldwell, guard.

1926

City Boxing Commission's Mr. Bartholomew asked to rent the Coliseum on June 14, "and from time to time thereafter for boxing exhibitions." The request was referred for policy decision, and on July 2 a successful motion kept the fighters off the grounds.

Professional hockey made a bid for Indianapolis on October 19. Bernie

Layman of Indianapolis proposed installing an ice floor and ice machine in the Manufacturer's Building for hockey and ice skating. Layman and his associates offered to invest $150,000 in their scheme to belong to one of two American hockey leagues. They proposed a sliding rental arrangement starting at $500 monthly, then up to $1,000. Layman proposed to make the entire investment. It was the first year for the Canadian-American Hockey League.

Layman endeavored to rent the Coliseum "for athletic purposes" one evening each week – boxing, professional basketball games and events "of National importance." He wanted a five-year lease with a five-year option; he'd pay $500, gradually increasing to $1,000 each month.

Barker wrote to Minneapolis and Detroit to find out what buildings they used for their hockey games and ice skating. The November responses were read and consideration was continued. That meant nothing came of it.

1927

Early in the year, the Indiana High School Athletic Association asked permission to build a 15,000- to 20,000-seat coliseum for basketball tournaments. IHSAA's proposal offered the building for State Fair use; other rental proceeds would be divided with the Board. IHSAA later abandoned the idea and negotiated for tournaments "at indoor Butler Athletic Field."

In another lost athletic venture, Adjutant General William H. Kershner, speaking on Marion County American Legion's behalf, failed to obtain permission to use the Coliseum for a May 28 Gene Tunney exhibition bout. Since the Board had already ruled against boxing, Tunney was counted out.

1928

In January, the Indianapolis Baseball Club filed a petition with the Indianapolis Board of Zoning Appeals asking permission to build "a modern Baseball Stadium" on the property between Kissell Avenue (now Coliseum Avenue) and the Monon Railroad and between Maple Lane Boulevard (now 38th Street) and Fairfield Avenue.

Remonstrators attending the January Board meeting believed a baseball park across from the Fairgrounds would cause the community to "suffer a depreciation of approximately $300,000." They called upon the Board to give "serious consideration to remonstrating against the location of a baseball park in this high class residential district."

The matter was immediately taken up, and by a 9-4 vote, the Board used "all the influence at our command to keep the baseball park from near or on the fair grounds."

A decade later, the property was vacant and the owners' agent was having difficulty unloading it. In '28, the baseball club's Norman Perry offered $70,000; a '38 appraisal set a price of $110,000, but a deal to build apartments there fell through. Then the agent wanted the Board to buy it. They didn't.

1932

"Tracy Cox, Indianapolis lightweight, easily defeated Prince Saunders, Chicago Negro, before a near-capacity crowd at the Coliseum last night," sports fans read in October 26's *Indianapolis Star.* "The bout went the limit of ten rounds in which the local lad was the winner of seven rounds with three of the number even.

"In the semi-windup of ten rounds between Kid Sammy Slaughter, Terre Haute Negro, and Jackie Purvis, Indianapolis middleweight, Slaughter won every round. Purvis was a punching bag and outclassed by the Terre Haute state champion."

Asked in early Spring to consider Friday night prize fights (three "good matches") during the Fair, the Board promptly moved not to sponsor boxing contests. Heavyweight, middleweight, and lightweight fights would have sold dollar, two- and three-dollar seats. But after the Fair, the fighting proposition was a rental issue, and that was another Depression Era matter.

The State Boxing Commission highly recommended the fight promoters, Barker reported; William C. Miller of the Pontiac Automobile Agency signed the contract.

1934

In November, Lt. Governor M. Clifford Townsend suggested creating an Athletic Department and adding "Farmers' Softball baseball finals. The Farm Bureau can handle that the best in the world." Townsend was confident Chamber of Commerce and Farm Bureau leagues could be arranged, with State Fair championship finals.

Townsend also envisioned bicycle races and reviving the horseshoe pitching contest, controlled by a "Contest Department." He saw possibilities at the county and district fairs.

After the Fair, Colonel W. T. Johnson's World Championship Rodeo rode into the Fairgrounds September 29-

Contestants in the 1932 Pushmobile Contest: (l-r) Alex Toth in Speedway City's Speedway Special; Billy Real in the Stewart Radio entry; Vearl Collins, piloting the Bowes Seal Fast Special; Norman Wade in another Bowes Seal Fast Special; and Ray Calhoun in the Iciere Special.

The man from Polar Ice tapes Ray Calhoun's hand during a Pushmobile pit stop.

Culver Military Academy alumni and the Fort Benjamin Harrison Army polo teams line up before moving to the Coliseum for the Night Show championship action.

Fans in the Grandstand on Opening Day of the 1936 Fair watched the state finals softball tournament in the center of the Track of Champions.

The Patrick Henry team from Marion took the state championship during the 1936 Soft Ball Tourney.

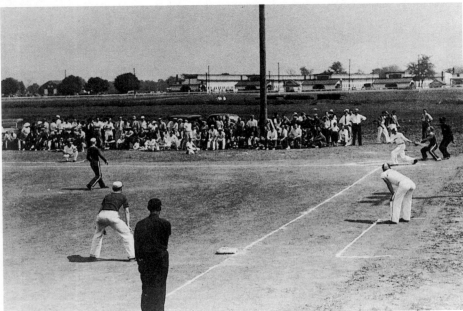

30 for two days of fourteen events each, "never twice alike!" Cowboys competed bareback on broncos named Fire Neck, Whiskey Jack, Polar Bear, Gates of Mountain, and Stubbs. Lucyle Roberts of Antlers, Oklahoma, rode Her Hero in the Cowgirls' Bronco Riding event.

Leonard Stroud of Rocky Ford, Colorado, and Tom Kirnan of Smithfield, Texas, put on trick and fancy roping exhibitions. E. Pardee, Lajunta, Colorado, won the calf roping contest in 20.2 seconds, just two-tenths faster than Fort Thomas, Arizona's Hugh Bennett.

Blackie Russell, Jack Quait, Tex Doyle, and Dick Anderton wrestled steers; Red Yale, Shorty Hill, and Cecil McKinney rode them. Jasbo Fulkerson drove "I'm No Angel" chariot-style. All 106 cowboys and cowgirls came from west of the Mississippi or western Canada except for Luther Marsh, who hailed from Manchula, Florida.

1935 In May, the Board learned the American League Bowling Conference would convene in Indianapolis for six weeks the following spring.

Herman G. Deupree, bowling's executive secretary, told the Committee in October that the tournament would bring 30,000 people to Indianapolis. Deupree proposed building thirty-two new alleys in the Coliseum, running north and south, for the March 10 to April 13 meet. The deal was made, and by next January the bowlers were installing a heating plant. The Board later learned the bowlers had broken 166 roof skylights.

1936 Opening Day hosted a big state finals softball tournament in the center of the Track of Champions, a Fair first. Six games led up to the final that evening at the Grandstand.

Program readers learned the September 11 horseshoe pitching championship of Indiana was a first, although "pitchin' 'shoes" at Fairtime went back much longer than that.

1939 Built in 1939 for $1,202,789.24, the Coliseum and Live Stock Pavilion became a pivotal Indianapolis landmark overnight. Along with a power house, the Coliseum originally had 7,839 permanent seats, a 125-seat cafeteria, ten snack bars, and eight rest rooms.

Long before the Coliseum was completed, Arthur M. Wirtz of Chicago Stadium proposed to operate it and bring in hockey, public skating, and ice shows. He told the Finance Committee his lease in Pittsburgh, where his minor league hockey team headquartered, had expired.

Wirtz was big business: his company owned and operated Chicago Stadium, Detroit Olympia, the Red Wing Hockey Club in Pittsburgh, and the Pittsburgh Hornets. He proposed bringing in the Pittsburgh hockey team.

Wirtz knew his business: "In hockey . . . it takes, roughly, two or three years to get a hockey team organized . . . before you can get it on a paying basis." He sweetened his offer with a certified check.

The Board soon accepted his deal, and in related action resolved a policy to rent the Fairgrounds buildings "for the purpose of bringing in revenue to maintain the continuing expense of the operation of said buildings."

So the Indianapolis Coliseum Corporation was born; Wirtz was its first president. He occupied the "committee rooms" under the seats on the Coliseum's north side. By September 29, Wirtz had set an opening day (although the ice floor apparently wasn't ready until November 6 or 7). He wanted to install the largest spotlights made to light the entire arena and the bandstand.

"People love the spectacular, and you can do it with this lighting. I want to have a spectacular opening. We will open with the regular hockey game [the Indianapolis Capitals], and then give a fashion show of winter sports clothes by the leading debutantes of the city. After that they could go in for public skating."

Wirtz spent $30,000 more than he intended installing the ice plant and other equipment for central Indiana's oldest and largest indoor ice rink. He leased the Cattle Barn for parking.

By mid-October, Fair Manager Harry G. Templeton relayed word that

Purdue University Dean/Board member J.H. Skinner presented the 1934 Fair's largest watermelon to Purdue head football coach Noble Kiser on behalf of the Purdue Alumni Association.

the Coliseum would be "substantially" completed by November 10 (the date turned out as November 16). A carpenters union carpenter strike had "put a crimp" into the overall timetable which "put us out of gear entirely," the contractor's general superintendent avowed. "The men worked seven hours, were paid for eight, and actually worked for six." Another strike held up hanging a roller door, while electricians threatened yet another.

After their first two games of the season on the road, the Capitals opened Coliseum action on November 11 against the Syracuse Stars, winning victory number three, 5-1. With their fourth home ice win on November 19 over the Cleveland Barons (3-0), they took over league leadership in front of a crowd of 7,477 cash customers. The night before at Cleveland, the score tied 1-1 in overtime.

1940 Herbie Lewis, Indianapolis' first pro hockey coach, guided the Indianapo-

lis Capitals as general manager, coach, and player, fully expecting an even better team than the '39-'40 season when the Caps won the International-American Western Division Championship.

The Hercules Athletic Club brought the Coliseum its first professional wrestling match on June 17. Crowds of up to 2,000 had been turned away from the club's smaller Tuesday night venue on Pennsylvania Street (the outdoor Sports Arena on 500 North Pennsylvania Street in warm weather, and indoors at Tyndall Armory at 711 North Pennsylvania).

Before the Board approved the match, Director Levi Moore posed the question, "whether the Board wanted this sort of thing on the Fairgrounds."

It was a five-bout "go." Lloyd Carter was the "matchmaker." In the second bout, 181-pound Frankie Wolf out of Cleveland was paired with Coach Billy Thom, two pounds lighter and from Bloomington.

Then in the Main Go, Jumping Joe Savoldi, 217 pounds, from Three Oaks, Michigan, was up against The Angel, from France, weighing in at 276.

After six months in the United States, The Angel was unbeaten. "Harvard University anthropology professors, after examining The Angel, declared him to be super-human and the strongest man they have ever seen or heard of."

Pitted against this invincibility was strength, fame, and home country advantage. Savoldi, a "top flight grappler . . . a star grid performer under Knute Rockne . . . ha[d] beaten just about every topnotch heavyweight wrestler in the game."

The Winter Club of Indianapolis, one of the oldest figure skating clubs in the United States, made its debut in the Coliseum, although under a different name – the Free Skating Club. Club skating began on October 20.

1941 Within four months of its beginning, the Free Skating Club changed its name to Winter Club of Indianapolis during a January meeting, and then, with fourteen charter members, joined the United States Figure Skating Asssociation. Regular skating sessions have continued every year since then. Names listed in the club's articles of incorporation filed on January 14 included Elmer F. Straub, Thomas A. Elder, Roy C. Pedigo, Robert B. Rhoads, V.B. McLeay, and P.B. Denning. The club's purpose has remained the same from its inception, "To improve, encourage and advance figure skating." Interclub competition was held annually until the mid-1970s.

1943 War in two theaters kept military men busy filling orders at the Fairgrounds Specialized Depot, but the Coliseum remained open for public use. In Indiana, that especially meant high school basketball.

Fort Wayne's Central High School, coached by Murray Mendenhall Sr., took the IHSAA state basketball championship title, 45-40, vanquishing Lebanon in March 23 tournament action in the Coliseum.

Central's team roster featured: Tom Shopoff, forward; Robert VanRyan, forward; Robert Armstrong, center; James Blanks, guard; Murray Mendenhall Jr., guard; Max Ramsey, forward; Edwin

Members of the Winter Club from many years ago: (l-r) "Red" Faucett, Louis Mount, two unknowns, Taylor Todd (with pipe), H. Jackson Hiatt, Paul Van Voorhees, two unknowns.

Lindenberg, forward; Robert Doty, guard; Raymond Chambers, guard; and Charles Stanski, guard.

Following the 4-H Club Fair, the Coliseum Corporation opened the "Winter Thrill Center" with "Entertainment to Keep You Mentally and Physically Fit" – thirty American League Hockey home games, two daily public skating sessions, and Sonja Henie with the internationally famous Hollywood Ice Revue. The Indianapolis Coliseum was "Indiana's Winter Wonderland."

1944 Evansville's Bosse High School, led by coach Herman Keller, dominated high school title competition two years in a row. In the March 18, 1944, final, Kokomo was the loser, 39-35.

The Bosse "Bulldogs" roster listed: Norris Keller, forward; Gene Schmidt, forward; Julius "Bud" Ritter, center; Bryan "Broc" Jerrel, guard; Jack Matthews, guard; Donald Tilley, forward; Norman McCool, forward; William Hollman, center; Erwin Scholz, guard; and Gene Whitehead, guard.

1945 In its March 17 return to IHSAA victory, Evansville Bosse trounced South Bend Riley 46-36. The Bosse roster included: Norris Caudell, forward; Norman McCool, forward; Julius "Bud" Ritter, center; Jack Matthews, guard; Bryan "Broc" Jerrel, guard; Don Tilley, forward; Bill Butterfield, center; Jim DeGroote, guard; Gene Whitehead, guard; and Alfred Buck, forward.

1948 The American Bowling Congress, dating to 1903, wanted to take over the Coliseum and Cattle Barn for 110 days in 1950, Executive Committee members learned on February 19. They would consider no other building except the "New" Coliseum for their tournament, according to Indianapolis Convention and Visitors Bureau manager Joseph Cripe and the bowlers' Neil King. Tentative dates were March 15 through July 20, with the tournament itself spanning April 1-June 10, 1950. A favorable Board response in long-range terms was sought.

An understanding with Arthur Wirtz already had been obtained, according to Cripe in a March 11, 1948, letter to Secretary-Manager Orval Pratt. Wirtz' lease on the Coliseum normally extended well into the bowlers' frame.

The event was "the world's largest sporting event held indoors," according to Cripe. In '48, more than 40,000 bowlers were expected in Detroit, along with "not less than 100,000 visitors"; the cash prize fund exceeded $525,000. Detroit's meet would last eighty days.

Forty new bowling lanes would be constructed in the Coliseum, and the Cattle Barn would be needed for concessions, dressing rooms, and displays.

Indianapolis hotels were willing to tackle this major influx "to the best of their ability," Cripe wrote, "even though they would be forced to turn away regular business during that period."

That regular business included Indianapolis 500 fans. Cripe asked for the Board's "whole-hearted approval." But

The Indianapolis Capitals from the 1944-45 American Hockey League season: (top row, l-r) "Fido" Purpur, Jimmy Skinner, Eddie Reigle, Morden Skinner, Connie Poitras, Cy Rouse; (middle row, l-r) "Moose" Sherritt, "Red" Kane, Jack Hewson, Larry Thibeault, John Forbes, Bill Thomson, Coach Johnny Sorrell; (front row, l-r) Trainer and Spare Goalie Les Tooke, Pete Leswick, Ted Garvin, Dick Kowcinak, Connie Dion.

due to "present commitments" with the Coliseum, on March 17 the Board deferred any negotiations until 1951. The next day, the Executive Committee agreed that "due to zoning," the Coliseum was out. Bowling discussion resumed the following year.

1949 The American Bowling Congress representatives tried to score with the Board again on January 24; "They were having a bowling tournament which they did not know what to do with." Here

Chainsawed risers and platforms from the Coliseum arena are heaped in a massive pile following the Wirtz Corporation's 1954 late-night parting gesture after a lease renewal disagreement.

they were, with an eighty-day tournament coming up in '50, with 35,000 bowlers set to play beginning in early March and no place to lay down forty lanes. Only the Coliseum would do.

Preliminary discussions had revealed that the Coliseum Corporation was willing to move some of its 1950 Capitals hockey games out of town and play the last game sometime around February 26. After the meeting, even though the Board knew the Manufacturer's Building wouldn't be accepted, Speed Superintendent L. Orville Miller recommended offering it to the bowlers.

Then on February 9, Arthur Wirtz and Coliseum manager Dick Miller were invited in. Complicated trouble was brewing. Wirtz had first tried to talk to the Board about disputes over cost and lease arrangements during the past summer, but that was the Board's busy time. So now that it was Wirtz' busy time, the Board was willing to talk.

"I did everything I could to not answer any of the questions asked by the newspapers [about lease term disagreements and rumors that the lease would not be renewed]," he said, "but finally you get to a spot that if you don't answer them the public thinks you are guilty. Over a period of ten years, we have tried to build up good will, and the public seemed to think that we were not creating good will."

Board President Homer E. Schuman acknowledged the Board didn't want any publicity about the issue, either.

Wirtz had heard about Anton "Tony" Hulman's overtures to four hockey leagues in a bid to get his own Coliseum hockey team. The Capitals were the farm team for his Detroit Red Wings, and so it wasn't remarkable that Wirtz had heard about it. "It happens that we are connected with all these leagues," Wirtz asserted, "and it would be impossible for him to get this franchise." But Wirtz wanted to "bury" all past differences which included disagreements over light, gas and water costs, and concessions payments. (Wirtz was certain that electric costs would drop if a separate meter was installed for the Coliseum.)

Schuman brought up the Cattle Barn. It was now "very much in demand and, frankly, we would like to have the Cattle Barn back." Uppermost in the demand was the '49 International Dairy Exposition. In two years, the Board would wish it had never heard of that event, but in 1949, there was no way of knowing that kicking out a profitable arrangement in exchange for a "not for profit" agricultural proposition was less than sound.

But for the moment, the Fairgrounds buildings were "a lot more in demand now than they used to be," Board treasurer Francis M. Overstreet said. He asked to know the chances that Wirtz would release the Cattle Barn, "letting us make some money out of it and you [could] use it whenever possible for parking?"

Wirtz wanted to know what the Board had in mind.

"Events like the Sportsman's Show and Home Show," Schuman replied. Dairy bull. By this point, both sides wanted the Cattle Barn and waivers allowing its use.

Wirtz had no problem with subleasing, with the exception of "music corporations. I want to give you the Cattle Barn for any events you want with the exception of amusement shows."

Back to the International Dairy Exposition and the Bowling Congress, the Board was especially interested in making the Fairgrounds the permanent site for the Dairy Exposition, and that event included the Coliseum.

No problem; but the Board had first told Dick Miller that the show was on October 1, and now it was October 8-15. That created a problem, since the Capitals opened their '49-'50 season with an October 15 home game.

Miller asked whether the Board favored the dairy show or the bowlers. Giving the bowlers the Cattle Barn was no problem on either side, or so the Board said.

"This is a two-way agreement," Schuman said. "We are for the International Dairy Show being held in the Coliseum. The Coliseum is out as far as the American Bowling Congress is concerned, but they can have this in the Cattle Barn."

Board minutes record that "this was agreed upon by consent." Everything was "fairly well ironed out," Schuman announced, "and I think we shall be able to get along fine together."

Now back to the bowlers. They were still in the market for a tournament, but a self-inflicted gutter ball got in the way. Lt. Governor John A. Watkins alerted the Board on April 21 of what was to come during the afternoon session. The General Assembly had enacted a law outlawing racial discrimination in public schools, and although bowling wasn't included in the language, the American Bowling Congress barred blacks from participating, and the Fairgrounds were, after all, a state facility.

Watkins had told "this colored group that they could present their problem . . . [T]hey want to have the rules and regulations let down so that the colored bowlers could hold membership . . . [W]e feel it is a private proposition.

"We can't tell the American Bowling Congress what to do," Watkins said. But using state property put a "different phase on it." Governor Henry Schricker and Watkins both felt "we would be involving the State if this property were rented to the A.B.C.," he explained. Their recommendation was not to rent any of the facilities to the Bowling Congress.

Board member Gilman Stewart immediately starting looking for a plausible reason not to rent to the bowlers. "It does not seem that our available facilities are adequate to take care of this large of an organization."

That afternoon, the Board was visited by William B. Ransom, president of the National Association of Colored Bowlers; Indiana director of Physical Education Randall Frakes; Charles Posner, acting director of Indianapolis Community Relations Council; and C. Ferguson, a director of the bowling association.

Ransom put it simply: "The only people who are permitted to bowl are people who belong to the 'male caucasian' race. I have here one of the tournament blanks which say in part, 'bowlers must come from members of the caucasian race' . . . [T]his policy should not continue . . . our position, as expressed to Governor Schricker, is that these public facilities should not be extended to them."

Posner made his point, too: "We feel that Indianapolis wants to go forward instead of backward."

Frakes revealed that the A.B.C. discrimination clause also excluded Japanese, Chinese, Indians, and others. Women also were prohibited.

"It would be very unfortunate for Indianapolis to have such national publicity if this congress is allowed to come to Indianapolis," Posner said.

Schuman promised an answer "in the next day or so." After their visitors left, Boardman Phares White remarked, "There is more to it than this. You know we cannot rent this place to the A.B.C. because of the law."

Purdue Dean Harry Reed commented, "We only have to tell the A.B.C. whether or not they can have the place." But the Board didn't speak up for civil rights in 1949. Five days later, the American Bowling Congress was called in.

Board members learned A.B.C. was "somewhat of a fraternal organization such as Elks, Masons, etc. . . . [W]hen we go into a community we leave a lot of money."

The group claimed to have letters from the Indianapolis Convention & Visitors Bureau, Governor Schricker, Indianapolis hotels, and the Fair Board "asking us to hold our bowling tournament in Indianapolis. We didn't ask to come to Indianapolis or to Indiana, we were invited." Also the proposal to rent the Cattle Barn for bowling was not "satisfactory." Once the alleys were installed, there wouldn't be room for spectators; and the lighting wasn't adequate for seventeen-hour playing times starting every day at 9 a.m.

A letter was in A.B.C. files inviting the bowlers, "asking us to come here and we are most embarrassed by your procedure," the Board was told. Wirtz had assured them that the Coliseum was "ready and willing to assist" the bowlers "in any way they could."

A letter from Schricker, the Board, and others inviting them was complemented with another, dated March 29, 1948, describing daily rental rates of $400. That surely was Pratt's letter to Indianapolis Convention & Visitors Bureau Manager Joseph Cripe when "the Board went on record officially as being favorable toward having the American Bowling Congress held in the Coliseum April 1, 1950, through June 10, 1950 . . .

[R]ental for the Coliseum will be $400 per day."

Yet only a few weeks before this meeting, the bowlers had received a rental quote double the original amount. The Fairgrounds had to cater to agricultural projects first, Schuman explained. "I don't mean we would scorn the Bowling Congress, but the dairy industry and agricultural interests would be very unhappy if the International Dairy Show was not given a preference," he said. "The Coliseum is out and we offered the Cattle Barn and up to the present that is how it now stands."

After a review of the minutes, the Board decided not to negotiate with the bowlers until 1951, since the Coliseum was tied up until then, "due to present commitments." Not a word was said about racial discrimination.

◆◆ The ABC was in the market for a tournament site, but a self-inflicted gutter ball got in the way.

The decision didn't sit well with the bowling delegation. "We are surprised that your organization is run in quite this way," bowling's Neil King said. (The Board didn't like anyone talking to them in quite that way.)

In a May 19 letter to Carl Tyner, who had replaced Pratt, American Bowling Congress tournament director Charles Treuter Jr. wrote, ". . . by now you know that we signed a lease for the Coliseum at the State Fair Grounds in Columbus (Ohio), and the 1950 . . . championships will start on April 15, running through June 4 . . . [T]he Congress membership voted for Indianapolis when an invitation was extended by your good city . . . in 1948 . . . [W]e tried every way to obtain a suitable building. The Coliseum was our best building from every angle, and when some of your local capitalists and business men could not find a solution to the problem we had to go elsewhere."

That wasn't his true feeling on the matter; it was somewhat more like *Indianapolis Star* sports editor Bob Stranahan's June 15 column "Straight Stuff" when he wrote, "City Not Too Popular With Keglers.

"As might be well expected, Indianapolis didn't fare too well in the *National Bowlers Journal*'s comments on the shift of the 1950 American Bowling Congress from the Hoosier capital to Columbus, Ohio, when no site for the big ten-pin tourney could be obtained here.

"[O]riginally scheduled for Indianapolis, the 1950 meet was transferred to the Ohio city when it developed the Indiana State Fair Board refused to honor its original commitments on the Coliseum and offered, instead, the use of the cow barn . . .

"When the ABC was awarded to Indianapolis a year ago at the Detroit convention, plans called for the close of the hockey season in the Indianapolis Coliseum on Feb. 26 . . .

"Since the Detroit convention, however, the Indiana State Fair Board set up a Dairy Show to run in October, taking up a part of the early hockey dates and forcing the hockey season to extend into April. Then came the offer of the cattle barn.

"After several days of discussion with Indiana State Fair officials the offer was rejected . . ."

"Indianapolis will suffer economically from the loss of the tournament," Stranahan editorialized, "but the Fair Board took the attitude that the buildings and grounds were the property of the entire citizenry of the state . . . not just Indianapolis. And the members are right in this.

"If Indianapolis had owned a municipal auditorium capable of caring for the big pin congress, this would not have happened here." One day Indianapolis would, indeed, own such a facility, and the Fairgrounds would suffer economically.

1950 The Coliseum Corporation lease came up in Board discussion on January 24. Schuman announced that Lt. Governor Watkins had presented a 3,000-name petition calling for the Capitals hockey team to stay in Indianapolis.

Board member Roger Wolcott, close friend to Hulman, remarked, "If I thought the franchise for hockey could be taken over by the State of Indiana at the end of the five-year lease, I would say that Mr. Wirtz should be out at the end of the five years."

Boardman Earl J. Bailey took a different tack. "I am not blaming anyone," he commented, "but I think the whole Board is at fault. We have handled this in the wrong kind of light. As I see it, the contract runs automatically for five years unless we pay Mr. Wirtz $50,000. I think we have no trading stock left."

After all, "these people came in and pioneered this work. We couldn't expect anyone to come in and start such a proposition as they did without tying it up for several years. Whomever it is given to, you would have to eliminate the outsider."

Although Schuman and Overstreet didn't appreciate a letter, contents unknown, from Wirtz, "we more or less asked for it. I think we are losing our power to make a bargain. I think we have a good tenant and he is paying us a good rent."

After more discussion, the Board voted not to exercise its option of paying him the $50,000 and terminating the Coliseum lease.

1954 Chicago played the New York Rangers in the last regular National Hockey League game of the season Feb-

◆◆ **The Winter Club of Indianapolis sponsored the 1952 Olympic Trials. Winter Club members Marilyn Meeker and Larry "Dallas" Pierce won the 1959 National Figure Skating Championship in Junior Dance.**

ruary 19. A Coliseum ad in the eighth annual *Indianapolis Times* "Ice-O-Rama" charity skating show program reminded fans that "your attendance is more than just a move to bring hockey back." The Capitals left after the 1951-52 season. Three years passed before the International Hockey League Chiefs brought hockey back for the 1955-56 season; they ended their first regular season 11-48-1.

Minneapolis squared off with Rochester and New York took on Milwaukee in a March 9 regular National Basketball Association double header. College All-Americans played the Harlem Globetrotters April 6 in the "World Series of Basketball – See [the] Greatest College Players of 1953-54." More than 16,000 people showed up to watch a Globetrotters game before Arthur Wirtz and company packed up and left, according to former grounds superintendent Jesse Stuckey.

Wirtz' Coliseum Corporation got mad that year and chainsawed all the risers and platforms around the entire arena, Stuckey recalled in 1991. "They left owing $85,000. They took the dasher rails and the ice machine."

Board President Gilman Stewart spotted it first and then reported it to the newspapers and the Board. A lease renewal disagreement precipitated the parting gesture.

"Everything was to stay except the [hockey] franchise and the players," former Secretary-Manager Estel Callahan remembered. "But they started hauling [things] out at night. They came in late at night and sawed [parquet seats in front of the box seats and the risers] up at night with electric saws. They wrecked the spotlights, too."

Melvin T. Ross, from the Murat Theatre, took over as Coliseum manager in June that year; his stay ended soon after the disastrous Halloween Night Coliseum explosion.

On the night of September 11, college basketball all-stars from Indiana and Kentucky met in the Coliseum for the second bout of a two-part basketball battle. They had fought first in Kentucky State Fairgrounds' Horse Show Pavilion.

For Kentucky, everything was legal. Adolph Rupp of Lexington was declared coach: "WHEREAS, the coach herein has been selected by poll of the sports writers and editors (Earl Ruby, *Louisville Courier-Journal* sports editor; Jimmy Finnegan, WHAS sports editor; Dean Eagle, *Louisville Times* sports editor; and Ed Kallay, WAVE sports editor) throughout the State of Kentucky and is ready, willing and able to undertake the selection, conditioning and training of eligible players for the said contests,

"NOW, THEREFORE, THE COACH AGREES,

"To provide his services as coach to the extent of his skill and ability and the services of a trainer . . . and to select, condition and train eligible players for the First Annual Kentucky-Indiana All Star Basket Ball Games . . . ."

That's certainly how all all-star games are played.

The All Star Games would be organized to acknowledge "the fact that the college basketball players of the states of Indiana and Kentucky have this year, as they have for many past years, gained national prominence, and being mindful of the great interest in basketball on the

part of the citizenry of the two states . . . in an effort to advance the educational, physical and cultural interest of the public and at the same time promote the progress of the state and stimulate public interest in the advantages and development of the state's educational institutions . . . ."

Only graduates of the two states' colleges and universities were eligible. Each team consisted of a coach, a trainer, and eight players. One of Indiana's players was Bobby Leonard. Leonard had led the I.U. Hoosiers to the NCAA Championship in '53. Some years later, he returned to the Coliseum and coached the last-place Indiana Pacers to three championships.

In the first skirmish, Indiana bloodied Kentucky soil, 49-45, so Kentucky crossed the river and returned the favor. In his September 12 story, *Indianapolis Star* sports editor Jep Cadou commented, "Kentucky gained an even break in its basketball Civil War with Indiana last night by trouncing the Hoosiers 69-56 in an exceedingly rough College All-Star game.

"A disappointing crowd of some 3,000 watched in dismay in the Indiana Fairgrounds Coliseum . . . Indiana lost the game at the free throw line. The Hoosiers hit only 20 of 40 charity tosses while Kentucky connected on 31 of 40." Leonard, of Indiana University, fouled out. So did Notre Dame's Joe Bertrand.

"Four Kentucky players were loaded with four fouls each when it ended," Cadou wrote. There was elbowing, pushing, holding, "and it developed mainly into a free throw shooting contest."

Worse yet, "in view of the scant crowd, a renewal of the series next year is problematic," according to Cadou. "The players participated in the receipts from the two games."

Indiana's first College All-Star Basketball team: (standing, l-r) Bruce Hale, Forest Jackson, Taylor U.; Charley Kraak, Indiana U.; Bill Sullivan, Notre Dame; Lou Scott, Indiana U.; Dick Rosenthal, Notre Dame; Bob Leonard, Indiana U.; Hugh Thimler, (kneeling, l-r) Norm Ellenberger, Butler U.; Dick Farley, Indiana U.; Coach Johnny Jordan, Notre Dame; Joe Bertrand, Notre Dame; Gene Loercher, DePauw.

1958 The Indianapolis Chiefs won the Turner Cup playoffs on April 1 that year, defeating Louisville in the final match-up of the best-of-seven contest. Hooray! Another Champion called the Fairgrounds home.

That summer, the *News*' Frank Salzarulo told readers, "The Indiana State Fair Board yesterday rejected a proposal of the Indiana Coliseum Corporation for a new lease on the Coliseum.

"That finishes hockey for Indianapolis," Corporation general manager

From that time on, Youth Hockey claimed ice time before most folks were out of bed.

Despite these hardships, hockey was growing in popularity, Jackson informed the governor. "You may recall that just a little over a week ago, on a Sunday afternoon, the Notre Dame and Purdue teams played to more than 5,000 here in our Indianapolis Coliseum."

A new Junior Hockey League was forming; Jackson called for the same amount of support found in Toledo and Columbus in Ohio, and – today's Indianapolis Ice's arch-nemesis – Fort Wayne.

Indianapolis needed "appropriate time on weekends" for twelve home games and two practice hours each week, "all of which we are willing and able to pay for . . . . Remember – keeping a boy on ice may keep him out of hot water."

Branigan took up the matter with Board President Edward McCormick two days later, and Jackson was put on the March 13 agenda for a preliminary hearing. All of fifteen minutes was allotted for Jackson's presentation on the youth-directed program – far less time than some Boards were known to spend discussing critical issues like Board sports jackets and ribbon colors. (A former Board member recounted years later that Board members once spent time individually sampling different brands of toilet paper before rendering their purchasing decision.)

Floyd Patterson kept his title in a May 1 world heavyweight championship bout with England's Brian London in front of a crowd of 10,088 fans at the Coliseum.

The title match had been planned for Las Vegas, but Indianapolis instead won the fight allegedly because "gambling interests were rumored to be interested in the venture," according to *Indianapolis News'* Frank Wilson. "New York money [was] 10 to 1" against London. The fight contract was signed in the lobby of the Indiana Senate. No one thought London had a chance.

The match-up, televised nationally on NBC (and blacked-out locally), was the first world title fight of any kind ever held in Indiana. Publicity touted the fight as "the most lucrative tune-up in history." Patterson was set to square off

"Mel" Ross responded. Ross had asked for a new three-year lease beginning on October 1 and a $12,000 yearly rental decrease. The current five-year lease was due to expire in May 1959.

The professional hockey program had operated "at a tremendous loss," for the past three years, according to Ross. Revenues were around $10,000 annually. While the championship could lead to an increase in future revenues, Ross remarked, "it would be foolhardy for us to continue hockey this coming season unless we were assured of a home for it for at least three years." The Chiefs, of course, stayed through the 1961-62 season, finishing sixth in a seven-team league.

1959 Indianapolis Youth Hockey took to the Coliseum ice in the winter. Coliseum manager Ross "shook hands"

with Harold "Hal" Jackson, a defenseman with the Indianapolis Capitals and set aside two hours each week, from 4-6 p.m., at no charge, as former Coliseum manager Bob Young recalled. Danny Laurin, later the Coliseum and Skate Shop pro, was a co-founder, along with Ross.

Soon scheduling developed headaches for everyone involved. According to a letter Jackson wrote in February 1968 to Governor Roger Branigan's secretary David Allen, 600 boys eight to eighteen signed up within two weeks – "Such a large number, that we were unable to handle them in the beginning, and . . . we lost many disappointed boys as a result."

Then, Jackson recounted, Thursday hours "were taken away from us, and we were reassigned to the unbelievable time of 5:30-7:30 a.m. on Saturdays."

Dick "The Bruiser" Afflis, called every name in professional wrestling's handbook, terrorized opponents during a career spanning nearly four decades.

for his "million-dollar" title defense against European champion Ingemar Johansson June 25 in New York.

Patterson won his ranking on November 30, 1956, after his fifth-round knockout of Archie Moore. He was guaranteed $75,000 and a $175,000 TV-radio fee; from that, he would pay London's $60,000 guarantee.

Patterson trained several weeks at the Fairgrounds, doing his early morning roadwork on the Track of Champions. The day before the fight, he "loped around the Fairgrounds mile oval 3-1/2 times, had two sessions with the small bag, did leg and body exercises, punched at shadows for awhile, and danced a bit in the ring," the *News'* Corky Lamm reported. He stayed in one of the Coliseum south side apartments during training.

Patterson told *Ring Magazine* editor Nat Fleischer he liked the Fairgrounds' training camp. "I'm training right here where I'm going to fight."

"I'll know how to fight [London] after the first round – first or second, whatever it takes," he told Lamm.

Patterson knocked London's lights out in the eleventh round with "two hard punches to the body, a right to the head and a crashing left to the jaw that knocked the challenger over backwards.

"The knockout was so complete," *Indianapolis Times* sports editor Jim Smith wrote, "that London stayed on the floor for more than a minute after the final count." London was "a mass of cuts and bruises from his waist to his head." Patterson, without a mark on him, never once fell behind in match points.

"At one point, London hit Patterson with about five straight lefts (but very high) and then crossed a right that also connected. The crowd roared its approval. Then Patterson came back and did the same thing to London, only a lot harder, and in the bargain laughed as if to say, 'That's the way you should do it.'" At another point, Patterson, believing he'd injured the Briton's ribs, almost helped him to his feet after a knockdown.

THAT JUNE, *Wrestling Life,* "the World's Largest Selling All-Wrestling Magazine" which proclaimed itself ". . . the reliable printed voice of professional wrestling," devoted its cover to Dick the Bruiser and Cowboy Bob Ellis at the Coliseum. Bruiser held a chair leg broken from *Wrestling Life* photographer Bob Luce's ringside seat. In the aftermath, Wilbur Snyder steadied the "badly bloodied Ellis after [the] savage Bruiser attack."

The "Match of the Month" had transpired on March 28: "Cowboy tackles a mat bull . . . Bruiser and Ellis were signed for this match more or less as a direct consequence of their wild, brawling 20-minute TV match in the television studios of Indianapolis' WFBM [on March 14] . . . which ended in a 'no decision' verdict – and the Cowboy looking the better off for wear.

"A rematch was indeed a natural for the huge 12,000-seat COLISEUM to bear. Fourteen days following their TV encounter, the Bruiser-Ellis grudge match

Dick the Bruiser

became a reality . . . with a capacity crowd storming the famous Fair Grounds Coliseum to witness the historic encounter.

"Billed as a no-time-limit affair – to the bitter, bloody end – the match actually turned out to be all of that and much more.

"In fact, not even this factual candid action report portrays the downright ugly brutality and sheer ruthlessness of the Bruiser as he beat Ellis into a hulking mass of blood. Here was the height of modern ring savagery as I [Luce] have never seen it before."

After the TV battle, 235-pound Ellis, the typically "quiet, congenial sort," said of 250-pound Bruiser, "The Brute reminds me of a Brahma bull. You protect yourself at all times or get your head busted wide open!"

Ellis promised, "I'm not going to use science on this palooka . . . just the

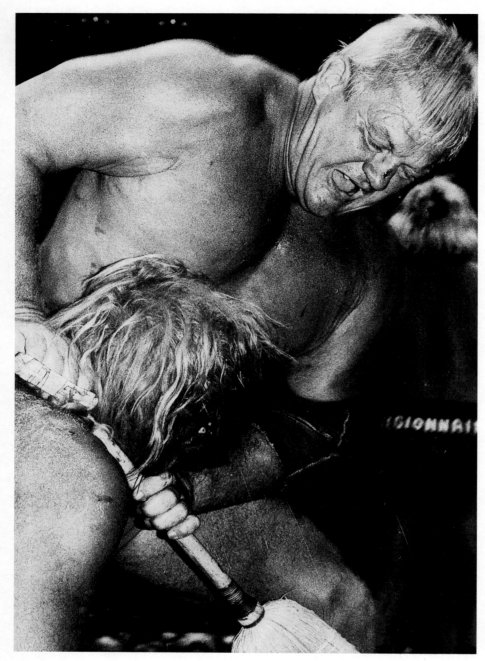

"I'm going to crush Bruiser's thick skull!" Roy Shire snarled for *Wrestling Life*'s benefit later that year. "Violent Feud Flares Up As A Result Of Thanksgiving Day 'Chair Beating' Of Roy Shire In Indianapolis Coliseum Which Sent Rebel Rouser To Hospital With Severe Brain Concussion. Bruiser Scoffs At Threat: 'I'm ready for Ray . . . Let Him Name the Time and Place!'"

In an exclusive interview, brother Ray Shire complained that Bruiser had beaten Roy "unmercifully with a steel chair, almost killing him . . . [I]f I see him on the street I'm going to walk up to him swingin' . . . and if I don't knock him down and out with my fists I'll grab a club and beat his brains out."

Shire called Bruiser "a Cave Man . . . a down and out nothing! An outcast from normal society . . . what the hell is the matter with this big lummox, can't he wage a fair battle in the ring? What's pro wrestling coming to when one big ape . . . can make his own rules as he goes along . . . [H]e's not a wrestler . . . he's a paid killer!" Bruiser's cousin The Crusher called the Shires "softheaded crybabies."

Yukon Eric teamed with Bruiser against the Shires December 12, and a standing-room-only crowd of 13,000 jammed into the Coliseum to watch the grudge match. The box office take: $27,000.

1960 "Amazing Archie" Moore defeated challenger Willi Besmanoff in a May 25 Coliseum pre-title bout scheduled to "provide the city with some added color for the '500' Festival." The *State Fair News* reported the bout would be nationally televised. Moore had been reinstated as world light heavyweight champion by the National Boxing Association provided he defended it against Germany's Erich Schoeppner later in the year. Moore's title had been vacated for failure to defend it within the required six months.

Moore, 43, "always the tactician, always the thinker, the man of surprise," won the bout in a tenth round technical knock-out.

"One thing is for sure: Archie Moore got the workout he came to Indianapolis for last night," *Indianapolis News'*

bony side of my arm and my bare fists! This thing is going to be settled here and now – either he beats the hell out of me or I'll knock his brains loose."

Action photos from the Coliseum match confirm what Luce called "The bloodiest, most savage bout of all time!" In one shot, Bruiser's closed fist "caroms off of the jaw of Ellis, contorting his face into [a] rubbery mass . . . [S]econds later, wild swinging Bruiser connects again . . . [sending] a partially dazed Ellis toppling out of the ring."

The third "out-of-the-ring toss by Brute busts Ellis' head open" and Ellis went berserk, attacking other wrestlers' attempts to help him.

Following a March 6 Coliseum match, the *Indianapolis Star* reported "a crowd of 11,689 paid a gross gate of $25,321 to see last night's professional wrestling show . . . Dick the Bruiser and Angelo Poffo won the main event, a tag team match, over Bobby Managoff and Yukon Eric . . . [A] traffic snarl developed on 38th Street as people attempted to get to the Fairgrounds to see the grapplers." According to one account, the event "created a traffic snarl that made a world's series game insignificant."

Bruiser used a chair on yet another Coliseum opponent when he teamed with 275-pound Yukon Eric November 26 against Roy and Ray Shire.

Frank Wilson reported. "The crowd of 2,633 persons, who paid $24,432, got their money's worth." Four other fights preceded the main bout.

Besmanoff, 27, recently of Indianapolis, was "young, eager, and, perhaps, just a bit too cautious." Moore, the "grand old light-heavyweight champion" who "nearly tipped the building" at 206-1/2 pounds, found 198-1/2-pound Besmanoff "a handful for nine rounds." Besmanoff had lost a decision to Moore in '58.

Fans "and a peeking national [ABC] television eye" saw Moore dropped once, in the second round. Besmanoff went down twice, "the second time the victim of a well-calculated right hand that caught him flush on his battered nose in the ninth." A bloody "gusher flowed."

Certainly, Besmanoff got in his licks and caught Moore by surprise in the second round, but Moore changed his tactics. Besmanoff had first met the canvas in the fifth round when Moore landed a right uppercut. In the first round, "a butt and a thumb, neither deliberate . . . raised a mouse on Willi's right eye.

"Willi said later that the only punch that hurt him was that brutal ninth-round smash. Even then he came back with a stinging left to Moore's mush."

In the tenth round, "red painted Besmanoff's white trunks, Moore's body and referee [Frank] Gilmer's white shirt. Still they went. Then Gilmer, looking more concerned as time fled, stepped in and held Moore's hand high." Besmanoff complained he wasn't hurt nearly as bad as he looked, "and a doctor attested to the fact.

"Most certainly, Gilmer had acted for two reasons . . . [H]e felt that Besmanoff was worse off than he actually was. Secondly, the spattered spectacle was not one conducive to kind thoughts about the fight business."

1961

There is a plaque in the Coliseum concourse – "In memory of the skaters from this rink, who, while on their way to the world's figure skating championships, perished in a plane crash in Belgium, February 15, 1961."

Winter Club's Larry Pierce and Diane Sherbloom, the new 1961 U.S. Dance Champions were scheduled to perform together at the U.S. championships. From Los Angeles, Sherbloom became Pierce's substitute partner when his original partner Marilyn Meeker of Indianapolis broke her ankle just before the compe-

Willi Besmanoff is down on one knee after "Amazing Archie" Moore connects during their 1960 Coliseum bout, which ABC televised nationally.

tition. Pierce, Sherbloom, and Winter Club coach Daniel C. Ryan, Coliseum pro since 1955, were among eighteen skaters and sixteen officials, coaches, and family members who died in the fiery Boeing 707 crash the morning after Valentine's Day.

In *Skating* magazine's account of the crash, Flight 548 had been in a holding pattern over Brussels airport.

"After circling twice, the plane descended to 600 feet on the final approach. The landing gear was lowered, then inexplicably retracted. The approach was aborted and the plane pulled up sharply and began to climb." For reasons never known, the control tower was unable to re-establish contact with the plane.

"There were unusual engine sounds and the plane made several zig-zag turns and began to shake. It then nosed over and fell into a series of spins." Upon impact, there was a "tremendous

explosion" and the plane disintegrated in a field near the small village of Berg four miles from the airport. No one aboard survived (there were twenty-seven other passengers and eleven crew members), a farmer working in his nearby field was killed and another man's leg was severed.

President Kennedy offered the country's condolences. On February 16, the World Championships, scheduled in Prague, Czechoslovakia, were cancelled. The season ended.

Skating's February 1991 edition recalled that "it seemed as though the world had stopped with the loss of the

brightest and best of U.S. skaters and that our future in the sport had been extinguished in the flames. The loss was and still is immeasurable."

The United States Figure Skating Association Memorial Fund was founded after the tragedy; through it, noted *Skating* magazine, "the spirit of the 1961 World Team continues to enhance the sport and the champions of today and the future." Jeffery A. Johnston took over as Coliseum pro following the tragedy. Ryan's wife Rose Ann stayed on as part of the Winter Club staff.

Youth baseball was allowed to use the Board's overflow parking lot at 46th and Carvel Streets in a May 19 decision. Five leagues already were using the lot. The Board originally signed a Little League contract for $1 in 1952, but hadn't authorized it since then. Board approval came January 28, and lot leveling and grass seeding began in the spring.

The Junior League Baseball Club was first to obtain Board approval. Permanent concrete stands, dugouts, backstops, and fences had been erected to accommodate the games.

1967
The American Basketball Association's Indiana Pacers opened their first season in the Coliseum, in a stay lasting until 1974.

The Saturday night crowd on October 14 far exceeded expectations; re-portedly 10,835 showed up for the Pacers' first game, a victorious 117-95 over the Kentucky Colonels. Starting players were guards Freddie Lewis (6') and Jimmy Dawson (6'1"), forwards Roger Brown (6'5") and Oliver Darden (6'6-1/2"), and center Bob Netolicky (6'9").

"A band blared, spotlights lit up the Coliseum," Pacer historian Mark Montieth wrote.

The Pacers won three ABA championship titles while based at the Coliseum – 1969-70 (First, East), 1971-72 (Second, West), 1972-73 (Second, West), Eastern Division titles 1968-69 and 1969-70, and a Western Division title 1970-71.

After the first title, the victorious team held a victory dinner at the Farmers' Building, "with the public welcome at $1.25 apiece."

The ABA was established on February 2, 1967, when owners of eleven franchises announced its existence. E.J. Bannon, president of Purdue National Bank, had the Pacers franchise.

The Pacers ended their first season in third place in the play-offs; they had created more than 3,000 "hard-core" fans at the Coliseum according to General Manager Mike Storen. The Pacers had become "'the thing to do' in wintertime entertainment."

The Fairgrounds Coliseum ticket was good for admission to the first ABA All-Star basketball game in January 1968 until far too many were sold – and the entire game moved to Hinkle Field House.

The Pacers left the Coliseum in 1974, moving downtown to bigger and newer quarters at Market Square Arena. The Coliseum's 9,479-fan capacity just wasn't big enough anymore. To date, the Pacers have yet to win another championship.

1968
On January 9, the First Annual American Basketball Association All-Star Game was scheduled to begin at 7:30 p.m. in the Coliseum. The tickets were sold-out; correction: too many tickets were sold, way too many. The game went on, but at Hinkle Fieldhouse. Rent was more than ten times greater than the Coliseum, but 10,872 fans were able to attend the game.

Pacer Mel Daniels led East Division scoring with twenty-two points, as East triumphed over West, 126-120. Roger Brown scored twelve points, as did Netolicky.

Winter Club members Judy Schwomeyer Sladky and James Sladky won the U.S. National Figure Skating Championship in Senior Dance and went on to win again the next four years. World Team members from 1967-72, they finished second in 1971 and third in 1970 and 1972 in the World Championships.

Skating together since 1966, the couple starred in the Ice Follies, Holiday On Ice, and Disney on Ice. In 1991, the Sladkys were in their thirteenth year as the "Campbell Kids."

1977 The first annual Sid Collins Memorial Horseshoe Pitching Press Tournament for Hoosier media types debuted in honor of the late and internationally recognized "Voice of the Indianapolis 500."

1978 The Fairgrounds events calendar was filled with activities in January and February: an eight-day Indianapolis Auto Show; IUPUI basketball; a busy Indiana Wizards basketball home schedule including games with New York, Kentucky, Rochester, Virginia, West Virginia; and a sale of oil paintings at the Farm Bureau Building.

The Wizards? After the Pacers left the Coliseum for bigger downtown digs, the All America Basketball Alliance was created, with headquarters in Princeton Junction, New Jersey. As of January 1978, the eight-team roster included: the Indiana Wizards, the Kentucky Stallions, the Rochester Zeniths, the New York Guard, the Carolina Lightning, the West Virginia Wheels, the Richmond Virginians, and the Georgia Titans.

"While other teams have looked to youth to build their AABA foundation, the Indiana Wizards have taken the opposite tact," league publicity said.

Former three-time Indiana Pacer All-Star Roger Brown (by the end of his first season with the inaugural team he lead in scoring – 520 – and tied with Netolicky in game point averages, 22.7) and now player-general manager, had "some players who have been around and have suffered with the growing pains of ABA. We'll be more than prepared for the first AABA season." Brown still had some shots left in him. He also was on the AABA board of governors.

Mel Daniels, 1969 and 1971 ABA Most Valuable Player and a National Basketball Association member in '77, was "still capable of intimidating the oppo-

nent." Nine-year ABA veteran Netolicky wanted another pro-ball year. Former ABA All-Star Freddie Lewis had eight years behind him; now he put his experience to work coaching and playing.

"These four players were the nucleus of the original ABA Indiana Pacer dynasty and they have every hope to regain that magic at the State Fair Coliseum, their former home with the Pacers.

"It's very special to be able to play our games in the Coliseum again," Brown said. "We've had so very many successes in the old 'barn' that I'm sure the fans will want to join us in regaining some of the magic."

The league lasted all of two to three games, Wizard teammate Billy Shepherd recalled in 1991. He didn't think any of the Wizards ever drew a paycheck and doubted whether the Coliseum rent

The highest ranking United States Dance competitors in the history of U.S. ice dancing, Judy Schwomeyer Sladky and James Sladky invented a dance called the "Yankee Polka," now compulsory in international competition. Their dance demonstration before the Olympic Committee in Grenoble, France, led to dance's inclusion as an Olympic event.

was paid. "We opened at the Coliseum [a doubleheader] and then went to Kentucky and played the Lightning." He remembered little else.

1981 Professional ice hockey returned in the fall after an eighteen-year absence. The Central Hockey League's Checkers, farm team for the NHL champion New York Islanders, moved to the Fairgrounds for forty home dates, with an October 7 season opener. They lost to Cincinnati.

for two lack-luster seasons.) The Ice claimed the best record in Indianapolis hockey history (53-21-6) during its '89-90 season and Indianapolis' second Turner Cup.

During that second season, 8,567 spectators came on "Heywood Banks Night," the greatest attendance since the 1950s. (The Capitals averaged an 8,000 home game attendance during their last five years.) It also was the first hockey sell-out in the Coliseum since the '40s. The Ice also claimed the season's best home game record in the IHL: 27-6.

1990 BMX bicycle racing made its first appearance April 22 in the Swine Barn, the first time for anything of the kind since the building went up in 1923. The quarter-mile track (National Bicycle League sanctioned track #1035), at 1,250 feet, was considered the longest in the nation. The track also was the official BMX venue for the White River Park State Games in 1990 and 1991.

◆◆◆

1982 The Winter Club of Indianapolis hosted portions of the United States Figure Skating Association's National Figure Skating Championship January 26-28 at the Coliseum ice rink. Main competitions centered at Market Square Arena.

Novice Men's, Ladies', and Junior Men's Figures opened the Coliseum's Championship contribution. Championship Ladies' Figures filled second-day competition. Junior Ladies' Figures and Championship Men's Figures rounded out the three-day schedule.

The Checkers won the Adams Cup championship; its pennant hung in the Coliseum. (They won the cup again in the '82-83 season, then suffered defeat in the finals during the next season). Goalie Kelly Hrudey was voted MVP after his Adams Cup playoff performance. Visiting players called the rink "the best in the league."

1987 An estimated 400 runners entered Family Fun Run competition. The 10K event, sponsored by the Indiana Farm Bureau and the Fair, offered $2,500 in cash awards.

1988 The International Hockey League's Indianapolis Ice brought pro hockey back to the Coliseum for the 1988-89 season. (From 1974-78, the Racers called Market Square Arena home. The Checkers skated at the Coliseum from 1980-85 before moving to Market Square Arena

Jubilant Indianapolis Ice players lift the Turner Cup aloft after clinching it at the end of their 1989-90 season; their regular season record, 53-21-6, put them first in the Western Division.

Coliseum Ice Hockey History

YEAR	TEAM	LEAGUE	RECORD	PLACE
1939-40	Capitals	IAHL	26-20-10	1st, West Div.
1940-41	Capitals	IAHL	17-28-11	5th, West Div.
1941-42	Capitals	IAHL	34-15-7	1st, West Div./Calder Cup
1942-43	Capitals	IAHL	29-23-4	3rd overall
1943-44	Capitals	IAHL	20-18-16	2nd, West Div.
1944-45	Capitals	IAHL	25-24-11	2nd, West Div.
1945-46	Capitals	IAHL	33-20-9	1st, West Div.
1946-47	Capitals	IAHL	33-18-13	4th, West Div.
1947-48	Capitals	IAHL	32-30-6	4th, West Div.
1948-49	Capitals	IAHL	39-17-12	2nd, West Div.
1949-50	Capitals	IAHL	35-24-11	2nd, West Div.
1950-51	Capitals	IAHL	38-29-3	2nd, West Div.
1951-52	Capitals	IAHL	22-40-6	5th, West Div.
1955-56	Chiefs	IHL	11-48-1	6 of 6
1956-57	Chiefs	IHL	26-29-5	2 of 6
1957-58	Chiefs	IHL	28-30-6	4 of 6/Turner Cup
1958-59	Chiefs	IHL	26-30-4	4 of 5
1959-60	Chiefs	IHL	25-40-3	6 of 8
1960-61	Chiefs	IHL	20-46-4	7 of 8
1961-62	Chiefs	IHL	19-49-0	6 of 7
1963	(Capitals)	Detroit farm team until Halloween explosion		
1974-78	RACERS AT MARKET SQUARE ARENA			
1979-80	Checkers	CHL	40-32-7	2nd place
1980-81	Checkers	CHL	44-30-6	3 of 9
1981-82	Checkers	CHL	42-33-5	3rd, North/Adams Cup
1982-83	Checkers	CHL	50-28-2	First/Adams Cup
1983-84	Checkers	IHL	34-36-2	4th overall
1984-85	Checkers	IHL	31-47-4	4th, West Div.
1985-87	CHECKERS AT MARKET SQUARE ARENA			
1988-89	Ice	IHL	26-54-2	5th, West Div.
1989-90	Ice	IHL	53-21-6	1st, West Div./Turner Cup
1990-91	Ice	IHL	48-29-5	2nd, West Div.
1991-92	Ice	IHL	31-41-10	5th, East Div.

Photo Acknowledgments

Index

The Tee Pee, Indianapolis' first drive-in restaurant, opened July 4, 1932. Albert Raymond "Mac" McComb leased the land on the Fairgrounds' southeast corner and built the summer-time frame and stucco refreshment stand, eventually expanding to feature full dining services. Sonja Henie visited, Floyd Patterson stopped by.

McComb died in 1960; his wife operated the drive-in until 1972; their son Charles ran it until 1978. Other owners sought to revive it, but to no avail. The Historic Landmarks Foundation vainly sought to save the venerable drive-in institution; a spokesman called it a rare surviving example of "road-side nomadic architecture." The Tee Pee finally closed in 1980 and the building was torn down in 1988. Today the site is a parking lot.

McDonald, M.A. 196
McEntire, Reba 189
McGowan, E.J. 31
McGuffeyites 170
McIlroy, Colonel 34
McKay & Charles 48
McKee, John F. 99
McKee, Will J. 142
McKeen Cadets 264
McKinney, Cecil 302
McLaughlin, Andra 285
McLeay, V.B. 304
McLoughlin Manufacturing Company 276
McManis, T.B. 265
McMillan, D. 4
McMurray, Floyd 169, 170
McNamara, Edgar C. 195, 217-218, 243, 249
McNamara, Leo C., Sr. 207, 209-210, 213
McNeal, Bruce 75
McNutt, Paul V. 36, 276
McQuinn, Harry 234
Meadow Jewel 217
Medley, Bill 59
Meeker, Marilyn 313
Mehner, Billy 250
Mellencamp, John 191
Mendenhall, Murray 304
Mercer, Mrs. 273
Merchants Association 267
Merchants Heat and Light Company 154
Meredith, Henry C. 64
Meredith, Solomon 7, 174
Meredith, Virginia C. 104
Merlau, John 23–24
Merry Maid 198
Messmer, Walter 299
Messner, Dan 200-201
Methodist Hospital 258
Meyer-Kiser Bank 16
Miash, Emmalyne 119
Michael, Catharine E. 104
Michigan City 143
Mid-West Quarter Horse Breeders Association 239
Mid-West Sports & Boat Show 281
Middleburg 98
Middletown 195
Milburn, Danny 257
Military and Knights Templar Encampment 264
Miller, Connie 52
Miller, Delvin 209, 210, 216
Miller, Dick 235, 281, 306
Miller, L. Orville 156, 212, 213, 215, 237, 306
Miller, Samuel Joseph 128
Miller, William C. 301
Millersville Eastern Star 169
Mills Brothers 48
Milne, Gordon 285
Milo S. 200
Milsap, Ronnie 59
Milwaukee, Wisconsin 56
Miner, Franklin 281
Minneapolis 31
Minneapolis, Minnesota 308
Minneman, Paul 278
Minor Heir 196, 201
Mishawaka 177
Mishler, Harry 35
Miskelly, S.M., Mrs. 104
Miss Alice Melville and Her Hollywood Troupe 36
Miss Harris M 202
Miss Royal and Her Horses 32
Mitchell, James 10
Mitchell, Randall 241, 242
Mitchell, Robert 174
Mittman, Dick 222

Mockler, Warren 258
Model Clothing Company 30
Moffett, Paul G. 171, 210-211, 237
Moline Plow Company 89
Monarch Jr. 196
Monon Railroad 12, 57, 138, 285
Monroe County 3
Monroe, James, Pres. 12
Monrovia 78, 98, 125, 196
Monte Cristo 199
Montgomery County 165
Montgomery-Ward 267
Monticello 49, 143, 276
Montieth, Mark 314
Moore, Archie 311-312
Moore, L.A., Mrs. 107
Moore, Laura 124
Moore, Levi 280, 303
Moore, Levi P. 126, 146, 155, 175, 208
Moore, Lou 235
Moores, Jacqueline 112
Moores, Merrill 266
Moores, Sheryl 112
Mooresville 89
Mooresville Times 232
Moreau, Donald W., Sr. 24, 25
Moreland, Charles 281
Morgan, George 47
Morrill, Justin Smith 70
Morris, Charles R. 45, 178, 206, 209, 210
Morris the Cat 185
Morrison, J.E. 82
Morse, Robert M. 22
Morton, Oliver P. 9, 10, 141
Mount, James A. 13, 64–65, 142, 144, 166
Mount, Louis 304
Mount Vernon 143
Mr. Borden 211
Mr. Green Jeans 48
Mt. Healthy, Ohio 29
Mtume 59
Muncie 138, 169, 171, 174, 176, 234
Muncie Central High School 299, 300
Muncie Star 23, 163, 218
Muncie State Normal School 125
Munson, David 267
Munson, L.C., Company 267
Murat Theatre 308
Murphy, Addie 119
Murphy, Charles 300
Murphy Shows 36
Murphy, Virginia 125
Murray, Anne 59
Muscletone 207
Mutual Broadcasting 157
Mutz, Jacob 88
Mutz, John 23
Myers, Howard 99
Myers, T.E. 235

N

Nabors, Jim 187
Naismith, James, Dr. 299
Nalon, Duke 234, 235
Namba Japs 32
Naomi 56
Nappanee 98, 266
Natiello's Band of Louisville 32
National Appaloosa Horse Show 294
National Association of Colored Bowlers 307
National Association of Short-horn Breeders 11
National Association of Swine Breeders 11
National Basketball Association 291, 308
National Bicycle League 316
National Bowlers Journal 307

National Boxing Association 312
National Broadcasting Company 37, 52, 310
National Hockey League 308
National Horsemen Association 211
National Pork Producers Council 294
National Saengerfest, N.A.S.B. 267
National Surgical Institute 159
National Swine Show 273
National Tractor Pulling Association 291
Nave, Lum 196
Naylor, Mary D. 105
Neal, Forest 175, 176, 273
Neal, William 300
Neese, Emily 125
Neilman Machine Works 266
Neiman, Mr. 237
Nellie S. 198
Nelson, Isaac De Graff 71
Nelson, Mark 278
Nelson Morris, Swift & Co. 32
Nelson, Nip 48
Nelson, Willie 59, 191
Nesbit, Mr. 196
Netolicky, Bob 314
Nevele Pride 208, 224
New Albany 6–7, 28, 104, 173, 263
New Albany Daily Ledger 6, 7, 173
New Bremen, Ohio 250
New Castle 143
New Harmony 70, 71
New Kids on the Block 57
New Orleans, Louisiana 105
New Palestine 23
New York City, New York 34, 44
New York Guard 315
New York Islanders 315
Newburg 118
Newby, Benoni 73
Newby, Daniel 73
Newby, William 73
Newhall Family 28
Newhard, Sandy 114
Newton, Irene 119
Newton, Louise 100
Newton, Wayne 59
Niblack, John 242
Nicholas, James 282
Nicholson, J.W. 104
Nicolai, J., Mrs. 3
Night Horse Show 280
Night Ranger 59
Nine Mile 265
Noblesville 59
Noe, A.M., Mrs. 105, 166
Nordhorn, Don 253
Norma Jean 52
Norrick, A.G. 155, 210, 211
North American Breeders Sale 294
North American Gymnastic Union 298
North, Levi J. 28
North-Western Farmer 64
Northway, Ina 119
Norwood, George N. 5
Notre Dame University 309, 310
Nowlin, H.L. 31, 201
Nutt, Cyrus, D.D. 70

O

Oak Ridge Boys 57, 59, 187
Oceola 7
O'Connell, Helen 57
O'Connor, Pat 47
Odd Fellows 31
Ohio County 73
Ohio Steam Dental Company 29
O'Keefe, Dennis 213
Oklahoma City, Oklahoma 32
Oldenburg 105
Oldfield, Barney 232, 234

Oldfield, Lee 234
Oliver, J.E. 130
Olsen & Johnson 154, 155
139th Field Artillery 36
O'Neill, Jane 52
Operation Beehive 150
Orin Welch Aircraft Company 272
Orleans 45, 176
Orman, John 267
Orme, Marcia 119
Orpheum and Keith 34
Orr, Joseph 166
Orr, Robert D. 23-24, 191
Osmonds, The 56, 57
Otterbein 107, 118
Outlaws 56
Overman, Glen 300
Overstreet, Francis M. 45, 178, 237, 306
Owen, David Dale 70
Owen, Lane & Dyer 262
Owen, Richard, Prof. 142
Owens, Buck 54
Oxford 200, 237

P

Page, Patti 47
Pain's Fireworks Company 30, 32
PAL Club 158
Palin, Septimus F. 202, 204-208, 210-214
Palmer, Fred 235
Palmer, Mr. 237
Palmgren, Larry 250
Panke, R.J. "Steve" 57
Pankratz, Wally 258
Paragon 98
Pardee, E. 302
Paris, Kentucky 79
Parke Davis & Company 266
Parker, Colonel 157–158
Parks, Carol 185
Parr, Josephine 76
Parshall, H.M. 208
Parsons, Johnny 240
Parton, Dolly 56, 114, 191
Pasco, Luke J. 37
Paswater, Dick 249
Pat Henry 199
Patrick, Mark 191
Patterson, Floyd 310
Patti, Sandi 185
Patton, Blaine 235
Paul Revere & The Raiders 54
Payne & Powell 194
Peace Corps 208
Peachy, Clem 32
Pearcy, Noble R. 21
Pearl, Minnie 52
Pedigo, Oliphant 265
Pedigo, Roy C. 304
Peed, Evan H. 198
Pendleton 21
Perry, Norman 301
Peru 138
Peter Astra 208
Peter Lind 217
Peter Pluto 204
Peter the Great 202, 215
Pfau, William H. 281
Pfeffer, Robert 255
Philadelphia 88
Phillip, John Sousa 27, 31
Phillips, Arnold W. 287
Phillips, Arthusia 119
Piatt, Ida 125
Pickens, Mr. 274
Pierce, Larry 313
Pierceton 98
Pioneer Hi-Bred International 68
Pittsboro 254, 258

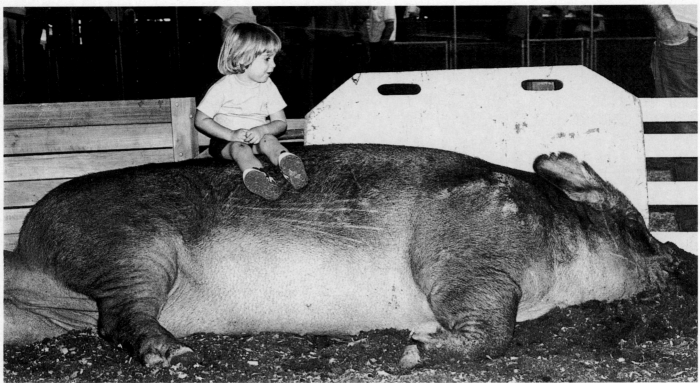